The $upertrader's Almanac

(REFERENCE MANUAL)

Second Edition

by Frank A. Taucher

Table of Contents

*"If you don't know where you're going,
any road will take you there."*

Chapter 1 - Preparation

Chapter 2 - You and Your Broker

Chapter 3 - Who Will Manage Your Money?

Chapter 4 - Analytical Techniques

Chapter 5 - Spreads

Chapter 6 - Mother Nature and The Markets

Chapter 7 - Computer Applications

Chapter 8 - Additional Products

Introduction

If you always do,
what you've always done,
then you'll always get,
what you've always gotten.

The past two decades have provided some of the best trading markets in the history of the country.

Yet many traders / investors have experienced only average, mediocre or even losing results during this exciting, yet volatile, period.

Consider the returns of your own investment program over the past several years. (You will have to choose the appropriate period of time. If you are over 50, 20 years may not be enough while if you are 25, 5 may be too many).

Do you have a formalized investment program? If so, what is its objective and have you been able to attain that objective? Were results satisfactory when compared with other investment results? Would you like to increase your rate of return? Would more consistent results be desirable?

"The $upertrader's Almanac" has been written to provide you with tools that will help you either establish an investment program or make changes to an already existing program, should such be your desire.

The Almanac is actually comprised of two separate books.

This book, "The $upertrader's Almanac Reference Manual", presents several different trading theories and techniques that successful traders use in making buy and sell decisions. Most of these trading techniques can be used separately on a stand-alone basis to provide profitable results over time.

NONE, however, will work without error or periodic losses (drawdowns)!

As you will see in the book, the individual trading techniques become particularly powerful when used in combination with other trading techniques resulting in fewer trades but a higher percentage of successful conclusions.

Those techniques that can be projected into the upcoming year and are TIMELY in nature (such as seasonality, cyclicality, anniversary dates, important change-in-trend dates, first notice day slammers, astronomical events, and so on) are summarized and listed in our companion book, "The $uptertrader's Almanac Calendar Book", which is published annually. (Again, the book you are presently reading is NOT the "Calendar Book" but the "Reference Manual").

To clarify a potential misconception, the reader should note that this is not a book about the stock market, the gold market, the bond market, the real estate market, the energy market, the grain market, or any other particular market. It is about the process of trading which, when learned correctly, will enable one to successfully navigate ANY liquid, freely-traded, public market be that market stocks in Japan, oil in Singapore, gold in London, soybeans in Brazil, bonds in the United States, and so on.

But the book does not stop with education about trading techniques. It is also about the philosophy of trading and of living - about celebrating the rewards of life that come with the joy of true financial freedom derived from implementing a successful trading program.

Some may find a sense of frustration in that the book does not provide a "Holy Grail", one-step magical formula that takes five minutes to read and makes you wealthy in the next 30 days.

Let's be realistic, however. IF such a formula existed, it would not be available anywhere near the price you have paid for this book.

The pages that follow therefore explain SEVERAL solid trading approaches that successful traders have used to multiply their wealth. The value of these techniques exists only when the trader, when confronted with the age-old dilemma of "buy / sell / hold", is able to draw upon the treasure chest of these techniques and arrive at an appropriate course of action.

Introduction

In the author's opinion, trading is a highly individualistic form of artistic expression. I would not write the same essay as you in an English composition class, would not wear the same clothes as you, would likely prefer a different make and color of automobile with different options, and so on.

Trading is the same. Those techniques that I prefer to use in my trading environment are likely to be different from yours. A business executive or full-time professional with little access to intraday price data and information will trade differently from one who sits all day in front of a computer screen.

Hence, it is not my place to TELL or even SUGGEST to others how THEY should trade.

IT IS UP TO THE INDIVIDUAL TRADER TO FIND THOSE TECHNIQUES THAT HE IS MOST COMFORTABLE WITH, CAN UNDERSTAND, AND CAN MOST EASILY ADMINISTER ON A DAILY BASIS GIVEN THE CONSTRAINTS OF HIS FINANCIAL OBJECTIVES, JOB REQUIREMENTS, FAMILY SITUATION, TOLERANCE FOR RISK, LIFESTYLE PREFERENCES, AND SO ON.

In short, each individual trader must himself seek those techniques that best fit his own trading environment.

I cannot stress enough how important to long-term success this basic concept of program customization is to one's trading approach.

YOU will experience greater long term success if YOU find those techniques that best fit YOU. No matter how well MY techniques may work for ME, YOU must find those that work for YOU!

Such is the spirit in which The Almanac is prepared. It is designed to help YOU find those methods that work for YOU in YOUR trading environment.

To accomplish this task, you are going to have to do some work!

Prior to doing so, however, it is fair for you to ask if these principles actually work.

The answer is a resounding "YES"!

As an example, the author engaged in a test from July, 1989 to April, 1990 on Financial News Network, a daily financial television program with a purported viewing audience of several million households, in which price forecasts were made each Tuesday of the 9 month period. The broadcast schedule was announced in advance to purchasers of The 1989 and 1990 Almanacs.

No compensation was paid by FNN to the author. The author's purpose in subjecting his work to these weekly interviews was to demonstrate to as large an audience as possible that one could pick up "The $upertrader's Almanac Calendar Book", turn to the pages in the book that coincided in time with the weekly interview, and use the information in "The Calendar Book" and the techniques in "The Reference Manual" to make highly reliable price forecasts of pending market price action DESPITE THE ALMANAC'S INFORMATION HAVING BEEN WRITTEN MONTHS EARLIER!

To vividly demonstrate to the reader the enormity of the task and the low probability of the project being even moderately successful, the reader may, right now, wish to simply project what stocks will be doing eight months hence.

Difficult, isn't it?

Most would admit that their projection is, at best, a haphazard guess.

So how did the project on FNN turn out? Again, using only the timing information listed in The 1989 and 1990 Almanacs (Calendar Books) and the trading techniques explained in this Reference Manual, I would venture to say that, had one followed all the recommendations made on that program, one would have EASILY and by a VERY wide margin outperformed ANY of the results published for the period for the very best of public money managers or by any of the tracking services which follow the best performing newsletters, etc!

The recommendations included a short sale of stocks on the EXACT DAY of the 1989 high in the S & P 500 just prior to the October 13th panic, purchase suggestions of March Orange Juice just prior to the December freeze of 1989 and just before the

Introduction

market traded at its maximum limit up 8 of 10 days, a purchase suggestion in gold 3 days before the 1989 low of the year in September (not all markets chose to bottom or peak on the exact day of the Tuesday interview - this one bottomed three days later on Friday, September 15th), and so on.

A second example of the value of these techniques that is of greater importance is the stack of letters that have been collected over the past few years from readers who have written to share their successful Almanac experiences "on the front line, in the trenches, and in real-time battle".

It is my sincere hope that you will shortly join this group of successful traders.

For now, please reread the quotation at the start of this introduction.

Good luck and good trading!

Frank Taucher

June, 1990

Chapter 1

Preparation

Perseverence

I do not think there is any other quality
so essential to success of any kind
as the quality of perseverance.
It overcomes almost everything, even nature.
           - John D. Rockefeller

Henry Ford's first company went bankrupt during its first year in the auto business. Undaunted, he tried again, this time achieving a greater degree of success in that he was able to postpone bankruptcy for two years. Since then, his third company has been doing just fine.

R. H. Macy's first 3 dry goods stores went broke.

The National Aeronautics and Space Administration (NASA) failed in 20 of its first 28 attempts to launch a rocket into space.

Remember reading about green eggs and ham in one of Dr. Suess' children's books? 23 publishers rejected Dr. Suess' first book. The 24th sold 6 million copies.

The Apple computer, developed in a garage, was rejected by both Hewlett-Packard and Atari. Operating on its own, Apple's first year sales hit $ 2.5 million.

In his book, "Market Wizards - Interviews with Top Traders", author Jack Schwager tells of champion trader Marty Schwartz and states "Schwartz spent a decade losing money on his trading before he found his stride as a remarkably successful professional trader." Schwager notes how Schwartz, a former securities analyst who "was always broke because of market losses" changed his methodology and transformed himself from a repeated loser to an amazingly consistent winner who averaged over 200 percent NONANNUALIZED return over a ten year period in trading championships he entered. He was reportedly up over 700 percent in his single complete one year entry.

What if Dr. Suess had given up after the 23rd publisher had rejected his book?

What if Schwartz had given up after his tenth losing year of trading?

You will encounter periods in your trading career when the weight of the world will seem to be upon your shoulders.

I have AND STILL DO!

When that happens, refer to this page and consider the perseverence displayed by the people in these pages.

Consider the acheivements they would have foregone had they surrendered their dreams!

Objectives

*Where you come from
is not nearly as important
as where you are going.*

When I attempt to quantify a rate of return as a future attainable objective with people, few seem to have given the matter much thought.

Let's put some numbers into perspective.

Over a long period of time, it is the rare money manager who is able to attain a rate of return equal to 1.1 times the average 90 day US Treasury Bill rate (the bull market in stocks in the 1980s will have altered the RECENT experience of the past few years).

Two primary factors will erode the purchasing power of your invested capital. Those two factors are the ravages of inflation and taxation.

As an example, if the combined erosion from all sources of taxation (federal, state, local, and other) on your investment return is fifty percent and inflation is five percent, the minimum rate of return needed JUST TO PRESERVE THE PURCHASING POWER OF YOUR CAPITAL is ten percent.

If you can make your money grow at a forty percent rate of return annually AFTER the effects of inflation and taxation, your capital will approximately double in real dollars every two years.

At such a rate, you will be outperforming the long term equity growth rate of virtually all the stocks on the New York Stock Exchange and the growth rate of by far the majority of investors in the United States.

Your problem will be in first achieving the above (or another) rate of growth and then in sustaining the growth rate over time. Also, even if successful in the next few years, as the amount of funds managed increases, the ability to sustain growth rates decreases.

Another problem, as previously mentioned, will again be sustaining the growth rate AFTER inflation and taxation.

To figure your required pre-tax growth rate, simply take the required after-tax growth rate and divide by 1 minus the expected rate of inflation and then divide again by 1 minus the expected tax rate from all sources (federal, state, local, and other). For the mathematically inclined, the formula is

$$R = \frac{A}{(1-i)(1-t)}$$

where R = the pre-tax, pre-inflation adjusted rate of return, A = the after-tax, after-inflation desired rate of return, i = expected rate of inflation, and t = rate of taxation.

For instance, if one desires an after-tax rate of return of 40 % in a 5 % inflationary environment and a 45 % tax bracket, the formula yields R = 40 / (1 - .05)(1 - .45) = 76.56 %

Many speculators have difficulty accepting such a rate of return as an acceptable objective because they feel it is too low.

Let me reiterate again, however, that such a CONSISTENT growth rate over long periods of time is extremely exceptional.

There is also one further important adjustment that should be made with respect to the income necessary to support your living standard.

If you have a job or are otherwise income-dependent, you should seek to attain a level of income from your trading program that is AT LEAST equal to the amount necessary to support your current standard of living. You should seek to accomplish this task as quickly as possible.

Once achieved, you will have attained the minimum level of financial freedom required for your own personal financial situation. Your investment income (again, assuming consistency) will have insured you against an unforeseen unemployment and afforded you the CHOICE of remaining or not remaining at your current employment.

Why Trade?

*The day you take
complete responsibility for yourself,
the day you
stop making any excuses,
that's the day you start to the top.*
- O. J. Simpson

Having lived in Oklahoma over the past few years with its agrarian and energy base, I have been provided with many examples of how easily informed, intelligent, and very astute investors and business people can overleverage their affairs and QUICKLY, within a period of but a few months, lose their entire fortune and see their life's work, earnings, and businesses vanish.

These people have received the ultimate margin call!

You may have observed the same occurring in your area of the country as the rolling recession of the 1980s has, at different times, hit basic industry, agriculture, natural resource, high technology, financial, and other sectors of the economy forcing business closures, job termination, job relocation, farm foreclosures, real estate deflation, restructurings, and so on.

And yet the period immediately preceding these recessions was marked by high double-digit inflation, booming oil and gold prices, a collapsing bond market, and a stagnant stock market.

Forbes magazine annually lists the wealthiest people in America. Many faces, such as the Hunts of Texas, who began the decade on or near the top of this list, have disappeared entirely.

In my opinion, many of these people have spun the economic roulette wheel of financial prudence and structured their finances in such a manner that they and their businesses benefitted primarily only if the price of the goods they were selling went up faster than the costs of acquiring or producing those goods.

With a friendly local banker or Uncle Sam eager to loan money to such thriving businesses, it was easy to borrow to finance such rapid growth when, after all, it was widely known that the price of oil would soon be at $ 60.00 or $ 100.00 (since worldwide proven reserves would only be sufficient to supply another eight years usage); or that stocks would soon be at 5,000 (since the business cycle had been permanently repealed); or that residential real estate prices HAD to continue going up (since they aren't making any more of the stuff)!

I call these people INVESTORS. Again, they were in a position to benefit ONLY if prices kept going UP. You know them in the stock market as "long term investors" or "blue chip investors". They will quote you statistics such as this one from Ibbotson Associates in Chicago, which states that "Over five-year time periods, you have a 94 percent chance of making money in the stock market. Over ten-year periods, you have a 99 percent chance of coming out ahead and your odds of making 10 to 20 percent on your money, compounded annually, are better than even".

GRANTED, THOSE ARE GREAT ODDS!

They and similar statistics and arguments are sufficient to convince most Americans that it is PRUDENT and PROPER that one should become an investor with one's money.

UNTIL, that is, something like the bear markets of 1973-74 or October, 1987 occur!

The trader, in contrast, not only seeks higher returns, but also seeks greater security and freedom by insulating himself from the one-way blinders that the investor wears.

Many this past decade have positioned their assets in such a manner that they prospered as investors normally do - e.g., only when the businesses and markets in which they are invested INCREASE in price or expansion occurs.

When business, industry, and their related markets contract, however, investors can be crucified, especially if they have leveraged (borrowed money to buy) their one-way bet!

Eventually, a greater fool is needed to buy their leveraged asset at a higher price if they are to profit.

Joseph Granville used to call these final purchasers "the bagholders" since they rush in and violently shove and push others aside in order to buy that which they so deeply desire to possess. Whatever was in the bag, it was increasing in price quite rapidly since it had been mentioned in the newspapers / magazines that there would soon be none left. Besides, it was also touted on television by the most respected analysts. So they push, and they shove, and they grab their precious bag. And when they have won and own the bag, they hold it high above their head for all to see. Then they lower the bag and look inside. When they see nothing, they realize the value of what they have bought.

Another market top has been made.

Contrast this one-way positioning to that of the trader who is always flexible to the extent that he is willing to buy or trade from the long side an industry, its products, its stocks, or its bonds during a period of prosperity and is just as willing to sell short or trade from the short side during periods of contraction when "the bagholders" are having to sell at any price and are pushing price downward in an ever-decreasing spiral.

Hence, the basic reason why markets FALL FASTER THAN THEY RISE!

Leverage, like the Bryan Adams song says, "Cuts Like a Knife."

Hence, who is in better position to prosper over long periods of time during the various periods of inflation/deflation, expansion /contraction, boom/bust, overbought/oversold, and recession/

stagflation/depression that always have characterized AND AL-WAYS WILL characterize one's investment environment than the well armed, educated, and prepared trader?

Besides being able to profit during periods of both proserity and contractions within a single industry, the trader additionally has several other advantages over the investor.

He can, for instance, easily move his assets from an industry that is stagnant to one that is either experiencing rapid prosperity or rapid contraction.

This ease of movement reflects the trader's total liquidity. Every day he knows the value of his holdings. Contrast the importance of such current information with the recent experience of Donald Trump. Trump claimed a personal net worth of $ 5 billion based on his own estimates of his holdings in 1989 (according to Cable News Network) versus various financial publications' estimates of his net worth in early 1990 of somewhere around $ 500 million. If both are correct, $ 4 1/2 billion of his funds had disappeared within one year and he apparently was oblivious to it. By June, 1990, banks were knocking at the door with their margin call on his empire in hand.

Did he not know the extent of the devaluation of his holdings? Were the markets he was participating in not liquid enough to allow for easy disposal of assets when the decline began.

Had Trump become the ultimate bagholder? Only time will tell!

Contrast this experience with that of a trader, however. When the equity value of a trader begins to decline, he can very simply flatten his positions, take some time to clear the cobwebs of his mind, and later approach positions again with a fresh perspective.

Finally, the most important reason for developing a trading program is the freedom of choice it affords the successful trader.

If a two-month vacation is desired, one can simply turn the trading process off for two months and return refreshed with the batteries recharged. (Not to mention the ability to finance the entire trip with one's trading profits).

The potential for earnings is limited only by one's talents and perseverence.

If one would prefer another area of the country to live in, electronic advancements of the past several years afford the opportunity to relocate and continue operations with little interruption other than the normal problems associated with moving.

If trading for yourself, you have only the Internal Revenue Service to deal with. There are no bosses. Employees and their attendant problems are nonexistant. There is no OSHA, EPA, CFTC, NFA, FBI, FERC, USDA, and so on, with which to deal!

Further, the pressures of "making a living" instead of "living a life" disappear when one can become a consistently successful trader.

Also, when successful, the trader experiences total freedom of thought, expression, and association at levels unparalleled in our society today.

Trading allows you to shuck the shackles of financial dependence and all the negative thoughts and stress associated with the dependency and insecurity of a job.

If you would like to support a particularly worthy social cause, it will be YOUR CHOICE whether to provide time, money, or both and you will, if successful, have ample supplies of both to contribute.

I simply cannot say enough about personal financial independence.

Why should you trade?

It's simple!

TO BE FREE!

My advice to you is to go out and succeed and enjoy yourself while doing it!!!

(And please write and tell me of your experience when you have arrived at your destination)!

About The Almanac's
Product Reviews

*It's better to help others
get on board than to tell them
where to go.*

Throughout "The $upertrader's Almanac", attempts have been made to identify products produced by other vendors and authors that best explain, discuss, and support the theories reviewed throughout this book.

Ideally, for each subject, an attempt is made to identify a book that the reader could refer to for more in depth information on the subject, a newsletter for current information on the subject, a hotline or fax service, a video tape, a software package (if applicable), a seminar, and so on.

Our original intent in listing other vendor's products in The Almanac was simply to make readers aware of what additional information was available on a particular subject area beyond our abbreviated articles.

Our concern from an image point of view grew, however, as I did not want to be associated as having directed our readers to "junk". It was thus decided that the best way to approach this subject was to perform "due diligence" on the products reviewed (to the best extent possible) and to weed out those that don't measure up.

Note that in performing such a service, I am not judging on the merits of, say, a weather newsletter or how successful the newsletter's recommendations have been over a given period of time. There are other services available in the industry that perform the "who's hot" function. What I am saying is that, for those people who are interested in following the weather and its effects on markets, here is the best newsletter I have been able to review that, in my opinion, covers and explains the subject; here is the best book; here is the best video tape; and so on.

My interest thus is whether or not the product can properly identify and explain the buy and sell signals that the theory generates (if followed properly). In my opinion, THAT is where the Almanac reader's interest lies.

Over a long period of time, if the subject has validity, the recommendations should digress towards the true value that the theory has in interpreting and profiting from market movements.

In such abstract subjects as The Elliott Wave, Gann, Cycles, and so on, judgment on the usefulness of these products can be subjective. Such opinion is unfortunate, indeed, but the issues involved are simply not black and white.

So why don't we have YOUR favorite weather (or whatever) newsletter, book, or other product listed? There are many possible reasons. First, I may not be aware of the existence of the product. Second, I may have contacted the vendor and received a stack of advertisements and letters on how good their product is, but until I have the product in my hot little hands and have had a chance to "kick the tires", we have nothing to review or recommend. Third, the vendor may not have responded to our inquiry. Fourth, we may have received a response but have not had time yet to review the product.

And, finally, the product may have just not measured up (in my opinion).

The Almanac's Trade of the Year

> *Don't gamble!*
> *Take all your savings*
> *and buy some good stock —*
> *hold it 'till it goes up,*
> *then sell it.*
> *If it don't go up,*
> *don't buy it.*
> *- Will Rogers*

We began listing a "Trade of the Year" with the publication of "The 1988 Commodity Trader's Almanac".

In 1990, we additionally listed a "Second Half Trade of the Year."

The objective of these trades was to provide the reader with an idea that, in our best estimation, was timely and might allow the $upertrader to apply some of the trading techniques discussed in The Almanac in a high-probability, low-risk situation.

We usually attempt to suggest a spread in this trade because of the lower volatility that spreads normally entail versus outright long or short trading positions.

The trade is usually presented within the context of a "Trading Matrix" which allows one to apply the principle of "Scaling-In" should one so desire (see "Scaling" in the "Analytical Techniques" chapter).

Since it is impossible to know the individual financial circumstances of each purchaser of The $upertrader's Almanac, the "Trade of the Year" suggestions are obviously not personal, individual investment advice but are general trade ideas with supportive information that one can use to make a determination based on one's own individual financial circumstances of whether the "Trade of the Year" is appropriate for each individual.

Nevertheless, since the introduction of this concept, we are happy to report that the "Trade of the Year" for each of the years the concept has been presented has proven to have been quite profitable and that these trades have so far returned each year several times the cost of this book for those who have chosen to participate.

The "Trade of the Year" is presented each year in "The Calendar Book" and reflects the author's best assessment of fundamental and technical factors in the upcoming year.

For Your Teenager

"When I was a boy of 14,
my father was so ignorant
I could hardly stand to have the old man around.
But when I got to be 21
I was astonished at how much
the old man had learned in 7 years."
- Mark Twain

Having a young man just a little older than the age of the boy in Mark Twain's reflection above always brings to mind the above quote when I am at the receiving end of one of "those" looks where the eyeballs roll upwards to the sky and a heavy sigh of exasperation spews forward from deep within.

Oh, but could I arrange for a pigeon to fly overhead at the moment and do what pigeon's do best to countless statues throughout the land.

Being unable to make such arrangements, however, I instead sent my son to 2 camps that he thoroughly enjoyed and learned from immensely. Your teenager will, too!

The first is The United States Space Camp at the NASA Space and Rocket Center, One Tranquility Base, Huntsville, AL 35807-0680 (800-633-7280).

What a quality program this is centered around the Space Shuttle and other scientific experiments and observations.

This will likely prove to be a truly richly rewarding experience for your youngster as (s)he explores various aspects of space and space travel.

The second is The Jefferson Institute Entrepreneur Bootcamp, 757A South Main Street, Springville, UT 84663 (800-672-6019)

This program is geared towards developing the entrepreneurial spirit in young people and allowing them some romping room in the Colorado Rockies in mid summer.

The highlight is the competition between young entrepreneurs when they each are given paper funds to invest in the stock market. The winner is awarded a real numismatic gold coin in this simulated experiment.

Your child will come home with several business opportunity ideas that will help him develop that creative business spirit that is so difficult to otherwise teach.

Both of these camps are highly recommended and will likely provide your youngster with valuable experiences (s)he will treasure for the rest of his/her life.

Physical Preparation

If I had known I was going to live this long,
I would have taken better care of myself.

It has been said that the markets make a cruel lover and that more emotions can be experienced in trading for a month than many will experience in five years. I would certainly not dispute those statements but do feel that there are some steps that one can AND SHOULD take to short circuit some potential problems long before they become problems.

The first concerns your health, and, especially, your physical well-being or wellness. After one reaches the early or mid-thirties, it becomes increasingly important that you maintain your physical condition. Two types of physical conditioning programs are involved. The first and most important is aerobic activity geared to increasing AND SUSTAINING your heart rate at a level of 80 percent of its maximum capacity for at least 15 minutes (and preferably longer) 3 or 4 times a week.

If you are feeling sluggish, you will be amazed at what a little aerobic exercise can do for you.

The computer screen may be better than apple pie as far as many active traders are concerned, but its also replacing the "t" in "stud" with a "p" and turning many into "computer potatoes". People sit in front of screens all day long and watch the ever-changing tick chart while their eyes slowly deteriorate and the rolls spring out around their waistline.

Vigorous, regular exercise will help you turn that "spud" in you around. It's ironic that something that will make you feel so good and is so good for you is ignored by so many. Also, because of the strain of the profession (most of which is self-induced), I would suggest that you not only get a regular physical examination, but that you also increase the frequency of the exams simply because of the nature of the business. Also, make sure your doctor is aware of and approves your exercise program if you are middle-aged or older.

Finally, how often do you watch . . . . (fill in the blank with the six o'clock news, the ten o'clock news, the morning show, a football game, the Johnny Carson show, Financial News Network, or whatever)? Consider this - if you regularly watch the 6 o'clock news, you can cycle on a stationary bicycle for 30 minutes while you watch your favorite program every evening (you will wind up feeling far better when the half hour is over than that news show is EVER going to make you feel)! I have a Bally's Lifecycle myself and highly recommend it. It has a little computer in it which simulates hills as it increases and decreases the resistance of the peddling. A 12 minute workout leaves one feeling "Energized" (but check with your doctor first if over 30). If you will implement such a program, you will still be able to watch the TV but will get more out of the time and will wind up feeling better. And your trading will probably benefit, too, from your increased alertness!

The second type of physical conditioning that one will benefit immensely from involves your strength and stamina. This doesn't mean reserving a space at Venice Beach, but it does mean supplementing your aerobic conditioning with some muscle conditioning. The product that I find ideal for our profession is the old Charles Atlas "Bullworker". If you cannot engage a personal weight trainer or otherwise enter a formal strength development program, you will benefit from this device as you assume your favorite "computer potato" position. The product is a spring resistance bar that you push and pull against, doing a type of isometric/isotonic exercise that is quite good for toning.

Will this keep people from kicking sand in your face at the beach?

I doubt it, but it will help your physical conditioning!

And I just simply cannot emphasize enough the importance of being in good physical shape if you plan on trading successfully!

Mental Preparation

*If you don't know
who you are, the market
is an expensive place
to find out.*
- George Goodman (paraphrased)

There are three basic elements involved in trading successfully - the first involves mastering the markets, the second involves managing your money, and the third involves mastering yourself. Most traders focus entirely on the first element. This exclusion of the other two elements is the major reason for the high rate of failure among novice traders. In order to succeed over the long term in the markets, you will have to master all three.

While experienced traders generally consider trading psychology to be important, if not critical, beginning traders generally consider it of little interest and value. Many professionals even believe that it is the mental and emotional side of trading which is the downfall of almost all traders.

Many of the qualities that will help a person in other parts of his life can hurt him in a trading program. For instance, ego may make you a good sales person, but it will ruin you in the markets. Greed may help your other businesses succeed but it will ruin you in the markets. Time may help you recover from a disastrous love affair, but it will kill you if you are long 5,000 shares of IBM that are dropping 75 cents per day.

By condensing and concentrating our emotional experiences, the markets amplify our experiences and thereby bring out the best and the worst in all of us. Learning to overcome psychological problems will make us not only better and more successful traders, but will help us in other facets of our lives as well.

As one's trading evolves, it will usually progress from trying to learn how to be a genius at predicting markets to buying expensive trading systems or vice versa.

SOME OF THE FORTUNATE FEW EVENTUALLY FIGURE OUT AT SOME POINT THAT ONE OF THE REAL KEYS IN MAKING CONSISTENT PROFITS LIES NOT IN PREDICTING THE MARKETS BUT IN KNOWING AND CONTROLLING ONE'S SELF.

Unfortunately, those who need to explore the psychology of trading the most are usually the ones who cannot be bothered by it. They are usually "too busy" or will "look into it later". The truthful answer, however, is often that they perhaps just do not want to face the answers.

Investment psychology is fascinating. Back in the days of 20-Mule Team Borax when I was a stockbroker, I was amazed to find out that when people bought stock from a broker, their subconscious comfort level was highest if, just after the purchase, the price of the stock went down just a little. Not a lot, mind you, but definitely not UP a lot, either. Why? If it went down a lot, the reasons for discomfort are obvious. If it went UP a lot, they were uncomfortable because they HAD to make another decision!

Do they buy more, hold, or sell?

Having to make another decision increases the level of discomfort! If the stock went DOWN just a bit, however, most investors were comfortable because they first of all did not have to make another decision. Secondly, they were able to rejoice in their correct first impression that "I KNEW that I was right and that I shouldn't have bought that stock and listened to that broker". In other words, they were not only able to transfer responsibility for the decision to the broker, but were able to avoid having to make another decision besides! Hence, the reason why the level of comfort was so high even though the stock had gone down a little.

Trading can present especially unique problems because, as discussed earlier, the leverage involved tends to magnify the psychological problems that arise. For instance, there are many people who find losses unacceptable, so they avoid having to make a decision that would result in closing out a position at a loss (perhaps YOU can remember once being in this situation). They HOPE that the market will turn and the loss will be avoided. As a result, the loss continues to grow until it is FORCED on the investor. A few such situations may at first be avoided, but eventually the habit catches up with this type investor. And when it does, the impact of forcing a large loss on the average investor who cannot accept even a small loss can be psychologically devastating!

Since our society places such a premium on winning, losses can be difficult to deal with. Yet the successful trader has learned somewhere along the line that an essential secret of winning is to make it O.K. TO LOSE! He will, in fact, often perceive the experience as an educational one and learn from it rather than dwelling on the negative aspects. Or he will be pleased that the loss has been taken because he is secure in the knowledge that some of those small losses would have otherwise developed into large, uncontrollable losses.

HENCE, THE ENTIRE PROCESS OF TAKING QUICK, SMALL, DISCIPLINED LOSSES IS VIEWED BY THE SUCCESSFUL TRADER AS BEING A NECESSARY AND POSITIVE ONE FOR IT WILL, OVER TIME, BETTER PRESERVE THE TRADER'S CAPITAL.

For most investors, dealing with profits can be equally difficult. What happens if one sells too soon and the price goes WAY up? What happens if one does NOT sell and the price goes back DOWN? Or if a stop is placed that is uncovered by floor traders or specialists who then reverse direction and run the price back

up! Which positions should be held and which should be liquidated? And so on.

Imagine yourself a merchant and you have two products. At the
end of the first month, one of the products has sold out and the
second hasn't sold. You would want to restock more of the
hotseller, right? In fact, it would make sense to take a loss on
the second product by selling it at a discount in order to raise
cash to buy more of the first. If such is the natural reaction, then
why do people reverse this process when they trade markets and
sell for small profits while keeping losers?

> *The fault, dear Brutus,*
> *is not in our systems,*
> *but in ourselves*
> *that we are losers.*
> *- William Shakespeare*

I once read where the developer of a successful trading system
canvassed his purchasers after the first year's experience of his
system and found that fewer than ten percent of the people were
still trading the system DESPITE the fact that the year had been
quite profitable.

Reading this upset me because I sell some day trading systems
myself. In fact, after reflecting on the situation, I added a portion
to our advertising that discusses the mental aspect of trading the
system. In an attempt to make it easier psychologically for the
purchaser to stick with the system and take every order, I
included a statement that the person who trades the system
should back the system with $ 10,000 per contract traded and
be willing to lose that grubstake (this amount of money far
exceeded the worst historical drawdown that the system had
experienced during a four year period in which it had run up over
$ 100,000 in profits).

The psychological ploy here was to get the purchaser to COMMIT
TO FOLLOWING THE SYSTEM rather than worrying whether the
next trade was going to be a loser or a winner, changing the
signals because the money supply report was up/down, trying to
outguess the algorithm, placing some orders and not placing

others, etc. The idea was to follow the system unless it lost the original $ 10,000.

I felt comfortable presenting the idea to people on this basis because of the expectation that they would be more apt to benefit from the system if they had committed themselves in advance to working with the structured rules and defined risk. Once I started including the mental aspect in our literature, however, our sales completely dried up! The only thing I could figure was that people just didn't seem to want to accept the DISCIPLINE involved in following the rules.

If you have a technique, a given set of rules, a trading system, etc., one thing you might regularly do is congratulate yourself at the end of each day you properly follow the rules of the system. Review and correct those days that you do not. NOTE THAT THIS REVIEW PROCESS HAS ABSOLUTELY NOTHING TO DO WITH WHETHER OR NOT YOU WERE PROFITABLE! Why? Because you are reinforcing the discipline needed to successfully trade by the rules of the system in your review process. If you are not following the rules of whatever system or technique you are trading, you are trading a different system for which you have no rules. You are not trading YOUR system! However, if you DO follow the rules and the system does not meet your objectives, you can make a conscious decision to alter the rules or to change systems entirely and then work with the rules of the new system.

> *"Deal the cards faster", cried the losers,*
> *as the winners laughed and told dirty jokes.*
> *- Thomas Lillard*

One of the most basic questions a trader should ask himself is whether he is trading to make money or for the fun of it. Silly as that may sound, many trade for the fun of it EVEN THOUGH THEY MAY THINK THEY ARE TRADING TO MAKE A PROFIT.

The two are conflicting approaches!

Conflict creates stress!

Recreational trading is free-form with little or no money-management control. Trades are entered to "see what will happen" and, especially, to "outsmart" the market. Losses are subconsciously expected.

Trading-for-profit is more like running a business. Costs (losses) are controlled and revenues (profits) maximized on a rather emotionless, calculated, mechanical basis. Trades are not entered unless certain risk/reward ratios are met.

Where do YOU honestly fit and could this be having an effect on your trading results?

If speculation
keeps you awake at night,
sell down to the sleeping point!

Much of the foreseeable future will be spent analyzing the ongoing battle between the bull and the bear, inflation and disinflation, growth and recession, and so on, just as it always has been. ALL WILL POSITION THEIR FORTUNES ONE WAY OR THE OTHER IN ORDER TO MAXIMIZE THE PROFITS AND MINIMIZE THE LOSSES OF THESE PERCEIVED PRICE AND ECONOMIC MOVEMENTS!

Some will correctly buy stocks, or bonds, or gold, or real estate, or businesses, or farmland, or CDs, or whatever. Some will do so incorrectly!

Those who correctly position themselves in whatever is "hot" for the next year or two will profit handsomely. In 1978 through 1980, it was oil, metals, and intangibles. In the early 1980s it was short positions in foreign currencies. From 1982 to 1986 it was paper assets with stocks and service industries continuing until 1987.

Denominating funds in the currencies of most foreign countries has been quite profitable since early 1985 through January, 1988. Subsequently, the grains took over when affected by the 1988 drought with meats following in 1989 and into 1990 and the food group performing quite well over the same period.

There is the other side of these perceived "opportunities" to consider, however.

Many people in this area of the country have had to close the doors to their energy-related business when they found out that they had positioned themselves incorrectly. As oil prices collapsed, they found out that their business could only profit if the price of oil went the other way (UP)!

Many family farms of generations back have been foreclosed in the last few years as farmers discovered that they were positioned incorrectly. They were able to grow their crops at a profit and service their debt only when prices were HIGH!

Many good, solid banks and the people who ran them have had to close their doors when they found out that their business was incorrectly positioned and was tied to an energy, agricultural, or real estate industry that was able to thrive only when prices remained HIGH!

Many workers throughout this great country of ours who had worked at basic-industry jobs for decades suddenly found themselves incorrectly positioned and unemployed in the early 1980s when foreign competition and dollar strength exported their jobs overseas!

Many get-rich-quick would-be millionaires of the no-money-down, even-get-some-back real estate television charades found themselves incorrectly positioned and holding unsalable real estate with large first, second, and third mortgages in the central, southwestern and, more recently, northeastern United States as the economies there went into virtual depression! (Talk about a margin call)!!!

Many are still holding the gold coins they bought in the early eighties and would just love to be able to sell them (if only they could break even) as would many who bought and held stocks in 1987!

Many have borrowed money through "junk bond" financing to have the privilege of buying a company at its highest price ever and taking it private (reminds one of the Petro-Lewis, Apache, Houston Oil & Gas, and Chase Econometrics $ 60.00/bbl oil price forecast in the early 1980s)!

Many very smart and learned people have bet their fortunes correctly in the last few years and made a killing. As we can see from the above, however, some didn't do so hot even though, at the time, everyone thought that the people who were making the above investments were QUITE ASTUTE!

What one business was able to profit from these market conditions BE THEY UP OR DOWN! If you guessed trading, you're on your way!

Despite it being so hard to succeed at trading, IF YOU EVER MAKE IT, YOU WILL HAVE GAINED THE GREATEST (material) SECURITY OF ALL!

That security is financial freedom!

If you can properly manage your business (your trading account) on a consistently profitable basis, you will be able to profit if the bull or the bear prevails, if we inflate or deflate, if growth is sustained or depression comes calling, and so on.

There will be only four risks you may possibly have to face - 1.) Revolution (i.e., we become the "United States of Something Else"), 2.) Exchange Insolvency (or what would have happened if The New York Stock Exchange HAD stopped trading on October 20th, 1987, or if you had the majority of your savings in one of those Ohio thrifts a couple of years ago and could only withdraw $ 750 of your own money per month, or if you were long Silver back in 1980 when the COMEX changed the rules to "liquidation only" orders), 3.) Your Brokerage Firm's Solvency, or 4.) government confiscation of whatever it is in which you denominate the majority of your assets.

The pot of gold at the end of the rainbow is large indeed!

To achieve it, you must master three things;

The first is the markets.

The second is the management of your money.

The third is yourself.

Money can't provide happiness,
but neither can poverty!

How to Use the Symbols

We are symbols,
and inhabit symbols.
- Essays: Second Series (1844), The Poet

(This article is also repeated in the back of "The Calendar Book" for convenience).

Symbols are used throughout the Almanac to refer to the various markets discussed. For the most part, the symbols used in The Almanac conform to those of most quote machines (hence, the reason why "CL" is used for Crude Oil). The notable differences are for BD, CA, CD, CF, GO, LR, NY, SU, TN, UL, VL, WK, and WM.

Here are the symbols for the various markets -

AD	- Australian Dollar	JY	- Japanese Yen
AL	- Aluminum	LB	- Lumber
BD	- United States Treasury Bond	LC	- Live Cattle
BO	- Soybean Oil	LH	- Live Hogs
BP	- British Pound	LR	- Leaded Gasoline
C	- Corn	MB	- Municipal Bonds
CA	- Canadian Dollar	NY	- NYSE Index
CC	- Cocoa	O	- Oats
CD	- Certificate of Deposit	OJ	- Orange Juice
CF	- Coffee	PA	- Palladium
CI	- CRB Index	PB	- Pork Bellies
CL	- Crude Oil	PL	- Platinum
CP	- Copper	PP	- Propane
CT	- Cotton	S	- Soybeans
DJB	- Dow Jones Bonds	SF	- Swiss Franc
DJI	- Dow Jones Industrial	SM	- Soybean Meal
DJT	- Dow Jones Transportation	SP	- S & P 500
DJU	- Dow Jones Utility	SU	- Sugar No. 11
DM	- Deutschmark	SV	- CMX Silver
DX	- Dollar Index	TB	- US T-Bills
ED	- Eurodollar	TN	- US T-Notes
FC	- Feeder Cattle	UL	- Unleaded Gasoline
GM	- GNMA	VL	- KC Value Line
GO	- CMX Gold	W	- CBT Wheat
GS	- Grain Sorghum	WK	- Kansas City Wheat
HO	- Heating Oil	WM	- Minneapolis Wheat

Hence, when we discuss the "WM" market, we are discussing Minneapolis Wheat.

Symbols are also used to refer to specific contracts of a commodity when we are discussing the futures markets rather than the futures market itself. This is done by combining the symbol for the market (as listed in the table above) and the symbol for a specific month (as listed in the table below).

Here are the symbols for the months of the year -

JAN	F	D	JUL	N	T
FEB	G	E	AUG	Q	R
MAR	H	I	SEP	U	B
APR	J	L	OCT	V	C
MAY	K	O	NOV	X	W
JUN	M	P	DEC	Z	Y

The first column is the symbol for the first year while the second column is the symbol for the second year.

As an example, bonds trade four contracts per year (March, June, September, and December). Using the table above, the symbol for March is "H" ("M" for June, "U" for September, and "Z" for December). Thus, to define the specific March bond contract, we combine the commodity symbol (BD) with the month symbol (H) and obtain "BDH".

If we wanted to refer to a specific year for the March US Treasury Bond contract, we would just add the year. BDH81 thus refers to the March, 1981 contract.

"BDI" thus refers to the second year of the March Bond contract. For instance, in January, 1991, "BDH" refers to the March, 1991 Bond contract, while "BDI" refers to the March, 1992 contract. Note that in April, 1991, "BDH" becomes the March, 1992 contract while "BDI" becomes the March, 1993 contract.

Chapter 2

You and Your Broker

Your Brokerage Relationship

If you want free service,
you'll have to pay for it!

There are eight main ingredients of a successful brokerage relationship -

1.) The solvency of the firm (it doesn't do any good to succeed at trading if the firm goes under and takes your capital with it (see the related article on "Brokerage Firm Solvency"),

2.) How good the fills or executions are (this varies from firm to firm AND FROM MARKET TO MARKET WITHIN THE FIRM),

3.) Commissions (a full-service firm charges more than a discounter but will provide more support, too (research reports, hand holding, recommendations, etc.). However, if that is not what you need, a no-frills discounter may be for you. It is my own personal opinion that most traders put too much emphasis on commissions instead of superior fills which winds up costing them more in the long run),

4.) Margins (they vary widely from firm to firm and CAN ALSO VARY WITHIN THE FIRM FROM CUSTOMER TO CUSTOMER),

5.) The firm's T-Bill and money market fund policies (how much of your own funds can you put to work earning interest?),

6.) Operations (are trades frequently messed up, do confirmations arrive promptly, does it take weeks to make trade corrections, do hours pass before you find out at what price your order was filled, can you easily interpret the monthly statements, etc.?),

7.) Service (does it take 5 rings before the phone is answered, are the brokers courteous, are requested items promptly forwarded and changes promptly made?), and

8.) Intangibles (does the firm make it seem like it is a PRIVILEGE for you to do business with them, does the firm provide a national watts line, does the firm provide a supplementary monthly newsletter, have you known the individual you deal with for years, is he/she a relative, and so on?).

I am frequently asked to recommend a broker, but would rather state that I do business with LIT America, Inc., in Chicago, a discount firm, and that speaks for itself. (Contact Mr. John Chalupa, Manager of the Special Services Division, 800-826-8035. Mention the Almanac and you will qualify for a special discount. Also, ask Mr. Chalupa about LIT's execution capabilities and to demonstrate their "arb" capability).

Brokerage Firm Solvency

*Bankruptcy is a legal proceeding
in which you put your money in your pants pocket
and give your coat to your creditors.*
- Joey Adams

The default at Volume Investors Corporation in 1985 spurred the following question; "How can the financial stability of a brokerage firm be assessed?"

Consider the following -

One of the major attractions of futures trading is the clearinghouse system. In short, the clearinghouse of each exchange acts as custodian of all funds so that all winners are assured receipt of their profits. Hence, the financial integrity of a trader's account is made secure by

1.) his own funds,

2.) the guaranty funds each brokerage firm is required to deposit with the clearinghouse,

3.) the clearinghouse's own cash reserves, and

4.) the joint responsibility of the collective membership of the clearing house.

It is because of these layers of protection that the futures industry points with pride that no customer has ever lost a single cent as the result of the failure of any commodity clearing house. NOTE, HOWEVER, THAT NOT ALL FIRMS ARE MEMBERS OF THE CLEARING HOUSE and also that SOME ARE MEMBERS AT ONE EXCHANGE AND NOT MEMBERS OF A DIFFERENT EX-CHANGE. Non-members would not necessarily be afforded the same protection as members in the event of failure.

Also, in times of brokerage firm failure, one should note that even with member firms, each exchange guarantees only that the futures positions will be transferred to another member firm AND NOT CASH BALANCES OR FUNDS INVESTED IN UNITED STATES TREASURY BILLS. These funds and securities can be left behind as they become subject to bankruptcy proceedings. For a non-member, both futures AND cash are subject to bank-ruptcy proceedings and are frozen. (Commodity accounts are not afforded the equivalent of Securities Investors Protection Corpo-ration (SIPC) or Federal Deposit Insurance (FDIC)).

Additionally, many commodity firms are owned as subsidiaries of larger firms, EVEN AT SOME OF THE NATION'S LARGEST FULL-SERVICE BROKERAGE FIRMS, and it is difficult, if not impossible, to ascertain just how safe your money would be in the event of a crisis (i.e., where the firm was faced with having to bankrupt its commodities division in order to survive)! There is also no way to ascertain at any one time what the credit worthi-ness of a firm's customers is, what the risks of the firm's and the firm's customers' positions are, or how diversified or concen-trated the risks of the firm's customers are (with a large number of customers being better than a majority of the risk being concentrated in a very few accounts)!

There are many safeguards built into the system, however. For instance, firms are required to maintain 6 percent of their assets in cash. If this percentage falls to 4 percent, the firm is subjected to monthly audits. The firm's accounts are then transferred to other clearing members if the cash falls below 4 percent.

There are additionally some steps that a trader can take on his own. For instance, each futures commission merchant (FCM) must file financial information regularly and is subject to quar-terly and spot financial audits. This information can be analyzed to provide an idea of the financial integrity of a firm. Ownership equity (including subordinated loans), for instance, will tell how much the people who own the firm have sunk into it. All cash, securities, and other property owed to nonrelated customers must BY LAW be held in separate accounts (customer segregated accounts) and is totaled and listed as customer segregated equity. One important relationship to look at is therefore the ownership equity to the customer segregated equity. Typical of these ratios is a range of 15-25 percent with a large number being preferable.

FCMs are required to meet and maintain funds above their minimum capital requirements. Funds above this requirement are excess capital. This figure should be compared to the firm's minimum capital requirement and to its largest liability, customer segregated equity (again on a ratio basis). For the latter, a ratio in the 5-10 percent range is typical with a large number again being preferable.

Margins

In God we trust;
all others must pay cash.
- American saying

Many investors are familiar with margin from their stock accounts. Margin as it pertains to a commodities account is different, however. It is so different, in fact, that, in this observer's opinion, the term should not even be used in conjunction with commodities. The reason is that it conjures up visions of stock market margins in the minds of those not truly familiar with the terms. A better name would be "deposit" or some similar term.

In stocks, margin is a down payment, the first installment of the purchase price for shares of stocks. In a sense, it is similar to a home mortgage in that a purchase consists of both equity (or funds deposited by the investor) and debt (or funds borrowed by the investor from the broker and upon which the investor pays interest to the broker). The total of equity and debt completes the purchase of the asset which is, in this case, shares of stock. A major difference is that there is not a definite time period over which the loan is extended when stocks are purchased on margin (versus, say, a typical 30 year mortgage on a home). Since the Great Depression, the Federal Reserve Board has regulated credit for purchasing stocks and has held the margin rate at 50 percent since 1974.

In commodities, margin is not a down payment on anything. When a trader enters a futures contract, he is making a promise to buy or sell something IN THE FUTURE. The margin is thus just a good-faith deposit or a sum of money that the trader puts up to show his intent to make good on his promise. It should be noted that both the buyer AND the seller are required to make margin deposit with their respective brokers to guarantee payment of profits to the winners from the losers.

Since futures margins are not down payments on loans, they have not historically been regulated by the Federal Reserve or any other governmental agency. Instead, they have been set by the exchanges. As a rule of thumb, futures margins usually amount to what the customer might reasonably expect to lose in one bad day in the market. Hence, as the volatility of any given commodity increases, so does the margin required to maintain the position. These margin rates are termed "Exchange Minimum Margins" or "Exchange Minimums". Each brokerage house may then set its own "house" requirements at any level it chooses so long as it is at least equal to or greater than the exchange minimum.

Some firms which treat commodities as a sideline to their major business of securities trading may set ridiculously high margin requirements. For instance, a while back I had a Coffee spread listed in "The Spread Investment Letter" at $ 250 which was right off the margin requirement sheet at my firm.

A subscriber called and related how he had checked the rates at three firms (one a full service and two discounters) and that the requirement for this spread was listed at $ 3,000, $ 7,000 and $9,000 (the full service firm was, surprisingly, the lower of the three)!

Some firms also have "layered" or "tiered" margin rates. They extend a low rate to their most credit-worthy customers and a second, higher rate to other customers. Some even go so far as to have three different margin levels. Using a T-bond contract as an example, the margin might thus look something as follows (assume an exchange minimum at $ 2,000) - level 1 margins (perhaps called "exchange minimums") might be at $ 2,500, $500 above the actual exchange minimum, with level 2 margins ("house minimums") at, say, $ 3,500 while level 3 margins ("firm minimums") might be set at, say $ 4,500.

These higher margin rates offer advantages to the brokerage house in the form of greater security and the use of free money upon which the firm can earn interest overnight. The disadvantages to the customer are that he does not have the benefit of interest earned on his own money and additionally forfeits the greater diversification and corresponding stability that lower margins are able to provide an account.

It is important to also be aware that the individual brokerage firm will usually have two margin rates - the INITIAL margin requirement and the MAINTENANCE margin requirement. The initial requirement is the amount of money that must be free in the account in order to enter into a new position. For instance, in our example above, if your account was afforded exchange minimum margins and you wanted to trade a T-bond long or short, you would need to have $ 2,000 in your account in excess of all other commitments.

If the maintenance margin requirement were $ 1,500 on this position, you would be able to maintain the position so long as your account had $ 1,500 in it. In other words, the account would be able to sustain a loss of $ 500 prior to a call being issued by the brokerage firm for more funds. Once your account value dipped below the maintenance requirement, however, you would be issued a maintenance margin call for additional funds and would usually have 2 days to meet the call or be forced to liquidate the position.

Some firms will allow favorable market action to meet this call while others will not. For instance, if your equity dropped to $1,200 and you were given a call, the call might be forgiven if the next day the bond experienced a favorable change which valued the account at more than the maintenance margin requirement.

If you are dealing with a discount firm, expect that they will ask you for either an overnight cashier's check or money order or a fed funds wire from your bank to their bank to meet a margin call. Besides noting that margins vary greatly between (and even within) firms, one should note that they also change rapidly as market volatility changes.

Such changes are shown in the following chart of November Soybeans during the 1988 bull / bear market. Note the changes in margin rates and the subsequent market action. Note, too, that these are the exchange minimum margins and that they may have been DRAMATICALLY higher at individual firms.

Finally, observe the fallacy in which some simulation studies engage when performing historical simulation studies of which a given static margin rate is assumed. In our Soybean example, for instance, although the simulation study may have shown a great short sale from early to late July based on a constant $ 1,500 margin rate (which was common for the 2 years preceding the 1988 bull market), when the exchange margin was $ 4,500, the trade may have not been executable in real time due to the increase in rates not accounted for in the study.

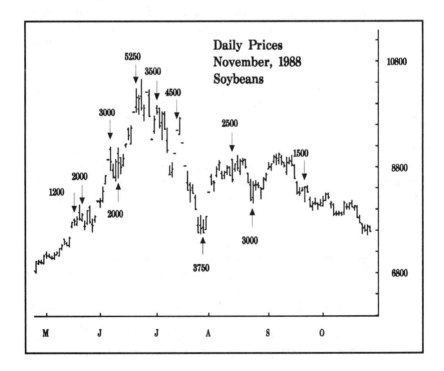

Collateralized US Treasury Bills

There were times
my pants were so thin
that I could sit on a dime and tell
whether it was heads or tails.
- Spencer Tracy

United States Treasury Bills can be purchased in commodity accounts in order to keep one's good faith money earning interest while it is on deposit at a brokerage firm. The usual minimum purchase is $ 10,000 although some firms require $ 20,000.

The reason why this use of funds can be especially important to the commodity trader is that the T-bill can be used as collateral to meet initial margin requirements on new positions. The amount that may be used may vary from firm to firm but generally amounts to around 90 percent of the face value of the T-bill. Thus, a $ 20,000 T-bill in your account would be serving double-duty by earning about $ 1,200 interest per year (@ 6 %) and by providing collateral to meet about $ 18,000 in initial margin requirements.

Some firms do not extend this T-bill courtesy to their small accounts while others only allow purchases in large multiples (say, in $ 20,000 increments) which, if you have a $ 25,000 account, would leave a $ 5,000 free cash balance (and small wonder, too, that firms would want to see that cash balance in the account since the firms get to invest the funds and earn interest on the aggregate daily cash balances left uninvested in customer accounts). A few firms additionally have money market funds available to handle these excess cash funds with some even providing automatic daily "sweeps" of excess funds.

One problem with using T-bills is that they cannot be used to meet a call for additional funds generated by a maintenance call. For example, you may have a $ 20,000 T-bill and $ 500 cash in your account when you enter a new position with a $ 2,000 initial margin requirement. The collateral of the T-bill meets the initial requirement. Now let's assume that the position drops in value the first day by $ 700. Your account would still show the T-bill but would now have a cash deficit of $ 200. You would be issued a T-bill Maintenance Margin Call. In other words, you would be forced to sell the $ 20,000 T-bill to meet the $ 200 cash deficit in your account or inject other outside funds.

Thus, although it is obviously advantageous to use T-bills in your account, they can create the above minor problems and some forethought should precede their investment.

Additionally, US T-Bills acquisition costs can be abnormally high at some firms with some even charging a "liquidation fee" or a "rollover fee" upon maturity of the T-Bill. These fees can be reduced by purchasing longer-term T-Bills. Determine first, however, the maximum maturity that your firm will recognize for collateralization purposes.

Getting a Quote from your Broker

No price is
too low for a bear or
too high for a bull.

Often times it is important to get a quote from the floor, especially when spread trading.

In asking your broker for such a quote, remember to get four items;

1. The bid price,

2. The ask price,

3. The last traded price, and

4. The time of the last trade.

Prices can and often do change rapidly, of course, so that the quote may have disappeared by the time you are prepared to enter your order.

Also, remember that, in a fast market, it will be difficult to obtain an accurate last price, let alone a floor quote.

How to Enter an Order

Captain Lincoln, in the Mexican War,
led his company to a fence
but did not know what order to give
to get them over.
"Halt", said he,
"the company will disband
and meet on the other side of the fence."

Market Order

For account _____ , I would like to (BY / SL) (quantity) (month) (market) at the market.

(EXAMPLE : For account 12345, I would like to BY 5 December Live Hogs @ the market).

Limit Order

For account _____ , I would like to (BY / SL) (quantity) (month) (market) @ (price).

(EXAMPLE : For account 12345, I would like to SL 5 December Gold @ $ 510.00).

Stop Order

For account _____ , I would like to (BY / SL) (quantity) (month) (market) @ (price) STOP.

(EXAMPLE : For account 12345, I would like to SL 5 December Gold @ $ 510.00 STOP).

Stop Limit Order

For account _____ , I would like to (BY / SL) (quantity) (month) (market) @ (price) STOP, (price) LIMIT.

(EXAMPLE : For account 12345, I would like to SL 5 December Gold @ $ 510.00 STOP, $ 508.00 LIMIT).

Market-if-Touched Order

For account _____ , I would like to (BY / SL) (quantity) (month) (market) at (price), MIT.

(EXAMPLE : For account 12345, I would like to BY 2 JUNE Bonds @ $ 510.00, MIT).

Market-on-Close Order

For account _____ , I would like to (BY / SL) (quantity) (month) (market), MOC.

(EXAMPLE : For account 12345, I would like to BY 2 March Silver, MOC).

Stop-Close-Only Order

For account _____ , I would like to (BY / SL) (quantity) (month) (market) @ (price), SCO.

(EXAMPLE : For account 12345, I would like to BY 2 March Silver @ 627, SCO).

One-Cancels-the-Other Order

For account _____ , I would like to (BY / SL) (quantity) (month) (market) @ (price) (qualifier) OCO (BY / SL) (quantity) (month) (market) @ (price) (qualifier).

(EXAMPLE : For account 12345, I would like to BY 5 April Live Cattle @ 6050 OCO BY 5 April Live Cattle @ 6210 STOP).

Spread Order (Like Units)

This is a spread order. For account _____ , I would like to BUY (quantity) (month) (market), SELL (quantity) (month) (market), (contract) (price) over (contract).

(EXAMPLE : This is a spread order. For account 12345, I would like to BY 5 March Corn, Sell 5 March Wheat, Wheat 110 cents over Corn).

Spread Order (Unlike Units)

This is a spread order. For account _____ , I would like to BUY (quantity) (month) (market), SELL (quantity) (month) (market), (contract) (dollars) over (contract).

(EXAMPLE : This is a spread order. For account 12345, I would like to BY 1 May Crude Oil, Sell 1 May Heating Oil, Crude $ 615.00 over Heating Oil).

(A convenient letter size sheet listing the above orders will be forwarded to those who enclose a SASE along with their request).

Reporting Levels

Clearing members, FCMs and foreign brokers are required to make daily reports to the CFTC showing each trader's positions on their books that, in any future month for a commodity, exceed the reporting levels as shown below.

The Commission issues its report of all reportable and nonreportable positions (i.e., total open interest) each month and further breaks the reportable positions down into commercial and noncommercial holdings, spreading, and numbers of traders. All of a trader's reported futures positions in a commodity are classified as commercial positions if the trader uses futures contracts for hedging purposes as defined by the Commission. Nonreportable positions are those below the reporting levels and are obtained by subtracting reported positions from the total open interest.

AL	25 Ctrs	**BD**	500 Ctrs	**BO**	150 Ctrs	**C**	100 Ctrs
CC	50 Ctrs	**CD**	50 Ctrs	**CF**	25 Ctrs	**CI**	25 Ctrs
CP	200 Ctrs	**CT**	5000Bls	**CUR**	200 Ctrs	**ECU**	25 Ctrs
ED	400 Ctrs	**FC**	25 Ctrs	**GO**	200 Ctrs	**HO**	150 Ctrs
LB	25 Ctrs	**LC**	100 Ctrs	**LH**	50 Ctrs	**LR**	50 Ctrs
MB	50 Ctrs	**MMI**	1000 Ctrs	**NASD**	25 Ctrs	**NY**	1000 Ctrs
O	60 Ctrs	**OJ**	25 Ctrs	**PA**	50 Ctrs	**PB**	25 Ctrs
PB	25 Ctrs	**PL**	50 Ctrs	**R**	25 Ctrs	**S**	100 Ctrs
SM	150 Ctrs	**SP 100**	25 Ctrs	**SP 500**	3000 Ctrs	**SPOTC**	25 Ctrs
SU	200 Ctrs	**SV**	150 Ctrs	**TB**	100 Ctrs	**TN**	200 Ctrs
TN5	25 Ctrs	**UL**	100 Ctrs	**US**	25 Ctrs	**VL**	100 Ctrs
W	100 Ctrs						

CFTC Speculative Positions Limits

The maximum number of agricultural futures contracts a speculator can hold was originally established in the Commodity Exchange Act of 1936. Congress, during the CFTC's 1986 reauthorization, agreed that the issue of position limits needed to be addressed (exchanges that trade futures on financial instruments and other commodities have been authorized since 1981 to set position limits in these contracts themselves, subject to CFTC approval).

Limits under the old CFTC rule were basically 600 contracts for corn, soybeans, and wheat in all months, any one month, or the spot month. The new position limits for speculators (hedgers have no limits) are the following:

Number of Contracts

	All Months Net	Single Month	Spot Month		All Months Net	Single Month	Spot Month
Cocoa	2000	1000	500	Coffee	1000	750	200
Corn	2400	600	600	Crude Oil	5000		1000
Currencies	6000			Gold	6000		3000
NYSE		5000		Live Cattle	450	300	
Oats	400	400	400	Silver	6000	1500	
S & P 500			5000	Sugar	6000	4000	
Soybeans	2400	600	600	T-Bills	5000		2500
Soybean Meal	2160	720	720	T-Bonds	10000		
Soybean Oil	1620	540	540				
Wheat	1800	600	600				

Trading Limits

There are two limits that confront the commodity trader.

The first, position limits, has just been discussed and is not applicable to most traders.

The second, trading limits, can be. The existence of trading limits in United States commodity markets has always been a concern of novice speculators. Stories abound how people have gotten into positions they couldn't get out of and no doubt this has happened (the best example being when the COMEX went to liquidation orders only in the Silver market in January, 1980, and the market locked limit down for 22 days).

Limits are supposed to protect the trading public from unjustifiable adverse price moves that might occur from unexpected news. They are also supposed to provide the losing trader more time to reconsider and finance his position rather than being forced to liquidate. They are set by the exchanges based on expectations of normal price ranges and are sometimes expanded as the volatility of the market increases.

Often when a limit day is experienced for two days in a row, the exchange will go to expanded limits on the third day. These expanded limits are normally 1 1/2 times the usual limit. If the situation continues for another two days or so, the exchange might increase the limits to twice or three times the normal level. This process will continue until the market has a non-limit day and will then usually revert back to normal limits.

Spot contracts (or the nearest active futures contracts) in many commodities are without limits. In the Sugar market, the nearest two spot contracts trade without limits.

The October, 1987 stock market crash has resulted in legislation that has introduced limits (breakers) on the trading of stocks and stock market derivative products. In this author's view, this is a well-intentioned but very misguided attempt (though popular with the public and misinformed media commentators) to control the downside risk that naturally exists not only in stocks, but in EVERY market.

TRADING HINT : If you are stuck in a position that locks-limit against you and you WANT to get out or HAVE to get out, look first to see if there is a spot contract that you can take an opposite position in until both contracts can be liquidated. If a spot contract is not available, have your broker contact the spread broker on the floor and get a quote to spread your way into a contract that is likely to be less impacted (spreads still trade despite the limit move. This trading occurs, of course, but at a price).

Third, investigate the existence of a long option hedge (i.e., if you are short a market that is limit up against you, try to buy a call and therein limit the upside potential damage).

Fourth, see if there is a similar commodity that can help hedge the move. For instance, if pork bellies have gone limit against you, perhaps you can still enter the live hog market and lessen the effect of the loss.

Finally, contact your broker and see if an exchange-for-physical (EFP) transaction can be arranged.

Permissable Exchange Orders

	COMEX	MGE	KCBT	CME	IMM	CSC	NYFE	CBT	NYME	NYCE
STOP - LIMIT	Yes	No	No	Yes	Yes	Yes	Yes	No	Yes	No
MIT	Yes	No	No	Yes	Yes	Yes	Yes	No	Yes	Yes
STOP CLOSE ONLY	Yes	No	No	Yes	Yes	Yes	Yes	No	Yes	No

Delivery

What about the stories you have no doubt heard of 5,000 bushels of soybeans or 40,000 pounds of beef-on-the-hoof being delivered on your doorstep due to an overlooked, expired market position?

The proverbial gossip about trucks dumping tons and tons of potatoes on your front lawn just is not going to happen! In the first place, "delivery" of grain (as well as most other commodities) takes place in the form of a warehouse receipt, NOT the actual commodity itself. With precious metals, "delivery" occurs in the form of a bank document which guarantees that the quantity and quality of the metal represented by the contract is actually in the bank's vault. There can be special problems with some deliveries, of course. Eggs, for instance, used to be subject to spoilage prior to your being able to inspect and resell them. World sugar is not a good commodity to take delivery of as it can be delivered at any of several ports in the world. Nevertheless, the delivery process for all these commodities starts with a piece of paper and not with the physical commodity itself.

Also, since your brokerage firm will have to help you arrange many of the details before actual delivery can occur (i.e., method of payment, shipping instructions, storage instructions, place of delivery, date of delivery, and so on), you are going to hear from them PRIOR TO ANYTHING BEING DELIVERED TO YOU.

They will contact you not only prior to last trading day (LTD) and first delivery day (FDD), but also prior to first notice day (FND).

That said, an interesting story is told by economists about a gentleman knocking impatiently on a neighbor's door on a cold English evening in the 1930s. The visitor needed desperately to borrow his neighbor's barn to store the corn about to be delivered on his front lawn against his futures contracts. The identity of this harried man? None other than John Maynard Keynes, the father of modern Keynesian Economics and an active commodities speculator!

Electronic Exchanges

A broker is a man on the right end of the telephone.

Isn't the Chicago Mercantile Exchange's proposed Globex system a breath of fresh air? Globex is an electronic trade execution system which will provide for trading in selected CME futures contracts outside regular trading hours.

The major advantage that the system offers is the ability to truly execute at the best bid, best asked price. It offers a transparent, open, and competitive means of trading futures contracts.

The initial contracts to be traded are expected to be the Australian Dollar, British Pound, Canadian Dollar, Deutschmark, French Franc, Japanese Yen, Swiss Franc, Eurodollar, US Treasury Bill, and IMM Gold with sessions open from 6:00 pm to 6:00 am Central Time Sunday through Thursday evenings. Globex transactions would be considered next-day business so that each trading day would begin with a Globex session and end with a regular trading session.

Since each of the contracts initially proposed to be traded through Globex have regular trading hours of 7:20 am to 2:00 pm, the trading days for these contracts would thus be 18 hours and 40 minutes.

It is unfortunate that the Globex system is not the first such system introduced on world exchanges. The Soffex system in Switzerland is already operational and, apparently, trading quite efficiently.

Perhaps the introduction of such a system will enable customers to finally achieve truly efficient execution of prices and such terms as "front running", "bucket trading", "slippage", "clipping" and so on will become relics of the past.

Kudos to the Merc and let's hope the other exchanges soon catch up!

Chapter 3

Who Will Manage Your Money?

Financial Planning

We invest for the long term
but worry every second.

One of the very first decisions an investor must make is how much of his funds are going to be placed in various investment sectors (such as stocks, bonds, real estate, collectibles, insurance, savings, speculative investments, and so on). Such decisions should, of course, be made in the context of one's long term objectives, risk tolerance, and so on. For most, the proper amount that will be available for trading purposes SHOULD BE DETERMINED through the process of elimination. Once all other commitments are met, the amount available for trading will be the amount that is left over. This amount will increase, of course, over time as one increases one's trading abilities and confidence.

Ask yourself this question - if you open up a trading account and lose the entire amount, is that something you can live with without it changing your lifestyle or keeping you awake at night? If the answer to this question is no, then you have committed too much to speculation and should go back and start the process over again.

Once you have found your comfort level, you are ready to begin. Start by opening your account with TWICE the amount you can afford to lose. If you ever lose 50 percent of that amount, CLOSE YOUR ACCOUNT! You have reached your maximum "risk" point.

If you want to try again, wait for another day when your speculative funds have been replenished or your personal financial situation has changed.

If your account is successful, WITHDRAW HALF YOUR PROFITS EACH MONTH until you have withdrawn your original seed capital. At this point, you will have restored your financial position to its original starting point BUT THE ORIGINAL RISK WILL HAVE BEEN ELIMINATED!

You will be betting on the house's money rather than betting the house itself!

Asset Allocation

In investing money
the amount of interest you want
should depend on whether
you want to eat well or sleep well.
- J Kenfield Morley, "Some Things I Believe", 1937

Asset allocation is one of the most basic of money management techniques. Here the main thrust is the determination of what percentage of an investor's assets should be allocated to each of several areas.

For instance, if an investor had $ 10 in August, 1929 and allocated all his assets to the stock market, it would have taken him until 1945 to recoup his losses. Had he allocated $ 5 or half his assets to stocks and half to bonds, however, and maintained the 50-50 split at the end of every month, he would have recouped his losses by October, 1935 due to his practicing careful "asset allocation".

The key to this example of asset allocation is continually returning to the original division among stocks and bonds. In practice, assets are constantly returned to their original mix be they bonds, stocks, cash, speculative investments, or whatever else one invests in.

A different form of asset allocation that professional money managers use consciously varies the percentage of assets allocated instead of using a constant division of assets as in our examples above.

Several reports have been written in the past few years regarding the importance of including a professionally managed futures account in an investor's overall asset mix and its stabilizing effect on long term stock market portfolio performance.

The technique is more successfully employed by the average investor when the percentage of his overall assets is allocated to managed futures accounts (note the plural). Here asset allocation is used to control the percentage of one's assets allocated to a group of managed futures advisers.

If you practice asset allocation, should you allocate a portion of your funds to futures?

Should you consider using a professionally managed account?

Who Will Manage Your Money?

When two men in business always agree,
one of them is unnecessary.

After one has made the decision to allocate a portion of one's resources to the markets, the decision has to be made regarding who will be responsible for the management of the assets in the various markets. There are four basic choices -

1.) make all the trading decisions yourself,

2.) allow someone else to suggest trades but retain final authority yourself,

3.) give someone else the authority to enter and exit trades on your behalf, or

4.) some combination of the above.

If you are trading for the excitement of trading, then you are not going to experience the same exhilaration and personal excitement if someone else is doing the trading. On the other hand, if you do not have the time to concentrate on trading, then perhaps a professionally managed account is for you.

It seems to make little sense, however, to SHARE decision-making authority over an account (as in our second choice above). The reason why is that making trading decisions is not a process that readily lends itself to decision by committee.

Most of these types of programs fall under various brokerage firms "guided accounts". Here the firm's trade recommendations are conveyed to the customer who must then make the decision whether or not to accept the trade. You and I fully know that if you have just stepped out of the shower, your frame of mind isn't exactly on whether or not you should be starting the day off with an extra 10,000 bushels of corn tucked around your belt!

Hence, it seems to make more sense to either

1.) manage the funds yourself,

2.) transfer decision-making authority to someone who has demonstrated the ability to profitably manage funds, or

3.) use some combination of the above two.

The Equity Cycle

*If there is one consistency
among successful traders,
it is the disciplined use
of a good plan.*

If you manage your own account, is it more important to place more emphasis on your trading techniques and abilities or on your money management capabilities?

The truthful answer to that question might be one of the keys that can take your trading to a higher level. Here's the reason why -

A trader with average ability but good money management techniques can prosper while a trader with good trading techniques but poor money management abilities MAY succeed but he will MORE LIKELY flounder. In other words, the money management system employed is often as important, if not more so, than one's trading abilities.

Perhaps an example will better explain the above statement.

An account that gains 100 % and loses 50 % in its equity cycle should be quite profitable, right?

NOT NECESSARILY!

It depends on the money management system used.

For example, let's take a $ 10,000 account that is always fully invested. If this account were to gain 100 %, the profit would be $ 10,000 and the account would be worth $ 20,000. However, if it were to then lose 50 % (of the fully-invested $ 20,000), the loss would be $ 10,000 and the account WOULD BE BACK TO ITS ORIGINAL BEGINNING EQUITY OF $ 10,000 !!!

Let's now take that same $ 10,000 account and assume a constant investment of only the original funds. On the 100 % gain, we have the same result as above and the account is worth $ 20,000 after the gain. Because only $ 10,000 is constantly invested, however, on the downside of the equity cycle, only $5,000 is lost. At the end of the cycle, the second account is thus worth $ 15,000 while the first account is back to the original equity of only $ 10,000!

Just as one can obtain a solid jagged line when plotting the daily closing price of a commodity, so can one plot the daily equity or value of one's account (be it self-directed or managed). And just as it is important to "buy on weakness, sell on strength", so is it important when analyzing The Equity Cycle of one's funds to increase commitments (scale up and increase trading commit-ments or begin new accounts) AFTER drawdowns have been experienced and to decrease commitments AFTER equity surges have been experienced.

Applying this to the above example, let's assume that, after the first Equity Cycle is completed, both investors scale up their accounts. The first investor thus trades his original account size of $ 10,000 on a fully-invested basis while the second investor trades his account size of $ 15,000 on a constant-dollar basis. We again assume the 100 % / 50 % results. Where are our two investors at the end of this second Equity Cycle? The first investor is back at his original $ 10,000, of course, while the second investor is now at $ 22,500 !!!

It is quite easy to carry this process forward and compute that after 5 cycles, the account value of our second investor would have grown to $ 75,938. If we assume that there are, on average, two equity cycles per year, then it would have taken 2 1/2 years for our second investor to have achieved this result. After ten repetitions of the cycle (5 years under our assumption), the second investor would have an account value of $ 576,650 !!!

The first investor would, of course, still be stuck with his original $ 10,000 (and had better enjoy trading one whole heck of a lot and have a very patient and understanding spouse). If someone were to show this investor this simple money management technique, he, too, would be able to experience the same results as the second investor, FOR IT IS THE ONLY DIFFERENCE IN THE TWO APPROACHES! (For him to change, however, he would probably have to experience modification of behavior).

IF THE ABOVE DOES NOT EXCITE YOU, GO BACK AND RE-READ IT MORE SLOWLY ! (Note, of course, that using different figures would result in different projections and that the assumptions used in this example were quite unrealistic and ignored internal compounding).

How can you apply the above to your own trading environment?

Easy! Go back and pull the daily equity runs of your trading account, NOT the individual trades (what, you don't keep a daily equity run of your account value??? For shame, for shame!)

Plot those equity values on a daily basis over as long a period as is possible (make sure and adjust for equity additions and withdrawals). The resulting graph or equity curve TELLS THE TRUTH ABOUT YOUR TRADING AND MONEY MANAGEMENT ABILITIES!

Which way does the curve trend?

If this curve were a stock or a commodity, would you buy that curve because it is breaking out and constantly making new highs?

Would you sell it short because it is constantly making new lows? Or would you stay away from it because it was trading sideways?

IF YOU WOULD NOT BUY YOUR OWN EQUITY CURVE, WHAT COULD THIS ANALYSIS POSSIBLY BE TELLING YOU ABOUT YOUR TRADING PROGRAM???

If it is trending upwards, you should be able to identify and figure the percent equity drawdowns that occur during the growth of the curve by simply taking the amount of drawdown from a highpoint to the lowest low attained prior to a new highpoint and dividing the result into the original highpoint. Next, determine how often the drawdowns occur and the range and average drawdown (both in percent).

The following equity curve shows such an example (though it is for only an abbreviated period of time). Note the 3 drawdowns over the 39 day period as indicated by the arrows. These draw-downs have occurred about every 13 days with a range of 7 % to 17 % and an average drawdown over the period of 12 %.

(Note : This equity curve is real and was created using nothing but information from The Calendar Book of The Almanac)

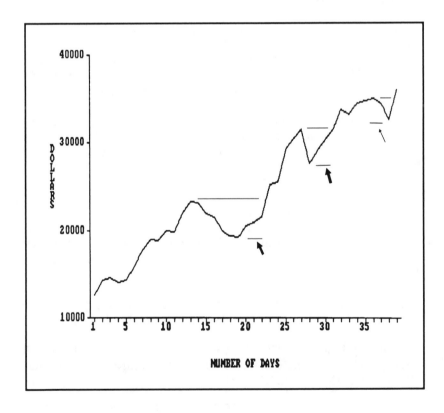

The Principle of the Tithe

If there is one consistency
among successful traders,
it is the disciplined use
of a good plan.

Assume you are trading your own account and that you have a trading system that you have employed for some period of time that is very average experiencing two $ 500 wins for every $ 400 loss (i.e., 67 % wins, an average profit of $ 200 per trade, and a won/lost ratio of 2 : 1). The margin requirement is $ 1,000.

You look back at your results over the years and notice that the system produces (on average) a $ 10,100 profit every 50 trades. Not bad! Assuming you put $ 10,000 in an account at the beginning of the year and that those 50 trades occurred over the course of the year, your account would thus be worth $ 20,100 at the end of the year!

Now let's add a very simple money management rule and see how we do. Let's assume that you start with the same $ 10,000 but that you make a small modification in the number of contracts you are willing to trade.

Your basic rule is that you will trade 1 contract for every $ 10,000 you have in your account (thus, if your account totalled $ 20,000, you would trade 2 contracts, 3 for $ 30,000, and so on. If equity dropped to $ 29,000, however, you would drop back to 2 contracts).

At the end of the first year, you would have traded 2 contracts once and your account would be worth only $ 19,700. Not a very good start! In fact, it is $ 400 short of the results for the other account! At the end of the second year, however, when the first account has grown to $ 30,200, your account has grown to $41,000 and you are now ready to trade 4 contracts.

At the end of the third year, the first account has grown to $40,400. Your account, because of money management, has now grown to $ 100,000, and you are now trading 10 contracts. After five years, the first account was worth $ 59,800 while your account would now be worth $ 599,100 and 59 contracts.

In the middle of the sixth year, in fact, you would bump up against exchange position limits of 300 contracts per trade with your $3,000,000 account versus the first account balance of only $76,600.

Now, I know that you're thinking that this can't be done and you're wondering why this guy is putting such hot air in this otherwise fine book?

But consider this - IF YOU ARE TRADING TO HIT A GRAND SLAM, IT IS EITHER GOING TO HAVE TO BE DONE IN A MANNER SIMILAR TO THE ABOVE OR BY PYRAMIDING YOURSELF INTO A HUGE, ONE-WAY MOVE !

Larry Williams won the United States Futures Trading Championship in 1987 by increasing a $ 10,000 account to over $1,000,000 in less than 12 months with real money. Do you think he could have managed such a Herculean task were it not for a money management system that allowed him to increase commitments as his equity increased and decrease commitments as his equity decreased ???

Here are a few more items about using the Principle of the Tithe. The actual investment amount to use is 10 % of the account equity. Once this amount is determined, it is divided by the current margin which tells you how many contracts you can trade.

For instance, if your account is worth $ 35,000 and the margin is $ 1,000 per contract, you can trade $ 35,000 X 10 % = $ 3,500 / $ 1,000 = 3 1/2 contracts = 3 contracts (when rounded down).

If you want to be even more conservative, some will lower the 10% investment amount to a 5 % figure. Others will divide the 10 % figure by the amount they can risk on any one trade. For instance, in our example above, if your stop was $ 500 on your next trade, $ 3,500 / $ 500 = 7 contracts. The problem here is that the margin on 7 contracts is, in this example, $ 7,000 (which, as a percentage of account size, is too high).

Hence, if you are going to incorporate risk only into the equation to determine the number of contracts you are going to trade, use the most limiting of the two numbers (margin OR risk) as the determinant for the number of contracts. Some will be even more conservative and will use the amount needed to capitalize the trade (margin PLUS risk) in determining the number of contracts to trade.

In our above example, this amount would be $ 1,000 + $ 500 = $ 1,500. When divided into 10 % of our account above and rounded down, the number of contracts to trade in this case is 2.

NOW COMES THE MOST EXCITING PART ! Consider this - in the example above, ONLY 10 % OF AVAILABLE EQUITY WAS EMPLOYED AT ANY ONE TIME !

The balance of funds was not even assumed to be invested in T-bills !

The actual Principle of the Tithe allows for a second position to be entered into with the balance of the funds in the account. For instance, in our example, if $ 35,000 - $ 3,000 = $ 32,000 was available for a second position and the margin was $ 700 per contract, $ 32,000 X 10 % = $ 3,200 which (when divided by $700) would allow for 4 contracts of this second position to be traded and would leave $ 32,000 - $ 2,800 = $ 29,200 in the account for a third position.

Is money management important?

From the above discussion, I think one would have to say that it is VERY IMPORTANT ! In fact, for most people, it is PROBABLY even more important than the trading system or technique being used !

Should you use money management techniques in the trading of your account?

Only you can answer that!

Larry Williams apparently does!

Money Management

Money is what you'd get on beautifully without
if only other people
weren't so crazy about it.
- Margaret Case Harriman

Without proper money management any trading system can become a loser, but with proper money management some unprofitable trading systems become profitable. Money management is a defensive tactic - it strives to protect the trader and his capital. If the trader can survive, profits will likely follow. Good money management is the trader's best insurance against failure and the reason to expect success!

Several examples of different money management approaches have been discussed and reviewed over the last few pages. The following presents three money management rules traders have traditionally used to manage their accounts -

1.) Total invested funds should be limited to 50 % of total capital. This means that, at any one time, no more than half of the trader's capital should be committed to the markets. The other half is backup or reserve.

2.) Total commitment in any one market should be limited to 10% of total equity. This rule helps prevent one from overtrading one's capital (one of the major causes of failure in the commodity markets).

3.) The total amount risked in any one market should be limited to 5 % of total equity. This 5 % refers to the amount a trader is willing to lose if the trade does not work out. Should one follow these rules or those on earlier pages?

That choice, of course, is yours to make!

The main point is to impress upon the reader the importance of good money management techniques and some methods that are used. From there, each must find that approach with which he is comfortable.

Modern Portfolio Theory

Whoever controls
the volume of money in any one country
is absolute master
of industry and commerce.
- Abraham Lincoln

Modern Portfolio Theory concentrates on investment decisions that effect portfolios of investments instead of individual investments. The main objective is to maximize portfolio return while stabilizing risk from a wide array of investment choices. One of the major assumptions in MPT is that performance will continue in the future as it has in the past, an assumption which puts the theory immediately in rather unstable territory (quicksand, for example)!

If a trader introduced silver into a portfolio that traded only gold, for instance, the equity curves of the two markets could be separately analyzed and then combined and analyzed. As gold and silver are quite similar in their price movements (are highly correlated), the introduction of silver into the portfolio would be expected to do little to reduce the overall risk or increase the overall return.

MTP seeks individual investments that have coefficients close to -1 or are negatively correlated in order to offer the greatest degree of stability to the overall portfolio instead of the near +1 that gold and silver would offer. Hence, the introduction of oats would be a better choice as the performance of oats would likely have very little to do with the performance of gold. This addition would tend to stabilize the overall performance of the portfolio as a period of poor performance by gold might be offset by the good performance of oats and vice-versa. A third market (lumber) might then be introduced, resulting in further stability but no reduction in results.

This process would continue over all the available choices for all markets thereby forming the efficient frontier of available portfolio choices until a feasible portfolio had been located for which no other portfolio 1.) had a lower risk for the same expected return, and 2.) did not have a higher expected return for the same risk level.

Once the portfolio was structured horizontally within, it could also be compared to other portfolios that followed a different investing technique for further stabilization. For instance, a trend-following portfolio could be compared to a counter-trend portfolio and the joint equity curve analyzed to further reduce risk and so on. Or a stock portfolio could be compared with a bond portfolio and then a futures portfolio introduced. (This just could replace diversification)!

A Self Evaluation

The most important commodity you can analyze is yourself.

What if you don't have the time or interest in trading and managing your own account or your results haven't lived up to expectations?

Is a managed account for you?

The following evaluation from the September, 1983 issue of Futures magazine might help you answer that question -

Y   N   I have some investment funds available.

Y   N   I have adequate life insurance, savings and/or other investments so that if I lose this money, it will not drastically affect my style of living.

Y   N   I am interested in the higher profit opportunities that trading affords and am willing to undertake the greater risks associated with trading in exchange for a chance at these higher returns.

If you answer "No" to any of the questions above, a managed trading account is not for you - otherwise, continue on

Y N   I have invested in stocks or bonds but have no experience in trading.

Y N   I have traded before but have never done very well.

Y N   I am tired of margin calls.

Y N   I am interested in trading but do not have the time to follow markets.

Y N   I do not understand the fundamental and technical factors involved in analyzing markets.

Y N   My best market information is advice from my broker or tips from my brother-in-law.

Y N   My heart pounds when I try to make investments myself. I get so excited!

Y N   My investment motivation is profits, not excitement.

Y N   I think a professional money manager could handle my investment funds better than I can.

Y N   I would be comfortable handing someone else a sizable amount of my money and asking them to trade it for me.

Y N   I could endure several losing months in a row without being tempted to close my account and would let an adviser have at least a year to trade my account.

Y N   Even though I could (or do) trade my own account successfully, I should have someone else manage a portion of my money so I can spread my risk or compare my results with theirs.

If you answered "Yes" to 5 or more of the questions above, you might benefit from a managed account. The key steps are having the money, a desire to trade, and the willingness to let someone else handle your money.

Overview of Managed Commodity Accounts

Investment professionals are people
who help you invest your money
until it's all gone.
- Woody Allen

From the time Richard Donchian began managing a futures fund in 1949 to the present, the managed futures industry has exploded. By the end of 1975, about $ 65 million was under management with $ 15 million of it in funds. Five years later the total had increased to about $ 750 million of which roughly $ 250 million was in funds. By the end of 1985, the total had increased to about $ 1.5 billion of which roughly $ 450 million was in funds. By mid-1987, the figure was up around $ 3.4 billion with funds accounting for approximately $ 1.3 billion.

Some of this especially rapid growth since 1983 was because of a report by Professor John K. Lintner of the Harvard Business School that offered empirical evidence that adding competently managed futures accounts to a portfolio of stocks and/or bonds would raise the total portfolio's rate of return without a corresponding increase in risk or would reduce the degree of risk given any specified rate of return.

Given our outlook for increased price volatility in our economy over the foreseeable future, the time appears right for investors to either begin honing their trading skills or else to perhaps consider investing in a managed account (if they have not already done so)! One has several choices in considering the latter investment.

First, there are many competent Associated Persons (brokers) to whom you can give a power-of-attorney over your account allowing them to enter buy and sell decisions on your behalf. The broker is registered with the National Futures Association as an AP because, in most cases, he is associated with a Futures Commission Merchant (FCM). An FCM is a brokerage firm that has the power to receive and hold customers money.

He may, however, be an Introducing Broker (IB) who is essentially an AP that has formed his own firm but still is associated with one or more FCM's on either a guaranteed or a non-guaranteed basis. Both of these people can manage your account on a discretionary basis and their only charge will normally be the commissions that the account generates. There is no standard performance record that must be supplied for such accounts.

The next alternative is a large pool of funds that is similar in theory to a mutual fund in that many investors invest in a common account that is run by a Commodity Pool Operator (CPO). This form of investment is normally used by those who only have small amounts of money available but still wish to participate in futures on a diversified basis. These funds are either close-ended (meaning that they cannot accept new participants after the initial sales period unless they reregister their offering) or open-ended. Solicitation of these funds is done through a prospectus that discloses, among other things, fees and past performance.

The final category is the Commodity Trading Advisor (CTA) who, for a fee, will manage your funds. The CTA must supply prospective customers with a disclosure document that states, among other things, fees, past performance, conflicts of interest, etc.

The CTA does not normally share in the account's commissions.

A recent trend has been investment into offshore funds that do not entail the onerous restrictions and regulations with which domestic (United States) funds are burdened.

Key Points in Selecting A CTA

*Some investments advisers don't have much to say,
but you have to listen a long time to find out.*

1. Decide your investment goals (i.e., what is your risk tolerance, what size capital commitment are your wishing to make, what is the time frame of your commitment, what is your target rate of return and how does it relate to inflation and taxation, etc.)

2. Gather disclosure documents.

3. Insure that the adviser is registered with the National Futures Association (if a domestic adviser) and determine if there is any past or pending legal action against him.

4. Review annual compound rate of return and largest drawdown information.

5. Review the adviser's intramonth daily trade data, if possible.

6. Determine how much of the adviser's money is in the program and the total amount of funds he manages.

7. Determine if different sized accounts are traded differently and, if so, what the rate of return of each is.

8. Determine if the fees and commissions are consistent with industry standards.

9. Determine if there is to be any change in the way the account is to be managed or in the fees charged versus how the track record was compiled.

10. Ask the adviser why he thinks that future returns may or may not be similar to the past.

11. Determine if the adviser is planning any significant increases in equity in the next several months that may affect his results, etc. Most of this information can be found in the disclosure document itself!

Key Points in Analyzing
a Fund Prospectus

Disclosure of trading results
should be done in a manner
that you wouldn't be ashamed
to sell the family parrot
to the town gossip.

1. Determine any conflicts of interest between the General Partner, the CPO and/or the CTA, and the FCM.

2. Investigate the background of the parties involved.

3. Determine the CTA compensation structure.

4. Investigate the track record, especially noting drawdowns and the type accounts that were traded.

5. Determine brokerage commissions and other charges.

6. Investigate the "Pro forma" table which should show what impact the fee structure proposed for the fund would have on the previous track record.

7. Determine how much of the fund's assets can be used for margin purposes.

8. Determine the level of the fund's aggressiveness and whether it suits your objectives.

9. Find out if the General Partner has invested in the fund and, if so, how much.

10. Determine if the fund has a "bail point" and, if so, where it is.

11. Determine any changes in the trading approach between the track record and the manner in which the fund will be traded.

12. Determine whether or not the track record was built on actual or hypothetical data.

Management Fees

*Whenever possible, the wage-contract
should be modified by a partnership-contract,
whereby the wage-earner is made to share
in the ownership, the management, or the profits.*
- Pope Pius XI, Quadragesimo Anno, May 15, 1931

CTAs normally charge two fees for managing money - 1.) a
management fee and 2.) an incentive fee. The management fee is
usually a percentage of the total assets in the account. The
incentive fee is a percentage of the new profits. The industry
standard has been a 6 % management fee and an incentive fee of
15 % with some additionally charging the interest income the
account may earn. Such fees have been softening over the past
few years with many managers now working for a fee of 20 to 30
percent of the new profits.

A fund or pool may, in addition, charge a one-time sales commission and/or an annual administrative fee. When commissions
are added in, one can see that the manager must, in some cases,
overcome a lot to be able to make the account grow!

Key Points in Analyzing a Track Record

*Success does not depend
upon having enough capital
but in deploying it properly.*

Isn't it ironical that the things that are supposed to make it easy
for the average investor to make an informed, accurate decision
are so complicated and difficult to understand that for most they
do nothing but confuse? One good example is that last sentence.
Another is a fund prospectus. A third still is the track record
reported in disclosure documents.

The CFTC requires that results for the last three years be included and reported on a quarterly basis (although most report results monthly). Other required information includes beginning net asset value, additions and withdrawals, net profits (losses), ending equity and rate of return. Some will go one step further and voluntarily include commissions, management and incentive fees, realized interest, and net asset value per $ 1,000.

The results purport to describe fairly how an adviser has performed. However, the following possible factors could possibly distort the figures in the record -

1. Because the performance is like a snapshot (i.e., it reports an adviser's performance at a particular point in time for the most recent period of time), performance may have varied drastically DURING the period from that reported at the END of the period in the record. Drawdowns are a particular case in point. If an adviser experiences a drawdown of 20 % during the month but then improves into the end of the month and finishes up 10 %, the record will only show that his performance was up 10 % for the month. If, at the end of the next month, his performance is down 5 %, his worst drawdown will be listed as having been 5 %. The 20 % figure will not show up in the track record.

2. In mid-1987, the CFTC issued a statement excluding "notional" funds from calculations. Notional funds are similar to "reserve" funds. It is money that the customer holds outside the account but agrees to furnish, if needed. If a $ 50,000 gain is reported on a $ 50,000 account, the performance is far different if that account is NOT backed by an additional $ 100,000 in notional funds than if it is!

3. Does the account reflect performance of an account that was traded differently than the one being proposed to you? This concern can be especially important if, for instance, the CTA developed his track record as a floor trader while not having to pay the commissions that will have to be paid on the new account.

4. The CFTC performance calculation is inherently distorted because of the formula it uses to compute Beginning Net Asset Value from which the rate of return is computed. The present CFTC method includes additions only at the beginning of the month and withdrawals at the end of the month. "Managed

Account Reports", for instance, includes additions and withdrawals DURING the month and therefore presents totally different performance results of the CTAs it follows.

5. Was the track record based upon the performance of the CTA's own individual account? If so, the account may not have been subject to the management and incentive fees of the new account. In such instances, a "pro forma" record is usually prepared.

6. One must keep in mind that the record is a COMPOSITE look at all the adviser's accounts in aggregate. Hence, if the adviser had one $ 100,000 account that made $ 30,000 for the month and six $ 10,000 accounts that each lost $ 5,000, his performance would be listed as even for the month. If you were planning to open a $ 10,000 account with this adviser, the performance of the smaller accounts would obviously be very valuable information to you.

ALMANAC OBSERVATION - Track records depicting performance of an adviser would be more accurate if figures used were compiled on a DAILY basis instead of a monthly or quarterly basis. This procedure would enable true return on investment calculations to be shown and additions, withdrawals, and drawdowns to be more accurately reflected. The figures would represent how the adviser did for the exact number of days that he had the funds in his possession to work with.

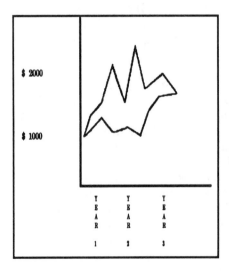

Also, if one is analyzing an adviser (or, especially, if comparing more than one adviser), it is most helpful if an Equity Graph is prepared which plots graphically the historical results of the CTA from one period to another. For instance, the two advisers below have the same ending results but have arrived by different routes. The graph clearly shows which is preferable -

Another way of analyzing an adviser's record is to construct a histogram with 10 % intervals and to then build a column of "X"s in the appropriate column for which each month's results are reported as in the graph on the right.

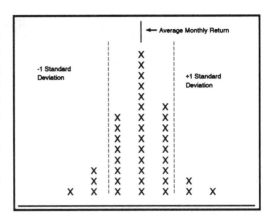

One could obviously average these results and arrive at the average return per time period. It would then also be possible to measure the degree to which the results "cluster" about the average. A manager with wide-swinging results, for instance, would have a smoother mountain than that shown in the graph while one with rather consistent results would have a very spiked peak as results cluster very close to the average each month.

The degree of clustering can be measured statistically by a technique called the standard deviation which simply contains about 68 % of all the data points (shown by the dotted lines in the graph). With this measurement, one thus has an objective and statistical measure of one kind of RISK.

Reward to Risk

Another good indication of superior performance is gained by taking the adviser's annual return and dividing by the maximum drawdown. Using this process and then ranking 96 advisers in late 1988 resulted in an average among the advisers of 1.97 with a range of from 20.28 to -0.44. (Thanks to Chris Starkey for the above information). These figures provide an excellent reward / risk ratio that is not commonly used by the public in analyzing advisers' track records.

The Sharpe and Sterling Ratios

The Sharpe Ratio was devised by Professor William Sharpe of Stanford University and combines both the average rate of return and the standard deviation into a single number by dividing the former by the latter. (The number is often adjusted first, however, by subtracting the equivalent 90 day US Treasury Bill rate from the average return). A higher number is indicative of greater consistency and lower risk in achieving a given rate of return.

The Sterling Ratio was originated by Deane S. Jones in 1986 and attempts to measure the risk one runs in achieving performance results. Here the 3 year average annual return (where a zero is used if the return is negative) is divided by the maximum annual drawdown (MAD) plus 10 percent. The MAD is defined as the worst percentage drop occurring from the end of one month to the end of any subsequent month during a calendar year. The resulting number reveals how many times greater the average annual rate of return was than the size of the adjusted average maximum drawdown. Any number above 1 is considered to be attractive (at the end of 1986, for example, the Dow Jones had a Sterling Ratio of .80, T-bills were at .79, and Gold was at .11).

Note the similarity between The Sterling Ratio and the Reward / Risk Ratio discussed above.

Montecarlo Simulation

The person who stands with one foot
in a bucket of ice cold water
and the other in a pan of boiling hot water
can tell you that,
on average,
he feels fine.

Perhaps the best method of analyzing performance is through Monte Carlo analysis where raw computing power is substituted for statistical technique. Here the actual results of an adviser's results are picked at random by the computer one data point at a time and a fictitious track record created. If a 3-year track record is constructed using monthly data, for instance, the computer will append 36 data points. Because of its speed, a computer can build many of these "track records" in a very small amount of time. Once a sufficient number have been constructed, an average return of the samples can be computed as well as a 90 % confidence interval (a statistical measurement that tells one where 90 % of the results would be expected to lie).

This confidence interval provides a guide as to what can reasonably be expected from a manager in terms of future performance. This expected performance can, in fact, be projected into the future in the form of a Montecarlo simulation "envelope" and can be used to look at the size of probable future equity erosions. An example of such an envelope is shown in the chart below for a 12 month period of time -

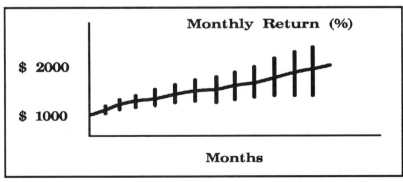

In such a projection, the average expected return for a $ 1,000 unit is drawn over time and an envelope that would be expected to contain 90 % of the possible future results projected. A narrow envelope would be more indicative of greater expected stability in the projection of the adviser's future returns.

Additional information that this technique provides enables one to analyze the probability of a given equity erosion after a given number of time periods have elapsed. For instance, the investor might want to know the answer to the question "What is the probability that my account will have declined by 5 %, 10 %, or 15 % after six months if I choose this adviser? After 12 months? After 2 years? . . . And so on. Montecarlo simulation techniques provide the ability to answer these questions.

An adjunct to Montecarlo simulation analysis is Risk / Return Space which plots return vertically versus risk horizontally. The appropriate variables to use from our above example would thus be to use the average projected monthly return on our vertical axis versus the standard deviation of monthly returns on the lower axis or, as an alternative, the 90 % confidence interval. This technique thus allows many money managers to be compared on the same chart.

The chart below, for instance, shows that A is the preferable manager because the same average monthly return is attained at far less risk.

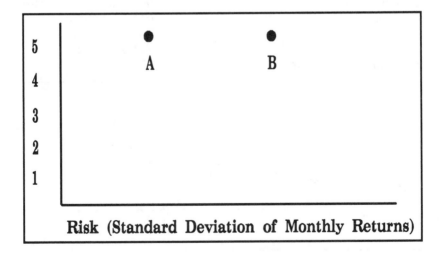

Adviser Diversification

Don't put all your eggs in one basket.

If it makes sense to diversify one's assets in a stock portfolio by spreading the risk among many different stocks, then why shouldn't an investor who is considering hiring (or already has hired) a professional Commodities Trading Adviser consider diversifying his assets over many different CTAs?

Inherently such a strategy does make sense because of the stabilization of equity growth that is achieved due to the averaging of poor performance periods that one adviser in the portfolio might experience with the good performance that other advisers might achieve during the same period of time. The key is, of course, in obtaining advisers who exhibit negative levels of correlation.

Which brings us back to Modern Portfolio Theory, Montecarlo simulation, and the conclusion of this entire discussion on measuring performance and choosing an adviser. If we can project the return of an individual adviser, then why not combine the investment results of the best advisers on a Risk / Return diagram, combine their equity projections, and inspect the resulting equity curve? If done, the result should be a projected equity growth curve whose envelope is far narrower than that of any one of the advisers. In other words, the same growth is projected to be attained at far less risk to the overall portfolio.

Those who practice this approach thus spend as much time and effort in the analysis and selection of the right PEOPLE to have manage their funds as most traders do in choosing which markets to buy and sell. And they do so with less risk to their invested capital.

But is a managed account for you?

Consider the following;

If you truly understand the discussion presented on the last few pages, who do you think, over a long period of time, is going to stand the greater chance of prosperity and success - the average trader of markets or the average trader of CTAs?

Perhaps reflection on this one single question will best answer the question of whether or not a professional money manager is for you!

If you have read this far, you obviously have interest in the subject and may find it helpful now to go back and reread the Self Evaluation section.

Advice

Every year, I receive many requests that generally follow 1 of 2 lines -

1. Do you manage money?

2. Do you have a particular adviser or fund to suggest?

The answer to the first question is that no, I do not, as of this writing, manage public funds although I am and have been for the past few years registered to do so through Trader's Expectations, Inc., a CTA registered with the National Futures Association (NFA).

My well-publicized experiences with the NFA are the main stumbling blocks towards my accepting public funds. The NFA's initiation, however, in 1990 of legal action attempting to force me to register "The Almanac" with the government may have precluded my ever being able to manage public funds in the United States (if I flat don't wind up in jail for writing this book)!

The answer to the second question is that no, I do not have anyone to suggest.

Chapter 4

Analytical Techniques

Fundamental vs. Technical Analysis

An analyst is someone
who can tell you something
you already know
and make it sound confusing.

There are two basic classifications of analysis used to analyze price movement - fundamental analysis and technical analysis.

Although both the fundamentalist and the technician attempt to solve the same problem of price direction, they differ in that the fundamentalist studies the CAUSE of price movement while the technician studies the EFFECT. The technician, of course, argues that the effect is all that he wants or needs to know and that the reasons for the price move are unnecessary. The fundamentalist, on the other hand, always has to know why.

A problem often arises in that the technicals and the fundamentals are often in conflict with each other, especially at the beginning of major market moves when the technicals act as a leading indicator of the fundamentals. This leads technicians to claim that the study of fundamentals is unnecessary. They support their argument by claiming that

1.) it is impossible to know all of the news and items that fundamentally affect price at any given point in time,

2.) even if this wealth of information were known, it is too rapidly changing to allow for interpretation and correct action,

3.) the news is dated and widely disseminated by the time it is received, and

4.) since money is either made or lost in the price movement, efforts should thus be concentrated on the study of price.

Their final conclusion is that chart reading, computerized chart analysis, or computerized system trading are thus short cuts to fundamental analysis.

Anyone who has ever traded markets, however, is well aware of the many times that price has attempted to lead a market to a major change only to be slammed back in the direction of the original move. In this instance, these false price reversal signals become "corrections" as the fundamentals again assert themselves.

Nevertheless, technical analysis can be said to include fundamental analysis. The reverse, however, is not true. Fundamental analysis does not include a study of price action. A good forecaster can go broke if he is not a good trader, while some good traders who are poor forecasters can generate profits.

That said, it must be noted that any important market move must be caused by underlying fundamental factors. Hence, they are important.

If one can find the time to analyze the fundamentals of a market and align those fundamental conclusions with technical trading signals (i.e., take those signals that only point in the same direction as the fundamentals), one is likely to improve trading results. Note, however, that such a statement implies that one is able to correctly analyze and interpret fundamental market information, a task that requires a large amount of time and dedication.

Fundamental Analysis

You have to beware the grain analyst
who can tell you the exact number of acres
being planted in Iowa and Nebraska
but can't tell you when to sell July corn.

Fundamental analysis is the study of the interreaction of supply, demand, and price. Cause and effect of price movement is reflected in the supply / demand curve.

Fundamentals are analyzed because -

1.) They provide information and insight unavailable to the pure technician,

2.) They sometimes portend a major price move well in advance of technicals,

3.) They can permit a trader to adopt a more aggressive stance than would otherwise be the case if the underlying fundamentals were not known and understood,

4.) They can allow a trader to remain with a winning trade longer than he otherwise might, and

5.) Knowledge of fundamentals and the way the market SHOULD versus DOES react to news can provide valuable information.

The two basic tools that the fundmentalist uses are the supply / demand table and the balance table (other tools include regression analysis, econometric forecasting, etc., and are beyond the scope of this discussion).

The balance table is used by fundamentalists to summarize the key components of current-season supply and disappearance. The table begins with beginning carryover from the previous campaign, identifies and adds sources of supply, identifies and subtracts sources of demand, and arrives at ending season carryover. It is the relative magnitude of this carryover figure that is considered the primary price-determining statistic. One should note that the balance table coincides with the crop year and not the calendar year. The major drawback to the balance table is that it does not include price anywhere in its analysis.

Technical Analysis

When to buy and sell
is more important
than what to buy and sell.

Technical analysis is the study of market action, primarily through the use of charts or computer aided analysis, for the purpose of forecasting future price trends. It involves two main sources of information - price and volume. In the futures markets, a third source of information, open interest, also can be added.

This information is used to distinguish between the two main types of markets, trending or trading. Trending market approaches buy high to sell higher (or sell low to buy back lower) while trading market approaches sell rallies and buy corrections in anticipation of prices returning to recent levels. Although most markets are in trading ranges 60 % to 80 % of the time, most profits are made by trades in the trending portion of market movements because of the enormity of the move. Longer-term traders normally will gravitate towards trending markets while the short-term oriented trader will normally find trading markets to be more appealing.

For the long term trader or trend follower, markets should be approached from a "tops down" viewpoint (discussed in the next two sections). One technique that can be used to establish the long term trend is obviously fundamental analysis. In the opinion of the author, another is long term cyclical analysis. Another approach might involve the analysis of a general price index such as the Dow Jones Industrials, the CRB Index, the Dow Jones Commodity Price Index, etc. Another might be to tabulate each day the number of advancing stocks, bonds or futures contracts (front and deferred contracts included) and to analyze these results in a manner similar to the way that stock market analysts compare the advance/decline line, number of new highs / new lows, percentage of contracts in uptrends, advancing / declining volume, etc., to the price action of the stock indexes. Once the major trend is determined, the daily bar chart, the basic working tool of the trader, should then be used to time entry in the direction of the major trend.

Degree of Trading

The market is where prophets tell us
what will happen
and profits tell us
what did happen.
- Robert Orben

One of the things we discuss throughout the Almanac is the LEVEL OF DEGREE at which one is trading. One may be trading, for instance, on bar charts of degree denominated in years, months, weeks, days, minutes, or even ticks. The level of degree is normally a function of time and time alone. The trend in one level of degree may be completely different from the trend at another level.

For example, the weekly trend in the stock market may be up, but the hourly trend may be down and may have been down for a long time IN TERMS OF HOURLY DATA. The long term trader of stocks might thus have a very successful trade in place and so may the long term trader of hourly stocks EVEN THOUGH the near-term direction would seem to be harmful to the weekly trader. Trend to him may still be defined as being up while the hourly trader may define it as being down (while the 5-minute trader may define the trend as having just changed direction to an up mode).

Another item we discuss throughout this book is that trading really consists of three disciplines -

1. Forecasting of price trend - traditionally done with fundamental analysis. If wrong here, the chance that the rest will work is lessened.

2. Timing - or the determination of the best specific entry and exit techniques. Timing is almost entirely technical in nature, even if the trader is fundamentally oriented.

3. Money management - which covers the control and allocation of available funds, composition of the portfolio, and acceptance of risk.

In short, price forecasting tells the trader WHAT to do (buy or sell), timing tells him WHEN to do it, and money management tells him HOW MUCH to commit to the trade.

"Tops Down" Trading

*Try to find something that works
and stay with it.
- Robb Sagendorph*

Cognitive psychologists tell us that the human mind has difficulty interrelating more than three separate variables at the same time.

With that in mind (pun intended) one may find it helpful to begin the trading process with a long-range view and then gradually work toward lower levels of degree. The end objective is to trade in the direction of the major trend when analysis at all levels of degree line up and point in the same direction, regardless of the level of degree that the trader finally uses.

For instance, initial analysis may define the weekly trend as up. If the level of degree that the trader is making his decisions in is the daily level, he would enter his positions only on the long side when his daily approach gave him "buy" signals. On "sell" signals, he would only exit the market and go flat since to go short would be in conflict with the next higher degree level, the weekly level. If he were trading at an hourly level, he would again only enter long positions and would do so as long as the weekly, daily, and hourly trends all pointed in the same direction.

Trading in this manner will insure that trades are made in the direction of the main trend and will simplify the decision-making process for the average trader as the concept is very easy to understand.

Basic Charting Techniques

Those who cannot remember the past
are condemned to repeat it.
- Santayana

The chart is the most basic of tools in the technical trader's toolkit.

The most popular of charts is the bar chart which is formed by recording time horizontally (or on the x-axis) and price vertically (or on the y-axis). For instance, if a trade of gold occurred at a price of $ 350.00 on June 1, 1990, we would go to the location on the time or horizontal axis that corresponded with June 1, 1990 and would then move up vertically to the location on the price or vertical axis that corresponded with $ 350.00. We would make a mark on our chart at the point where the day June 1, 1990 and the price $ 350.00 intersected. In similar manner, we would continue to record all the trades that occurred during the day at various prices. Our horizontal location would not change for that day, but a scattergram would soon appear representing all the different trades that had occurred during the day. At the end of the day, after trading had halted, four prices would become evident on our chart. First would be the first price at which a trade had occurred during the day (the opening price). Next would be the highest price and lowest price at which trades had occurred during the day. Finally, the last price at which a trade had occurred during the day would be recorded (the closing price).

The following chart shows several such daily bar charts for gold from June 14, 1990 to June 27, 1990. Opening prices for each day are noted by the horizontal tick mark to the left of each daily bar chart. Closing prices are noted by the horizontal tick mark to the right of each daily bar chart. The solid line represents all POSSIBLE trades that MAY have occurred during the day between the highest price of the day (which is at the top of the solid vertical line) and the lowest price of the day (which is at the bottom of the solid vertical line). Note that the solid line does NOT mean that gold has traded at all points between the high and low price of the day. For instance, the final trading day for June, 1990 gold on June 27, 1990 recorded an opening price of $ 350.70, a high of $ 351.50, a low of $ 350.50, and a close of $ 351.40. Gold MAY or MAY NOT have traded at $ 351.00 (or some other price between the high and the low that day).

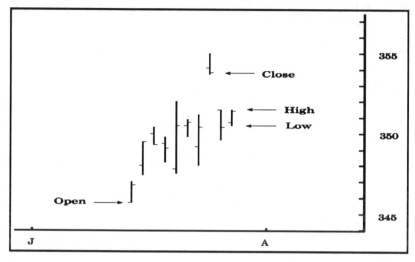

Note that trades can be recorded and a bar chart formed over any period of time such as all trades for a year, a quarter, a month, a week, a day, an hour, several hours, a half hour, one minute, and so on.

The Day's True Trading Range is sometimes defined as the high price minus the low price adjusted for the previous day's closing price. The following examples illustrate -

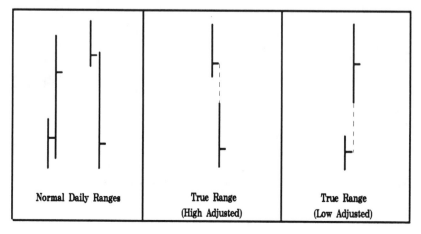

Ringed High Days are surrounded by days with lower (or equal) highs.

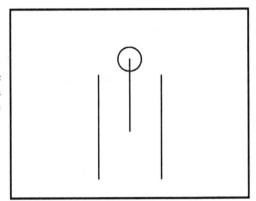

Sometimes these days are surrounded by two days on each side and sometimes three.

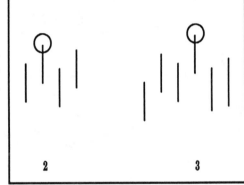

The reverse is, of course, the case for Ringed Low Days.

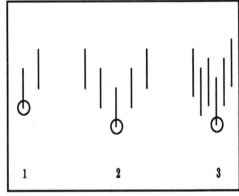

The next 3 charts show, in order, 1 Day Ringed Highs and Lows, 2 Day Ringed Highs and Lows, and 3 Day Ringed Highs and Lows for an actual market. Note that, for the true chartist, the market depicted by these charts is inconsequential. It could be a chart of an individual stock, a stock market index such as the Dow Jones Industrials, wheat, gold, ocean shipping rates, housing starts, etc. For the true chartist, the analysis will always be the same regardless of the market.

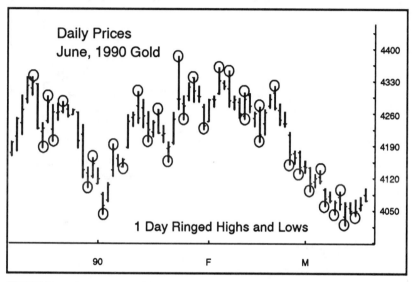

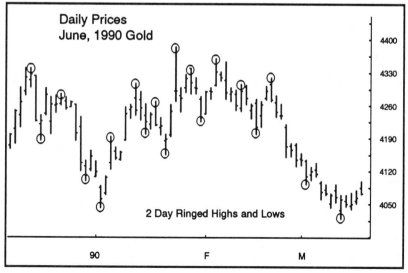

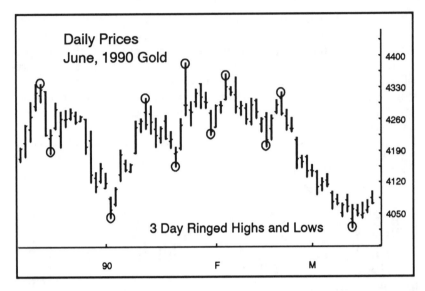

Some traders connect the swing highs and lows to indicate trend and / or reversal points. The following chart, for example, connects two day ringed highs and lows.

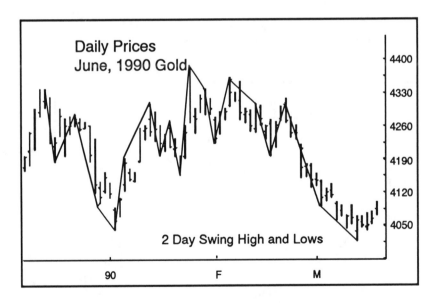

The following chart is a daily bar chart of the December S & P 500 futures contract from 871027 to 871216. It depicts a basic entry / exit approach used in conjunction with 1 day ringed highs / lows. An entry is made on the close of the day that the ringed price is first able to be determined. For a 1 day ringed high, for instance, the first day that this determination can be made is the day following the ringed high day (the day after the ringed high day must, of course, have a lower high for the ringed high day to be a ringed high day). If a ringed high is formed, a contract is sold on the close on the day after the ringed high day. No stops are used in illustrating this concept. No commissions or slippage is

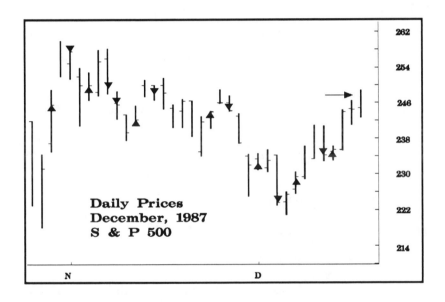

Daily Prices
December, 1987
S & P 500

assumed, either. Other variations of this concept enter at the low of the ringed day, the low of the day after the ringed low day, only sell if the close is down, and so on. Note that this data is as it originally appeared in The 1988 Almanac and has not been updated. Data that covered a longer period of time would obviously show different results.

The following assumes one contract for this period -

871029	BY @ 24570		
871102		SL @ 25775	+$6,025
871104	BY @ 25015		+$3,800

Date	Action	Exit	P/L
871106		SL @ 24910	-$ 525
871111	BY @ 24220		+$3,450
871113		SL @ 24760	+$2,700
871123	BY @ 24410		+$1,750
871125		SL @ 24430	+$ 100
871201	BY @ 23185		+$6,225
871203		SL @ 22360	-$4,125
871207	BY @ 22950		-$2,950
871210		SL @ 23435	+$2,425
871211	BY @ 23545		-$ 550
871216		OUT @ 24750	+$6,025

SUMMARY : 9 WINS, 4 LOSSES (69 %), $ 32,500 WON, $ 8,150 LOST, $ 24,350 GROSS PROFIT, 34 TRADING DAYS, $ 7,075 WORST DRAWDOWN,

RETURN ON INVESTMENT

(assume $ 25,000 margin) = 97.4 % (51 calendar days)

    = 697 % ANNUALIZED.

If one used a "tops down" approach and traded only in the direction of an upward trend, only buy signals would have been accepted and vice versa if the trend assumption was down.

For instance, the weekly trend could be determined by using weekly charts in the same manner as they were used for the daily chart. Also, the ringed period requirement of 1 day could, of course, be varied to 2 or 3 days. Note that a computer is not required to use a technique such as this. Note also the relative simplicity of the concept.

WARNING ! WARNING ! WARNING ! WARNING ! WARNING !

This technique is listed here for educational purposes only in order to provide you with some ideas that you can use on your own. It is not, under ANY CIRCUMSTANCES, being suggested as a stand-alone "trading system". It can, however, be used in instances when one is looking to enter a market in a particular direction and is in need of an entry technique.

For example, in the April 12, 1988 issue of "The Almanac Reports", it was noted that the New York Stock Exchange CASH index was not CONFIRMING the New York Stock Exchange June, 1988 futures index, that the NYSE Utilities and Transportations were not confirming the Industrials, and that volume was dropping off as the Industrial averages moved to new highs.

In short, it was time to sell short and make some money!

The technique we used in this instance to gain entry was the technique described above. Entry was achieved on April 13, 1988 @ the closing price of 27210 as indicated by the arrow in the following chart of daily June, 1988 S & P 500 futures prices.

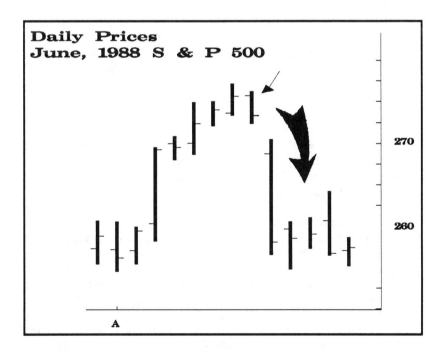

**Daily Prices
June, 1988 S & P 500**

270

260

A

Trendlines

KISS !
(Keep It Simple, Stupid!)
- United States Army saying

Although most traders tend to dismiss the importance of trendlines, they can, in fact, be one of the most important tools in a trader's toolkit.

Traders draw trendlines in many different ways but, generally speaking, the key to drawing proper trendlines is to draw them by connecting ringed highs and lows.

A trendline drawn off 2 day ringed highs or lows will provide fewer lines but the lines that are drawn will be of greater importance than those drawn off 1 day ringed highs or lows.

Trendlines become "tentative" once two ringed lows (or highs) can be identified and connected. The line is "confirmed" when prices retest and bounce off the line a third time.

TRADING HINT : Buy (sell) this test with a close stop just under (over) the line.

Trendlines become more significant the longer they are intact and the more times they have been successfully tested. The more significant the trendline, the more important its penetration when it is eventually broken.

Very often, the breaking of the trendline is one of the best early warnings of a change in trend, especially if price closes below (above) the line. It is especially important to monitor volume on the trendline break. Once broken, the trendline becomes resistance (support) and price will often retest the line from the bottom (a good short selling opportunity).

Often a series of retests of the old highs (lows) will be made that fail, creating a number of lower trendlines that appear as a fan. The breaking of the third trendline is usually an indication that prices are ready to enter a panic selloff (buying panic).

The most important trendlines will normally approximately 45 degrees. If a trendline is too steep, it usually indicates that prices are advancing too rapidly. The breaking of that steep trendline is often just a reaction back to a more sustainable slope closer to the 45 degree line. The opposite of the above applies to downtrend lines. Examples follow.

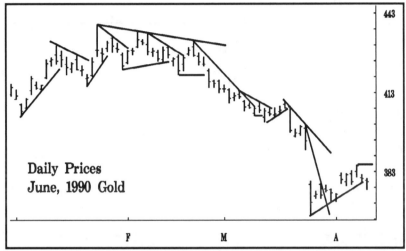

Daily Prices
June, 1990 Gold

The above chart shows trendlines drawn off 1 day ringed highs and lows. Note that Keltner's Rule should be applied when trading trendlines (i.e., in order to have entry, price should not only break the trendline but should also break the low (in the case of a sale or short sale) of the previous day.

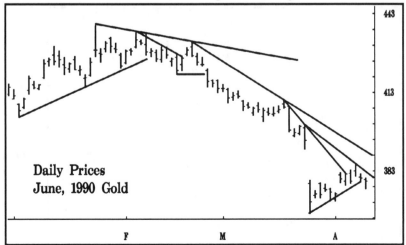

Daily Prices
June, 1990 Gold

The above chart shows trendlines drawn off 2 day ringed highs
and lows. Note that there are fewer lines and, therefore, fewer
trades. Note, too, that this approach draws the line right through
a cluster of highs or lows as in the down trendline drawn in
mid-February. Such will often be the case when drawing
trendlines off multi-day ringed high and low points, especially if
Keltner's rule is applied.

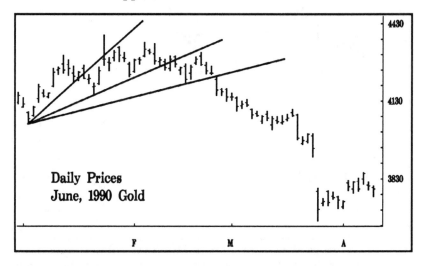

Note how the third successive break of the fan lines shown in the
chart above preceded the downward break in this market.

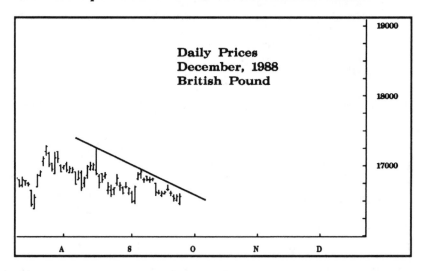

In the September 20, 1988 issue of "The Almanac Reports", we combined projected cycle low information for the British Pound from The 1988 Almanac along with fundamental analysis to state "Note that it has now been two months since the July 18 low marked the 20 month cycle low but that, listening to news reports, one would think that the Dollar had been quite strong over this period of time. British interest rates have meanwhile increased from 7 1/2 % to 12 %. We will buy one contract on a break of the August 16 to September 7 down trendline and the previous day's high."

That break did not occur until seven days later on September 26, 1988 but note that, once long positions were entered, they were never at a loss position (see the chart that follows which shows both the trendline entry point and the exit point as shown by the down arrow).

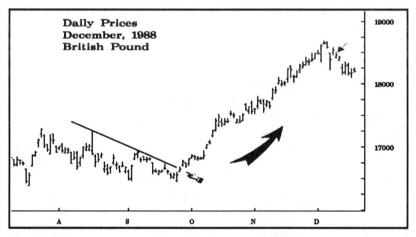

This position was exited December 9, 1988 @ 18430 in accordance with exit instructions from the December 7, 1988 issue of "The Almanac Reports" for a profit of over $ 11,000 per contract in less than three months.

Note that the technique used to time entry into this position was none other than a simple trendline break.

Note, too, that the December 5, 1988 high marked the high in the British Pound for the next eighteen months (at least) and that this high preceded a 37 point drop, six month decline in the British Pound.

Not all trendlines are straight. An interesting variation is the curved trendline which is drawn with a "French Curve" and can be just as valid as a straight trendline. An example is shown below.

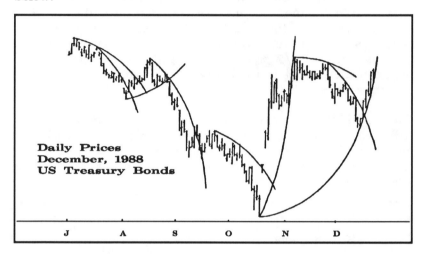

Daily Prices
December, 1988
US Treasury Bonds

The following example from the April 14, 1988 issue of "The Almanac Reports" shows daily June, 1988 Crude Oil prices where we combined the resistance of a straight trendline on the upper trend of price movement along with support provided by the curved trendline to enter short positions in this market. Prices peaked two trading days later @ 1884. The peak marked the high in the Crude Oil market for the rest of 1988.

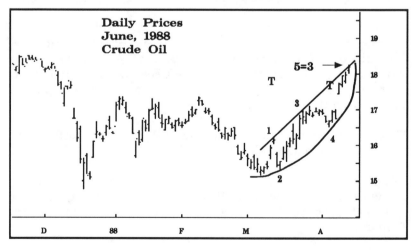

Daily Prices
June, 1988
Crude Oil

Those who have interest in Fibonacci numbers, Elliott Waves, and the like will note the two target projections marked by the two "T"s. These are Fibonacci price projections and project the extent in terms of price to which a next successive Elliott Wave may extend (see the section on Fibonacci price projections). The five wave Elliott wave sequence is as labeled in the chart. The observer can note that, in this analysis, the assumption was that four of the five waves had been completed and that the move was in the fifth wave of an expected five wave movement. In Elliott Wave terms, the length of the fifth wave often equals the length of either the first or the third wave (length of a wave is simply the distance in price that the wave has covered. In our chart, the third wave covers the distance from the number two to the number three or, specifically in terms of price, from $ 15.35 to $ 17.10 = $ 1.75). Since the fifth wave was already longer than the first wave, if the fifth wave was to approximately equal either the first or the third wave in length, the only wave left to choose from was the $ 1.75 third wave. Adding $ 1.75 to our assumed fourth wave low of $ 16.53 gave a projected top of $ 18.28. Note that our projection was also right up against the up trendline drawn off the tops of the first and third waves. The curved trendline fit especially well in this instance since it connected the March 7 beginning of the entire move @ $ 15.19 and the lows made by the second and fourth waves.

TRADING HINT : Those who are interested in trailing their trading signals with the Parabolic trading system but are not computerized and do not wish to perform the laborious calculations everyday may instead wish to simply use a chart and curved trendlines drawn from a French curve available at your local office supply store in order to derive their stops.

Point & Figure Charting

. . . I tried other methods
and consulted practically every known
writer, guide, and authority
in the financial field at that time.
These efforts were finally rewarded when at last
the point and figure method
was developed to such an extent
as to be one of the most valuable aids
of my vocation . . .
Like Archimedes, I was able to say,
"I have found it!"
- Victor de Villiers, 1933

Point and figure charts comprise a trading method of their own; that is, the charts themselves generate "buy" and "sell" signals which may be used to enter and exit the market. Point & figure charts are kept without regard to time or volume. "X"s are used to mark price advances and "O"s are used for the declines.

Each time the price reverses, a new column to the right is started. The signals are more precise than on bar charts and the entry and exit points are quite specific allowing the trader to achieve greater discipline.

The trader can adjust two parameters on Point and Figure charts which are the size of each box and the number of boxes needed for a reversal. Floor traders use very small box and reversal criteria whereas long term position traders use larger box sizes and reversal thresholds. The charts can be adapted to almost any need by varying the box and reversal sizes. They are easy to plot and easy to read.

SIGNALS - Simple reversal signals are given for buys when a column of "X"s tops a previous column of "X"s (often used for stop placements). The breaking of double and triple top formations are said to provide particularly good entry signals. Trendlines are noted with a 45 degree line drawn off the most recent significant reaction low (high). Note that P & F trendlines do not connect points on the chart like bar chart trendlines do. P & F charting also provides multiple signals that can be used for pyramiding purposes.

In 1965 "Profit and Profitability" was published by Robert E. Davis. Mr. Davis analyzed two stocks from 1914 to 1964 and 1100 stocks from 1954 to 1964 claiming that 80 percent of the transactions were profitable with an average profit of 25 percent.

Davis identified the ascending triple top formation (87.9 percent reliable) as being the best buy signal and the breakout of a triple bottom (93.5 percent reliable) as being the best sell signal for stocks. The two patterns follow.

```
                        X - BUY  |       X           X
              X           X      |   O   X   O   X   O
  X           X     O     X      |   O   X   O   X   O
  X     O     X     O     X      |   O   X   O   X   O
  X     O     X     O            |   O       O       O
        O                        |                       O - SELL
```

Here are some parameters to use for P & F charting

BO - .20 X 4	GO - 2.00 X 5	S - .04 X 2
C - .02 X 2	LC - .40 X 1	SM - .20 X 4
CP - .40 X 5	LH - .40 X 4	SU - .10 X 4
CT - .40 X 2	PB - .40 X 3	SV - .10 X 4
FC - .40 X 1	PL - 5.00 X 4	W - .02 X 4

Some examples of Point & Figure charting signals follow on the next page.

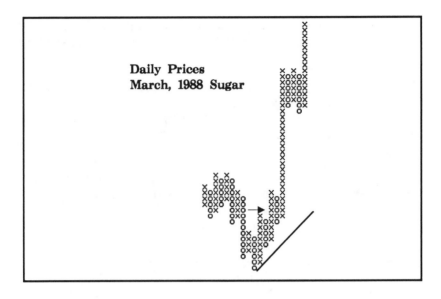

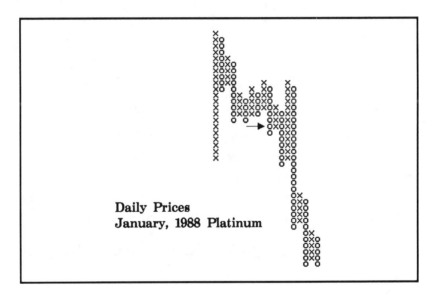

Buy prices in the March, 1988 Sugar shown in the top chart were at 7.40 cents as noted by the horizontal arrow while the sell in January, 1988 Platinum was at $594 prior to the November/December, 1987 $110 drop.

Continuation Chart Patterns

Big money isn't always smart money,
but it is seldom stubborn money.
- Zendal

Once one has become familiar with the basic bar chart, the trader interested in charting prices will want to become familiar with basic chart patterns and their implications for future price movement. Two basic patterns exist, continuation patterns and reversal patterns. We will first discuss continuation chart patterns in this section.

If the trend is your friend, then so are continuation chart patterns, for they trade in the direction of the trend. Continuation patterns are usually shorter-term in duration than reversal patterns. They consist of flags and pennants, triangles (symmetrical, ascending, and descending), wedges, and rectangles.

One requirement for both flags and pennants is that they be preceded by a sharp and almost straight line move. They are among the most reliable of continuation patterns and only rarely produce a trend reversal. An important requirement is that volume should dry up noticeably while each of the patterns are forming (correcting).

A triangle should break out between one-half and three-fourths the horizontal distance to the apex with diminishing volume occurring as the price swings become narrower. On the breakout, volume should increase. If a symmetrical triangle, the formation is essentially neutral. An ascending triangle (which usually has a flat top) is bullish while a descending triangle (with a flat bottom) is bearish. The fourth try at the top of the ascending triangle (or the bottom of a descending triangle) is the one to buy (sell).

Wedges have a noticeable slant, usually against the prevailing trend. Falling wedges are considered bullish while rising wedges are considered bearish. Wedges sometimes occur in the fifth wave of Elliott Wave formations. Wedge patterns usually move at least two-thirds of the way to the apex before breaking out. Like other continuation patterns, volume should contract during formation and increase on the breakout.

The way to trade these formations is in the direction of the prevailing trend upon entering the formation. Orders can be placed just above the trendline forming the breakout side in the direction of the trend.

Examples follow.

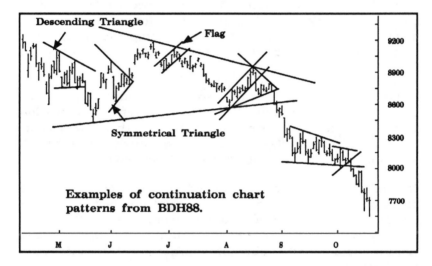

Examples of continuation chart patterns from BDH88.

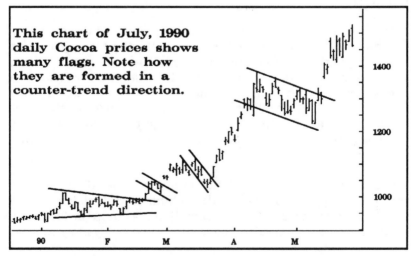

This chart of July, 1990 daily Cocoa prices shows many flags. Note how they are formed in a counter-trend direction.

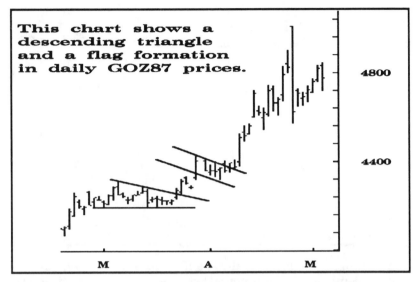

This chart shows a
descending triangle
and a flag formation
in daily GOZ87 prices.

4800

4400

M   A   M

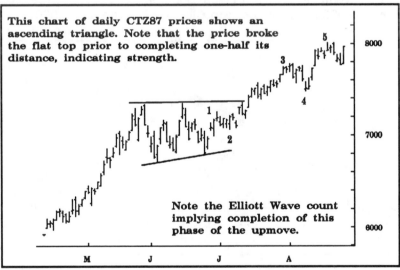

This chart of daily CTZ87 prices shows an
ascending triangle. Note that the price broke
the flat top prior to completing one-half its
distance, indicating strength.

8000

7000

Note the Elliott Wave count
implying completion of this
phase of the upmove.

6000

M   J   J   A

The following example is from the July 29, 1988 issue of "The
Almanac Reports." The chart insert shows daily September, 1988
Municipal Bond prices. In this issue, we wrote that "This market
has formed a very bullish ascending triangle formation as shown
in the chart . . . ".

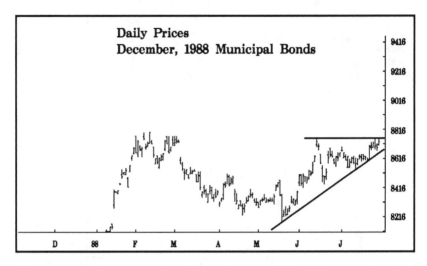

Daily Prices
December, 1988 Municipal Bonds

The ensuing three month rally is shown in the following chart of daily December, 1988 Municipal Bond prices. The rally produced over $ 6,000 in profits per contract on a margin of $ 1,500.

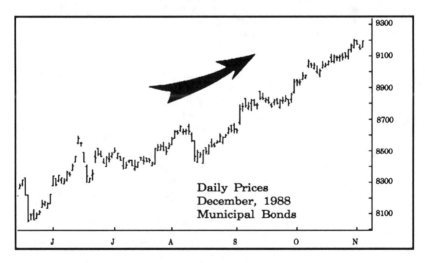

Daily Prices
December, 1988
Municipal Bonds

Note that nothing was required to take advantage of this situation other than a chart book and recognition of the ascending triangle formation and its implications for continuation of the move. You did not need a fancy computer, you did not need to be a subscriber to "The Almanac Reports" or any other service, and you did not need to be interpreting moon phases, Kobala numbers, or any other exotic technique!

All you needed was to be awake, to have the courage to believe what you were seeing, AND TO THEN ACT ON YOUR CONVICTIONS !!!

Thrust

> *It isn't as important*
> *to buy as cheap as possible*
> *as it is*
> *to buy at the right time.*
> *- Jesse Livermore*

The concept of thrust was originally developed by William Dunnigan in the early 1950s and included several different approaches to the subject ("Thrust Method", "One-Way Formula", double thrusts, repeat thrusts, etc.). The basic objective was to provide a way to enter an existing trend on minor reactions on the daily bar chart.

Key to the signals was the set up. In an uptrend (downtrend), a "downswing" ("upswing") was required and was defined as a day which had both a lower high and a lower low than the day preceding it. Inside days did not count and were treated as though they had not occurred. The intention was to buy minor reactions against the trend. At least one downswing day was required before a thrust day could occur.

The thrust signal to buy occurs when the high of the current day exceeds the high of the previous day. The order was good for one day only.

Should this situation occur, the long position is entered and a protective stop placed below the low of the day of entry. (An alternative approach places the stop above the high of the signal day if it is higher than the high of entry day).

Variations are that more downswing days are required before the signal can be given, that the day must close above the signal day's high, that the entire day's range must be above the signal day's high (but need not occur on the day after the signal day as with the other approaches), etc.

An example for the US Treasury Bonds follows for late 1987. Keep in mind that thrust works best in a trending market and that markets trend only about 15 to 30 % of the time. Note also that thrust allows a position to be pyramided as in the following example.

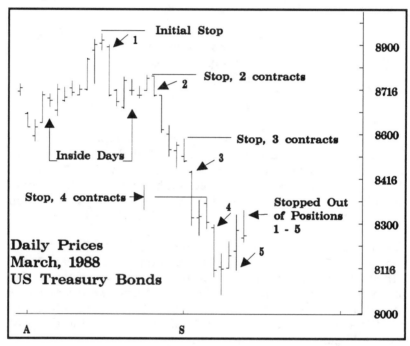

Note how the stops were lowered each time a new position was added and how signals involving inside days were ignored. This technique produced a profit of over $8,000 in only 18 trading days.

If you are going to use thrust, you should develop parameters that define whether a market is in an uptrend or a downtrend and should be willing to accept signals only if they occur within N days of a major high (low in a bear market).

Japanese Candlesticks

*Fools try to prove
they were right.
Wise men try to find
when they are wrong.*

One recent development in 1989 was the reintroduction of Japanese Candlesticks, a centuries-old charting method that expands upon the basic bar chart by including graphical representation of the difference between the open and closing prices of a particular time period. This difference is displayed by a widened box versus the horizontal tick marks that normally accompany a bar chart and represent opening and closing prices. The box is solid if the close is lower than the open and empty if the close is higher than the open.

Traditional Western charting techniques apply to Japanese Candlesticks as do such formations as umbrellas, spinning tops, and so on.

The following chart of June, 1990 US Treasury Bonds is charted in Japanese Candlesticks. Note how the solid boxes turned to empty boxes after the trend change on April 27, 1990 from down to up.

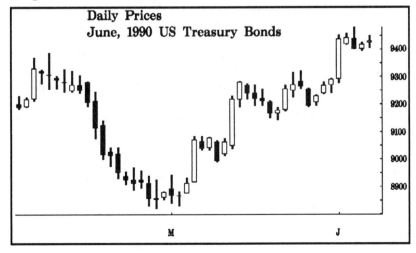

Reversal Chart Patterns

*Pay closer attention
to what the market is telling you,
rather than what you think it should do.
In a bull market,
an "over-bought" condition typically lasts longer,
while an "over-sold" condition ends very quickly.
The reverse is true in bear markets.*
- Alan Shaw

Chart patterns are divided into those that indicate the trend will continue (continuation patterns) and those that indicate the trend will reverse (reversal patterns). This section discusses reversal or change-in-trend patterns.

The major reversal patterns are the head and shoulders, double tops (bottoms), triple tops (bottoms), spikes, rectangles, the extended trading range (usually found at bottoms), the rounding saucer pattern, and the expanding triangle top (bottom).

In order to have a reversal pattern, there must, of course, first be something to reverse (a trend, even if it is sideways), and one of the first signals of an impending trend reversal is often the breaking of a trendline. Better detection of which of these signals are real as opposed to which are just corrections will result if analysis includes volume and open interest.

Generally speaking, the larger the pattern, the greater the subsequent move. If the pattern is a topping one, it is likely to be of shorter duration and more volatile than a bottoming pattern since prices tend to decline faster than they rise. In the early stages of market tops, volume is not as important as at bottoms, where an increase in volume is an essential ingredient.

Although not essential, in a head and shoulders top reversal, volume should decline as the head makes new highs and should definitely be lower on the right shoulder. Once the neckline is broken, it will often be retested. This retest should occur on light volume and should not recross the neckline. When the new trend resumes, volume should increase. On bottoming patterns, volume should increase on the rallies and definitely on the breakout. Retests are more common on bottoms than on tops.

An alternative entry technique used by some traders enters at the lower of the two dips for topping patterns instead of at the neckline. Additionally, it is especially bearish if the neckline is sloping down on the topping pattern. Also, if a head and shoulders top or bottom formation is suggested by price action and volume is CLEARLY confirming the developing pattern, some traders will sell the rally from the right shoulder dip at a 50 % retracement to the top of the head.

Another choice is to sell on the close of the day that the ringed high of the right shoulder is formed (reverse, of course, for bottoming patterns).

In a double top (bottom) it is essential that the previous reaction low (high) be broken, confirming the double top. These tops (bottoms) are often referred to as 1-2-3 tops (bottoms). A 2 day ringed low (high) at the reaction point will help to filter out some of the bad signals. The trends that result will be longer term trends. If the trader has a definite reason for believing that a trend reversal has taken place at the "1" point, the alternative entry techniques listed above can be used as can a trendline break if the pattern is large.

Spike reversals are usually accompanied by news. Technically, the only valid reversal signal that occurs is often the breaking of a very steep trendline (either straight or curved - see section on Trendlines) or an unusually high open interest figure (many longs added at very high prices). Sometimes the turn is marked by a key reversal day or an island reversal day that occurs on very heavy volume.

The rounding saucer pattern is rare.

The extended trading range pattern is discussed elsewhere and is normally most useful at market bottoms where price has consolidated for an extended period of time. This pattern is often approached on a scaling-in basis. Others approach it by buying the lower part of the trading range, especially if open interest is expanding.

Examples follow.

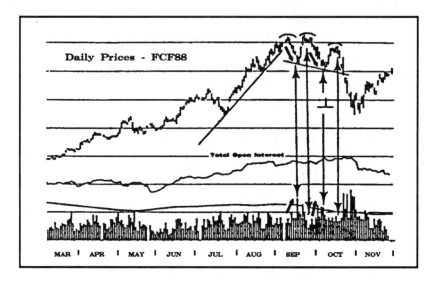

This chart of daily January, 1988 Feeder Cattle prices shows a textbook head-and-shoulders formation at the top of the meat market in the fall of 1987. Note the initial indication of a potential top was the trendline break in early September. Also, notice how volume, which is shown by the dark vertical lines at the bottom of the chart, increased on the initial selloff and then dried up as the "head" was formed. Next was the volume increase on the next selloff, followed by the drop in volume as prices moved up in the formation to form the right shoulder (which is EXACTLY what should happen at this critical point). The down-slanting neckline as indicated by the down trendline was an especially bearish indication. When broken, volume increased and prices cascaded. The target (the upside-down "T") was projected by measuring the distance from the head to the lower right neckline and subtracting from the neckline.

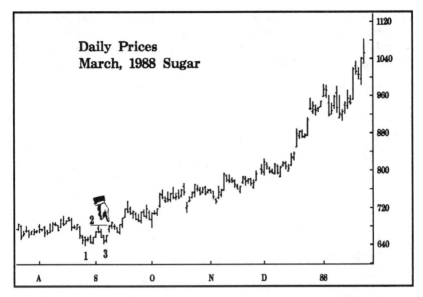

The chart above shows the rather popular 1-2-3 double bottom or "W" formation (with an "M" being formed at tops). (Note that there is also a minor 1-2-3 double bottom formation separately formed and completed between the "1" and the "2" in the chart). Results with this formation will be improved if point "1" is the lowest low for the past eight days (high at tops), if point "2" is a 2 day ringed high (low), and if point "3" has retraced at least 50 percent of the distance from point 1 to point 2.

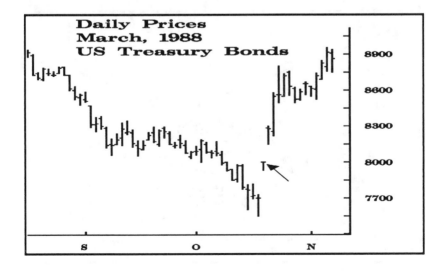

The previous chart shows the spike bottom reversal created in the bond market as the stock market dropped 508 points in October, 1987 and Federal Reserve Chairman Greenspan announced that the Fed would be the "lender of last resort".

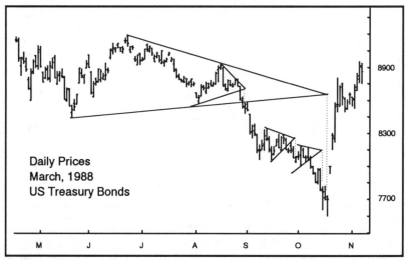

Daily Prices
March, 1988
US Treasury Bonds

Some traders believe that a change in trend is projected IN TIME at the point at which the two sides of a triangle converge in the future. The above chart of the March, 1988 US Treasury Bonds shows four such examples. The following chart shows weekly crude oil prices and is from the April 30, 1988 issue of "The Almanac Reports."

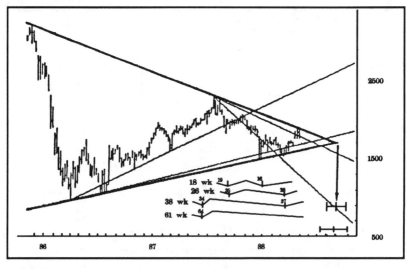

In this issue, we noted that the apex shown in the following chart of weekly Crude Oil prices (the point where the two thick lines meet) forecast a turning point in early September, four months hence. The 10 percent time bands were drawn at the bottom of the chart for the 18 week, 26 week, 38 week, and 61 week linear cycles. These projections were exactly as "The 1988 Almanac" listed them in the "Weekly Linear Cycles" section of the book. Note how the cyclical and triangular forecast coincided quite well.

Also, in the April 30 Report, note how prices had rallied right back to and been turned back by the (thick) long term down trendline. This RESISTANCE allowed us to observe at the time that "The major trendlines from the late 1985 high and early 1986 low additionally are drawn and show the importance of the current $ 19.00 resistance in the Crude Oil market".

We were thus able to conclude in that April 30, 1988 issue of "The Almanac Reports" that "The cycles are thus arguing for lower oil prices."

The result, of course, can be seen in the lower chart where prices did work much lower throughout summer, 1988 where they bottomed in fall, 1988 as projected by the 1988 Almanac amid a flurry of bearish comments and forecasts in the media. The subsequent rally covered over $ 13.00 per barrel over the next eight months.

Note how this trade was SET UP from weekly information and analysis. Actual timing of entry was done with analysis at a level of lower degree.

In the April 30, 1988 issue of "The Almanac Reports," we combined the following Head and Shoulders reversal pattern in the daily price chart of the June, 1988 Deutschmark along with Elliott Wave information, linear cycles listed in The 1988 Almanac, CIT (Change-In-Trend) Fibonacci Cycle turning point projections from Page 67 of The 1988 Almanac (which were right on the money), and some divergences that were occurring in the currencies at the time to enter short positions in the June, 1988 Deutschmark and other currencies.

The Deutschmark proceeded to drop over 900 points ($ 11,000) over the ensuing four months.

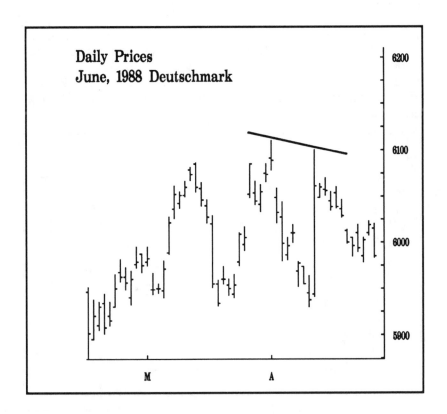

The next example is also from "The Almanac Reports." In the May 18, 1988 issue, we combined the Head and Shoulders pattern shown below in the chart of daily June, 1988 British Pound prices with some Elliott Wave and 20 month linear cycle projections from The 1988 Almanac to enter three short positions in the 18650 area. The ensuing price collapse was worth over $6,000 per contract by June 3rd in this market (2 weeks).

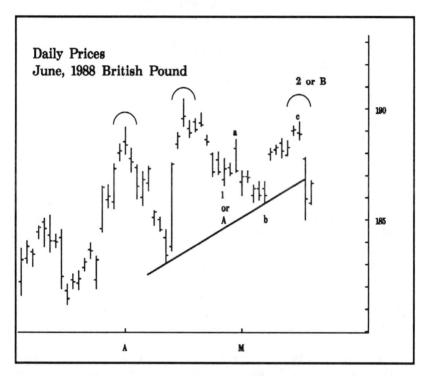

We wrote in the Report, "A possible Elliott Wave count is included which implies that we are in wave 3 of an expected 5 waves down which should be commencing immediately . . . In anticipation of lower prices into the June twenty month cycle lows, we will add to shorts on a break of the May 18th low @ 18570 and on a break of the May 17th low @ 18500." Prices dropped over $ 15,000 per contract over the next two months and, two years later, had still not recovered these May, 1988 levels.

Expanding Triangles

*It is no disgrace
to guess wrong,
but it is a disgrace
to stay wrong.*

The expanding triangle top (bottom) has been given many names ("broadening top", "broadening formation", "five wave reversal", "reverse point wave", "reverse wave", etc.) and is normally not given as much credence for use at market bottoms as at market tops.

In this formation, trendlines diverge in a broadening formation, creating a picture that looks like an expanding triangle. The market makes a series of higher highs and lower lows in this formation. In a textbook example, volume expands on each of 5 swings that occur instead of contracting as it does in a normal converging triangle. This expansion of volume occurs because the market has become extremely emotional due to an unusual amount of public participation. It is for this reason that this formation is usually seen at market tops and not at market bottoms (at long term market bottoms, markets are more "dead" than "emotional"). One must not confuse this formation with an Elliott Wave "flat" (see the section on the Elliott Wave).The basic pattern is given in the examples that follow.

The following daily price chart shows an expanding triangle top in December, 1987 Cotton. The insert in the upper right corner is a blow-up of the August top. Note that in both the August and November tops that price was too weak to even challenge the top trendline of the formation implying great weakness. Can you identify all five waves leading to the November top (the 5th is marked)?

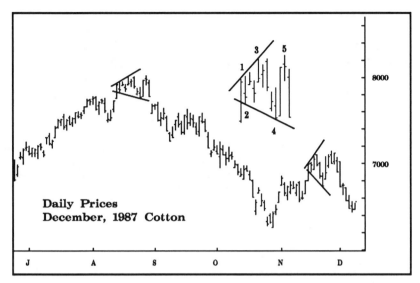

The chart that follows shows the March, 1987 low in Soybean Oil. Note how the challenge of the bottom trendline failed miserably. The expanding triangle formation is of greater validity if it can also be counted as the 4th and 5th waves of an Elliott Wave.

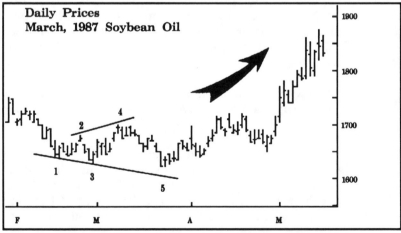

The chart that follows shows daily March, 1988 US Treasury Bond prices. As bonds traded into the 32 week cycle highs listed in the "Weekly Linear Cycles" section of The 1988 Almanac on February 5, 1988, this sell signal @ 9504 was issued in the February 5th issue of "The Almanac Reports" with stops @ 9519 (or just above the high of the move).

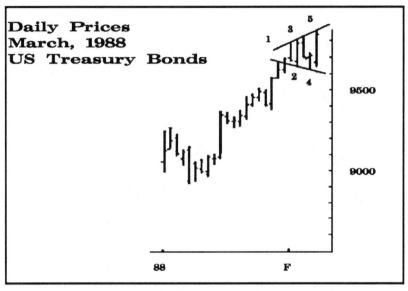

Daily Prices
March, 1988
US Treasury Bonds

News at the time was INCREDIBLY bullish spurred by such comments as that of Federal Reserve Board Chairman Greenspan's in testimony to Congress that " . . . the Fed's been loosening of late . . .". This news was also accompanied by a huge drop in the price of crude oil. March, 1988 US Treasury Bonds were sold short into the news and dropped to 9316 where they were covered on February 12th for a $ 1,625.00 profit per contract. Shorts were later again reentered shortly thereafter @ 9504 and @ 9420.

By May, just 3 months later, interest rates had risen dramatically and bonds had dropped in value over 10 points (or $ 10,000 per contract).

The following chart shows daily June, 1988 S & P 500 prices. The expanding triangle chart formation shown in the chart formation was one reason why a sell signal was issued in the March 21, 1988 issue of "The Almanac Reports" @ 27060. The position was stopped out on April 6th @ 26300 for a $ 3,800 profit.

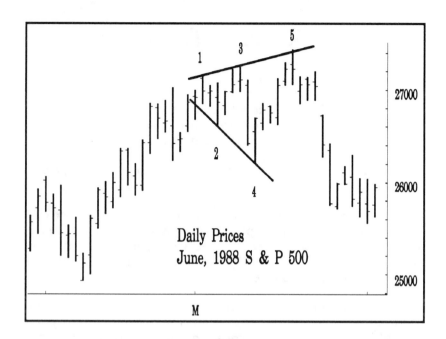

Note that the 5th wave was able to extend beyond the upper trendline connecting the tops of waves one and three. This break was one small signal that the expected down move was to be but of minor dimensions (which it was).

The entry @ 27060 on March 21st was on the close of trading. Why? Because this day was the first day that a ringed high day had formed at the wave 5 high.

The initial stop was placed above the wave 5 high of the move which occurred at 27445.

TRADING HINT : Expanding triangles are easy to spot and fun to use. The $upertrader should constantly scan markets for such formations. They can be especially profitable when they coincide with a "Weekly Linear Cycle" 5 percent time band listed in "The Calendar Book" of The Almanac. Just make sure that, if the Almanac is projecting a cycle low, that the expanding triangle formation is a "buy" pattern and not a "sell" pattern.

Reversal Days

Blessed is he who expects nothing,
for he shall never be disappointed.
- Alexander Pope, October 6, 1727

A reversal day occurs when a new high (low) made in an uptrend (downtrend) is followed by a lower (higher) close.

What happens is that an attempt is made to sustain the up trend early in the day. The attempt fails and prices reverse and begin to cascade in the other direction. The wider the range for the day and the heavier the volume, the more significant the signal for a possible near-term trend reversal.

Sometimes an outside day (where the high is higher than the previous day's high and the low is lower) will occur on the reversal day. Although this effect carries more significance, it is not a requirement for a reversal day.

Sometimes these days will mark the end of a trend and will be termed "key reversal" days. The problem is that time is needed to determine whether or not the reversal day actually reversed the trend or just temporarily corrected it. Hence, key reversal days cannot be ascertained for some time later.

Arnold did a brief study of outside days on the currencies, metals, and financials and concluded that the formation reasonably predicts consistent price movements for the next 3 days.

Sometimes the reversal day will occur over a two day period and is termed a two day reversal. In an uptrend, for instance, a new high for the move would be set with the close near the day's high. The next day, however, prices open roughly flat instead of continuing the trend and then close near the day's low. This second day of the two-day reversal can provide especially good entries when the price of day one has closed near or at limit down. To enter, stops should either be placed above the early morning price range or positions should be taken at the market with stops below the low of the day or the low of the previous day.

Another uncommon 2 day reversal day occurs when prices make a new high for the move and close near the day's high on day one. After opening much lower on day two, prices rally for most of the day, closing near the high of both days one and two. This situation is caused by early morning sellers having to cover their shorts at the end of the day. If the previous day's high cannot be exceeded, the market has provided a signal that short covering is fueling the rally, that the market is basically weak, and that it should be sold on the close.

Examples follow with both charts from daily December, 1987 US Treasury Bonds prices. The first chart shows 1 day reversals with 2 day reversals shown in the second chart. Two different types of reversal days are shown for each chart. In both instances, note how much better the signals are when taken in the direction of the major trend versus the normal contra-trend, reversal approach.

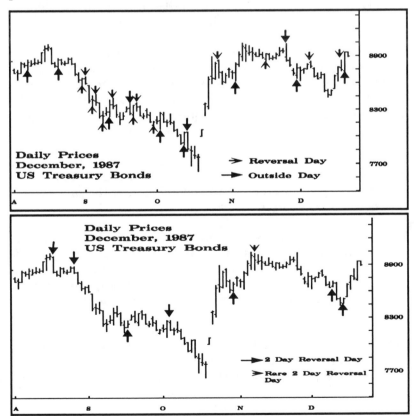

Gaps

*No profession requires
more hard work, intelligence,
patience, and mental discipline
than successful speculation.
- Robert Rhea*

Gaps can be classified as both continuation and reversal chart patterns, depending on the type of gap. They are fun to trade and consist of four general types - the common, breakaway, runaway (or measuring), and exhaustion gaps.

The common gap is the least important for trading purposes. It usually occurs in thinly traded markets or in the middle of horizontal trading ranges and has no importance.

The breakaway gap usually occurs at the completion of an important price pattern and usually signals the beginning of a significant market move. Increased volume on the breakout is important if the gap is to be believed. Breakaway gaps are usually not filled, especially if volume is quite heavy. If the gap is filled, it is an indication that the movement was a false breakout.

Runaway or midway gaps usually occur in Elliott third waves midway through the move. These gaps are usually not filled and provide a target objective for the completion of the move (since they occur midway in the move).

Exhaustion gaps usually occur near the end of the movement on one final burst of buying (selling), usually accompanied by news. Also, there is normally a marked increase in volume and open interest. Sometimes prices will form a breakaway gap over the exhaustion gap in the opposite direction forming an island reversal.

HOW TO TRADE - On a breakaway gap, enter the market in the direction of the move on a retest of the gap (especially if you can enter IN the gap). Stop the position just under the point at which the gap would be filled unless the gap was not accompanied by increased volume (this strategy does not apply to common gaps). Examples follow.

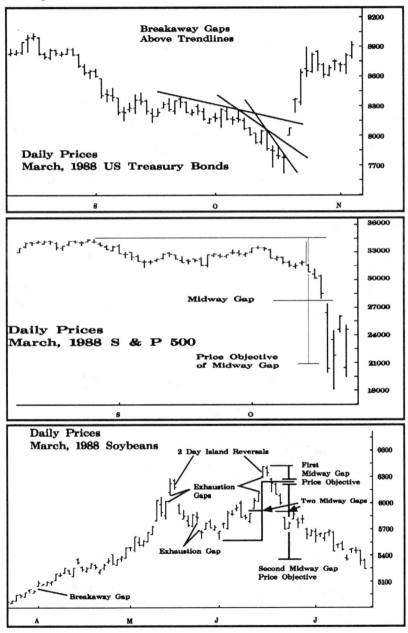

Swing Chart Analysis

*Success is getting up
one more time
than you fall down.*

Swing chart analysis is a trending approach that has been traced as far back as 1700 A.D. to Japanese rice merchants. Price is the only consideration as time, volume, and open interest along with all other technical measures are ignored.

Swing charts are somewhat similar to point-and-figure charts in this respect and in that a swing is defined as a movement of a minimum size (the swing filter) regardless of the time it takes to achieve that move.

New positions are entered at points where the new swing penetrates the level of the prior swing in the same direction. Secondary signals are also given if the new signal is in the direction of the main trend. Stop-loss orders can be placed at trend reversal levels or at a fixed dollar loss point.

Historical Trading Ranges

*One of life's most painful moments comes
when we must admit
that we didn't do our homework
and that we are not prepared.*
- Merlin Olsen

Long term trading ranges of five to ten years become very important as a market approaches the high or low end of the range. Support or resistance is usually encountered on the initial attempt at penetration and the market is turned back. Should the price linger at the highs, however, and especially if the market is making its fourth attempt at penetration, then expect a success-ful penetration to carry through. The longer the period of time that the market spent testing the highs, the greater will be the subsequent breakthrough.

At the lows, look for markets that for an extended period of time have been in an historically low level at or below the cost of production. The market should have gone through an extensive base-building period with a narrow trading range and the indus-try should be experiencing shutdowns of capacity or other im-proving fundamentals. (At a very minimum, the base building should have taken place over three weeks AFTER a three month trend has ended). Place resting buy orders above this trading range OR (if more aggressive) above a descending long term (3 months or longer) downtrendline (uptrend for such interest rate markets as T-Bills, T-Bonds, Eurodollars, and so on).

How effective is this trading technique?

In The 1987 Almanac, ALL OF THE MARKETS SUGGESTED EXPERIENCED SIZABLE MOVES THAT COULD HAVE BEEN CAPTURED BY USING THIS TECHNIQUE. These markets in-cluded Soybean Oil, Corn, Silver, Copper, Sugar, Crude Oil, US Treasury Bills, and Eurodollars (the latter two being both sell short suggestions). Results from entry point to the maximum extent of the subsequent price move were as follows; soybean oil (IN 1560, OUT 1982 = $ 2,500), corn (IN 156, OUT 202 = $ 2,300), sugar (IN 675, OUT 851 = $ 1,900), copper (IN 6135, OUT 13250 = $ 17,700), silver (IN 555, OUT 1175 = $31,000), crude oil (IN 1590, OUT 2276 = $ 6,800), US Treasury Bills (IN 9460, OUT 9167 = $ 7,300), eurodollars (IN 9015, OUT 9375 = $ 9,000).

These results are hypothetical, of course, for no one could have held to the exact top tick. However, if but HALF the move of the above had been captured, the moves would have been worth over $ 39,000 versus initial margins of about $ 7,000.

Weekly charts illustrating these moves suggested in The 1987 Almanac follow.

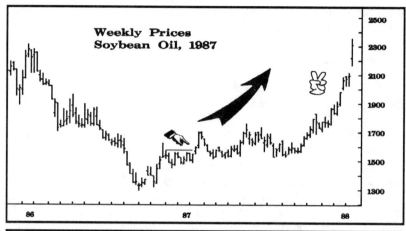

Weekly Prices
Soybean Oil, 1987

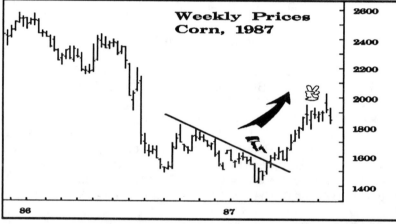

Weekly Prices
Corn, 1987

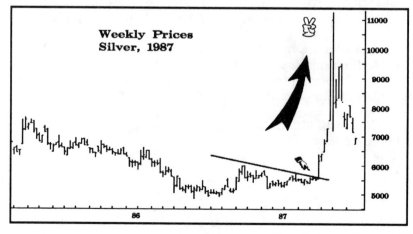

Weekly Prices
Silver, 1987

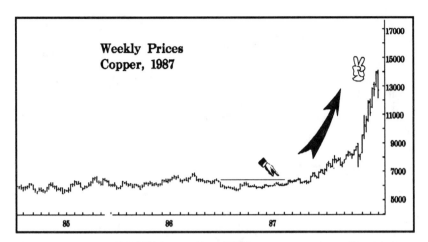

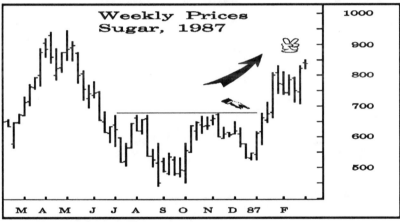

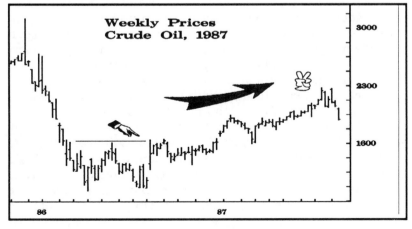

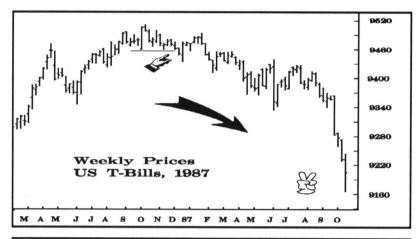

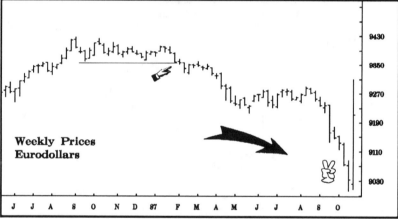

(The reader should note that 1987 was an unusual year in that
the major bear markets that had begun in the early 1980s in such
markets as grains, the soybean complex, the energy complex,
metals, and so on had ended the previous year. Termination of
these long term bear markets and the initiation of long term
multi-year bull markets along with such natural phenomena as
a change in moisture patterns from wet to dry and a change in
sunspot activity from decreasing to increasing had been correctly
anticipated and forecast in The 1986 Almanac. Hence, with many
markets at or below the cost of production, with the Democrats
having had just recaptured control of The United States Senate
in November, 1986, and with markets following quite well the
outlook in The 1986 Almanac, the forecast in this "Historical Price

Ranges" section The 1987 Almanac of these major long term bull markets, though correct in every instance, was really not much of a forecast at all since it merely was a continuation of the outlook in The 1986 Almanac and was but a reflection of Nature)!

Markets chosen from The 1988 Almanac were corn, cocoa, coffee, palladium, sugar, CBT wheat, Kansas City wheat, and Minneapolis wheat. Charts on these markets along with the breakout points shown in The 1988 Almanac follow.

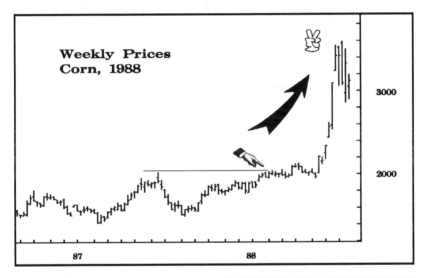

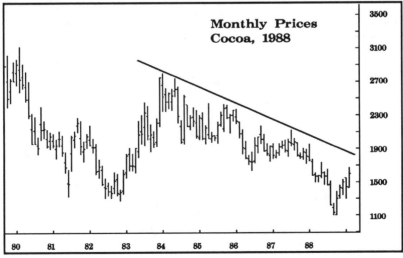

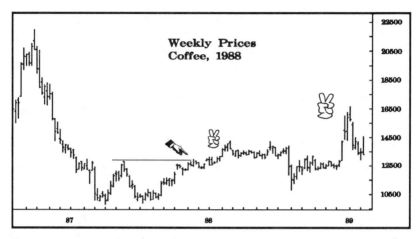

Weekly Prices
Coffee, 1988

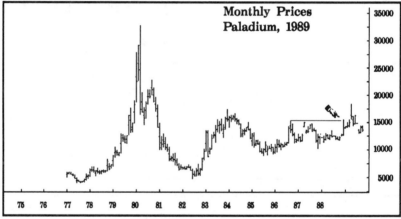

Monthly Prices
Paladium, 1989

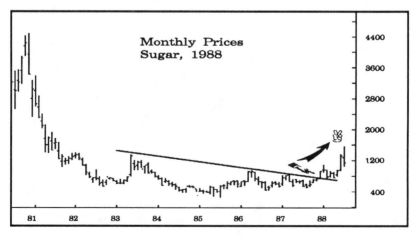

Monthly Prices
Sugar, 1988

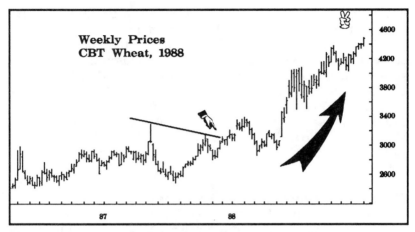

Weekly Prices
CBT Wheat, 1988

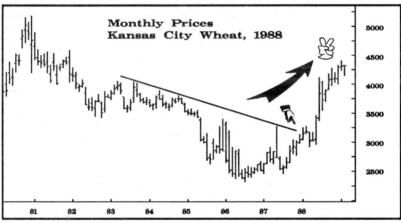

Monthly Prices
Kansas City Wheat, 1988

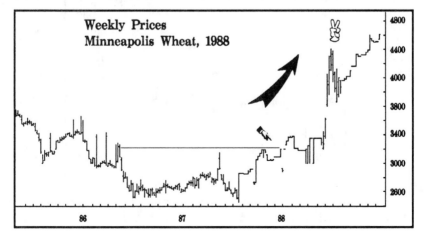

Weekly Prices
Minneapolis Wheat, 1988

Again, the charts are hypothetical, of course, with HALF the move of the charts reviewed in The 1988 Almanac totalling over $21,000 versus initial margins of about $ 5,700. The breakdown of the results from the entry point to the maximum extent of the subsequent price move was as follows; coffee (IN 12825, OUT 14275 = $ 5,438), corn (IN 204, OUT 359 = $ 7,750), sugar (IN 760, OUT 1564 = $ 9,005), CBT wheat (IN 309, OUT 449 = $7,000), Kansas City wheat (IN 320, OUT 440 = $ 6,000), and Minneapolis wheat (IN 285 1/2, OUT 461 = $ 8,775). Cocoa and palladium failed to attain their breakout points and therefore did not trade.

(The reader should realize that 1988 was an unusual year in that a severe drought that hit the United States Great Plains resulted in crop damage and high grain prices. The true technician, of course, would argue that such was EXACTLY what this simple breakout technique was signalling at the end of 1987 for these markets BEFORE the bad weather occurred. He who doubted probably ended the summer with nothing to show for his efforts but his air conditioning bill.)

Markets chosen from The 1989 Almanac were Lumber, Japanese Yen, Palladium, Platinum, Silver, and Unleaded Gasoline. Charts on these markets along with the breakout points shown in The 1989 Almanac follow.

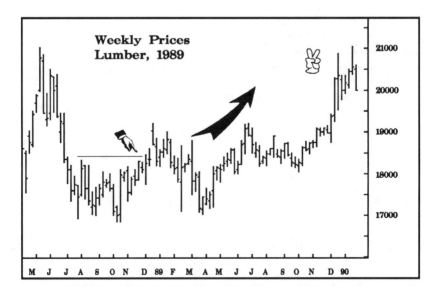

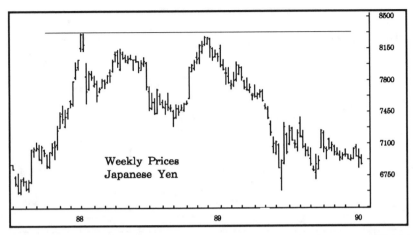

Weekly Prices
Japanese Yen

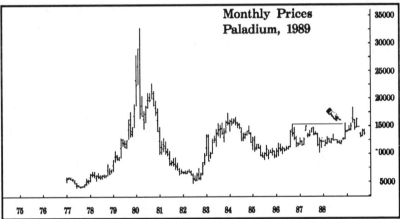

Monthly Prices
Paladium, 1989

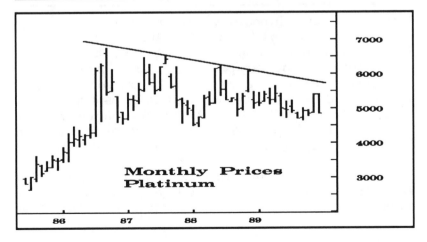

Monthly Prices
Platinum

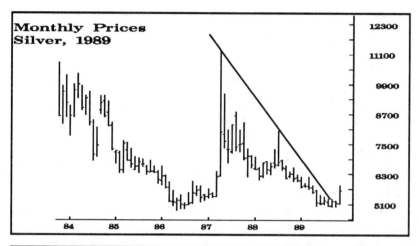

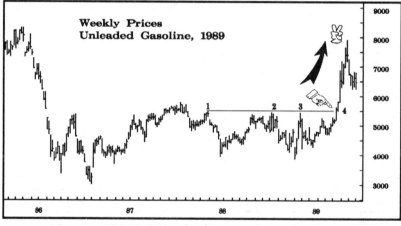

Again, the charts are hypothetical, of course, with HALF the move of the charts reviewed in The 1989 Almanac totalling over $10,000 versus initial margins of about $ 4,900. The breakdown of the results from the entry point to the maximum extent of the subsequent price move was as follows; lumber (IN 18350, OUT 20890 = $ 3,810), palladium (IN 15310, OUT 18400 = $ 3,090), silver (IN 53000, OUT 58740 = $ 2,870), and unleaded gasoline (IN 5460, OUT 7920 = $ 10,332). Platinum and the Japanese Yen failed to attain their breakout points and therefore did not trade.

For The 1990 Almanac, this section was inadvertently left out of The Calendar book. This was the first year of our two volume format which provided some confusion regarding what should be presented in which book and this section was regrettably an unintended sacrificial offering.

The only interview I gave regarding the 1990 outlook was with The Wall Street Journal and did involve this (and a few other) techniques, however. The market was Cocoa, and The Journal stated that I was the first and only analyst to suggest long positions in the Cocoa market. A chart of the ensuing price action and the key breakout point follows.

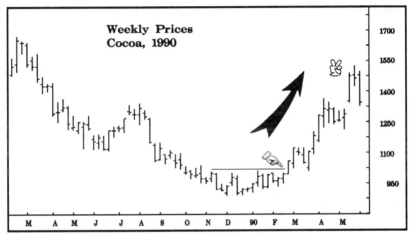

Should you incorporate such long term, trending information in your trading approach?

That is, of course, a question only you can answer! Many traders feel it is inappropriate because their "degree of trading" consists only of 5 minute bar charts, etc., because it is overly simplified, and so on.

I pay attention to this type information, but that does not mean that it will suit YOUR trading personality and approach.

Should you choose to use such information, however, you will find it listed in the "Historical Trading Ranges" section of each year's Calendar book.

HELPFUL HINT : This type analysis is incredibly simple and easy to do. It only takes a chart book and a few minutes every few weeks to review about 40 markets. If you are uncomfortable sitting with a long term position that may take several months to unwind, however, then simply let the breakout, if attained, define the direction for the next several months and trade in a lower degree (i.e., with daily, hourly, and so on data) and take trades that are only in the direction of the breakout.

If you doubt the potential effectiveness, go back and look at the weekly and monthly charts in the preceding pages.

Perhaps now you will want to begin each year with a review of The Calendar Book's "Historical Trading Ranges" section.

Support and Resistance

There is only one side of the market
and it is not the bull side
or the bear side,
but the right side.
- Jesse Livermore

Support and resistance levels are high and low prices that have previously formed during the normal course of trading. Orders can therefore be expected to be placed at these levels by a good percentage of the trading community.

In an upward rising market, for instance, sell orders are placed at or just under a previous high forming a resistance level (see the horizontal line in the weekly 1989 Japanese Yen chart in the previous section as an example). The first attempt at penetration of these resistance levels will often fail and price will be turned back. If the attempt is a fourth try, however, the attempt is especially likely to succeed and break through. The weekly 1989 unleaded gasoline chart in the previous example is a good example with the first three resistance points (points 1, 2, & 3 in the chart) and the fourth-try breakout point (point 4 in the chart) clearly marked.

TRADING HINT : FOURTH-ATTEMPT POINTS ARE HIGH-PROBABILITY BREAKOUT POINTS !!!

The alert trader should therefore CONSTANTLY scan the markets for such breakout points and be prepared to "go with the flow" if the point is broken REGARDLESS of the level of degree of trading ESPECIALLY if volume has been decreasing on corrections away from the breakout point!

Which brings us to the second set of orders at support / resistance levels, and that is the stops that are placed on the opposite side of the price level (in the case of a resistance level, it would be the buy stops placed just the other side of the price levels corresponding to the highs that form the resistance).

There are four characteristics that govern how strong a given support or resistance level is likely to be -

1. The amount of time spent at the price level (the longer the amount of time that price trades above / below a support / resistance level, the more significant that level becomes),

2. The amount of volume that occurs at the price level (the greater the volume, the more significant that level of support / resistance is likely to be),

3. How recently the trading occurred (the more recent the trading, the more significant the price level), and

4. The degree in which the support / resistance level was formed (i.e., weekly resistance levels are more important than hourly resistance levels).

Horizontal price levels are not the only levels of support / resistance that occur. Trendlines, channels, Elliott Wave formations (covered later), speed resistance lines , gaps, and so on can all provide support / resistance to prices. So, too, can round numbers, especially those that are multiples of 5 and 10 (i.e., 45, 50, 55, 60, etc.) and squares of numbers (for instance, 20 X 20 = 400, a significant number in the S & P 500, or 55 X 55 = 3,025 (a squared Fibonacci number), a significant number to the Dow Jones Industrial Averages. (One should thus not place orders right at round numbers but instead should place sell orders just under the rounded number and buy orders just above the rounded number).

Stops should be approached in just the opposite manner. Sell stops should be placed just below the round number in the expectation that the round number support might be enough to turn price back up. Buy stops should be placed just above the round number in the expectation that the round number resistance might be enough to turn price back down.

An example from the March 31, 1988 issue of "The Almanac Reports" shows how we combined this principle of resistance in the 1988 May Copper market with other techniques to enter a short position.

In late March, May Copper was approaching its early January highs as can be seen in the chart below. We noted in the March 31 Report that the 45 week cycle was listed in The Almanac under the "Weekly Linear Cycles" section as being due to bottom in eight weeks, that the 17 month cycle low had bottomed on February 1, 1988, and that the 24 week cycle low had bottomed on February 26, 1988. These lows had all been attained on schedule as projected in The 1988 Almanac which provided greater confidence in a successful projection of the upcoming 45 week cycle low.

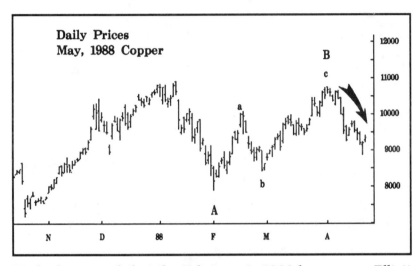

We had assumed that the February 1, 1988 low was an Elliott "A" Wave and that we were in the process on March 31, 1988 of completing an Elliott "B" Wave that was back near the early January resistance highs.

In the March 9, 1988 Report, we had projected a target of the expected "B" Wave of 106. Prices at that time were at 9725.

In the April 4, 1988 Report, we further noted that the deferred contracts were making new highs that were not being CON-FIRMED by the front month. This DIVERGENCE thereby indicated that the front May month was experiencing Comparative Relative Weakness.

With the 45 week cycle low due in eight weeks, with divergences present, with an Elliott Wave count supporting our interpretation of future market action, AND WITH PRICES TRADING UP INTO A PREVIOUS RESISTANCE AREA, it was time to enter short positions. These short positions were entered by using three different trading techniques; one was a simple trendline break and the other two were pattern recognition breaks.

Our first short position was entered on April 7 @ 10280 and the other two were entered on April 11 @ 10265.

The positions were exited two days later for a profit of $ 4,650.00.

In analyzing this trade, note that although our original March 9 prediction of a 106 high was VERY close to the eventual 10750 "B" wave high on April 4, 1988, we WAITED for the market to break and FORCE us into the position rather than fighting the uptrend and selling into strength as the market double topped.

Finally, note that the preparation and patience required for this two day trade to set up covered about one month but that, by the time the trade had formed, there were a sufficient number of other favorable clues that the odds of the trade working were very high (and, therefore, the risk very low)!

Is this the approach YOU would have used, or would you have sold into strength?

Where would you have placed your stop?

Would you have analyzed this trade differently? If so, how and why?

A second example from the April 30, 1988 issue of The Almanac Reports pointed out the double top that had formed in the June, 1988 Swiss Franc (as shown in the chart below) and combined this information with Elliott Wave analysis, the long term cyclical outlook as projected in The 1988 Almanac for the Swiss Franc, and several DIVERGENCES that were occurring in the currencies to predict that the top was the end of a large "B" wave that had been forecast to occur in an early February issue of "The Almanac Reports."

This issue also stated that the "C" wave would carry downwards to late summer cyclical lows.

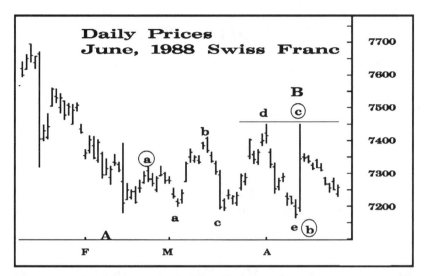

The same April 30 issue of "The Almanac Reports" concurrently projected that the late summer cyclical lows would traverse 840 points to a level of 7310 in another currency, the Japanese Yen. A chart of the September, 1988 contract is shown below.

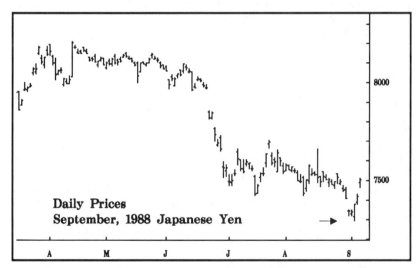

The actual bottom in the September, 1988 Japanese Yen occurred on September 2, 1988 @ 7296. This was the only day that prices traded below the 7310 level. The ensuing three month rally was straight up and covered almost 900 points.

Characterization

*The surest way
to go broke
is to sit around
waiting for a break.*

Characterization is the tendency of a given market or industry to trade in a particular manner. Markets as a whole, for instance, are more prone to spike tops and extended trading range bottoms with the exception of the financials (which are inverted) and the currencies.

Hence, when buying lows, market entry is more likely to be successful by using entry techniques that penetrate short term (4-8 week) cycle tops or penetrate 4-8 week (or longer) highs of sideways, trading range markets.

On market tops, however, trendlines that connect significant ringed low points tend to work better upon when combined with cyclic analysis (sell the market top after the trendline break).

These are CHARACTERISTICS of markets in general.

In specific markets, copper, gold, soybeans, and wheat are considered good charting markets while orange juice and pork bellies are not. Cotton charts have historically displayed many rounded tops and bottoms while soybeans have favored triangles. Head and shoulder formations abound in wheat charts. Currencies tend to be the best trending markets (perhaps due to government policies that, once adopted, tend to remain in place for years until new political leadership is assumed or radical fundamental changes are made). Hence, trend following approaches tend to work best in these markets. Cyclical analysis tends to work best in the meats.

Robert Joel Taylor in August, 1972 discussed the Technical Reliability Index that was created to measure the frequency and reliability of a number of commonly used chart patterns in different markets. A 70 % reliability rating is usually required before a chart pattern is rated as reliable. These reliabilities also exhibit seasonality, being higher in some months and lower in others. Updated results and reliability ratings through early 1986 are listed below.

Head and Shoulders Top - LC (69 %) CC (78) CP (77) C (81) CT (70) GO (70) LH (72) PB (87) SV (77) S (82) SM (72) SP (79) BD (77) W (81)

Head and Shoulders Bottom - LC (71) CC (72) CP (73) C (70) GO (74) LH (72) PB (85) SV (73) S (70) SM (70) SP (74) BD (75) W (75)

Double Top - C (73) CT (72) LH (71) PB (75) SV (71) S (73) BO (72) SP (77) BD (79) W (77)

Double Bottom - C (73) GO (71) PB (72) SV (70) S (76) SM (74) BO (71) BD (71) W (74)

Descending Triangle - SV (70) SM (71) BO (73)

Ascending Triangle - SM (71) BO (74) SP (71)

Island Reversal Top - CC (71) CP (81) PB (77) SU (72)

Island Reversal Bottom - CP (71) PB (74)

Saucer Bottom - LC (73) CC (73) C (75) CT (71) GO (76) SM (72) BO (70)

Trading Range Breakout, Up - LC (75) CC (71) CP (77) CT (81) GO (77) LH (74) SV (76) SM (77) BO (77) SU (71) SP (74) BD (77) W (71)

Trading Range Breakout, Down - LC (72) CC (71) C (73) CT (75) GO (72) LH (73) SV (73) SP (74) BD (72)

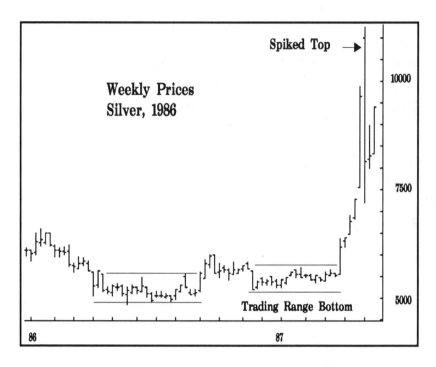

Weekly Prices
Silver, 1986

Spiked Top →

Trading Range Bottom

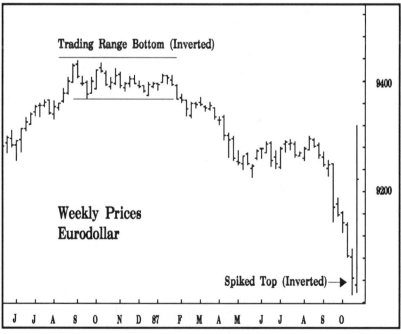

Trading Range Bottom (Inverted)

Weekly Prices
Eurodollar

Spiked Top (Inverted) →

Channeling Techniques

*I go long or short
as close as I can to
the danger point,
and if the danger point
becomes real,
close out
and take a small loss.*
- Jesse Livermore

No, this has nothing to do with Shirly MacLaine or spiritual mystics from the Land of Oz. Channels are simply barriers that contain price movement over a given period of time.

Once a trend is established, a trendline can be drawn on a chart that reflects the trend. Once the initial or tentative trendline is drawn and in place, a line can be drawn parallel to the tentative trendline from the apex of the move between the beginning point and the second point on the trendline. This parallel line and the trendline itself form a channel within which prices often stay for an extended period of time.

The channel can be used to form expectations of future price movement by the manner in which the prices move within the channel. For instance, in an upwards trending channel, an attempt to trade up to the upper trendline that falls short of the line is a sign of weakness. One therefore should be quite sensitive to the market breaking the lower line and should tighten sell stops. This rule can be generalized to state that the failure of any move within an established price channel to reach one side of the channel usually indicates that the trend is shifting and increases the likelihood that the other side of the channel will be broken.

Note in the daily chart that follows of December, 1988 US Treasury Bonds daily prices, for example, that such a failure to reach the other side of the channel can be seen at the late May trend change from down to up.

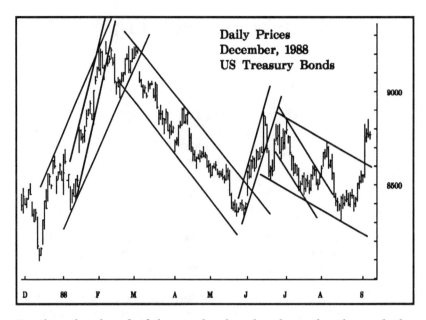

Daily Prices
December, 1988
US Treasury Bonds

On the other hand, if the market breaks above the channel, the breakout is a sign of strength and indicates higher prices. In both cases, once the channel line is broken, traditional analysis implies that the extent of the breakout has an objective that is at least the width of the channel.

Like trendlines, the longer the channel has been in effect, the more significant the penetration when the channel line is eventually broken.

Channels can also be constructed mathematically through the use of regression analysis. A line is first drawn through the center of the channel to obtain a "best fit".

Note in the chart that major channels can also contain channels of lesser degree.

Speed Resistance Lines

You can succeed in your trading,
but success depends not only
on the price of hogs, cotton, and sugar.
It also depends
on your own personality
and ability to solve problems
which are inherent in any game
of speculation.

Speed resistance lines (or speedlines) were developed by Edson Gould of Anametrics and combine the concepts of trendlines and percent retracement.

To construct a speedline, find the highest point in the current uptrend and draw a vertical line from the high point towards the bottom of the chart to where the trend began. Divide the vertical line into thirds and draw a trendline through the 2/3 and 1/3 points on the vertical line. These two trendlines are the 2/3 and 1/3 speedlines. These lines are said to provide support in an uptrend. That's all there is to it.

The above approach is, of course, reversed in a downtrend.

A strong market will remain above the support of its 2/3 speed resistance line and a weak market will tend to remain below the resistance of its 2/3 speed resistance line.

In bull markets, attempts to rally are likely to take place from ascending speed resistance lines. In bear markets, declines are likely to resume from areas where rallies test descending speed resistance lines.

Penetration of the 2/3 line in a bull market implies that price will decline to the 1/3 speed resistance line.

Penetration of the 1/3 speed resistance line implies a basic and rapid change in the primary trend of the market.

Some traders analyze speed resistance lines on a GROUP basis.

In using speed resistance lines, the trader should be aware that each time price makes a new high, a new set of lines must be drawn. (Reverse the process in a downtrend, of course).

Examples follow.

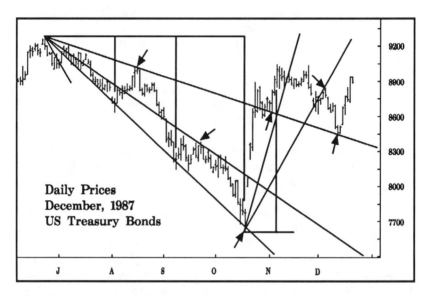

The chart above of daily December, 1987 US Treasury Bonds shows various groups of Speed Resistance Lines. The main lines are drawn in darker.

Note the tendency of price to not only decline from July to mid-October, but to remain below the 2/3 line (with the exception of the early April rally). When price broke the 2/3 line in early April, it was attracted to the 1/3 line in mid-April where the rally failed and moved back to the 2/3 line. Once the 2/3 line was broken in early September, the best this market could do for the next 1 1/2 months was to rally back to the line. Finally, when the 2/3 line was broken in mid-October, prices were again able to quickly rally back to the 1/3 line. Once the 1/3 line was broken, it became support instead of resistance and halted the early December sell-off as noted by the up arrow in the chart.

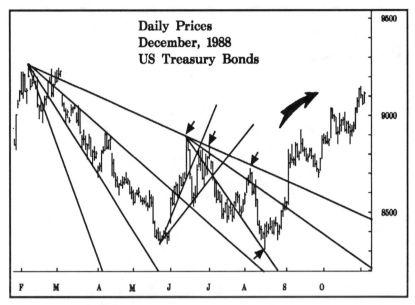

Daily Prices
December, 1988
US Treasury Bonds

Note how in the chart above of daily December, 1988 US Treasury Bond prices the minor 1/3 Speed Resistance Line supported the February to May decline 9 times with successive attempts at downside penetration becoming less and less potent. When prices finally broke away from this line and broke the main 2/3 line in June, they rallied directly to the main 1/3 line which then proceeded to halt 3 rallies from June to August as shown by the down arrows. Support was provided by the minor 2/3 line as shown by the lowest up arrow and, when price broke the minor 1/3 line in late August, the up move experienced immediate acceleration and shortly thereafter exploded above the main 1/3 line. Note that the breaking of the 1/3 line occurred on the fourth attempt.

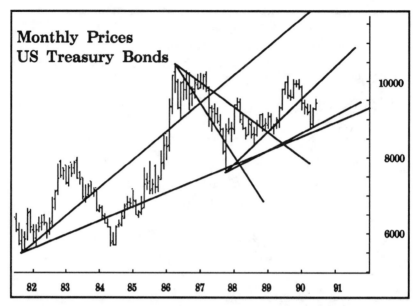

Monthly Prices
US Treasury Bonds

10000

8000

6000

82   83   84   85   86   87   88   89   90   91

The same technique can, of course, be applied to different degrees of trading. Here we see the monthly US Treasury Bond price chart. Note how important the main and minor Speed Resistance Lines have been to this market since the beginning of the early 1980s advance.

In the September 12, 1988 issue of "The Almanac Reports," we combined several techniques with the Speed Resistance Lines shown in the chart of daily December, 1988 US Treasury Bonds as shown in the following chart. Our position at the time was long two contracts from the August 25, 1988 issue of "The Almanac Reports" at prices of 8416 and 8425. We had just previously taken a $ 2,375.00 profit out of a short position in the September, 1988 bond contract. The entry date for our two long positions was August 29.

In Elliott Wave terms, it was anticipated that we were in a circled "C" wave and were nearing completion of that wave, that the resistance at the .618 Fibonacci retracement price level of 8900 or so would be stiff, that the upper Speed Resistance Line would combine with the above to further stiffen resistance, that the April and June highs would FURTHER add to resistance at that approximate level, that we were peaking the 28 day cycle in the December, 1988 US Treasury Bond contract, and that we were in the process of peaking a MAJOR 32 week linear cycle high projected in the weekly linear cycles section of "The 1988 Almanac." It was additionally observed in the September 12th issue of "The Almanac Reports" that the circled "A" wave rally had covered 177/32nds and that the current move had covered 176/32nds (providing virtual exact wave equality), that the September 9, 1988 Friday high was reached one day before the Saturday New Moon date, that Sunday September 11 marked a two year important anniversary date in the US Treasury Bonds, and that there was a divergence between the price on the September 9th high and the Stochastics and Relative Strength Indexes.

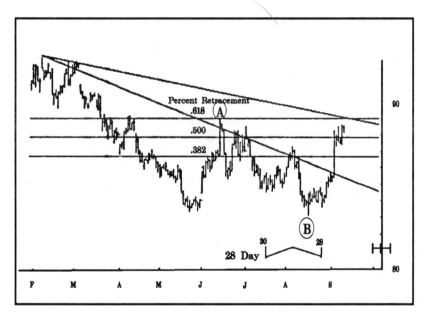

Our recommended action was to prepare to not only take profits on our long positions, but to reverse the market and sell short. The trigger came from an up trendline break on September 16th at 8805 which provided profits of over $ 6,700 on our two long contracts.

I can still remember as I write this now how, at the time, I thought that "This short position is going to be one of those pyramid position trades that pay off a lot of subscribers' mortgages and buy a couple of extra vacation homes besides!!!"

So what happened to our short?

It was stopped out on September 21st at 8802 with but a skimpy $ 92.75 profit.

Prices shortly thereafter rallied strongly through the above-mentioned resistance levels and gained momentum after the bottoming of the 28 day cycle on October 6th.

Did I suggest to my subscribers that they participate in this move?

No, I did not!

I have found out over the years that there are plenty of trading opportunities in the markets and that, if one is not analyzing accurately price movements that are occurring, it is best to stand aside and watch.

It is not important to attempt to trade every movement that occurs in every market. I have learned to accept the fact that there will be some moves in which I just simply do not participate.

When I do participate, however, it is important that I be on the right side of the market or else be out quickly with my trading capital intact.

The above example was thus one of MANY examples that demonstrate that even the best-looking of setups do not always work !!!

Chart Trading System

The trend is your friend.

In the July, 1986 issue of "Technical Analysis of Stocks and Commodities", William F. Eng, a professional floor trader at the Chicago Board of Trade, described a method he uses to trade markets that combines elements of our earlier "Tops Down" discussion, ringed highs and lows, and swing trading.

To follow the method, simply connect successively higher prices with a swing line in an uptrend (lower prices in a downtrend). Continue the process until two consecutive days are experienced where the lows are lower and the highs are no higher than the preceding day (vice versa for lower prices). When such has been encountered, begin connecting successively lower prices until the situation is again reversed. The series of peaks and valleys that are formed by using this process define the trend.

The trend is up when the last point broken is a peak and down when the last point broken is a trough. The opposite trough (peak) becomes the stop point.

The "Tops Down" approach further defines and filters the trend by combining daily, hourly, and 15 minute bar charts. The trend is up when the daily, hourly, and 15 minute trends all point up and down when the daily, hourly, and 15 minute trends all point down. Otherwise, they are flat and no position is taken.

In the example following of June, 1990 S & P 500 futures prices, the arrows note the entry points for the various signals. The horizontal lines represent the stop points. Note how small a portion of the daily chart the final 15 minute period represents.

Note also how "choppy" this period was and that the technique navigated this difficult 3 1/2 day period profitably.

The beauty of this system is its simplicity, the close proximity of stops, and its trend-following nature. If you would like more information, you may wish to order the 1986 volume of articles in "Technical Analysis of Stocks and Commodities" (for address, see "Periodicals" section).

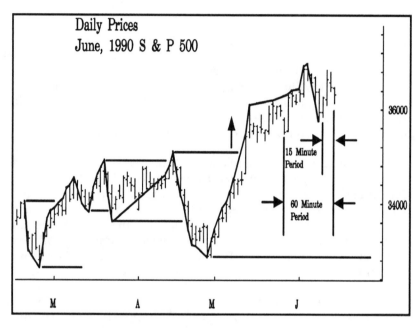

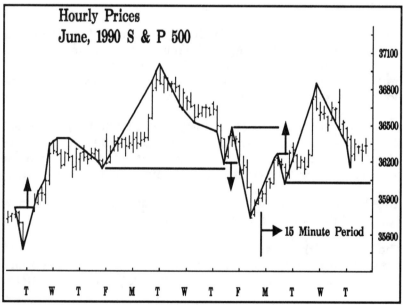

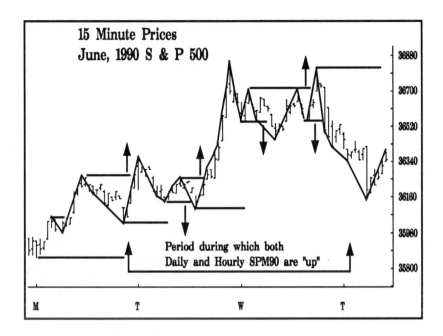

Three long positions would have resulted from use of this approach over the period analyzed had this approach been followed with the hypothetical trading results summarized below.

BY 611 @ 36265	SL 612 @ 36110	-150
BY 612 @ 36255	SL 613 @ 36545	290
BY 613 @ 36705	SL 613 @ 36545	-160

The net result over the 3 days trading would have thus been -20 points (\$ 100.00) exclusive of slippage and commissions. The reader should note that the period chosen was a very choppy four day period in which the short term trend reversed from up to down. A variation that uses trendlines will draw the appropriate trendline off the two most recent peaks or valleys formed by the lines.

Comparative Relative Strength

The gods always favor the strong.
- Tacitus : Annals, IV, c. 110

Relative strength is primarily a stock market term that is unfortunately used only sparingly in other markets.

There are three basic uses of the concept -

1. First, if one were expecting prices in general to begin rising (inflation), one could inspect the various group indexes that are available which chart the movement of an entire group of markets (i.e., the grains, industrials, precious metals, livestock and meats, oilseeds, imports, currencies, interest rates, energies, and so on would all be different groups and have their own group index in the same manner that the S & P 500 stock index is an average of several different stocks).

In using our "tops down" approach, one would first want to inspect the individual group indexes to see which was refusing to break a low that others had gone below, or which had held its gains better than the other groups, or which had a tendency to rally more, or which had made new recent highs when the others had not, and so on. In other words, what we are inspecting for is the strength of one group RELATIVE TO other groups and relative to an average of all markets.

Once this group has been identified, we would want to concentrate our long positions in the group exhibiting the most relative strength. Conversely, the same process would be used to identify the weaker groups, too. Shorts would be concentrated in those areas that were exhibiting the LEAST relative strength during periods of anticipated downward price movements.

2. Once the appropriate group had been located, we would want to select the individual markets within that group to either buy or sell (depending on the strength of the whole group).

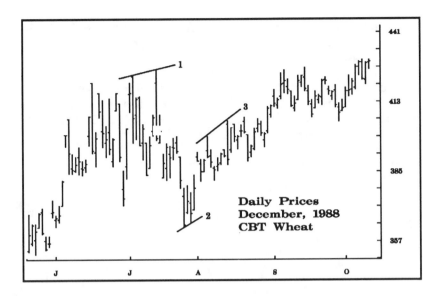

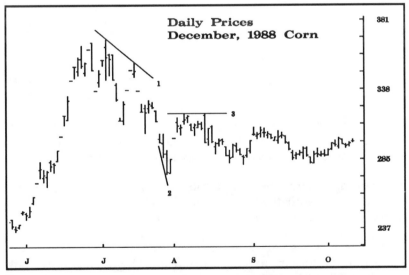

As an example, note in the two charts above of daily prices of December, 1988 CBT Wheat (WZ88) and December, 1988 Corn (CZ88) how much stronger WZ88 was than CZ88 at several key junctures indicated by lines 1, 2, & 3 in the 1988 campaign. These differences provided several clues that WZ88 was stronger than CZ88 because of its Comparative Relative Strength. Therefore, the trader wanting to trade grains would have been better off from this analysis to trade WZ88 from the long side and CZ88 from the short side OR to have entered the spread long WZ88 / short CZ88.

How did it turn out? The next chart of the spread between the two markets depicts the breakout at line 3 in the upper charts and shows that WZ88 went on to gain over $ 3,500 over CZ88 (350 %) over the next 4 months into early December.

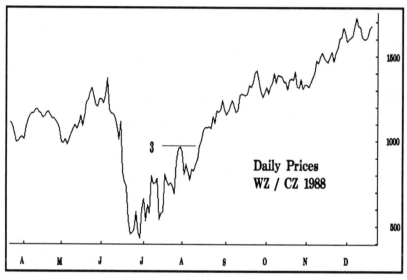

Note that nothing was needed to take advantage of this price move other than timely analysis of Comparative Relative Strength.

Such comparisons are very simple and easy to make, take very little time or sophisticated analytical equipment (a simple chart book will do), and occur continuously in the markets.

The same process can be used, of course, in the stock market. Here, one would want to purchase stocks of high relative strength rankings RELATIVE TO those rankings of other stocks and to sell short stocks of low relative strength rankings RELATIVE TO those of other stocks. Preferably, rankings of 95 or higher would be used for purchases and rankings of 5 or less for sales. A good source of such Relative Strength Rankings is "Investor's Daily Newspaper" which lists daily such rankings for a multitude of stocks.

3. In other markets, once the individual market has been identified, we would want to inspect the relative strength of the various available stocks or futures contracts within that market.

For example, in the WZ88 / CZ88 spread just discussed, note that the lines in the daily charts of WZ88 and WN89 shown below and labeled 1, 2, & 3 indicate that the WZ88 chart was relatively stronger than the WN89 chart. Hence, the appropriate wheat contract to trade from the long side was the WZ88 as indicated by Comparative Relative Strength analysis instead of the WN89 contract.

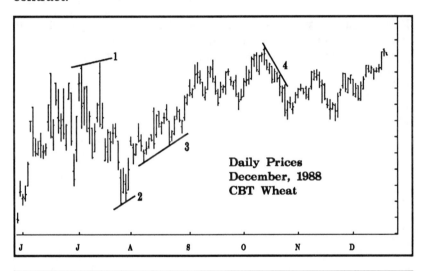

Daily Prices
December, 1988
CBT Wheat

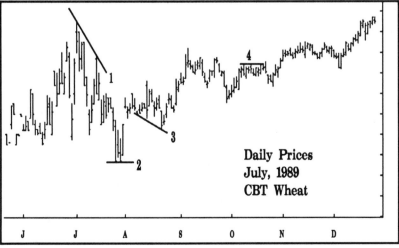

Daily Prices
July, 1989
CBT Wheat

Continuing the analysis of this market, note the change in relative strength that occurred at line 4. At this point, the WN89 contract began to outperform the WZ88 contract and to make new highs that were not matched by the WZ88 contract. A switch, therefore, from trading the WZ88 contract to trading the WN89 contract on long positions OR from a WZ88 / CZ88 spread to a WN89 / CZ88 spread enhanced profits another $ 1,750 above and beyond the results of the original WZ88 / CZ88 spread.

Such analysis, of course, is just as valid when trading at other levels of degree (such as weekly, hourly, and so on).

This method is strong enough, if fact, that, when mastered, it is sufficient to stand alone as an analytical tool (though it will perform best when used with other confirming indicators).

Confirmation and Divergence

The Chinese word for "Crisis"
is composed of two picture-characters . . .
the one meaning "danger"
and the other meaning "opportunity".

Confirmation and divergence are two of the most important concepts that one can use in analyzing markets. They are of such importance in trading that they are not only mentioned here but are discussed in other areas of The Almanac as well!

Perhaps the first theory to use these principles was The Dow Theory which was developed from the writings of Charles H. Dow, one of the founders of the Dow Jones Company and the first editor of The Wall Street Journal. (Incidentally, it should be noted that The Dow Theory received its name from S. A. Nelson in his 1902 book, "ABC of Stock Speculation" (in which he summarized a collection of Dow's editorials) and NOT from William Peter Hamilton, as is erroneously believed by many). The theory essentially stated that, in a true bull (bear) market, new highs (lows) in the Industrial Average should be confirmed by new highs (lows) in the Transportation Average. (Observation : I would suggest spending neither time nor effort in either following this theory or listening to the supposed importance of its signals as they are discussed by market seers on television)!

Confirmation and divergence apply to futures markets in several ways. For instance, when the spot contract moves to new highs (lows), those highs should be CONFIRMED in the back months as well (i.e., in the metals markets, if, in the month of May, June gold moves to new highs (lows), the move should be confirmed by the August, October, December, next February, April, and so on contracts doing the same for the move to be truly believed as asserting a trend).

The futures move should additionally be CONFIRMED by the cash market for gold making new highs (lows).

Further, within a particular complex, one would expect a move to new highs (lows) to be CONFIRMED in other contracts as well (i.e., in the metals markets, if gold moves to new highs (lows), the move should be confirmed by silver, copper, aluminum, palladium, and platinum doing the same).

Also, if one is using a technical indicator to track the market (for example, the Relative Strength Index), a move to new highs (lows) in price should be CONFIRMED by RSI also moving to new highs (lows).

Finally, if favorable news is received, the market should CONFIRM the news by acting in a favorable manner.

DIVERGENCE is the failure to CONFIRM and is one of the most important indications of pending price reversal that the trader has at his disposal.

Especially important is when a market fails to advance (decline) on bullish (bearish) news! This DIVERGENCE between news and market price action is an ominous warning (for if favorable news cannot drive a market, what can)? (If one is going to use this form of divergence, one needs to learn not to judge the news itself as being bullish or bearish, BUT THE MARKET'S REACTION TO THE NEWS)! (The ability of one to properly identify such divergences also requires a high level of MARKET knowledge or education so that one can accurately interpret news events and how they should effect various markets (see the "Cause and Effect" section for basic direction in this area)).

Another good DIVERGENCE signal is when prices make new highs (lows) but a momentum indicator (such as the Relative Strength Index, Stochastics, etc.) does not. If this pattern sets up three times in a row (i.e., 3 successive new highs (lows) not being confirmed by new highs in the last two oscillator peaks (troughs)) then the odds especially favor the market being ready for a panic sell-off.

Volume and open interest divergences are also especially important. New highs made on lower volume are an indication that the rally is in trouble.

DIVERGENCE among different contracts of the same commodity or versus the cash commodity is also important and a sign of a pending price reversal.

HOW TO USE - Although divergences are among the most important indicators of a potential market reversal, they are usually not strong enough in themselves to warrant market positions. They do indicate, however, that one should be tightening stops on existing or proposed market positions and should be willing to ACT upon the first sign of reversal in price (for instance, try applying the market entry technique in the Basic Charting discussion to the examples of divergence that are given on the following pages). Note that examples of confirmation would be just the opposite of those shown.

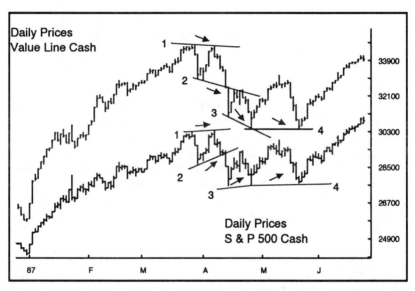

The above chart shows daily prices for the cash Value Line Index in Spring, 1987 on top with daily prices for the cash S & P 500 Index below.

Note the divergence that occurred both at the beginning of the April correction and twice at the April and May lows. The lines noting the divergences vividly illustrate the strength exhibited by the S & P 500 cash Index relative to the Value Line cash Index throughout the March to May correction period. The stock market proceeded to move from these lows to new highs on August 25, 1987 prior to the October crash. Is it any wonder that the S & P 500 cash index moved to new highs in June while the Value Line cash Index failed to confirm these new highs as shown in the right portion of the chart?

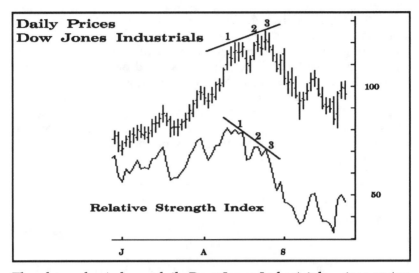

The above chart shows daily Dow Jones Industrials prices on top at their 1987 high and illustrates the nonconfirmation of price and a technical indicator (the popular Relative Strength Index) shown on the bottom. Note how price made new highs in late August, 1987 that were not confirmed by the RSI. In fact, if one looks closely, it is apparent that three consecutive highs were made with lower highs in the RSI. A panic followed into early September that was worth over $ 15,000 per S & P 500 futures contract.

While many complained on news programs of how program trading was destroying our markets and scaring off the small investor, the *small trader* who did little else but follow such buy and sell signals as this one reaped an enormous profit on his margin (which at the time was but $ 6,000 as it had been over the previous five year bull market in stocks). Thanks to such complaints, margins have increased to $ 25,000 and have locked out many small traders or would-be traders.

Was it any surprise to past Almanac purchasers that the same pattern again emerged at the 1989 stock market high and that the result was again the same panic-type selloff? The divergence is shown in the chart that follows of daily Dow Jones Industrials prices on top for the fall of 1989 and the Relative Strength Index on the bottom for the same period.

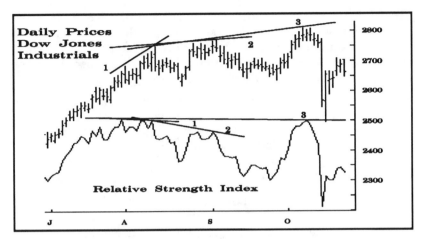

This divergence was one of several reasons we issued a NOT-very-famous sell signal on Financial News Network that resulted in short positions being instituted in the S & P 500 futures contract on the VERY HIGH DAY of the 1989 rally.

The upper chart that follows shows daily Dow Jones Transportation prices while the lower chart shows daily Dow Jones Industrials prices. Note the classical divergence which signalled the ensuing selloff when the Transportation Average did not confirm the Industrials. In mid-October, the Industrials broke support and were confirmed by the Transportations on October 15th. Black Monday, October 19th, occurred 2 days later. Two subsequent divergences at the lows successfully signalled two sharp rallies and suggested that the upcoming period would experience strength in the Industrials relative to the Transportations.

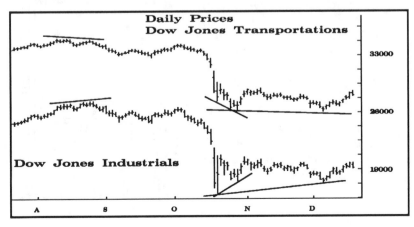

The following example of divergence between the S & P 500 cash stock index and the number of advancing / declining issues is a textbook example and was signalled not only by the nonconfirmation between the March / August peaks, but also by nonconfirmation of both new highs made in August.

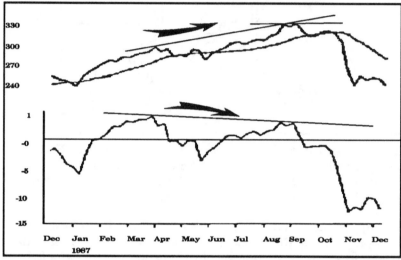

In the chart on the right from The Wall Street Journal, we were able to show in the April 12, 1988 issue of "The Almanac Reports" that the new highs being made in the Dow Jones Industrials were not being confirmed by the Dow Jones Transportations and were definitely diverging from the Dow Jones Utilities. At the bottom of the chart, note how volume was also diverging from price and not supporting the upward move.

Additionally, a divergence between the cash New York Stock Exchange Index and the New York futures contracts was noted as shown in the chart that follows.

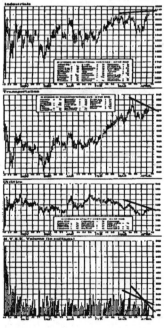

This information was used in combination with the entry technique shown in the Basic Charting Techniques section to enter short positions in the stock indices that resulted in over $ 8,500 in profits by the end of the month beginning with a drop of eight points ($ 4,000 per contract) THE VERY NEXT DAY !!!

The chart that follows illustrates divergence between cash and futures as the fall 1986 lows in the cash market were never broken during the late winter, 1987 bear move in November, 1987 soybeans. Note also that the new highs in April were confirmed in both the cash and futures market.

The subsequent three month move covered $ 1.60 / bushel ($8,000 / contract) in the November soybean contract.

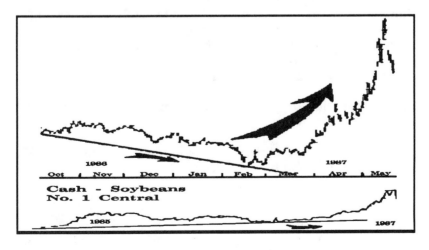

The chart that follows illustrates divergence between the cash and futures market in crude oil. The chart on the top is the November, 1987 crude oil futures contract while the lower chart is cash crude oil.

The subsequent drop in crude oil from August 3, 1987 to August 24, 1987 was a whopping $ 3.50 / barrel ($ 3,500) per contract!

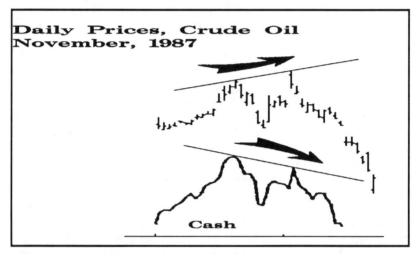

The charts that follow illustrate divergence among contracts of the same commodity. The top chart is April, 1988 Live Hogs, the middle chart is February, 1988 Live Hogs, and the lower chart is December, 1987 Live Hogs.

The February and April contracts failed to confirm the new highs in the spot December contract in early September, 1987. (Further inspection would also have revealed that the new highs in the spot December, 1987 contract were also not being confirmed by the Relative Strength Index, either).

The 2 month decline that followed this major peak covered over 8 cents per contract (over $ 2,400).

If you had to sell one of these three contracts in September, 1987, which one would you have chosen?

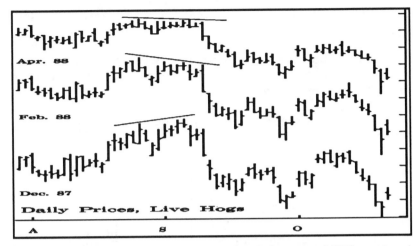

The correct answer, of course, is the February, 1988 contract (middle in the chart) since it was the one displaying the most weakness relative to the other two contracts!

The charts that follow show on the left daily prices for December, 1988 gold (top) and October, 1988 gold (bottom) while on the right are daily prices for December, 1988 US Treasury Bonds (top) and June, 1988 US Treasury Bonds (bottom).

What is the connection between these two markets?

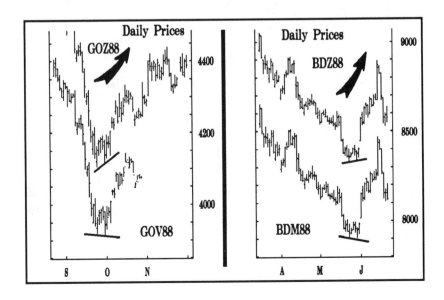

Obviously, the spot contract diverged from the deferred contracts in both cases.

Additionally, however, note that both markets formed the divergence right at the end of a FND Slammer and that a quite dramatic rally promptly ensued after the Slam and divergence.

Note, too, that in both cases, the FND Slammer ended quite long and pronounced bear markets!

The chart at right shows divergence among markets of the same complex. The charts show December, 1987 gasoline (top), December, 1987 heating oil (middle), and December, 1987 crude oil (bottom).

Note how the two products (gasoline and heating oil) failed to confirm at the August top and also foreshadowed lower prices just prior to the mid-August break by not confirming the attempt to hold the early August lows by crude oil.

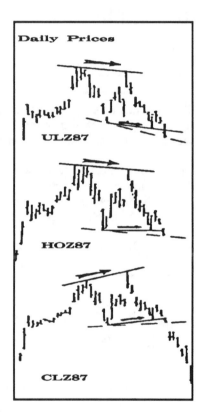

In the chart that follows of daily September, 1988 Soybean Oil prices (top) and daily September, 1988 Soybean Meal prices (bottom), note the divergence that occurred at the peak of the 1988 grain bull market. Similar divergences also occurred between corn, wheat, soybeans and so on.

Which of these two markets was best to sell?

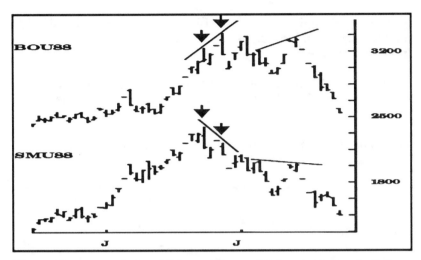

The soybean meal should have been sold due to its early failure to confirm the move to new highs that occurred in the soybean oil at the down arrow in the chart. Perhaps the greatest divergence that occurred at this time, however, was the divergence between news and subsequent market action.

If the reader can recall, 1988 was a severe drought year in the bread basket of the United States. It was in mid-June that most of the weekly news magazines ("Time", "Newsweek", etc.) chose to highlight dryness and the greenhouse effect ON THEIR FRONT COVERS! These stories broke right about the time THE MARKETS WERE PEAKING !!! The most NOVICE of traders could walk past a newsstand, see these stories plastered on all the front pages, and realize that these markets were in trouble WHEN PRICE COULD NO LONGER ADVANCE IN THE FACE OF SUCH BULLISH NEWS ! (Are all such stories as timely?)

Had these magazine editors read "The Outlook" section in "The Calendar Book" every year since we began printing in 1986, they would have known that such a trend toward dryer and warmer weather had not come as a surprise to Almanac purchasers!

The following divergence in the British Pound was noted in the April 30, 1988 issue of "The Almanac Reports" and, when combined with several other indicators, led to sell signals being suggested. Note the large nonconfirmations that preceded the panic selling of late May/early June as the 20 month cycle low was completed. Note also the divergences that CONFIRMED additional future weakness across the lows into early May as indicated by line 3.

Daily June, 1988 British Pound prices are on top with the Relative Strength Index in the middle and Slow Stochastics on the bottom.

Shorts off this setup led to profits of almost $ 5,000 by mid-June in positions entered May 2, 1988 forward.

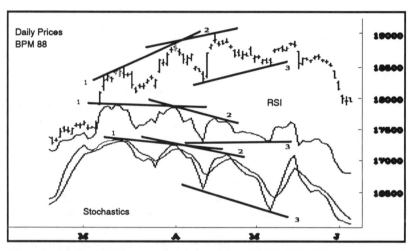

The chart that follows of September, 1988 US Treasury Bond prices is from the August 19, 1988 issue of "The Almanac Reports" and was one factor leading to the purchase recommendation of December, 1988 US Treasury Bond contracts. The middle chart is Slow Stochastics while the Relative Strength Index is on the bottom.

This position was also supported by our assumed Elliott Wave interpretation as shown by the letters in the top chart. Note the projected price movement to the circled "C" which later became reality as the prices shown in the chart marked the lows in the US Treasury Bond market for the next two years.

It should also be noted that the 32 week cycle high as listed in the "Weekly Linear Cycles Section" of "The 1988 Almanac" was due 3 to 5 weeks later which supported the circled "C" wave projected upmove.

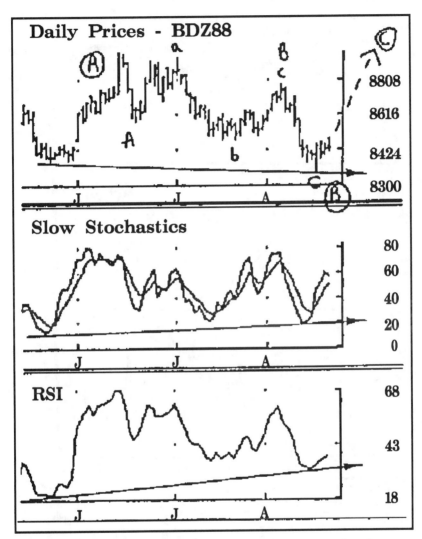

Such divergences between technical indicators and price can occur over any period of time. The charts below, for instance, plot 30 minute bar charts and the corresponding Relative Strength Index (middle) and Slow Stochastics (bottom) for March, 1989 US Treasury Bonds.

Note how timely the 3 Sell / Buy / Sell signals were during this 5 day period of 30 minute bar charts.

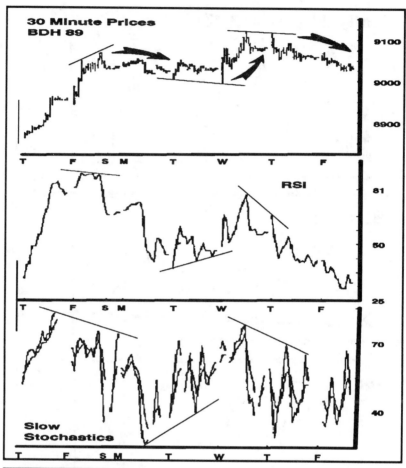

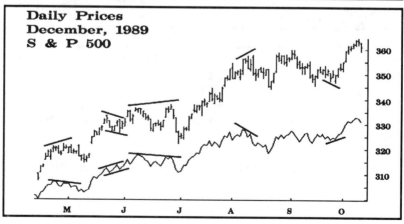

Percent Retracement

*You can
make a fortune
by following
this one rule alone.*
- W D Gann

Burton Pugh, a successful trader in the early 1900s, stated "This remarkable form of market action is the safest and surest movement on which the trader can base his moves."

Edward Dobson was so impressed he wrote a complete book on the subject.

All were discussing the popular 50 % retracement level which also is an important support point in the Dow Theory and Elliott Wave Analysis.

Retracement is normal in a bull (bear) campaign as prices pause or "exhale" before resuming their advance. The key, of course, is in distinguishing between a trending market that is experiencing a correction and a market that is experiencing a reversal of trend.

One key that can improve the ability to distinguish between the two is volume analysis (which should contract on the correction). Accuracy will also be improved if the correction coincides with an expected cycle low (high), a Gann support (resistance) line, the end of an Elliott corrective wave, a Fibonacci cycle count, and so on.

With the 50 % correction being so popular, it is no wonder that many market corrections are well supported at or near the exact 50 % correction point. Other retracement levels do exist, however, the most popular of which are the 1/3 and 2/3, the 75 % and 25% levels, the 40% and 60 % levels (2/5 and 3/5), those levels divided by 8 (87.5 %, 75 %, 62.5 %, 50 %, 37.5 %, 25 %, and 12.5%) (a method popularized by Gann), and the 61.8 % & 38.2% Fibonacci retracement levels.

These retracement levels are illustrated in the following chart which shows the origin of some common retracement levels. Note that the 50% retracement level is the most common in this chart (appearing 5 times) and that the next most common retracement is the 1/3 and 2/3 which both appear 3 times and are quite close to the popular .382 and .618 Fibonacci retracement levels.

100/	2	3	4	5	6	7	8	9	10
									10.0%
								11.1%	
							12.5%		
						14.3%			
					16.7%				
				20.0%					20.0%
								22.2%	
			25.0%				25.0%		
						28.6%			
									30.0%
		33.3%			33.3%			33.3%	
							37.5%		
				40.0%					40.0%
						42.9%			
								44.4%	
	50.0%		50.0%		50.0%		50.0%		50.0%
								55.6%	
						57.1%			
				60.0%					60.0%
							62.5%		
		66.7%			66.7%			66.7%	
			75.0%				75.0%		
								77.8%	
				80.0%					80.0%
					83.3%				
						85.7%			
							87.5%		
								88.9%	
									90.0%

Many will take these hard numbers and create a "band" around the retracement level similar to the manner in which time bands are created around the center of a time cycle. These "windows" are usually 10 % price bands and are the areas within which the correction is most likely expected to end. It is rare that a move that has experienced a correction of 70 % of the original move will again be able to assert itself, but it does happen.

One of the better ways of trading a correction is to allow the market to stop oneself into the position by trading at the next lower level of degree once the 50 % correction has been reached. For instance, if one were trading on a daily basis and price had just experienced a 50 % correction, one would turn to hourly, half-hourly, etc., price charts in order to determine an entry point. An entry stop order would then be placed ABOVE the market in the case of a buy order (below if selling short). This approach would prevent entry in many of those cases where the market had just experienced a trend reversal that was not yet recognizable. The method is similar to the scaling-in techniques discussed elsewhere in this book.

Retracements are normally calculated with respect to price only but can also be figured with respect to time. An aid that will help is the "squared retracement" line. This line can be easily drawn from the extent of the move to the original price level extended forward in time an amount equal to the amount of time required to cover the original price move.

An example is given by the diagonal lines in the following chart for weekly sugar prices. Note that this line contains all the price and time levels at which the corrective price action is "squared" with corrective time (not to be confused with Gann's squaring of price and time).

Especially important to this type of analysis is the 50 % retracement level which is shown in the chart by the horizontal dotted lines for each "power center" pyramid.

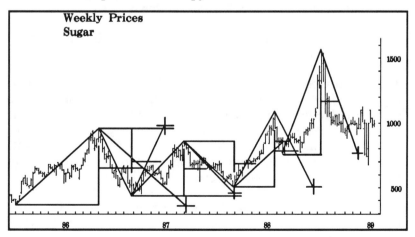

Price Objectives

*Fortunes are made
by buying low
and selling too soon.
- Baron Rothschild*

Once in a position, one is faced with the problem of selecting an exit price level. Most traders will simply trail their position with an exit "stop" order, but many others are more comfortable using price objectives.

These price targets are normally "chart based" or determined by analyzing the strength of the chart pattern and projecting the appropriate target upon breakout from the formation.

A second method is the "measured move". Here, the extent of the original price move is added to (subtracted from) the low (high) point of the ensuing correction.

A third method developed by Arthur Sklarew ("The Rule of 7") involves projecting 7/5, 7/4, and 7/3 the original move if upward and 7/5, 7/4, and 7/3 the original move if downward.

Fibonacci adherents project off the Fibonacci ratios, of course, and Gann enthusiasts project off squared prices and Gann angles, all of which will be discussed later.

Cycle enthusiasts project by using the average amplitude of the cycle being analyzed.

Many of the techniques discussed previously, such as constructing a "window" around the price objective, or tightening stops once the objective is approached, or tightening stops and trading at a lower degree, or using chart-generated exiting procedures such as trendlines, the technique discussed under the Basic Charting section, the techniques discussed in the pattern recognition section, and so on, still apply. Examples follow.

In the June 15, 1988 issue of "The Almanac Reports," we found ourselves short August, 1988 feeder cattle at prices of 7847,

7832, 7830, & 7722 and wrote "Meat is being sold by ranchers due to heat stress which depresses near-term contracts but results in smaller numbers later".

We combined The Elliott Wave count shown in the chart of daily August, 1988 feeder cattle prices that follows along with a Fibonacci price objective calculation to project the end of the 3rd wave in this market. The objective was obtained by simply taking 1.618 times the distance of the assumed first wave of the move which, in this case, was the distance from the top of the move to the circled "1" wave shown in the chart. This distance is marked by the upper "down" arrow in the chart.

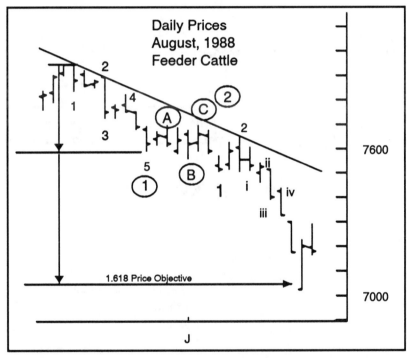

We issued instructions to exit all contracts at 7032 (which, the reader should note, was just above the round number 7030 price).

The exit occurred on the opening of June 16 as can be seen in the updated chart shown below. Note that the market opened at limit down with sellers. Prices were not at these levels but for a few minutes and then rallied the rest of the day bouncing almost 200 points off the 7027 lows which were but 2 ticks below our 7032 order. The trade provided a total profit of $13,657.60 in but 19 days.

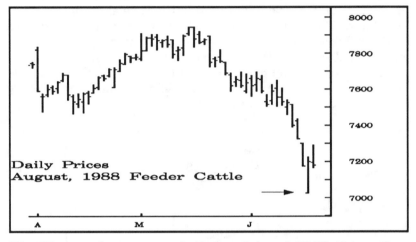

The 5th wave low was made 5 days later at 6915. Prices then proceeded to rally over 1300 points over the next two months to over 8200!

Moving Averages

*The person who stands with one foot
in a bucket of ice cold water
and the other in a pan of boiling hot water
can tell you that,
on average,
he feels fine.*

Moving averages are one of the most popular of indicators. They are on chart services, newswires, discussed on television talk shows, form the basis for some popular mutual fund trading systems, and so on.

They range from a simple one-dimensional moving average to crossover moving averages to the 4-9-18 day triple moving average to weighted moving averages to exponential moving averages to moving average convergence/divergence to triple exponential moving averages to step-weighted moving averages to moving averages with percentage bands to moving averages of high and low prices to Fibonacci moving averages and on and on and on.

Averages can be led, lagged, or centered. The main function they serve for most traders is that they are a confirming indicator of trend. Some will use moving averages on a stand-alone basis although a great deal of discipline is required along with a lot of patience in order to survive the whipsaw periods. Others will use a long term average to define long term trend and then will trade in the direction of the long term average only by using the short term average to time entry and exit of trades. If the long term average is down, for instance, then only short positions would be accepted when the short term average turned down, too. When the short term average turned up, the short position would be liquidated.

The simplest moving average of all is, of course, the single moving average. The direction can be easily ascertained by simply comparing the day being dropped with today's price. If today's price is greater, the average is up.

The advantage of moving averages is that they do trade with the trend. The disadvantage, as mentioned above, is that they tend to get whipsawed in choppy, nontrending markets. Richard Donchian has apparently successfully traded the 5 & 20 moving average system since 1961, however, which attests to the fact that, although they may not be the best of market indicators, they can be used profitably.

The moving average with percentage-band system employs an exponentially smoothed moving average plus a band both above and below the average of the amount indicated by the band. A signal occurs whenever the closing price breaks outside the band. The exit occurs when the price recrosses the moving average. A variation requires that the price close on either side of the bands.

Following are listed optimized dual crossover moving averages and percentage-band figures. Either system should provide much improved results over standard 5 & 20 day moving averages and can also be used as an indication of trend direction.

The format for the crossover systems is "ST/LT" where ST=short term average and LT=long term average.

For the band, it is MA / % BAND where MA=moving average and % BAND=the amount added to and subtracted from the average in order to form the upper and lower bands.

Some examples then follow.

BD 3/37 39/0.4%	CT 16/25 37/3.7%	PL 19/24 20/0.6%
BO 14/58 28/0.8%	DM 6/18 36/0.4%	S 23/41 76/0.9%
BP 5/50 47/0.0%	GM 6/33 39/0.4%	SF 7/50 66/0.9%
C 12/48 38/2.7%	GO 9/50 29/1.0%	SM 22/47 40/3.1%
CA 6/25 21/0.5%	JY 8/35 80/1.3%	SU 14/54 40/3.2%
CC 14/38 43/2.0%	LC 23/48 24/1.8%	SV 3/26 29/1.0%
CF 6/51 36/0.0%	LH 7/21 75/3.0%	TB 6/18 24/0.5%
CP 17/32 25/1.5%	PB 25/46 27/0.0%	W 12/48 63/2.9%

The trading simulation below shows the standard 5 & 20 day moving average which is widely followed and its ability to track the December, 1988 US Treasury Bond contract in 1988. The system generated signals as follows;

880115	BY 8730	880112	SL 8413	$ -3,531.25
880115	BY 8730	880219	SL 9028	$ 2,937.50
880225	BY 9106	880219	SL 9028	$ -312.50
880225	BY 9106	880308	SL 9002	$ -1,125.00
880413	BY 8827	880308	SL 9002	$ 1,218.75
880413	BY 8827	880415	SL 8703	$ -1,750.00
880603	BY 8610	880415	SL 8703	$ 781.25
880603	BY 8610	880708	SL 8522	$ -625.00
880802	BY 8624	880708	SL 8522	$ -937.50
880802	BY 8624	880811	SL 8406	$ -2,625.00

880831 BY 8516	880811 SL 8406	$ -1,312.50
880831 BY 8516	880928 SL 8702	$ 1,531.25
881004 BY 8822	880928 SL 8702	$ -1,625.00
881004 BY 8822	881109 SL 8902	$ 375.00
881130 OUT 8815	881109 SL 8902	$ 593.75

These trades thus add up to about $ -5,400 in closed profits during the 11 month period in 1988 and another $ 600 in open equity profit as of November 30, 1988.

The figures below show the popular 4-9-18 day moving average approach for daily December, 1988 US Treasury Bond prices. Here the results are analyzed on the basis of the long positions being held only when the short is above both the middle and long averages and the middle above the long. Vice versa for shorts.

880115 BY 8730	880113 SL 8510	$ -2,625.00
880120 BY 8729	880212 SL 9019	$ 2,687.50
880224 BY 9124	880222 SL 9101	$ -718.75
880301 BY 9127	880307 SL 9009	$ -1,562.50
880316 BY 8924	880310 SL 8925	$ 31.25
880408 BY 8902	880318 SL 8905	$ 93.75
880427 BY 8621	880415 SL 8703	$ 437.50
880531 BY 8401	880429 SL 8602	$ 2,031.25
880606 BY 8613	880620 SL 8530	$ -468.75
880627 BY 8624	880628 SL 8718	$ 812.50
880630 BY 8728	880707 SL 8619	$ -1,218.25
880725 BY 8529	880713 SL 8430	$ -968.75
880802 BY 8624	880810 SL 8412	$ -2,312.50
880822 BY 8331	880815 SL 8330	$ -31.25
880831 BY 8516	880920 SL 8728	$ 2,375.00

881003 BY 8828	880928 SL 8702	$ -1,812.50
881006 BY 8825	881017 SL 8924	$ 968.75
881020 BY 8920	881024 SL 8907	$ -406.25
881028 BY 9024	881107 SL 8908	$ -1,500.00
881111 SL 8821	881130 OUT 8815	$ 187.50

The results for the 11 month period would thus be about $ -4,200 with an open equity on November 30, 1988 of about $ 200.

The numbers below show the popular Moving Average Convergence Divergence (MACDM) method applied to daily December, 1988 US Treasury Bond prices. Crossovers of the indicators are used to yield the following results for the December, 1988 contract.

880115 BY 8730	880111 SL 8419	$ -3,343.75
880115 BY 8730	880212 SL 9019	$ 2,656.25
880411 BY 8812	880212 SL 9019	$ 2,218.75
880411 BY 8812	880415 SL 8703	$ -1,281.25
880513 BY 8525	880415 SL 8703	$ -1,312.50
880513 BY 8525	880518 SL 8324	$ -2,031.25
880601 BY 8523	880518 SL 8324	$ -1,968.50
880601 BY 8523	880707 SL 8619	$ 875.00
880801 BY 8530	880707 SL 8619	$ 656.25
880801 BY 8530	880926 SL 8716	$ 1,562.50
881007 BY 9012	880926 SL 8716	$ 1,562.50
881007 BY 9012	881019 SL 8909	$ -1,093.75
881031 BY 9113	881019 SL 8909	$ -2,125.00
881031 BY 9113	881107 SL 8908	$ -2,093.75
881130 OUT 8815	881107 SL 8908	$ 781.25

A summary of this trading activity for the first 11 months of 1988 would show about $ -6,200 for the December, 1988 US Treasury

Bond contract in closed profits and around $ 800 in open equity profits as of November 30, 1988.

Some people display this study as a histogram as shown below of the same daily December, 1988 US Treasury Bond contract prices and then trade off changes in momentum as defined by the peaks and valleys shown in the chart below.

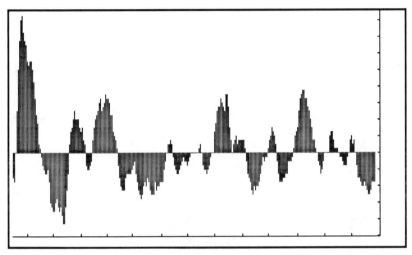

Following this approach on the December, 1988 US Treasury Bond contract would have yielded the following results in 1988.

880113 BY	8510	880126 SL 8816	$ 3,125.00
880128 BY	9020	880126 SL 8816	$ -2,125.00
880128 BY	9020	880201 SL 9106	$ 1,562.50
880202 BY	9204	880201 SL 9106	$ -1,062.50
880202 BY	9204	880203 SL 9108	$ -875.00
880223 BY	9124	880203 SL 9108	$ -1,500.00
880223 BY	9124	880225 SL 9106	$ -1,562.50
880226 BY	9120	880225 SL 9106	$ -1,437.50
880226 BY	9120	880304 SL 9020	$ -1,000.00
880311 BY	9012	880304 SL 9020	$ 250.00
880311 BY	9012	880316 SL 8924	$ -625.00

880317	BY	9014	880316	SL	8924	$	-687.50
880317	BY	9014	880318	SL	8905	$	-1,281.25
880323	BY	8818	880318	SL	8905	$	687.50
880323	BY	8818	880324	SL	8817	$	-31.25
880325	BY	8830	880324	SL	8817	$	-406.25
880325	BY	8830	880328	SL	8729	$	-1,031.25
880329	BY	8806	880328	SL	8729	$	-281.25
880329	BY	8806	880414	SL	8718	$	-625.00
880422	BY	8619	880414	SL	8718	$	968.75
880422	BY	8619	880428	SL	8600	$	-593.75
880503	BY	8600	880428	SL	8600	$	.00
880503	BY	8600	880517	SL	8417	$	-1,468.75
880524	BY	8323	880517	SL	8417	$	812.50
880524	BY	8323	880609	SL	8614	$	2,718.75
880614	BY	8823	880609	SL	8614	$	-1,281.25
880614	BY	8823	880616	SL	8631	$	-1,750.00
880622	BY	8707	880616	SL	8631	$	-250.00
880622	BY	8707	880627	SL	8624	$	-468.75
880628	BY	8718	880627	SL	8624	$	-812.50
880628	BY	8718	880706	SL	8625	$	-781.25
880715	BY	8515	880706	SL	8625	$	1,312.50
880715	BY	8515	880718	SL	8427	$	-625.00
880719	BY	8508	880718	SL	8427	$	-406.25
880719	BY	8508	880727	SL	8504	$	-125.00
880729	BY	8514	880727	SL	8504	$	-312.50
880729	BY	8514	880805	SL	8603	$	656.25
880817	BY	8400	880805	SL	8603	$	2,093.75
880817	BY	8400	880822	SL	8331	$	-31.25

880823 BY	8415	880822 SL	8331	$ -500.00
880823 BY	8415	880912 SL	8729	$ 3,437.50
880929 BY	8724	880912 SL	8729	$ 156.25
880929 BY	8724	881012 SL	8904	$ 1,375.00
881027 BY	9012	881012 SL	8904	$ -1,250.00
881027 BY	9012	881102 SL	9020	$ 125.00
881103 BY	9106	881102 SL	9020	$ -562.50
881103 BY	9106	881104 SL	8924	$ -1,437.50
881115 BY	8831	881104 SL	8924	$ 781.25
881115 BY	8831	881116 SL	8805	$ -812.50
881122 BY	8801	881116 SL	8805	$ 125.00
881122 BY	8801	881130 OUT 8815		$ 437.50

A summary of this trading activity for the first 11 months of 1988 would show about $ -7,300 for the December, 1988 US Treasury Bond contract in closed profits and around $ 400 in open equity profits as of November 30, 1988.

The chart that follows shows daily September, 1988 US Treasury Bond prices with an overlay of the suggested moving average (3/37) listed in The 1986-90 Almanacs. Note how this chart well displays the ability of moving averages to capture the large portion of major price moves when markets trend.

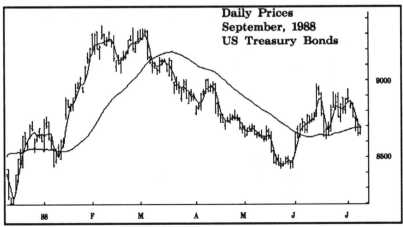

If one were trading this moving average in 1988, one would have had the following trades in the first 6 months of 1988;

880113	BY	8603	880111	SL	8512	$	-718.75
880113	BY	8603	880307	SL	9106	$	4,812.50
880603	BY	8705	880307	SL	9106	$	4,031.25
880603	BY	8705	880630	OUT	8824	$	1,593.75

Note that, as of 880630, these 3 trades totalled over $ 8,000 in closed profits and over $ 1,500 in open equity.

Oh, boy! Now we're getting somewhere!

Martha, call the bank and see what 2nd mortgage rates on the house are running these days!

The chart that follows shows daily December, 1988 US Treasury Bond prices and carries forward the first 6 months experience from June 30, 1988. The chart also shows the drawback to using moving averages and that is their poor performance during choppy markets such as that experienced from June to August, 1988.

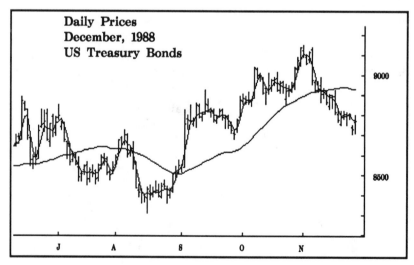

**Daily Prices
December, 1988
US Treasury Bonds**

Results from trading this set of parameters through November 30, 1988 would have been the following;

880630	BY	8728	880712	SL	8519	$	-2,281.25
880803	BY	8619	880712	SL	8519	$	-1,000.00
880803	BY	8619	880809	SL	8521	$	-937.50
880831	BY	8516	880809	SL	8521	$	-156.25
880831	BY	8516	881109	SL	8902	$	3,562.50
881130	OUT	8815	881109	SL	8902	$	593.75

Although the period was somewhat flat, ending with a loss on closed positions of a little more than $ 800 and an open equity profit of around $ 600, many traders would have lost patience with the approach by the time the 880831 buy signal rolled around and two months and four straight losses totalling around $ -4,400 had slipped through their fingers.

(What do we do now about that 2nd mortgage on the house???)

Sure hope Martha doesn't find out about this)!!!

Note that the $ 9,000 from the optimized moving average system is about $ 14,000 better than the standard, popular systems listed earlier in this section.

That $ 9,000 per contract in 1988 is also a lot better than one heck of a lot of people did trading US Treasury Bonds that year, too!

And, when compared to the margin of $ 2,500, it's actually not too shabby!

How did YOU do?

Are moving averages something YOU should use in YOUR trading environment?

Only you, of course, can answer that question!

The Weekly Rule

Civilization
and profits
go hand in hand.
- Calvin Coolidge

One of the best known trend-following techniques is the weekly rule. This technique has many of the benefits of the moving average but is less time consuming and simpler to use.

In 1970, a booklet entitled the "Trader's Notebook" was published by Dunn & Hargitt's Financial Services in Lafayette, Indiana. The best-known mechanical systems of the day were computer-tested and compared. The final conclusion of all the research was that the most successful of all the systems tested was the four-week rule, developed by Richard Donchian. In 1983, "Managed Account Reports" chose Donchian as the first recipient of The Most Valuable Performer Award for outstanding contributions to the field of commodity money management and now presents annually The Donchian Award to other worthy recipients.

The four-week rule is a reversal system (always in the market) but can be modified to make it noncontinuous by using a shorter time span (i.e., 1 or 2 weeks) for liquidation purposes only. The rules are quite simple -

1. Cover shorts and buy long when price breaks the highs of the four preceding calendar weeks, and

2. Liquidate longs and sell short when price breaks the lows of the four preceding calendar weeks.

HOW TO TRADE - Although used as a stand-alone system in the past, the weekly rule is best used as a confirming long term trend indicator to provide long term direction. Trades can then be entered in the direction of the weekly rule's defined long term trend by using shorter term methods.

Weekly Price Channels

The only limit
to our realization
of tomorrow
will be our doubts
of today.
- Franklin Roosevelt

From the weekly rule, the question obviously arises that perhaps a different number of weeks would be better to use than four. Perhaps three in some market and five, eight or eleven in others would better reflect the underlying cycles in different markets.

This possibility for improvement led to a study by Frank Hochheimer of Merrill Lynch in February, 1979 called the "Weekly Price Channel". In it, Hochheimer not only varied the number of weeks used in defining the weekly channels, he also varied the day on which the channels ended (Monday through Friday).

The study produced the following results for the best number of weeks and ending day of each channel -

BO	(9-M)	PB	(8 - W)
C	(7 - TU)	S	(2 - M)
CC	(10 - M)	SM	(11 - F)
CP	(6 - TU)	SU	(5 - TH)
CT	(9 - TU)	SV	(2 - TH)
LC	(2 - TU)	W	(4 - F)
LH	(1 - TU)		

(One should note that the study included prices from 1970 to 1976 only and that the parameters would most assuredly be different if the study were performed today on updated data).

The study was, in fact, updated one year later in February, 1980. The original parameters were applied to data from 1977 to 1979 and did quite well averaging, hypothetically, a $ 1,631 profit per $ 778 loss.

Besides the original channels for a few commodities, the portfolio also contained various moving average techniques.

Finally, Mr. Hochheimer issued another report in 1982 summarizing the earlier results.

In September, 1981, David Barker with Commodity Systems Reports issued a series of computerized commodity trading reports, one of which was an analysis of the outside price channel. This report optimized the number of days to be used in constructing the appropriate channel for each commodity. Executions were made if the closing price was above (below) the highest price of the last n-days.

Oscillators

When a woman has a run of bad luck,
she buys a new hat.
When a trader has a run of bad luck,
he buys a new system.

Any indicator which fluctuates up and down between overbought and oversold levels can be referred to generically as an oscillator. Oscillation is another of those market concepts that can be a little confusing. Some restrict the classification to include only those rate-of-change indicators which fluctuate between +1 and -1, +1 and 0, or 100 and 0 (as in percent). Hence, under this interpretation, such overbought/oversold indicators as momentum would not be included as an oscillator.

Pure oscillators are normally computed as the difference between two moving averages. Thus, as prices become overextended and gather too much velocity, the oscillator will alert the trader that the market has gotten ahead of itself or "overbought" ("oversold"). These signals indicate that a market might be losing momentum long before it shows on a chart.

There are many popular oscillation-type systems (Relative Strength Index, Moving Average Oscillators, Momentum, Rate of Change, Stochastics, etc.). Signals given, though different in format, usually look somewhat similar as prices fluctuate.

The risk of oscillator-type systems is that, in a major trend move, they will signal an early entry against the move and then stay in the "overbought" ("oversold") condition for some time thereafter as the market continues to advance against your wrong short (long) position.

In trading range markets, however, and when used to time entry on correction IN THE DIRECTION OF THE MAIN TREND, oscillators can be particularly effective.

If you can tie the oscillator to the underlying trading cycle (one-half the number of periods in the cycle), the oscillator will more accurately reflect the market you are trading and give you better signals.

Many traders consider the crossing of the zero-line to be a low-risk entry point when done in the direction of the main trend.

Oscillator parameters can be varied to provide more sensitive signals by shortening the time period over which the oscillator is constructed (a 9 period Relative Strength Index, for example, is better to use in looking for divergences than the standard 14 period RSI).

In using most such systems, look for divergences as prices make a new high (low) and the oscillator, in overbought (oversold) territory, does not. Use one of the other methods (such as chart patterns) to enter the position.

These price/oscillator divergences can be especially important when there are three in a row (i.e., three new highs in price that are unconfirmed by new highs in the oscillator) and often lead to panic reversals. (The British Pound is such an example in the section on "Confirmation and Divergence").

Lagging Markets

The stock doesn't know you own it
- Adam Smith

Lagging markets are those within the same complex that do not follow the movement of the other contracts in the complex.

For instance, in the Soybean complex, when Soybeans go up (or down), sometimes Soybean Meal will move with the Soybeans, sometimes Soybean Oil will, and other times both will. In the former instance, it is usually only a matter of time before the second product follows the first. If Rapeseed runs and Soybean Oil does not (or vice versa), follow the Soybean Oil closely as a "lagging market" and be prepared to enter on any signal in the direction of the Rapeseed Oil.

Another example would be the movement of big capitalization, "blue chip" stocks versus small capitalization issues. Other complexes such as energy or currencies are, of course, similar.

HOW TO TRADE - In the early stages of a move, go with the contract exhibiting the best relative strength. Watch the spread between the leading and the lagging commodity. When the spread stops widening, look to the laggard for entry signals to confirm the halt in momentum in the spread. Position in the direction of the original move of the leading contract. (Buying the laggard and selling the leader when this momentum slowdown occurs is normally wrong - it equates to picking a top in the leading contract, and, if one were that sure that the top had been reached, it would make more sense to simply short the leading contract)!

Pattern Recognition

PSST! Got a minute?
If you have,
I'll tell you how to make money
in these here markets!
It's easy! Simply
BUY LOW AND SELL HIGH!
Now, if you have
ten or twenty years,
I'll tell you how to figure out
whether the market's high or low!

Pattern recognition forms the basis for most trading systems and is the tendency of price movements to repeat themselves. Although there are many types of pattern recognition, only one will be discussed here. All attempt to capitalize on recurring price movement.

The following is for purchases (reverse to sell).

1.) Look for a period that is an 8 period low (i.e., the previous seven periods all have higher lows).

2.) Look for an upclose.

3.) Look for a downclose.

4.) Enter a buy stop above the high of the downclose day.

5.) If entry is not achieved and prices again close down, lower the buy stop to the high of the new downclose day.

6.) If entry is not experienced and a new low is made, begin the process over again.

Exit can be obtained by projecting a fixed dollar profit (say, $1,500), by trailing with a stop, by exiting at a target equal to the initial surge added to the high (or close, or low) of entry day, and so on.

Set up for this pattern is shown below. For instance, in the first example, period # 1 is the 8-period low while period # 2 experiences an upclose (thus satisfying the first two requirements listed above). In the second example, period # 1 satisfies both requirements by being an 8-period low and by closing up. In the third example, the 8-period low is made in period # 1 but the upclose is not experienced until period # 3.

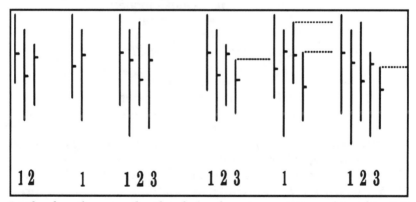

In the fourth example, the downclose is experienced on day # 3 and the buy stop is entered at the high of the day in accordance with rules 3 and 4 above. In the fifth example, the buy stop is lowered twice as two successive downcloses are experienced.

The process should not continue indefinitely. Usually about 6 periods past the 8-period low are sufficient to obtain an entry (if one is going to be obtained).

A real time example showing hourly prices from the March, 1988 S & P 500 in December, 1987 follows. Four appropriate signals are marked. Each of the four signals was worth a minimum of $1,500 over the six day period covered.

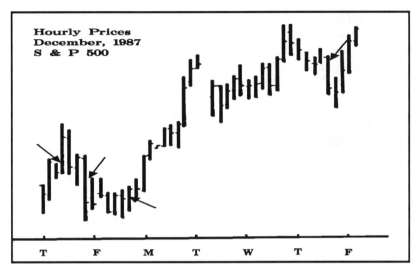

Hourly Prices
December, 1987
S & P 500

T   F   M   T   W   T   F

Pattern recognition is also used with the power of the computer to determine the probabilities of tomorrow's price action given the experience of the last n days. For instance, if today is the first day in five that price closes up, the computer can be used to determine the probability that price will be up or down tomorrow based on this 5 day pattern.

In the May 23, 1988 issue of "The Almanac Reports," this pattern was combined with other information to anticipate a major trend change from down to up on the June, 1988 S & P 500 futures contract. Specifically, in the May 18, 1988 issue, we had written that "(The percentage of) investment advisers bearish has reached the highest levels since July, 1982, just 1 month prior to the stock market explosion (that began the entire 5 year bull market)". This observation was combined with the third key astro turning point date of the year projected on page 254 of "The 1988 Almanac" for May 22, 1988.

Hence, we believed at the time that the market was SETUP or READY to change trend from down to up.

What was needed was a technique that would provide a specific entry buy point and TRIGGER the trade.

The TIMING technique that was used to enter the market was the above pattern recognition approach which resulted in a buy signal being issued on May 23, 1988 on a break of the May 20th high at 25405. (Purists will note that the entry point should actually have been lowered to the high of May 23, 1988 at 25370 given the second down close that day). The entry is shown by the arrow in the chart below of daily June, 1988 S & P 500 prices.

This trade was exited in accordance with instructions in the June 3, 1988 Report at the horizontal arrow on June 8, 1988 at 27095 for an $ 8,350 per contract profit.

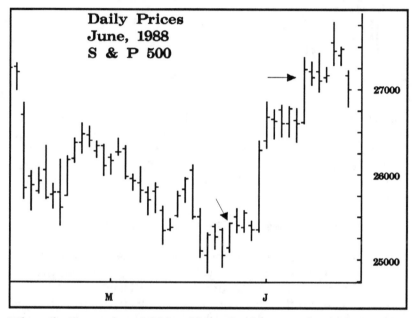

**Daily Prices
June, 1988
S & P 500**

When the December, 1988 gold market bottomed in late September, 1988, after a FND Slammer in the October contract, this pattern recognition approach both provided an excellent entry technique and several trading opportunities afterward as shown by the arrows in the chart of daily December, 1988 gold prices that follows.

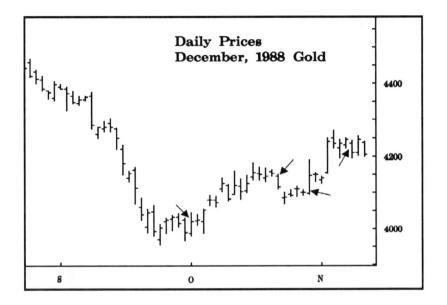

**Daily Prices
December, 1988 Gold**

Next Day's Trading Range

*When everyone is bullish,
a market must go down
because there are no buyers left;
conversely, when everyone is bearish,
a market must go up
because there are no sellers left.*

The most popular approach for projecting tomorrow's high and low price first involves calculating today's pivot point by adding together today's high, low, and close and dividing the total by three.

Once this pivot point is obtained, tomorrow's low is forecast by

1.) subtracting the pivot price from today's high and

2.) subtracting this difference from the pivot point.

The forecast high is made by

1.) subtracting the low from the pivot point and

2.) adding this difference to the pivot point.

If prices penetrate these levels, the next support/resistance level is projected to be the pivot point plus/minus the amount of today's range. Such a relationship is shown in the chart on the right.

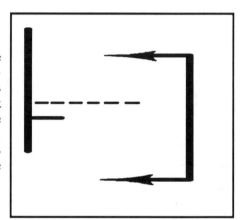

A variation of the above is that sometimes twice the distance between the day's pivot point and the high and low extremes is used in calculating the next day's range.

Chart-generated ranges are formed by connecting the highs and lows of successive trading days to determine the projected range for the following trading day. An example is shown in the chart on the right.

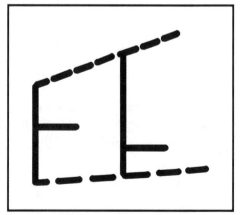

In the examples above, the reader must determine whether or not to use the true high / low in determining the next day's range with the true trading range being the preferred method.

Expiring Contracts

Speculation,
in its truest sense,
calls for anticipation.
- Richard Wycoff

IT IS POSSIBLE TO MAKE MORE IN THE LAST FEW DAYS OF AN EXPIRING CONTRACT THAN IT IS IN THE PREVIOUS SIX MONTHS OF TRADING THAT CONTRACT !

1. Trade in the direction of the long term prevailing trend (arrow)

2. Look for defined trend assertion within the last two months (see #1 in the chart that follows)

3. Look for trend acceleration and a move to new highs within the last 30 trading days (# 2)

4. Look for an Elliott Wave corrective pattern following the new highs (preferably a quick and simple A-B-C) (# 3)

5. Enter on the break to new highs (# 4)

6. Enter your stop below point # 3

7. Reverse the process for shorts

These trades normally occur because product is
in extremely short supply, because product is in
extremely ample supply, or because contracts
are being held in the hands of weak, inexperi-
enced traders who are getting ready to get their
innards "squeezed" out of them !!!

REMEMBER that margins on spot contracts will
be CONSIDERABLY HIGHER THAN NORMAL !!!

LAST TRADING DAY (LTD)

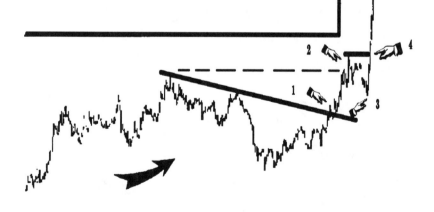

Oct   Nov   Dec   Jan   Feb   Mar   Apr   May   Jun   Jul   Aug   Sep

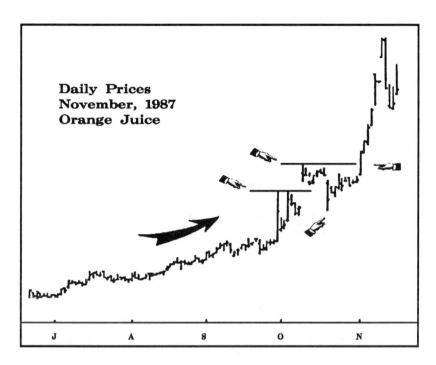

Daily Prices
November, 1987
Orange Juice

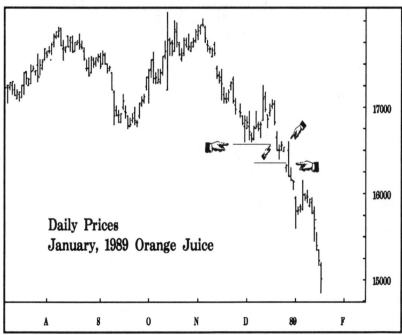

Daily Prices
January, 1989 Orange Juice

Basis Trading

When a falling market becomes
a screaming buy
because it cannot conceivably
drop any further,
place your order to buy
30 percent lower.

One good technique to use in the stock market is to analyze the buy and sell decisions of insiders. The same is true in the commodities markets!

But who are the insiders?

The insiders in commodities markets are the commercials or the dealers. These are the people whose business is the actual cash commodity product. In the grains, they are the large grain companies, Pillsbury, General Foods, Quaker Oats, etc. In the meats, they are the large meat packers, cattle feeding operations, large ranchers, etc. In the financials, they are the government securities dealers, commercial bankers, etc. In lumber, they are the large timber producers like Weyerhauser, International Paper, the sawmills, etc.

How can you tell what these people and companies are doing?

There are several ways (and remember that, despite their importance, they are but one of many players in the markets and are sometimes wrong in their positions, too, or may have other reasons for assuming them)!

One of the ways to follow commercials is through the basis chart. The basis chart is determined by plotting the cash price for any given commodity less the spot futures price.

The cash price can normally be obtained from news sources such as the Wall Street Journal (although there are some discrepancies - for instance, the Journal price is for fresh Pork Bellies instead of frozen Pork Bellies, Cotton is quoted in Memphis, Oats in Minneapolis, Soybean Meal and Soybean Oil in Decatur, and so on. Although these points are not in Chicago or New York, that is not as important as is the RELATIONSHIP between the cash market and the futures market in analyzing the basis).

Commercials buy product by pricing it against the nearest futures contract. Assume a commercial was willing to pay 15 cents under the nearest futures contract for corn. If futures drop 10 cents the next day and he still does not need corn, his bid might still be 15 cents under. If demand picks up, however, (let's assume the Russians start buying corn), his bid might go to 10 cents under, then 5 cents under, then even, then maybe 10 cents over, etc.

Hence, the first thing that the basis tells us is whether or not the cash product is in demand RELATIVE TO the current futures price.

Now, if the basis is 10 cents under, indicating that the commercial does not want the cash product, THEN WHY SHOULD YOU?

In other words, if the commercial has no need for the commodity, THEN WHY WOULD YOU WANT TO BUY THE FUTURES CONTRACT?

Likewise, when the basis is 10 cents over (futures below the cash), the commercial is bidding for cash product.

If the commercial aggressively needs the cash product, THEN WHY WOULD YOU WANT TO SELL FUTURES?

The general rule of thumb regarding basis trading is that you want to enter positions on the short side when futures are above cash and on the long side when futures are below cash. One benefit of following this general rule is that IF cash just stays level, your futures contract will become profitable as it converges on the cash price.

Hence, when you plot the basis on a chart, it will fluctuate around a zero line.

Remember that the general rule states that you want to SELL when the basis is BELOW the zero line and BUY when the basis is ABOVE the zero line.

The other main use for basis charts is in analyzing the CHANGE in the basis.

In our example of Russian corn buying above, note that the basis changed from very negative to very positive. Sometimes the basis will be one of the very first warnings of a potential major change in trend as the basis crosses the zero line or otherwise changes dramatically. These changes are more important when the basis has been steady over an extended period of time and indicate that stops should be tightened.

Although the basis can be a very important tool for analysis, it should not be used by itself just as insider trading information in the stock market should not be used exclusive of other analysis.

Also, it is important to note that the further one is from the expiration of the spot futures contract, the less reliable is the basis. For instance, a basis chart on February Pork Bellies in September is not going to be very reliable (especially since Bellies stored prior to November 1 cannot be used for delivery against the February contract).

Sometimes futures prices lead cash prices and overrun basis analysis. A good example is the Live Hog market in the summer of 1987. Many were claiming that the futures were a screaming "buy" because they were trading several dollars under the cash market. Futures were only forecasting the cash market, however, and as futures dropped about $ 10 into the end of the year, cash dropped around $ 20. In this instance, futures not only LED cash but remained UNDER cash all the way down.

One might note also that the basis works best in life-cycle commodity markets. Futures and cash markets in the metals, for instance, are too closely correlated to get the independent movements needed to track basis.

Finally, one should note that the basic concept of S & P 500 index arbitrage is a form of basis trading.

Backwardation

No one can trade successfully
if he does not
buy into weakness and
sell into strength.
- Charles Stahl

A glance at commodities prices in a newspaper will show several different months quoted for each market.

For instance, on December 11, 1987, Soybean prices were

January, 1988	590,
March, 1988	598,
May, 1988	606 1/2,
July, 1988	610 3/4, and
November, 1988	584 1/2.

Plotting these prices yields a graph like the one on the right where the July contract is priced higher than the January contract.

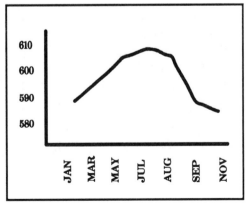

This is the normal relationship that exists in commodity markets due to the fact that the deferred months reflect the increased costs of storage, insurance, and interest (the carrying charges) for those holding the physical commodity (additionally, note how the August, September, and November contracts are priced to reflect the increased supply that the fall harvest usually brings).

Many major commodity bull markets will begin FROM this relationship. A particularly good clue is given when deferred contracts are selling at a premium to their calculated value given current carrying charges.

For instance, IF carrying charges through July were 10 cents, the implied value for July would be 600 (590 + 10). With the July selling at 610, the implication would be that the market and commercial interests in particular perceived higher prices in July and were willing to bid prices up for that period of time relative to the present.

This situation, when it exists, is normally bullish long term for prices. Note, however, that since the near term prices are at a discount to the deferreds, the implication is that the cash commodity is not PRESENTLY in demand.

Prices do not always trade at a discount or follow this normal relationship, of course. For instance, a chart of Copper prices for December, 1987 through December, 1988 contracts is shown on the right with prices as of December 11, 1987.

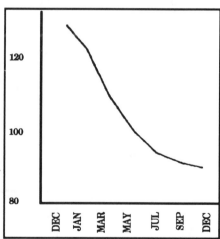

When prices in the near contracts are higher than they are in the deferred or distant contracts, the market that exists is called a PREMIUM market and the relationship is called BACKWARDATION.

This type market indicates that demand for the cash commodity by commercial interests is high. They are either able to sell it readily in the cash market themselves because of high demand, can use it in the normal operations of their business, or want product to store in anticipation of higher future demand and prices. They are thus willing to bid prices higher in the near term in order to obtain product. This backwardation is bullish for prices SO LONG AS COMMERCIAL DEMAND FOR THE CASH PRODUCT CONTINUES TO EXIST.

HOW TO USE - The key signal that backwardation or premium markets give to indicate future price increases is when the spreads go from a discount market to a premium market. This change occurs when the spread crosses the zero line or the price at which the two contracts are equal in price.

An example is seen in the two charts that follow of daily December, 1987 copper and November, 1987 orange juice prices.

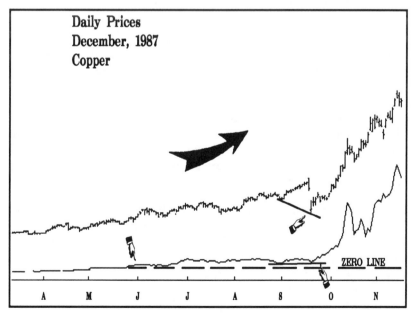

In the first chart, note that the spread went from a discount to a premium market in early June AND THAT IT REMAINED ABOVE THE ZERO LINE DURING THE ENTIRE COPPER ADVANCE in the second half of 1987, correctly indicating the higher prices for the entire year.

Indeed, when prices dropped sharply in mid-October and made a new low, note that the spread made a HIGHER low. This divergence correctly forecast higher prices as commercials bid up spot prices in order to attract product.

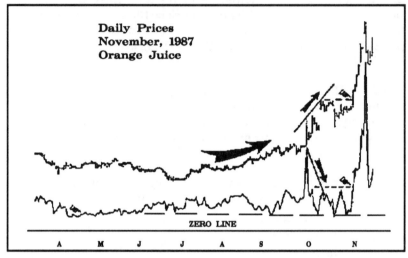

Daily Prices
November, 1987
Orange Juice

ZERO LINE

A   M   J   J   A   S   O   N

In the November, 1987 orange juice, the market first went premium in mid-April, but prices of November juice were not able to hold the advance, making new lows in late June. Note, however, that the spread not only remained above the zero line, but that it also was trading much above its June lows as prices were making new lows, signalling a divergence and possible future strength. This possible strength was confirmed in mid-July and then in August when prices made new four month highs. The strength continued through contract expiration.

When markets have been trending higher, failure of the spread to confirm higher prices often is a sign that the rally may be stalling. Note, for instance, the orange juice example. Prices at the up arrow in mid-October made a new high while the spread was not confirming, suggesting that an exit might be appropriate (or, at the very least, that the deferred contracts were starting to catch up indicating that long positions were better placed in the deferred contracts).

This stall lasted into the third week when, after completion of an Elliott Wave A-B-C correction, price broke to new highs at the first of the next month. The spread confirmed the move by breaking above the dotted line congestion zone and thus signalled reentry (or that positions should be moved from long deferred contracts to long the spot or near contract).

The old rule used to be that, in a true bull market, the nearby contract will gain on the deferred (backwardation). Hence, long positions in the nearby contract were the ones that would have the most potential. This rule has not been as reliable as it once was, as many markets in recent history would attest (crude oil is the most glaring example, trading premium consistently for the last few years despite a bearish market environment). (Precious metals always trade discount and the discount increases as markets increase or as interest rates increase, reflecting increased carrying charges).

One should note, however, that the rule was distorted by the general bear markets of the early to mid 1980s.

In summary, although the relationship between the near and deferred contracts should not be used as a signal by itself, it can provide important information to the observant trader regarding how commercial interests perceive future price direction.

Rolling Forward

I don't know where speculation
got such a bad name,
since I know of no forward leap
which was not fathered
by speculation.
- John Steinbeck

This technique is used to take advantage of a market that is experiencing backwardation. The expectation is that the market strength that exists in the spot contract will be carried over to the next contract after the spot expires and converges on cash product prices. The objective is to squeeze the near term contract for all it's worth and to then buy the next spot contract at a lower price and ride it to at least the same price as was experienced in the old spot contract. This movement should occur as the new contract converges on the cash price.

Note that the key to this technique working is that backwardation must be present and the cash price must either hold steady or increase. One should, therefore, insure that the futures (especially the new spot contract) are trading at a discount (below) to the cash price. As an example, let's look at our November, 1987 orange juice example in the Backwardation section. Note two things;

First, if the price were rolled on the close of the last day of trading for November orange juice, the juice would be sold at 163.50 and January orange juice bought at 158.75 for a 4.75 cent ($ 712.50) improvement in juice holdings (assuming, again, a constant or increasing cash price).

Second, because of the strong backwardation (indicating commercial demand for cash product), the November orange juice high of 174.00 on November 10, 1987 implied that the January orange juice contract would meet or exceed that high price (which it did by trading at 175.00 on November 30, 1987).

The charts that follow illustrate this relationship;

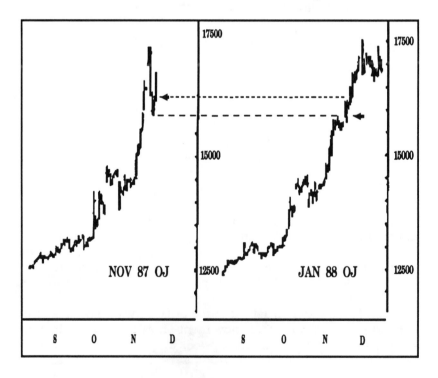

Another example was the wheat market of the mid 1980s. Despite huge supplies of wheat, most of it had been forfeited to government loan programs, leaving little in the cash market. Tightness in cash drove prices up relative to the price of deferred contracts. The same effect was experienced in late 1988 in the cotton market.

The reverse, of course, applies as well. In fact, the sugar market from 1983 to 1985 provided excellent opportunities to sell the new spot contract short and hold it into successively lower and lower expiration prices. Spot contract prices continuously sank relative to deferred contracts as sugar supply outstripped demand.

Scaling

If sugar is indeed
going up to 20 cents,
then we have a sacred duty as traders
to see to it that we have something
for sale at that level.
- Henry Van Kessel

There are two types of scale trading that can be used, scaling-in and scaling-down.

Scaling-In

In scaling-in, one places buy stop orders above or sell orders below a congestion zone and allows the market itself to force one into the position, entering at successively higher prices.

The main benefit of using this method is that it is very simple to use, requires little time, and yet can be quite effective. All that is needed is a chart book and a market that is in a base-building, sideways-trading congestion zone.

The scaling-in example that follows is from the sugar market, 1977-1980. As noted in The 1988 and 1989 Almanacs, the reason sugar has been used as an example is that, on a monthly basis, it is currently in the midst of a move that appears to be VERY similar to that of the late 1970s just prior to the movement depicted in the chart (please note, however, that the bull market lasted approximately 1 1/2 years. As this is being written in mid-1990, all Sugar contracts are priced about the same with a minor backwardation present).

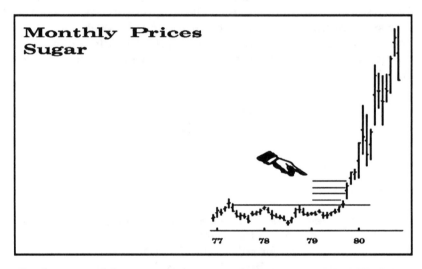

The horizontal lines represent purchase points SCALED-IN at about one cent intervals from 10 to 15 cents. Five contracts would have been purchased each of which would have been worth over $ 30,000 when sugar peaked in late 1980.

There are two major benefits of scaling-in;

1.) By making the market force you into a position, it automatically keeps you OUT of the market in a great many trades that otherwise would wind up losers, and

2.) it automatically regulates the size of positions that you will have (i.e., you will have large positions with profitable cycles and small positions with unprofitable cycles).

(This statement is such a natural that it hardly needs explanation, but stop and think about it for a moment. Isn't a good trading approach supposed to provide you with large positions in big moves) ???

If your positions are in the near contracts and the market exhibits backwardation, you will be able to benefit from the process of rolling forward (commission costs will be higher, however, than if positions are initiated in the back contracts).

Scaling-Down

If a very automatic, mechanical approach that provides consistent winners is more to your liking, then perhaps you will want to consider scaling-down.

The logic of scaling down lies in the fact that low prices must ultimately result in a reduction of supply as costs make it unprofitable to produce any given product. Since low prices increase demand, the combination of reduced supply and increased demand must ultimately result in higher prices.

When applying the concept to the futures markets, one great attraction of scaling-down is that one is purchasing part of an entire INDUSTRY instead of the stock of an individual company (a COMPANY can go bankrupt, but an entire INDUSTRY virtually cannot and MUST eventually recover (obsolescence excepted)). It is for this reason that this technique is usually used for long positions only and not short positions (with the exception of the short term interest rate markets such as US Treasury Bills and Eurodollars where yields are unlikely to go below 5 % or so over the foreseeable future).

The way this method works is that one

1.) determines the 10-year or longer price range for various markets,

2.) determines the lower 20 percent of that long term price range,

3.) identifies available capital for conducting a scale-trading program,

4.) determines appropriate price levels at which to scale into a market based on available capital,

5.) purchases the market at those price levels, making sure to not enter new positions in a particular market within the last four months of expiration of options or futures, and

6.) enters an order to liquidate the position at the next higher scale level immediately upon purchase.

An example is shown for March, 1988 Sugar using a 1/2 cent scale.

Daily Prices
March, 1988
Sugar

A 45 cent trading range over the last 10 years yields 11 cents as the lower 20 percent of the range (if one wanted to only use the lower 10 percent, purchases would be initiated only at 6 1/2 cents or lower). Purchases were initiated at the up arrows and liquidated at the down arrows.

There were five trades over this period. Five were winners with no losers for a gross profit of 2 1/2 cents (about $ 2,800). If the margin per contract was $ 1,000, then the maximum amount needed to support these positions during this 8 month period was about $ 4,800. The scale trader would have thus walked away with an approximate 58 percent return for his efforts in 2/3 year which annualizes at over 85 %.

A second example comes from the July 29, 1988 issue of "The Almanac Reports" where a scale-down approach was suggested for the July, 1989 cocoa market, a daily price chart of which is shown below.

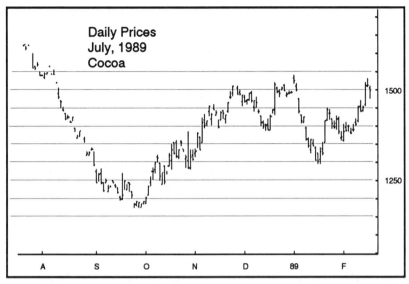

Note that this is not a good example of a good scale-down trade in that into the late September lows, there were virtually no bounces with which to provide interim profits - the market simply went straight down. Usually the normal volatility of the market will provide several opportunities for interim profits that can be taken between scale purchases as in the two trades in April / May in the March, 1988 sugar example above.

By following the scale-down approach in July, 1989 Cocoa as outlined in the July 29, 1988 issue of "The Almanac Reports," one would have had the following trades assuming a 50 dollar scale and an eventual stop of $ 800.

Scale	Bought	Price	Sold	Price	Profit	Multiple
1500	880810	1492				
1450	880812	1445	881123	1500	550	1100
1400	880819	1395	881109	1450	550	1650
1350	880826	1320	881104	1400	800	3200
1300	880831	1300	881018	1350	500	2500
1250	880901	1250	881010	1315	650	3900
1200	880916	1200	880919	1250	500	3500
1200	880919	1200	881005	1250	500	3500
1250	881011	1240	881017	1300	600	3600
1300	881026	1300	881027	1350	500	2500

1300	881027	1300	881102	1350	500	2500
1400	881115	1400	881121	1450	500	1500
1450	881207	1450	881220	1500	500	1000
1400	881215	1400	881220	1450	500	1500

Note as of the end of the year that this approach had experienced 14 trades, 13 of which had worked and 1 of which was open with an open equity profit of $ 260. The scale-down trader had made a gross profit of $ 7,150 on a maximum capital requirement of $17,494, had come full-cycle in less than 5 months, and was now ready to either sell the final contract at 1550 or to add another contract at 1500, at 1450, at 1400, and so on.

In other words, he would be in position to begin the entire process again. Or perhaps this time he would want to trade two contracts on this market.

Note in the example that 5 of the 13 trades had resulted in profits of greater than $ 500 due to gap openings that can occur on either the buy or the sell side and which further enhance profits.

A variation of the above approach is shown in the last column on the right.

Here another contract is added at each successively lower purchase price (i.e., at 1450, two contracts are purchased, at 1400, three contracts are purchased, and so on). The theory is that the lower the price, the closer one is to the ultimate reversal point.

A summary of the above approach would show 59 contracts traded with 58 profits and 1 contract open at the end of the year which had an open equity profit of $ 260. The approach would have made $ 29,200 on a maximum required capital investment of $ 54,866 which is a 53 % return (over 135 % annualized).

The only way that one can theoretically lose when using this method is by setting the scales too close together (i.e., buying too many contracts for the available capital in a down market), by failing to follow through with the original plan, by not allowing for a sufficiently low price when initially planning the trades, if the market remains in a perpetual bear market (an impossibility as such would dictate an eventual price of zero), or a market that remains permanently in a carrying charge market (where the near contract is worth less than deferred contracts).

Some major advantages of the method is that it is very simple to understand and use, is very mechanical, benefits from volatility, can produce trading profits during the course of the scale-down trading cycle, and can be totally planned in advance to allow for virtually all contingencies prior to entering the first position.

It does, however, take an incredible amount of patience to execute a scale trading program. One should note that the narrower the scale, the more trades and more interim profit, but the more capital required to execute the strategy.

This type approach is obviously not for everyone. There are some, however, who do not relish trading or simply do not seem to be able to become successful at trading for whom this portion of the book will be by far the most valuable.

If you fall into the above category, the best way to take advantage of the above information is to use the six-step formula given at the beginning of this section in conjunction with the Linear Cycle information. Locate in the weekly linear cycles section of "The Calendar Book" an upcoming major Linear Cycle low projection for the market of interest. Begin the scale-down process at least four weeks prior to one of the projected major lows.

Here are the points at which to begin a scale down program based on 20 % of the 10 year price range;

BO	2000	PL	330
C	210	S	600
CC	2000	SM	160
CF	12500	SU	1100
CL	1500	SV	900
CT	4300	UL	4500
GO	260	W	300
HO	4500	WK	300
LB	14500		
LH	3800	**Scale UP on**	
O	140		
PA	110	ED	9200
PB	4100	TB	9300

The same approach can be used to scale-down spread relationships.

A special section in "The Calendar Book" lists the favorite scale trades for the year.

Additionally, one of the most popular sections in The Calendar Book is the "Trade of the Year". We usually discuss several ways of approaching the "Trade of the Year" one of which involves the scale-down approach and lists an accompanying detailed trading matrix. Look in this section of The Calendar Book for more detailed information.

The above Cocoa market was again listed as one of our favorites for scale-down trading in The 1989 Almanac. So how did it turn out?

The chart below shows the same July, 1989 contract reviewed and suggested in The 1989 Almanac from December, 1988 to February, 1989.

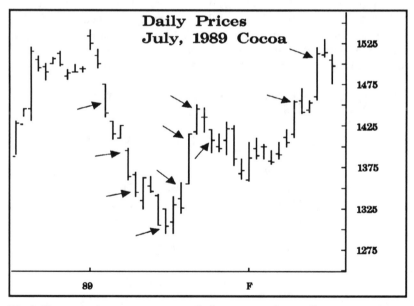

Had the exact same approach been used on the exact same contract, the following results would have been approximately recorded;

SCALE LEVEL	BOUGHT	PRICE	SOLD	PRICE	PROFIT	MULTIPLE
1500	880810	1492				
1450	890105	1450	890214	1500	500	1100
1400	890110	1395	890123	1450	550	1650
1350	890111	1350	890120	1400	500	2000
1300	890117	1300	890119	1350	500	2500
1400	890125	1400	890209	1450	500	3000

This technique would have thus added an additional $ 2,500 over the next 1 1/2 months for those using the technique.

In fact, the technique worked so well from 1989 through 1990, as can be shown in the following chart of weekly cocoa prices, that we suggested the technique on national television on Financial News Network during several interviews in the fall, 1989 and on several other media outlets.

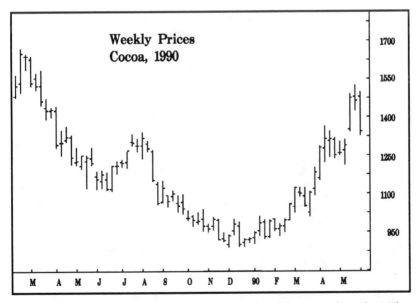

Those who followed these suggestions should remember that The 1989 Almanac was predicting major lows in this market in early 1990 which fit quite well with a scale-down program and its accumulation of long positions on price weakness.

How did the early 1990 projections of a major bottom (which were based on the information contained in the "Monthly and Weekly Linear Cycles" sections of the Calendar Book of The 1990 and 1989 Almanac) in this market work out?

I think you can judge for yourself from the above chart !!!

If YOU are a former Almanac purchaser, did you participate in the rewards of such a scale-down trading program in cocoa?

Did you begin such a program anew in mid-1990 as price again moved into the 1100s?

Pyramiding

The commodity future's game
is a money game -
not a game involving
the supply-demand
of the actual commodity
as commonly depicted.
- R. Earle Hadady

As mentioned in the discussion on The Principle of the Tithe in the Money Management Section, pyramiding is one of two ways to hit a grand slam on a major price move. Many well-known traders and trading advisers feel, in fact, that pyramiding is one of the most important - if not THE most important - of money management techniques.

There are two main pyramids - the upright pyramid and the inverted pyramid.

The inverted pyramid is the ultimate fantasy of traders - i.e., where one enters a position with one contract and increasingly uses the profits of established positions to buy more and more contracts. In this type approach, the trader is increasingly dependent on higher and higher (or lower) prices. Such a position is highly dependent upon two things:

1.) an almost vertical one-way move with little or no corrections, and

2.) an ability to time the exit of the position prior to a devastating correction. Because both of these abilities are extremely rare in the markets, inverted pyramids involve a high probability of almost certain ruin.

Upright pyramids, however, have a far higher probability of success. Here a large number of contracts are opened on the initial trade and successively fewer contracts added at each successive entry point. In an ideal pyramid, the number of contracts in the base or first level will be approximately equal to half the total number of contracts in the pyramid. The base should begin with an odd number of contracts and should then subtract a constant even number of contracts from the prior lower level for symmetry.

Pyramids are normally constructed on a SCALING-IN basis. If a long pyramid is being built, positions are entered by using successively higher BUY STOP orders and vice versa for short pyramids.

Exiting is normally done by use of a stop order. It is constructive, however, when initially building the pyramid, to have an exit objective defined.

Also helpful is a reflective pyramid where prices are exited in the reverse image that they were entered (i.e., the last contract added is the first exited while the first contracts added (the base) are the last contracts exited).

Here are a few other guidelines -

1.) When adding positions, each successive layer should be smaller than before,

2.) Additions should not be made unless the last unit shows a profit,

3.) Add only to winning positions,

4.) Do not add to an existing position if the intended stop point would imply a net loss for the entire position, and

5.) Never add to a losing position.

Candidates for pyramiding should come from those markets that are completing either a major cyclical top or bottom or are completing an intermediate top or bottom whose next thrust will be in the direction of the prevailing major cycle. If the first and second Elliott Waves can also be identified, the ensuing major third wave movement is the most profitable place to begin building pyramids once the cycle bottom (top) is in place.

The Almanac's pyramid choices had not missed through 1989, having chosen live cattle in 1986, the CRB index in the spring of 1987, and corn in Spring, 1988. Corn was recognized by Forbes Magazine in early 1989 as having been the best performing commodity market in 1988.

The choice of silver in The 1989 Almanac, however, broke this string of successful pyramid suggestions. The 1990 Calendar Book did not contain a pyramid suggestion due to oversight. The pyramid candidate of the year is a major feature of each year's "Calendar Book."

The chart that follows shows the setup for the corn trade as presented in The 1988 Almanac while the second chart following shows the results.

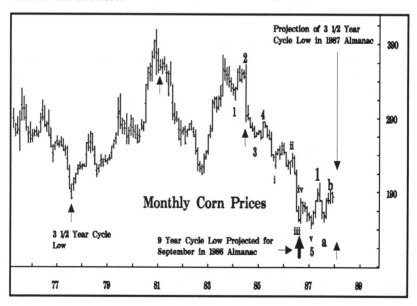

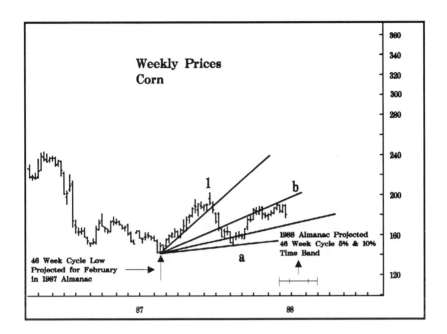

Weekly Prices
Corn

46 Week Cycle Low
Projected for February
in 1987 Almanac

1988 Almanac Projected
46 Week Cycle 5% & 10%
Time Band

HOW IT CAME OUT

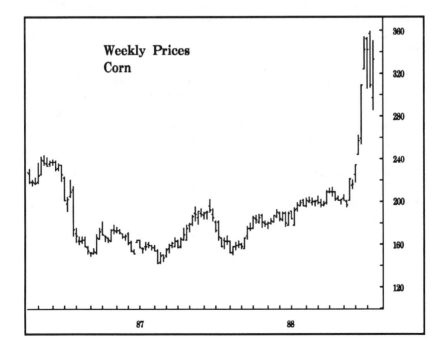

Weekly Prices
Corn

Entering and Exiting Positions

Life consists
not in holding good cards
but in playing those
you do hold
well.
- Josh Billing

You have decided to buy a particular market. Maybe the source of your decision is a seasonal trade, a cycle you think has bottomed, fundamental analysis, or whatever.

What is the best way to enter the market?

Walt Bressert tried to answer that question with his 40-page booklet, "Market Entry and Exit: How to Trade With the Professionals". The technique combines seven key price level pivot points with four time periods. The seven pivot points are the previous day's high, low, and close and the current day's open, high, and low. The four time periods are today's open, 30 minutes after the open, midday, and 35 minutes before the close.

The idea is to use the pivot points as a timing device when the trader believes the market is topping or bottoming, as mentioned above. The buy or sell signals occur when the pivot points are broken during the day. Signals occurring late in the day are stronger signals than those that occur early.

As the day progresses, signals are moved closer to price activity than their beginning points. Some modified examples for entry into a long position are given below. Note that the initial entry price stop is computed by subtracting yesterday's low from yesterday's close and adding it to yesterday's high price (see discussion on "Stops").

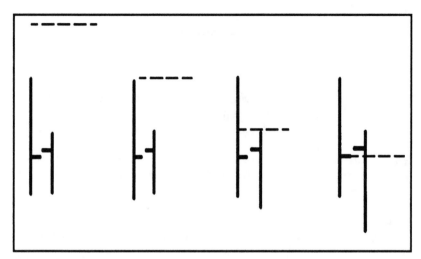

In the first example, the initial range stop based on the above formula is placed prior to the market opening.

In the second example, the stop is lowered after the first 15 minutes to the high of the previous day OR the high of the early morning's price range, whichever is greater.

In the third example, the stop is lowered 15 minutes prior to lunch hour to either the morning high or the previous day's close, whichever is greater. Note that lunch hour for New York markets occurs one hour earlier than Chicago markets.

Finally, in the fourth example, the entry stop is lowered 30 minutes prior to the close to either the day's high or the previous day's close, whichever is lower but still above the current trading price.

If a long position is absolutely desired prior to the market's closing, entry can be made at the close if none of the stops are hit during the day. Otherwise, begin the process again tomorrow by using the range entry as the initial buy stop.

Stops

*I go long or short as close as I can to the danger point,
and if the danger becomes real I close out and take
a small loss. - Jesse Livermore*

You've entered your trade and now must choose a stop point.
Where should you enter the stop? Here are some ideas;

If you are chart-oriented, enter a good-till-canceled (GTC) order
at the same time the trade is entered at or before the point at
which price movement causes a transition in the technical picture.

For instance, if you are in an uptrend and breaking an uptrend
line would indicate that the trend may have changed, then enter
your stop just below the trendline. If a position has been entered
that involves a trading range market, enter the stop on the other
side of the trading range. If a possible 1-2-3 pattern may be
forming in the direction opposite to your position, the stop should
be moved to just beyond the "2" point.

After a correction has ended and price has resumed its trend,
stops should normally be moved at least up to the point just
outside the range of the correction. Ringed highs and lows often
provide points below (above) which stops can be placed.

If your stop is too far away, a money stop (which risks only a given
amount of money) can be used. A general rule of thumb, however,
is that IF YOU CANNOT DEFINE A STOP POINT, THE POSITION
SHOULD NOT BE ENTERED.

If you are trading with a computerized trading system, stops can
be optimized by testing historical prices to define the best range
of stop level to use. This process can be especially valuable if the
stop is tied to the recent volatility of the market being traded.
Such flexibility allows the stop to be tightened at times and
loosened at other times.

Volatility is normally determined by taking the average day's trading range over a given period (for instance, the last 10 days). Stops then become a function of this average range, usually being determined by multiplying by a factor.

Another approach simply increases (decreases) an initial stop by the amount that today's high (low) price is above (below) yesterday's high price. The initial stop may be determined by several of different methods. For instance, the average daily trading range for the last 20 days may be calculated and multiplied by 1.5 in order to arrive at a value that can be subtracted from (added to) the entry price.

An excellent approach upon initially entering a position is to use the "Hardcastle Breakeven Stop" and to move the initial stop up to just below the low (above the high on short positions) of the first day that results in the stop being profitable.

For instance, if a Gold position is entered at $ 420.00 and 5 trading days later the low for the day is $ 423.00 (and that day is the first day whose low is above the $ 420.00 entry price), the stop would be moved up to $ 422.90.

A couple of basic rules regarding trading and stops are worth mentioning here; first, never, ever if you can possibly avoid it, let a profit go into a loss.

Second, if you are corn-fused (as they say in Iowa), then get out.

Finally, if you feel that the market may possibly be changing trend, then move your stops up tighter by using another method of calculating the stop (if you have to).

A good example at the end of 1987 was the copper market. Although the Rolling Forward procedure would tend to indicate higher prices for March, 1988 copper prices as mentioned in the earlier discussion regarding Rolling Forward techniques, the spot March and back month contracts had been setting up a classical divergence. The indication was that stops should be tightened considerably which proved to be valuable insight as prices proceeded to plunge.

Daytrading

*For my money,
a good day trading system
would have an accuracy of
somewhere in the area over 50%.
The average risk reward ratio
should be 2 : 1 with
the average profit
at least twice as large
as the average loss.
The average profit per trade
should be at least $ 150.00.
- Larry Williams*

Day trading is the ultimate for the person wanting lots of "action". The term means that positions are both opened and closed on the same day.

Day trading has several advantages, one of the largest of which relates to margin. At most firms, margin rates will at least be reduced considerably, while at many firms, they will be essentially eliminated altogether (so long as you have equity in your account and do not over leverage the funds available).

The advantages are potentially tremendous. If one has a system that makes 15 percent per year on equity by trading overnight positions (spreads, outright long and short positions, arbitrage, etc.), and is able to make an additional 15 percent from day trading, then one is able to double the return on the same amount of equity by piggybacking one's daytrading approach onto the overnight system.

There are two basic types of day trading approaches.

The first includes those methods that analyze prices in a "live" environment.

The second analyzes the prices prior to commencement of trading each day and enters orders to both open and close positions without any need to check prices during the day. The orders are either filled or they are not filled and at the end of the day, the trader collects his profit/loss and proceeds to the next day in a very mechanical fashion.

In order to daytrade, one has special needs. The margin factor mentioned above is one very important need.

Another is reduced commissions. $ 75.00 commissions and above will simply not enable survival in a day trading account.

Additionally, order execution is an absolute necessity. If orders are constantly coming back $ 25 to $ 50 off the mark, I would strongly suggest having someone else represent your orders in the pit (unless, of course, one is trying to day trade in illiquid markets [see "Contract Liquidity"]).

Also, since prices change so rapidly in the day trading environment, an incredible amount of self-discipline is required to execute whatever method the trader is following.

It is also important that the day trader be trading those markets that are sufficiently volatile that the price moves provide enough opportunity for profit to justify the effort.

The importance of having a rather simple method to follow cannot be overemphasized. One simply cannot be attempting to day trade in a live environment and be so congested that clear and precise decisions cannot be rapidly made.

That said, I must confess that every-so-often when I become "bored" with routine, I will trade the S & P 500 free-form off a one-minute bar chart (by free-form, I mean that one simply marshals all of one's knowledge and expertise to enter and exit trades). I find it invigorating and challenging but not sustainable for too long simply because of the intensity of concentration and time commitment demanded.

Volume

The turnover is highly important,
whether it's in business
or when the alarm clock
goes off in the morning.

Volume is the sense of urgency and should expand in the direction of the trend if the trend is to be sustained. In like manner, volume should contract on corrections. Changes in this volume pattern often warn of a reversal in trend before it actually happens.

For example, if an uptrend has been proceeding normally, with higher volume on rallies and lower volume on reactions, only to suddenly have volume subside on the rallies and increase on the reactions, it is likely a signal of a pending price reversal.

This DIVERGENCE is especially important if penetration of a previous high (low) occurs on declining volume.

When analyzing volume, a moving average over, say, the last 5 days will often provide greater clarity in volume interpretation.

Volume analysis is not as useful in commodity futures as in stocks. One reason is that there is a one-day lag in reporting the actual numbers. Another is that total volume for all contracts is used to analyze individual contracts. This volume figure often contains large professional spreads that are traded for a multitude of different reasons. Also, lock limit days will usually show light volume since few contracts are able to be traded. Finally, important information available to the trader of stocks, such as upside-downside volume and the number of issues traded on upticks versus downticks, is not available for the futures market trader.

As a general rule, the resolution of all price patterns (the breakout point) should be accompanied by heavier trading activity if the signal given by the breakout is to be believed (i.e., trendlines, trading range breakouts, gaps, chart patterns, and so on).

Technicians have experimented with many volume indicators to help quantify buying and selling pressure. The most basic is cumulative volume analysis. Here a running total of volume is kept by adding daily volume if prices close up and subtracting volume if prices close down. It is the direction of the volume line that is important, especially as it relates to price, and not the actual volume numbers themselves. Divergences between the volume line and price (i.e., price makes a new low and volume does not, providing a buy signal) are very important to cumulative volume analysis. The line should move in the same direction as prices.

Volume accumulation assigns only a percentage of the volume as plus or minus depending on where the close is in relation to its daily trading range instead of the entire day's volume. There are several versions of this formula, some relating the open to the close, some the close to the median or average price of the day, and so on. In these methods, downside volume is subtracted from upside volume to create a cumulative line that is used in the same manner as the volume line described above.

Another interesting volume technique is Equivolume charting. Here the volume for a particular day is indicated by the width of the bar on a chart.

Still another way to approach volume/price analysis is through the amount of volume required to move a market up one price unit and the amount required to move a market down one price unit. As a rule, an increase in the shares required to move a market up indicates a weakening position. The same applies to the downside.

Often a ratio is created by dividing selling momentum by buying momentum with a number greater than 100 being bullish.

Perhaps the most interesting of the volume indicators, however, is three dimensional charting. In this method, accumulated volume is charted on the y-axis, time on the x-axis, and prices are noted on significant high and low points. Divergences are noted quite clearly by lower peaks made with higher prices.

All of the above techniques can be averaged over several days for greater clarity, of course.

Volume is more important on the upside than on the downside, at least in the early stages of a price move.

As a rule of thumb, if the volume on a particular day is three times the average volume of the last five days, it is an indication someone is interested and is time to take a look at the market.

Examples for both volume and open interest follow the open interest discussion.

Open Interest

Results? Why, man,
I have gotten a lot of results.
I know several thousand things
that don't work!
- Thomas Alva Edison

Open interest represents the total number of outstanding contracts that remain unliquidated in a given futures market and is probably the most misunderstood concept in the markets. It is the number of outstanding longs OR shorts and not the total of both.

Open interest increases when a new buyer purchases from a new seller and decreases when an existing long sells to an existing short. If a new buyer purchases from an existing long or a new seller sells to an existing short, open interest remains unchanged. Markets with open interest levels below 5,000 contracts or volume levels below 1,000 contracts should be avoided.

It is the change in open interest numbers that provides forecasting value. Rising open interest indicates that new money is flowing into the market and increases the odds that the present price trend will continue. Declining open interest shows that money is leaving the market and that the amount of funds committed to new positions is not sufficient to make up for those being liquidated.

To be really significant, the increase or decrease in open interest must exceed the seasonal tendency (the smooth dotted line on open interest charts). Rising (declining) prices accompanied by greater than normal seasonal open interest declines indicate that the rally is being caused primarily by short covering (long liquidation). Money is leaving rather than entering the market.

These situations can be summarized in the table below -

Price	Volume	Open Interest	Market
Rising	Up	Up	Strong
Rising	Down	Down	Weak
Falling	Up	Up	Weak
Falling	Down	Down	Strong

Summing up, if volume and open interest are both increasing, then the current price trend will probably continue its present trend, be that up or down.

A seasonal pattern in open interest may be created by a commodity that is put into storage, increasing open interest. As it comes out of storage, open interest declines as the hedge is lifted.

Here are some other open interest guidelines -

Toward the end of major market moves where open interest has been increasing, a leveling off or decline in open interest is often an early warning of a change in trend. A high open interest figure at market tops can be considered bearish if the price drop is very sudden because all recent new longs are trapped at high prices.

In a trading range market, if open interest expands dramatically during a market rally to the high of the trading range and prices are unable to sustain the advance, it is an indication that large commercial and dealer interests are expanding their short or hedge positions. Since commercials deal in the actual physical commodity and can deliver product, the ensuing sell off can be quite rapid and volatile as speculators are forced to liquidate positions.

Conversely, a move to the lower end of the trading range accompanied by a sharp drop in open interest is often followed by a sharp upmove after large commercial interests have covered their short positions on the price drop.

The two above rules are difficult to spot and require a tremendous amount of vigilance to catch but are high probability moves when they do occur. In fact, my personal experience is that this is the best use of open interest.

Open interest should confirm breakouts just like volume.

In blowoffs and selling climaxes, prices suddenly jump after a long advance accompanied by a large jump in trading activity. The key to recognizing the top (bottom) is the sizable decline in the open interest that often occurs.

Individual contract open interest numbers can be helpful by indicating which contracts are the most liquid for trading.

Finally, here is a daily model for using price, volume, and open interest -

If price is	UP	UP	UP	UP	DN	DN	DN	DN
If volume is	UP	UP	DN	DN	DN	DN	UP	UP
If open interest is	UP	DN	UP	DN	DN	UP	DN	UP
The daily value is	1	0	0	-1	1	0	0	-1

Gary D Powell was kind enough to draw to my attention that the Daily Value is given by the formula $DV = P \times (V + OI)/2$ where P (price), V (volume), and OI (open interest) are each assigned a value of 1 if up and -1 if down.

The daily values can then be cumulated over several days and indicate confirmation / divergence of trend.

Examples follow of both volume and open interest.

The late July / early August, 1987 rally in crude oil to new highs was unconfirmed by volume as shown in the chart to the right of February, 1988 prices.

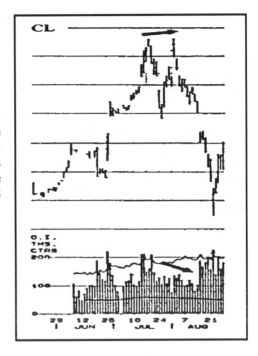

Both volume and open interest failed to confirm the September, 1987 highs in oats as shown in the chart to the right of daily March, 1988 oats prices.

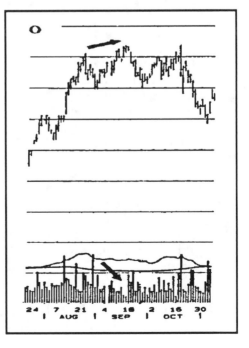

The rally in June, 1987 that occurred in the March, 1988 US Treasury Bond contract did so on progressively lighter volume and was an indication of market weakness (which soon was forthcoming) as shown in the chart to the right of daily BDH88 prices.

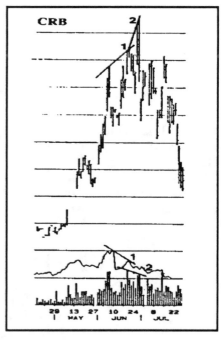

Note the divergence at the June, 1988 high in the CRB Index. The mid-June high was not confirmed by open interest (as indicated by points "1") and then, at the very top in late June, the high was not confirmed by either open interest or volume (as indicated by points "2"). Such divergences were also common at the 1988 highs in the Grain and Soybean complexes.

Note, in the chart to the right of daily March, 1988 Palladium prices, how an attempt to break through the two month trading range in October was "stuffed" by commercial interests as indicated by the surge in open interest when prices rose to the top of the trading range just prior to the fall selloff.

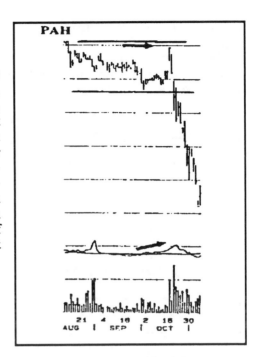

In the chart to the right of daily May, 1989 sugar prices, lower prices at point "1" were not confirmed by volume or open interest.

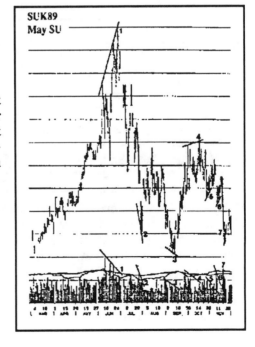

The same divergence occurred again shortly thereafter as shown at point "2". Note the sharp rally after the drop off in open interest at the first up arrow but note, too, that such was the normal seasonal pattern as indicated by the average open interest of the last five years.

After staying in the trading range marked by the two horizontal lines for the next two months, open interest declined to new lows for the move as commercials covered their hedge short positions in preparation for the rally that ensued shortly thereafter as indicated by the second up arrow.

Can you spot the volume / open interest divergences that occurred at point "3"?

Note how volume increased to a high for the move at point 4 just three days before the two successive limit down days in late July!

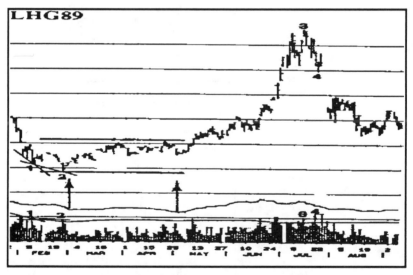

Volume and open interest told quite a story in the live hog market as shown in the chart above of daily February, 1989 live hog prices. Note at point "1" the divergences between price and both volume and open interest that occurred at the early February lows.

Next, at the late February lows, both volume and open interest again diverged with price.

At the early July highs at point "3", a major volume divergence again occurred prior to the selloff to point "4" in mid July where lows were not confirmed by volume.

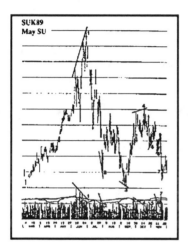

The chart on the left of daily May, 1987 sugar prices shows several volume/open interest divergences with price beginning with the rally to new highs in June. The volume spike at point "7" occurred one day prior to the late November lows and was unconfirmed at the new price lows the following day as can be seen in the chart.

The final example involves Accumulation / Distribution.

Note in studying the chart of daily March, 1989 US Treasury Bond prices and the A / D line that the major signals are given when price and the A / D line diverge.

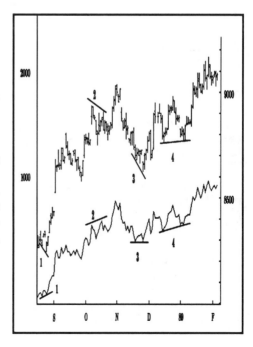

Should you use volume and open interest in your analysis of market price movement?

Only you, of course, can answer that!

It is the next logical step that many traders undertake in their trading careers as they look to improve analysis performed only on price alone.

The next level of technical analysis that most traders usually study after volume and open interest involves time.

The Commitment of Trader's Report

*The foolishness
of the many
is the opportunity
of the few.*

The Commitment of Trader's Report is released by the Commodity Futures Trading Commission (CFTC) on or about the 11th of each month and shows open interest statistics as of the end of the previous month in the nation's futures markets.

The report breaks down open interest into three categories (large hedgers, large traders, and small speculators) and indicates who is long and who is short in a particular commodity.

Futures traders who deal in large enough quantities to reach reportable levels in each market (see discussion on Reporting Levels) must report those levels to the CFTC daily. It is from these numbers that the Commitment of Trader's Report is compiled.

The total open interest less the reporting levels of hedgers and large traders is presumed to be small speculators.

Of particular importance in analyzing this report is the position of the commercial interests. Commercials are the actual dealers in a particular commodity. Their business is to know their commodity better than anyone else as that commodity is their business. Small speculators are deemed to be the less astute traders. The relationship between the commercials and the small speculators is somewhat akin to the specialist on the NYSE and the "odd lotter".

In analyzing open interest, the month's net figures for each of the three categories should first be determined by subtracting the month's short position from the month's long position. If commercials are bearish on a particular commodity, for instance, this net figure will be negative. When commercials are net long, the market is in a particularly bullish posture. The reason why is because the natural position of commercials (since they are basically hedgers) is a net short position.

Commercial interests should also be compared to speculative interests. When the commercials are net long and small speculators are net short a particular commodity, the interests are out of balance and the price is most likely to move up in the favor of the commercials.

It is important to not only analyze the composition of the market, but to note the change in composition over time as well. Do this by subtracting the current month's net figure from last month's net figure for each of the three groups. If this figure is positive, the group being analyzed has become more bullish on the commodity since the last report. The most bullish indication of this report would thus be a large net long commercial interest position that has become more positive since the last report accompanied by a large net short speculative position that has become more bearish since the last report.

Each group additionally follows certain seasonal trading patterns. It is the departure from these normal seasonal habits that provides an additional indication as to the various group's attitudes and future market direction.

HOW TO TRADE - Use the report for long term market direction and position yourself with the "smart" money (commercials). Keep in mind that the figures are reported around the middle of each month and are compiled as of the last day of the previous month and are thus about 12 days old by the time you receive them.

Hence, it is of greater value if bullish figures reported at mid-month are combined with price that has decreased since the end of the last month and vice versa.

RELIABILITY OF THE COMMITMENT OF TRADER'S REPORT

EXCELLENT - CC, SU, LH, CP, SF, W, ED, OJ, SV

GOOD - LC, GO, HO

POOR - PB, CA, AL, TB, BP, LB

REVERSED -DM, JY, BO

Note that, for the currencies, the Report's figures are backwards as the futures markets act to mirror the commercial's true intentions which are often carried out in the interbank market.

Particularly favored for those wishing more information on The Commitment of Trader's Report is the newsletter The Bullish Review by Steve Briese. Mr. Briese was quite instrumental in lobbying the CFTC to adjust their reporting of the Commitment of Trader's index from once to twice per month which they did in September, 1990.

The advantage of this newsletter is that it creates The Commitment of Trader's Index which varies from -100 % to 100 %. This number allows for easy comparisons and for historical seasonal positioning among the three groups. Hence, what may seem to be a bullish COT Report may not show up quite the same in the Commitment of Trader's Index.

An example is seen in the November 30, 1988 Commitment of Trader's Report that listed the following information;

	Long	Change	Short	Change
Large Traders	5,105	+312	6,895	+313
Commercials	42,946	+1,281	43,212	+285
Small Traders	28,662	-76	26,606	+919

At first glance, there is no apparent imbalance as all groups appeared to be in balance.

The Commitment of Trader's Index, however, rose 2 % to a 100% reading (most bullish). Prices, which had been going down for five straight months, soon reversed and rallied over 200 points in the next 3 weeks. (The reader should note that a buy recommendation was NOT issued in "The Almanac Reports" because, as mentioned earlier, by the time the information had been received in mid-November, prices had already risen. As mentioned earlier, it is important that prices be LOWER than they were at the end of the previous months for high readings (vice versa, of course, for low readings).

If you mention that you are an Almanac purchaser and contact Steve Briese at The Bullish Review, 14600A Blaine Avenue East, Rosemount, MN 55068 (612-423-4949) a free copy will be sent.

Contrary Opinion

When all agree,
in harmony,
it's not too long,
'till they're all wrong.

Early study on the subject of Contrary Opinion was primarily related to the stock market. It was first popularized some 30 years ago by the late Humphrey B. Neill in his biweekly "Letters of Contrary Opinion" that he wrote for more than two decades. In January, 1954, a collection of his writings under the title "The Art of Contrary Thinking" was published (Caxton Printers, Caldwell, ID 89659).

The Odd Lot Theory, formulated by the late Garfield A. Drew about 4 decades ago, was also an early contributor (odd-lotters, who trade less than an even 100 share round lot, represented about 1/8th of NYSE volume back then, however, verses less than 1/2 of 1% now). The subject was further advanced in 1962 when Abraham Cohen quantified stock market sentiment.

In its simplest form, Contrary Opinion seeks to measure the psychology (sentiment) of a market by determining the degree of bullishness or bearishness among participants. This measurement is made by canvassing various analysts, newsletter writers, advisers, and so on in order to arrive at a figure that represents their collective attitude toward the market.

The number is expressed on a scale of 0% to 100% with 0% indicating that there are no bulls and 100% the opposite (all bulls). Ratings above 70% (below 30%) are said to represent markets that are overbought (oversold) and are normally regarded as being significant.

The norm is 55% with extremes at 90% and 20%. Bull markets usually experience ranges of 50% to 80% (20% to 50% in bear markets). Figures can remain at extremes as long as open interest increases steadily.

Generally, a change in weekly direction of 5% is considered significant enough to warrant consideration of a contrarian trade. Such is also the case if contrary opinion is at an extreme and open interest levels off, providing a sign that traders are fully positioned in the direction of the move and that the market is ready for a correction.

Additionally, good (bad) news that fails to move a market up (down) when the consensus is high (low) is an excellent indication of market fatigue (see also the section on "Confirmation and Divergence").

Composition of open interest is important when used to confirm contrarian positions. Since hedgers have effectively removed themselves from both the cash and futures markets, the ideal contrarian position is one opposite to a large number of speculators. For instance, it is particularly bearish if small long speculators and short hedgers and short large traders coincide with a high contrary opinion number.

Interpretation of contrary opinion figures is particularly prone to error in thin markets, disorderly (runaway) markets, and markets with sharply rising open interest levels.

Many rely more on put/call ratios as a better measurement of market sentiment since they can be tabulated daily and measure the way the players are actually positioned with their money (as opposed to their OPINIONS of how SOMEONE ELSE should be positioned).

Which brings us to the two main problems with using contrary opinion, and they are

1.) obtaining an accurate reading of the trading community's actual opinion, and

2.) releasing the sentiment measures on a timely basis without delay.

Perhaps the following expresses the Principle of Contrary Opinion best -

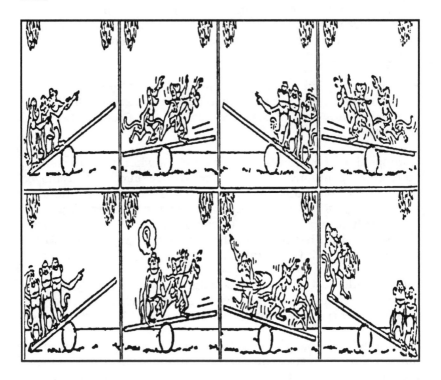

Dual Vertical Bar Trend Indicator

Every trading system makes money -
if you can sell enough copies.
- Jim Welsh

The following trading technique, "The Dual Vertical Bar Trend Indicator", is an easy method for determining trend direction and has been provided courtesy of Kent Calhoun, a commodity trader and system innovator.

Step 1

Buying pressure (BP) and selling pressure (SP) are measured as defined by the following formulas;

$$BP = C - B$$

$$SP = A - D$$

If BP>SP, an uptrend exists that is defined as higher highs and higher lows. The uptrend is said to be confirmed if the market closes up as in the first example.

If BP<SP, a downtrend exists that is defined as lower lows and lower highs. The downtrend is said to be confirmed if the market closes down as in the second example.

If the closing price does not confirm the action of the highs and lows, the uptrend / downtrend is said to be unconfirmed and divergent.

The third diagram shows an unconfirmed divergent uptrend.

The fourth diagram shows an unconfirmed divergent downtrend.

Inside days are treated as nontrending days with unconfirmed price action. An example is shown in the fifth diagram.

Outside days are treated as potentially the best buy and sell days if the outside bar consists of the following;

1.) A wide range,

2.) Heavy volume, and

3.) A close above / below the midrange and the previous day's close.

An example is shown in the last diagram.

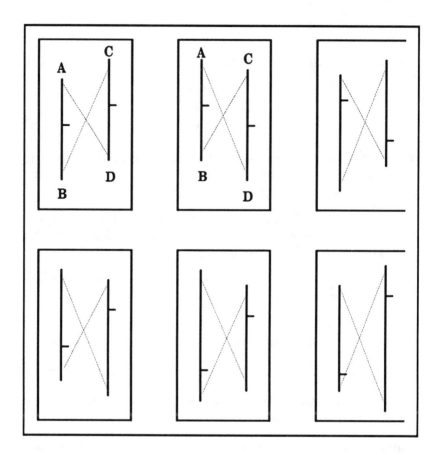

The proper way to use such information is in accordance with a "Tops Down" trading approach.

For instance, the technique can be used on monthly charts to determine long term trend. Weekly charts should be analyzed next. If they confirm the monthly trend, then daily charts should be analyzed for trend confirmation signals.

If one's degree of trading is on a daily basis, signals at this level will determine entry / exit points. Daily charts can further be broken down into hourly, half hourly, 15 minute, and so on time periods. Each of these time periods use the exact same approach and trade in the direction of the major trend on successively smaller and smaller time periods.

Note that if such an approach is used, many potential trades will be eliminated and long periods (several months) may pass when there are no trades at all. An offsetting advantage, however, is that it would be very difficult to experience a major move without this technique capturing a major portion of the move.

As an example, the charts below show monthly, weekly, daily, and hourly prices from the 1990 campaign in June, 1990 US Treasury Bonds.

The reader should note that the monthly trend (down) was in conflict with the weekly periods shown in the charts below. Therefore, no trades would be available using the tops down monthly / weekly / daily / hourly approach. In order to illustrate the concept, however, we will assume that the trader has been trading on a weekly / daily / hourly approach.

Note in the weekly chart, that the "up arrow" at point 1 defines an uptrend for the month of May (which is the time that the weekly data overlaps the daily data and the daily data overlaps the hourly data). These overlaps are as indicated in the appropriate charts.

Since the weekly trend is up, the only time that the weekly data AND the daily data are both up is from 900503 to 900509, from 900510 to 900516, and from 900522 to 900525.

The hourly data only shows prices from 900503 to 900516.

There were thus 12 trades during this period when weekly, daily, and hourly prices "lined up". These 12 trades are summarized below;

BY May 3	8908	SL May 4	9019	$1,375.00	$1,325.00
BY May 3	9023	SL May 3	9021	-62.50	1,262.50
BY May 7	9015	SL May 8	9020	156.25	1,418.75
BY May 8	9025	SL May 9	9020	-156.25	1,262.50
BY May 9	9008	SL May 9	9006	-62.50	1,200.00
BY May 10	9012	SL May 10	9013	31.25	1,231.25

BY May 11 9119	SL May 11 9118	-31.25	1,200.00
BY May 11 9126	SL May 14 9217	718.75	1,918.75
BY May 15 9216	SL May 15 9213	-93.75	1,825.00
BY May 16 9216	SL May 16 9131	-437.50	1,387.50
BY May 16 9206	SL May 16 9207	31.25	1,418.75
BY May 16 9209	SL May 16 9207	-62.50	1,356.25

In summary, the 12 trades resulted in a $ 1,356.25 gross profit though being correct on only 5 of the 12 trades. Notice that the two largest trades were both profitable which is what one would expect when trading in the direction of the major trend.

Fibonacci Numbers

*To those who search,
life reveals its mystery.*

Not far from the Leaning Tower of Pisa, Italy, is a small statue of a thirteenth century mathematician, Leonardo Fibonacci. Fibonacci published three major works, the best known being "Liber Abaci" (having nothing to do with the modern day flamboyant piano player). This work introduced to Europe the Hindu-Arabic number system which you and I use today and which gradually was to replace the older Roman numerals. He also introduced a series of numbers as a solution to a mathematical problem involving the reproduction rates of rabbits (pork bellies weren't trading at the time).

The number series was formed by adding two consecutive prior numbers beginning with 0 and 1 (i.e., 0 + 1 = 1, 1 + 1 = 2, 2 + 1 = 3, 3 + 2 = 5, and so on) giving rise to the sequence 0, 1, 1, 2, 3, 5, 8, 13, 21, 34, 55, 89, 144, 233, 377, 610, 987, and so on. This number series became known as Fibonacci numbers.

The sequence is such that any of the numbers when divided by the next smaller number approaches .618 as the numbers increase and when divided by the preceding number approaches 1.618, giving rise to Fibonacci ratios (i.e., 55/89=.618, 89/55=1.618). Additionally, the ratio between alternate numbers in the sequence approaches 2.618 or its inverse, .382 (i.e., 55/144=.382, 144/55=2.618). Here are some interesting properties of these four ratios (.382, .618, 1.618, and 2.618);

$$2.618 - 1.618 = 1.000$$
$$1.618 - .618 = 1.000$$
$$1.000 - .618 = .382$$

$$2.618 \times .382 = 1.000$$
$$2.618 \times .618 = 1.618$$
$$1.618 \times .618 = 1.000$$
$$.618 \times .618 = .382$$
$$1.618 \times 1.618 = 2.618$$

Now the rabbits were not exactly thrilled at these astounding revelations, nor were most Italians. Nor was anyone else until one Charles J. Collins agreed to help a convalescing accountant by the name of Ralph Nelson Elliott begin his career on Wall Street by introducing him to the editors of Financial World magazine. Elliott spelled out his theory in a series of twelve articles in 1939. In 1946, just two years before his death, Elliott wrote his definitive work on the Wave Principle that bears his name, "Nature's Law - The Secret of the Universe".

The basis for his work was the mathematical relationships defined by the Fibonacci sequence (the Fibonacci numbers).

The ratio 1.618 to 1 is known as the golden ratio, gives rise to the golden spiral, and is found in the universe to such an extent that it still is often referred to as "Nature's Law". Elliott in fact theorized that man's progress throughout history was following a natural law of growth and decay based on the Fibonacci sequence. This growth pattern is believed to follow the Logarithmic Spiral defined by the Fibonacci sequence. It was believed that this spiral not only describes the growth pattern seen throughout the entire Universe as galaxies spiral outwards, but that it also maintains its constant form down to even the smallest elements of nature.

Lucas introduced a sequence similar to Fibonacci numbers (formed by the same process of adding two prior numbers in the sequence) with the exception that the numbers began with the series 1 & 3, giving rise to the sequence 1, 3, 4, 7, 11, 18, 29, 47, 76, 123, 199, 322, 521, 843, and so on. The ratios of these numbers, when compared to each other as in the Fibonacci sequence, also approach the .381, .618, 1.618 and 2.618 ratios.

Harahus combined the two sequences to obtain 1, 2, 3, 4, 5, 7, 8, 13, 18, 21, 29, 34, 47, 55, 76, 89, 123, 144, 199, 233, etc., in order to fill in the gaps left by large Fibonacci numbers.

The numbers are used by market observers in many ways to arrive at market timing decisions.

Some use the pure numbers themselves to project Fibonacci turning points on yearly, monthly, weekly, daily, hourly, or other data sequences.

Others use the ratios of the numbers to overlay market moves and project areas of support or resistance.

Still others use the ratios as a guide to determining retracement levels during market corrections or to project change-in-trend market turning points.

These techniques will be discussed on the next few pages.

Fibonacci Time Projections

*There is one thing stronger
than all the armies in the world,
and that is an idea
whose time has come.*
- Victor Hugo

The Elliott Wave Theory is composed of three parts - wave form, ratio, and our present subject, time.

Some traders base many of their decisions on the forecasting of time periods during which a change in the existing trend in the market is expected. There are two methods of making change-in-trend time projections based on the Fibonacci sequence. The first is Fibonacci cycle counts and the second is Fibonacci ratio time projections.

Fibonacci Cycles

Fibonacci cycle counts are made by counting forward from significant tops and bottoms with the expectation that future tops or bottoms will occur on or around specific Fibonacci time periods (i.e., that the market will change direction on the 13th, 21st, 34th, 55th, 89th, and so on Nth Fibonacci time period from the initial significant top or bottom). The technique is quite simple to use and can be used on yearly, monthly, weekly, daily, hourly, half-hourly, or any other time period charts.

An example follows in the chart below of hourly June, 1990 US Treasury Bond prices.

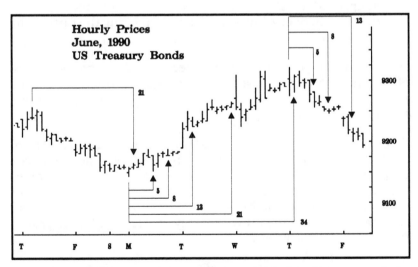

Note that in all cases shown, price unfolded in this example in the manner suggested by the Fibonacci Cycle sequence by experiencing at the very least a minor CIT (Change-In-Trend) that was marked by at least a two-period ringed high or low day occurring exactly on or within one period of the expected CIT day.

(The prevailing trend was the trend that was in effect the few periods prior to the expected CIT projection).

Note that a projected CIT Projection does not forecast whether or not the change will be in either an up or a down direction. Nor does a change from an up to a down projection have to be made from a significant low (or high) point (it can be made from either one).

"The Calendar Book" of The Almanac summarizes major weekly and monthly Fibonacci time cycle counts in the "Monthly Change-In-Trend Projections" section and the "Weekly Change-In-Trend Projections" section.

Monthly CIT Fibonacci Cycles are projected off major five month ringed high and low months.

Weekly CIT Fibonacci Cycles are projected off major ten week ringed high and low months.

The reader should be aware that, since these projections in "The Calendar Book" are static in a dynamic market environment, they become more in need of adjustment and updating the further the year progresses.

Because of the enormity of the project and the dynamic nature of markets, it is not possible to list daily projections in The Almanac. When using such data, one must distinguish between trading and calendar days.

Fibonacci Cycles Change-In-Trend projections for gold have been made in this section beginning with The 1987 Almanac. The projections that were made for each year are listed in the tables that follow. The charts that show how those projections came out are shown at the end of the tabular listings which summarize all the years' projections for the monthly, weekly, and daily projections made for each year.

1987

1987's projections were made off the major highs and lows of January, 1980, June, 1982, February, 1983, February, 1985, and October, 1986. The projections are as follows;

CIT PROJECTION	CYCLE	PROJECTED FROM
NOVEMBER, 1986	21 M	850225 LO
DECEMBER, 1986	55 M	820621 LO
MARCH	5 M	861008 HI
JUNE	8 M	861008 HI
JUNE	89 M	800121 HI
SEPTEMBER	55 M	830215 HI
NOVEMBER	13 M	861008 HI
DECEMBER	34 M	850225 LO
W of 861114	89 W	850225 LO
W of 861212	233 W	820621 LO
W of 870306	21 W	861008 HI
W of 870501	377 W	800121 HI
W of 870605	34 W	861008 HI
W of 870807	233 W	830215 HI
W of 871030	55 W	861008 HI
W of 871204	144 W	850225 LO
870105	89 D	861008 HI
870301	144 D	861008 HI
870529	233 D	861008 HI
870701	1597 D	830215 HI
871020	377 D	861008 HI
871109	987 D	850225 LO

1988

1988's projections were made off the major highs and lows of August, 1976, January, 1980, February, 1983, February, 1985, and December, 1987. The projections are as follows;

CIT PROJECTION	CYCLE	PROJECTED FROM
W of 880506	610W	760825 LO
880104	21D	871214 HI
880117	34D	871214 HI
880205	4181D	760825 LO
880207	55D	871214 HI
880312	89D	871214 HI
880506	144D	871214 HI
880803	233D	871214 HI

1989

1989's projections were made off the major highs and lows of August, 1976, January, 1980, February, 1983, February, 1985, and December, 1987. The projections are as follows;

CIT PROJECTION	CYCLE	PROJECTED FROM
SEPTEMBER	55 M	850225 LO
SEPTEMBER	21 M	871214 HI
W of 890825 (34)	233 W	850225 LO
W of 890825 (34)	89 W	871214 HI
W of 890106 (1)	55 W	871214 HI
890713	1597 D	850225 LO
890816	610 D	871214 HI

1990

1990's projections were made off the major highs and lows of August 25, 1976, January 21, 1980, February 15, 1983, February 25, 1985, December 14, 1987, and June 9, 1989. The projections are as follows;

CIT PROJECTION	CYCLE	PROJECTED FROM
JANUARY	8 M	890609 LO

JULY	89 M	830215 HI
OCTOBER	34 M	871214 HI
W of 900202 (5)	34 W	890609 LO
W of 900511 (19)	377 W	830215 HI
W of 900921 (38)	144 W	871214 HI
900128	144 D	890609 LO
900314	2584 D	830215 HI
900519	987 D	871214 HI

These dates were the most major of CIT Fibonacci Cycle turning point dates projected in each year's Almanac for the gold market. They are, of course, also listed in each year's Calendar Book under the "Monthly Change-In-Trend Projections" and "Weekly Change-In-Trend Projections" sections.

If one were going to use such projections for other markets, one might want to summarize the year's activity in a manner similar to that above.

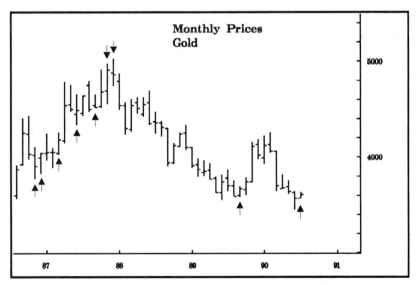

As can be seen in the chart above of monthly gold prices and in the chart that follows of weekly gold prices, the month of September, 1989 was quite important in halting and reversing the 21

month downtrend. In The 1989 Almanac, we wrote on page 298 specifically that " . . . the month of September is very important to this market and, in particular, the 34th week of the year is especially important to the Gold market in 1989 . . .".

This observation, made over nine months prior to the September bottom in this market, was based on the Fibonacci Cycle projection technique explained above.

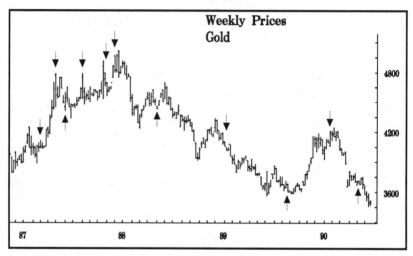

Daily projections are shown in the following charts.

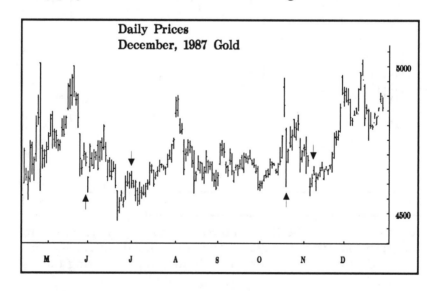

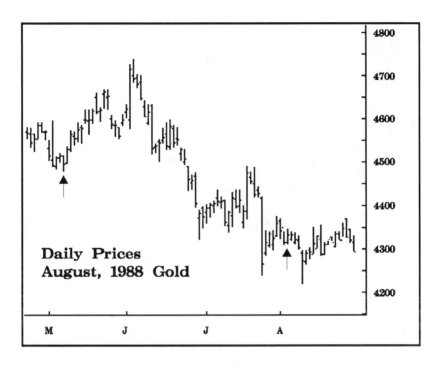

Daily Prices
August, 1988 Gold

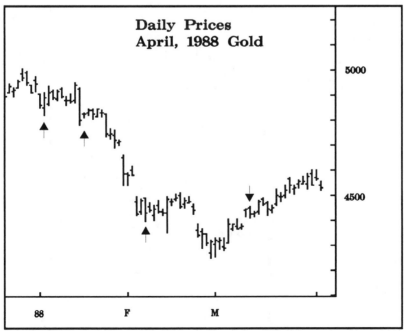

Daily Prices
April, 1988 Gold

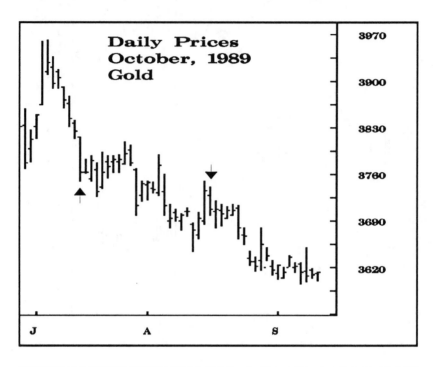

Daily Prices
October, 1989
Gold

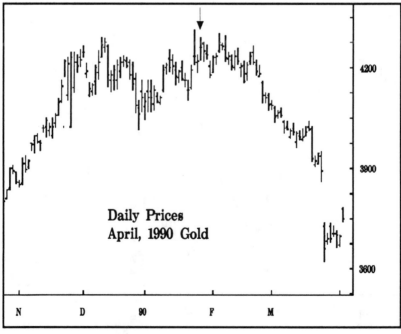

Daily Prices
April, 1990 Gold

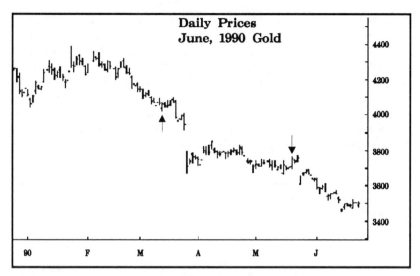

A quick glance at the following chart of monthly US Treasury Bonds prices will show how well this market has been reacting to Fibonacci time cycle Change-In-Trend turning points (the numbers count the number of weeks).

Note that these turning points have been especially important off the 1981 low and the 1986 high.

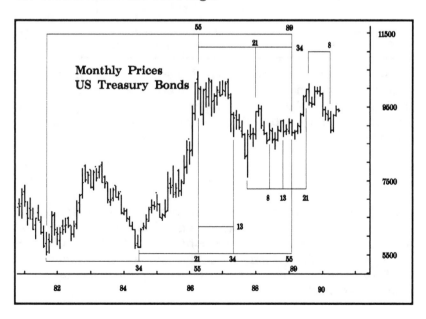

An example from the March 3, 1988 issue of "The Almanac Reports" is shown below in monthly soybean meal prices. The arrow points to the major 21 month Fibonacci time cycle low projected in The 1988 Almanac. Also projected in February were the 31 month and 44 week major linear cycle lows. Hence, the chart shows an example of combining Linear Cycles and Fibonacci time cycles to arrive at a forecast point in time at which trend was expected to change. In this case, a clear Elliott Wave A-B-C correction formed off the December, 1986 highs into the February, 1987 lows.

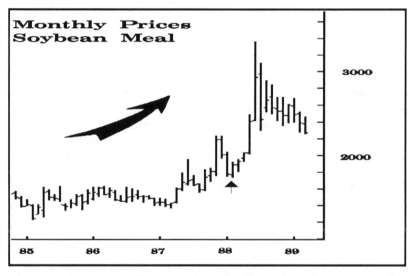

These techniques, when combined, allowed us to write at the time, "In light of the fact that so many cycles were due to bottom in January / February (and appear to have come in right on schedule), it appears that this market is primed for considerable advance."

And as you can see in the chart, CONSIDERABLE WAS the advance!

Another example from the same March 3, 1988 issue of "The Almanac Reports" is shown below in the chart of daily May, 1988 silver prices. Here we combined Fibonacci Time Cycle Change-In-Trend projections from The 1988 Almanac with Linear Time Cycles and Elliott Wave counts to forecast a point in time at which trend was expected to turn.

The Elliott Wave count assumed is as shown. It was assumed that we were in the circled "5th" of 5 waves down and that we were also in the 5th wave of the circled 5th. The wave counts from the March 3, 1988 issue are shown as presented at the time.

Additionally, a 52 week Linear Time Cycle low projected by The 1988 Almanac in the "Weekly Linear Cycles" section was due during that period of time. February 29, 1988 was 91 days since the circled 4th wave high on November 30, 1987 and 144 days from the August 4, 1987 major silver high the preceding year. February was also the 21st month since the major May, 1986 silver low. (Do you also recognize the FND Slammer on February 29, the date of the up arrow?)

With such a confluence of information, we were able to confidently write, "Even though only 3 days have passed since the February 29 lows, I think that there is a good possibility that the 52 week cycle low has been made on that exact date".

Three different entry techniques were used to enter long positions, one of which was the trendline shown in the chart. The pattern recognition technique discussed in the section on pattern recognition was used in this instance to provide a second entry point. The 1-2-3 technique provided the third entry point and, with so many trading techniques suggesting that a turn was at hand, the position was traded with multiple entry techniques, as noted above.

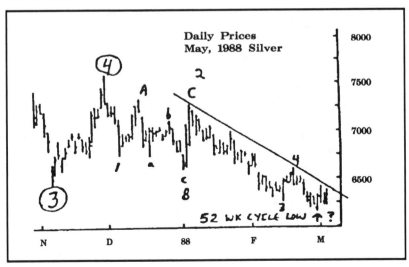

Initial stops on all three positions were just below the February 29 low (the day to which the up arrow is pointing).

We additionally wrote that "The expected move should cover about $ 1.00 to the previous wave 4 high".

As can be seen in the following chart, the observation of the cycle low on February 29, 1988 later proved correct as did the projection that prices would achieve their wave 4 high as represented by the horizontal arrow (it was actually exceeded by about 30 cents).

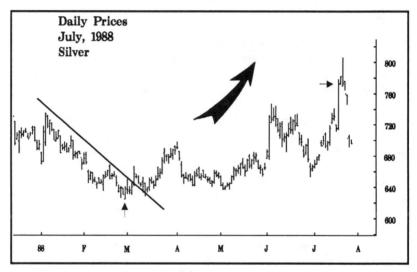

The trendline break used for entry in one of the three positions is also shown in the chart.

Note how absolutely minuscule the risk was as defined by the initial stop in relation to the projected move!!!

These highs would prove to be the highs for the rest of the year for silver prices.

The entire move was worth over $ 15,000!

If you would like to use Fibonacci Cycle projections, you will find the most important weekly and monthly ones listed in the "CIT Projections" section in "The Calendar Book."

Fibonacci Ratios

The second way of making change-in-trend projections by using the Fibonacci number sequence involves the use of the ratios listed in the "Fibonacci and Lucas Numbers" section. Basically, the distance as measured by the number of time periods between two points is determined (be they hours, days, weeks, etc.) and is then multiplied by one of the Fibonacci Ratios. The three most commonly used are the .618 : 1, 1 : 1, and 1.618 : 1 relationships. The resulting product is then added to the original time period to reflect the natural orderly growth process of the Fibonacci sequence as it evinces itself in the markets.

For instance, if the distance between two successive market lows is 20 days, then multiplying by .618 would yield 12 days, by 1 would yield 20 days, and by 1.618 would yield 32 days. These numbers are then added to the original time span that the original move covered (20 days in our example). Hence, on the 32nd (20+12), 40th (20+20), and 52nd (20+32) day from the beginning of the original move, a change in trend would be anticipated.

If the market is moving up into the turning point, one would look for a high to form.

If the high does not form, move to the next change-in-trend projection. (Vice versa, of course, if the market is moving down into the turning point).

Some traders additionally use the .382 and 2.618 projections although such use is not as common.

The Calendar Book projects the .382 : 1, 1 : 1, and 1.618 : 1 ratios for monthly and weekly data. The projections are listed in the "Monthly Change-In-Trend Projections" section and "Weekly Change-In-Trend Projections" section.

Information at the front of the Calendar Book in the "How to Use the CIT Projection Information" explains in detail how to interpret the nomenclature used in the monthly and weekly pages if you would like to use this type information.

Fibonacci time ratio projections can be made from bottom to bottom, from top to top, from top to bottom, or from bottom to top (although some purists will only use the top to top or bottom to bottom relationships). One of the problems in using them, however, is the multitude of possible relationships. These relationships can always be found after the fact, but it is not always clear which of the relationships is relevant to the current trend at any given point in time.

One solution to the above problem is to use two period ringed highs and lows, three period ringed highs and lows, and so on, when defining the points from which projections are made, instead of the more common (and more frustrating) projections off one period ringed highs and lows. (The greater number of periods needed to provide the high / low pivot point, of course, the fewer turning points will be projected).

"The Calendar Book" uses ten period ringed highs and lows for the projections made in the weekly section and five period ringed highs and lows for the projections made in the monthly section.

A second solution that some traders follow is to use only pure Fibonacci numbers in making the ratio projections.

A third solution used by some is to only use the top to top or bottom to bottom projections.

Many traders will start the entire series over again upon penetration of the 89th period (i.e., on the 90th period which, coincidentally, is also 90 degrees from the beginning of the move). Others will switch to Lucas numbers from the 90th period forward.

Additionally, just as time bands are used with Linear Time cycles, some traders use time bands of the exact expected turning point period to provide 10, 5, 3, or 2 percent time bands within which the market is expected to change trend (for both Fibonacci Time Cycles and Fibonacci Ratios).

For instance, in our example above, a five percent time band constructed around the projected 32nd day turning point of the move would add and subtract 1.6 days from the 32nd day in order to construct a likely turning point time zone. This time zone or time band would begin on the 30th day and run through the 34th day with the 32nd day being the center of the time band.

Others will simply add and subtract the day after and the day before the projected turning point period in constructing their most probable turning point time band.

Another technique is to plot on a chart in advance the projected turning point dates and to look for areas in which several projections tend to "cluster" or bunch together.

When using this technique, many traders will, of course, record both Fibonacci Time Cycles and Fibonacci Ratios and may additionally add other change-in-trend turning point projection techniques such as linear time cycle forecasts or astro turning point projections and so on.

Five examples from December, 1987 gold prices have been drawn on the chart below to illustrate the procedure. Note that these ratios project only the 1.618 : 1 Fibonacci Ratio Time Change-In-Trend projections.

An example is provided from the November 10, 1988 issue of "The Almanac Reports" where the reader can note the combination of Linear Cycle analysis, Fibonacci Time Cycle analysis, and Fibonacci Ratio analysis in the weekly Live Hog chart shown below. Note the late 1988 lows predicted by the Linear Cycles and the Change-In-Trend projections from the other two techniques.

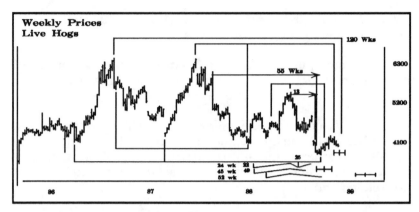

In the following chart, note the result of the time-based CIT projections from the Live Hog chart and how prices exploded out of the projections.

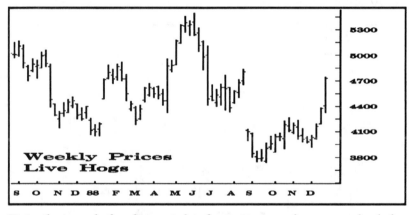

Note that such fundamental information such as supply / demand, etc., was not a determinant in this trade (for it was quite literally IMPOSSIBLE to find anyone saying anything positive about the live hog market at the time)!

By the end of the year, however, prices had increased over 1,000 points! In fact, within two years, prices had moved up over 3,000 points and had almost doubled off their fall, 1988 lows. In fact, those fall lows were STILL not broken over two years later!

If you would like to use time-based Fibonacci Ratios in your analysis of markets, you will find the most important monthly and weekly ratios listed in the "CIT Projections" section of "The Calendar Book."

Fibonacci Price Projections

Wall Street's graveyards
are filled with men
who were right
too soon.
- William Hamilton

Fibonacci ratios are used to establish price objectives in the direction of the trend and to establish market entry points during market corrections. Price projections are created by determining the difference in two prices and multiplying by one of the ratios (1.618, 2.000, 2.618, or 3.326 (which is 2 X 1.618)) in order to obtain price projections.

(Fibonacci price projections should not be confused with the Fibonacci ratios (.382, .500, and .618) applied to percent retracement during counter-trend market corrections).

The price projections are especially useful when combined with Elliott Wave analysis. As an example, were gold to rally from $410 to $ 420, the difference of $ 10.00 multiplied by 1.618 would provide an expected move of $ 16.18 for the next wave. When added to the top of the previous wave ($ 420), a target of $ 436.18 would be established as the next expected resistance point. If the $ 10.00 move above were the first of three expected Elliott impulse waves, the $ 436.18 would be the projection for the second impulse wave (third Elliott Wave) and 2.618 X $ 10.00 + $ 420.00 = $ 446.18 would provide a (but not the only) price objective for the entire five wave move or for the third wave were the third wave to extend.

Fibonacci fan lines are drawn in the same manner as speedlines except the lines are drawn through the .618, .500, and .382 retracement levels along the vertical line that measures the impulse wave. They are usually used with Fibonacci arcs which incorporate time in the projection process.

The example below of weekly gold prices shows a Fibonacci Fan drawn off the December 14, 1987 high and point 1 (in the case of the lower three lines). The reader can easily ascertain the importance of these fan lines to the gold market through mid-1990.

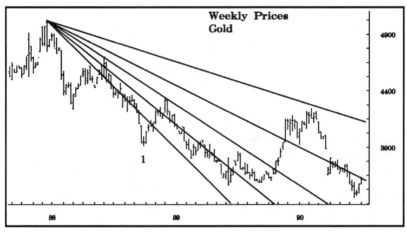

In the following example of 5 minute March, 1989 S & P 500 prices, the distance from the beginning of the move to point "1" was multiplied X 1.618 to obtain the objective at point "2". Point "2" marked the end of the third Elliott Wave for the move. The entire move ended with the wave 5 distance (as marked by the "3") equal to the distance from wave 1 to the top of wave 3. Point "4" marks a 50 % retracement of the entire five wave move. Note how well this 50 % retracement level supported prices.

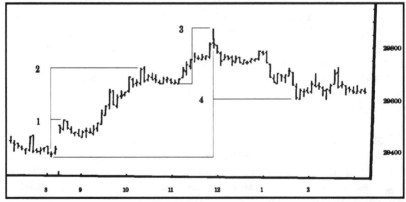

In the chart below of monthly US Treasury Bond prices, note how the .618 retracement levels of each successive previous leg provided an excellent reversal entry price objective over the 4-plus years through late 1988 as noted in The 1989 Almanac. Note, too, how each successive retracement contracted and how US Treasury Bond prices were coiled for an extended breakout move. The 1989 Almanac was thus able to observe that this successive contraction indicated the period of coiling was about over and that a large price move would soon be experienced. We also wrote that Fibonacci Time Cycles would suggest that whichever way price first breaks out early in the year, it would be reversed in February.

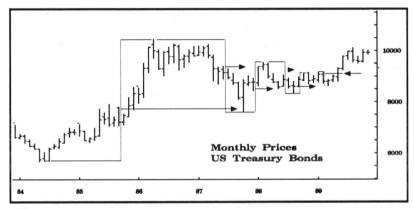

Monthly Prices
US Treasury Bonds

One can see that the initial January thrust was rerouted in February. The extended upmove that then began after the March cyclical lows covered about 15 points over the next five months.

Elliott Wave Patterns

The only success we have is profit.
- Rex Beach

As mentioned previously, the Elliott Wave Theory is comprised of three parts;

1. wave form,

2. ratio, and

3. time.

This section discusses the third part which is wave form or patterns of the Elliott Wave. The theory states that markets follow a basic eight wave pattern of five advancing and three correcting waves per complete cycle. The five advancing waves are labeled 1 through 5 while the three corrective waves are labeled A, B, and C.

Waves 1, 3, and 5 are impulse waves - in the direction of the trend (indeed, they DEFINE the trend) - while waves 2 and 4 are corrective waves, correcting the advancing waves 1 and 3. After the entire 5 wave advance is completed, a 3 wave A, B, C correction begins. The following chart shows the basic wave form.

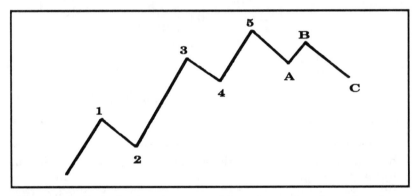

Elliott categorized nine degrees of trend ranging from two hundred years to only a few hours and found that the basic 8 wave cycle form remains constant regardless of what degree of trend is being studied. In a manner similar to our discussion of a "tops down" trading approach, each wave subdivides into smaller waves of lesser degree and is itself part of a larger wave of the next higher degree.

Some of the more basic tenants that the Wave Theory holds are that, in a 5 wave advance, one of the 3 impulse waves (usually the 3rd) will extend (or be much larger than the other 2 waves), that a market will never correct in 5 waves, that triangles will normally occur in the 4th wave, and that the 4th wave of next lower degree will usually contain the corrective process that occurs if the move is to expand.

These relationships can be seen in the chart. Note that impulse wave 3 is longer than waves 1 or 5 (i.e., is extended), that the

A-B-C correction is in the form of three waves (not 5), and that the end of the correction at the bottom of wave C coincides roughly with the bottom of wave 4.

As mentioned earlier, the Fibonacci series forms the mathematical basis for the relationship of the various waves to each other and for the entire Wave Theory itself.

The Wave was originally developed to explain aggregate decisions made in the stock market (and, therefore, to reflect man's aggregate behavior and economic progress). Several of the basic Elliott Wave assumptions do not seem to be reflected in the commodity markets, however, making the entire basic assumption of the Wave questionable (i.e., that it is truly reflective of the Natural Order and unwinding of the Universe).

In the mid-1980s Almanacs, we wrote that the alternative to the above statement was that, if the Wave Principle IS valid in the commodity markets, we may be facing some rather explosive price moves in the next few years as the bottoms of the 4th wave from the 1932-34 lows appear to be in place in many commodities (there are also other possible interpretations of current long term wave structure, of course).

The chart that follows of monthly soybean prices which is reprinted from previous Almanacs best illustrates this long term interpretation. The same basic pattern can be found in several other commodity markets.

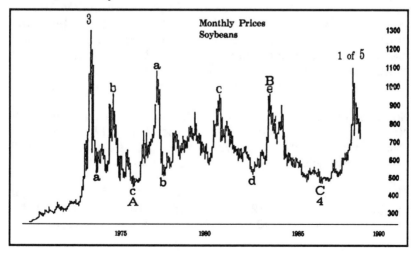

Let's explore, however, some reasons why the Wave Principle may just not apply or often seems irrelevant to the futures markets.

First, only a few thousand participants may be in any one contract or market at any one time as opposed to the stock market indices (which is where the Elliott Wave Theory has enjoyed its most pronounced success). In the stock market, AGGREGATE human behavior is better reflected (indeed, some have even stated that the Elliott Wave is ineffective on individual stocks).

Second, the unbreakable rule in stocks that the fourth wave should not overlap the first wave often occurs in futures (it is argued that one should therefore use cash markets to properly gain Elliott perspective on commodity markets, but have you ever tried to get hourly charts on Robusta Coffee or Number 1 Yellow Soybeans?).

Perhaps the most significant difference, however, is the observation that major bull markets in futures can be "contained", meaning that bull market highs do not always exceed previous bull market highs. This occurrence has been quite frequent within the futures markets in the last fifteen years.

Granted IT IS VERY POSSIBLE that the futures markets have been in a major 4th wave correction of major long term upward movements OR HAVE JUST RECENTLY COMPLETED THAT CORRECTION, as mentioned above. If so, these corrections have a high probability of having ended within 1 year of 1987 since, as noted earlier, the time portion of the theory makes 1987 a potential change-in-trend year for many markets (1987 being the 55th year off the major 1932 bear market lows for stocks and many futures markets, 1988 being the 55th year off major 1933 market lows for other futures, and 1989 being the 55th year off the major market lows of others still that bottomed in 1934).

Noteworthy among the above is the stock market. The 1987 change-in-trend projection given by the 55 year Fibonacci Time Cycle combined with Elliott Wave analysis is as classic as we will probably experience in our lifetime in any market.

This interpretation places the beginning of the five wave stock market move at the 1932 lows, the end of the third wave at the 1966 highs above 1,000 in the Dow Jones Industrials, and the end of the 4th wave at the 1974 recession lows (when the very survival of capitalism itself was pondered). Note that this low occurred eight years after the 3rd wave 1966 high, that the 3rd wave high occurred thirty-four years after the move began, and that the 1982 beginning of the upward acceleration began eight years after the 1974 4th wave low. The entire five year bull market from 1982 to 1987 was equal in time to the first wave of the bull market which lasted from 1932 to 1937.

The 1987 top occurred fifty-five years off the 1932 low, twenty-one years off the 1966 3rd wave high, thirteen years off the 1974 4th wave low, and five years off the 1982 low.

Additionally, Gannophiles will concur that 1987 was 90 years from the 1897 April 19th and April 23rd lows at 38.49 !!!

If this peaking in 1987 does indeed prove to be the correct interpretation (and subsequent action in such indexes as The Dow Jones Industrials Averages have stretched the credibility of this outlook), then the major 1987 PEAKING in stocks would fit quite well with the major 1986 to 1988 BOTTOMING in several other markets such as industrial metals, energy, grains, beans, and so on.

Also supporting this possibility are the bottomings of several major linear time cycles in such things as Soybeans, Corn, Wheat, Cotton, Copper, etc., in the last few years, as reviewed, projected, and updated in the last several Almanacs.

If the end of the 4th wave correction that began in 1973 in Soybeans, for instance, did indeed end in September, 1986, then that correction lasted 13 years, which is exactly what would be expected by Fibonacci Time Cycle adherents.

The bottoming of this 4th wave along with the bottoming of the 9 and 27 year linear time cycles projected in The 1986 Almanac for September, 1986, occurred EXACTLY when it should have occurred. Such would thus support the argument that we are and have been since 1986 in the throes of a multi-year markup stage in beans.

Similar analysis applies to other markets.

The assumed Elliott Wave 4th wave correction in monthly soybean prices is shown in the preceding chart from the assumed peak of the 3rd wave in 1973 that completed the advance from the 1930s to the 1986 assumed 4th wave low.

The Elliott Wave count was the preferred wave count at the time of our writing of The 1989 Almanac. Subsequent price action has forced an alternative outlook to label the entire move up from the 1986 low to the 1988 high as the first of an assumed five wave upmove to follow. Such an interpretation suggests that, if correct, price action since the 1988 high has been a 2nd corrective wave.

One reason why this outlook is plausible is because it is the same basic outlook that we have discussed in all previous Almanacs. It is so far following that general script. If you purchased The 1986 Almanac, you may recall that we assumed that such an increase, should it become reality, would BEGIN with a devaluing dollar in the face of onerous supplies. Such is EXACTLY how this major advance began!

This anticipated price movement is additionally supported by our weather-related projections into the mid-1990s as discussed elsewhere in this book. Such a scenario would, in fact, fit quite well with the well-publicized Elliott Wave interpretation of the stock market where the 5th and final wave since the 1932 lows is assumed to have now been completed or else is close to topping. In fact, it would be quite plausible for the stock market to be experiencing a declining phase as the commodity markets begin their long term advance to their final fifth wave tops off those same 1930s lows.

As we wrote in earlier Almanacs, "If this scenario is to occur, it will probably be initiated by monetary inflation (a currency that becomes less valuable to hold) and will culminate with true shortages as the 1990s evolve".

Since developing this scenario in the mid-1980s, we feel that the outlook is and has been in progress and is on track.

The unexpected opening up of Eastern European markets has added another factor boosting the demand side of the equation in the early 1990s.

The other alternative, of course, as mentioned at the beginning of this section, is that the importance of the Wave Principle simply is not as large in the commodity markets as a true Law of Nature would suggest it should be (I've probably just lost half my subscribers with that statement).

To summarize, the understanding of Wave structure and Fibonacci relationships can, at times, be an invaluable aid in analyzing markets. One should therefore definitely know how to recognize and use wave patterns and apply the principles of Elliott Wave analysis when the market is acting in accordance with those principles.

But if you find yourself having to connect "a-b-c"'s and insert "x" waves over and over again in what seems to be an unending "corrective pattern", then there is no use in trying to force Wave analysis.

In some market situations it just does not seem to fit or the wave form does not become clear until well AFTER the move has occurred. So if you find yourself confused, then turn to other forms of analysis, try other markets, or analyze the wave form and trade the market on a different level of degree.

In the chart below of monthly GO prices, updated from The 1989 Almanac, the count implies much more down movement in prices. Since the assumed next wave is assumed to be a "C" wave, it should break down into 5 waves and accelerate the downward movement if it is to occur.

A bullish alternative is that the "C" component of the "B" wave that lasted from 1985 to 1987 was actually a "1" wave up which puts us now in the "2" corrective wave.

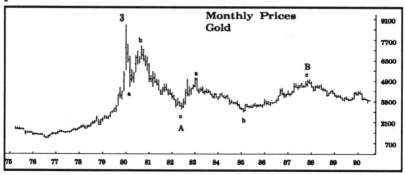

Elliott Wave Guidelines

*If you are scared
to go to the brink,
then you are lost.*
- John Foster Dulles

(Rules given are for bull markets and
apply in reverse to bear markets)

1. Expect Elliott Wave reversals to be made inside linear cycle time bands (use time cycles for market orientation and to confirm wave counts).

2. The 3rd wave should not be the smallest of the impulse waves in a primary move. If it is, you need to recount (reconsider your analysis). (The 3rd wave CAN, however, be smaller than either the 1st OR the 5th wave, although this is a rare event).

3. Primary waves occur in waves of five and nine. Corrective waves occur in waves of three and seven. Hence, if you cannot quite determine the count, look for moves of seven or nine waves.

4. During a primary five wave move, two of the waves will usually be about equal in length and one of the waves will extend. Hence, if you are observing a market that has extended in the third wave and the third wave is much longer than the 1st wave, the 5th wave is likely to be equal in length to the 1st wave. Such a relationship is shown at the beginning of the "Elliott Wave Patterns" section. Likewise, if waves 1 and 3 are equal, expect wave 5 to extend.

5. A wave 4 "e" wave of a triangle or a "c" wave of a double three corrective wave is normally an especially good, low risk entry point, particularly if the 1st and 3rd waves have not extended and are equal in length.

6. If the 2nd of five waves is a simple "abc" correction, expect a complex 4th wave correction and vice-versa (Rule of Alternation).

7. One way to enter the beginning of a possible 3rd wave or to add to existing positions is on a break of the trend line connecting the first wave peak with the "b" wave peak. Stop the position under the assumed beginning of wave 1 OR the low of wave 2 depending on your risk tolerance.

8. A five-count diagonal triangle that forms an ascending wedge and itself forms the 5th of five waves provides an excellent entry point at the break of the lower trend line of the 5th wave. Minimum objective is the 4th wave. (See rule 11)

9. A contracting triangle in an assumed 2nd or 4th wave provides an excellent entry opportunity for entry in the direction of the primary wave upon a break of the upper trendline and in the direction of the primary thrust.

10. With the exception of a diagonal triangle, the 4th wave of a primary five-wave movement should not overlap the 1st wave. If it does, then you need to recount. (Thus, if you think you are in a 4th wave correction, an especially good time to enter the market is just above your assumed 1st wave peak with a stop just below the 1st wave peak).

11. Upon completion of a five wave advance, the ensuing correction will usually carry no lower than the 4th wave of the next lower degree. (Hence, place orders to reenter the market just above the bottom of the 4th wave with close stops). (See rule 5)

12. Volume should increase in waves 1, 3, and 5 and decrease in waves 2 and 4. It is also likely that volume would decrease throughout the corrective wave.

13. If you are in a 5th wave that has experienced an increasing open interest and open interest suddenly levels off as prices advance, be prepared to exit the market.

14. Breakaway and midway gaps, panic market entry, limit days, etc., normally will occur in the 3rd wave and be supported by an expansion of volume.

15. If you are expecting a corrective "b" wave and it has 5 waves in it, you either need to recount or you have just finished only the "a" portion of what will likely be at least an "abc" corrective "b" wave.

16. When using Elliott Wave analysis, use a "tops down" approach by analyzing the wave of next higher degree for the major trend direction and the wave of next lower degree to confirm market timing decisions. (For example, if trading daily charts, analyze weekly charts for major trend direction. Then, if looking for the completion of a 2nd or 4th wave to provide an entry point, go to hourly charts (if you have access to them) and look for a "c" wave consisting of five waves that terminates the corrective process to provide that entry point.

17. When in doubt about the count of a particular wave, try to analyze the structure in the next lower degree to resolve the count.

18. If your correction has 5 waves, you need to relabel or recount as only primary waves can have 5 waves. Usually, if a correction has 5 waves, it is the "a" or "c" wave of an "a-b-c" correction known as a 5-3-5 zig-zag. At the end of the "a" wave, you thus know that two more corrective waves at least are yet to come.

19. If you can identify the "b" wave of a flat correction, either through volume or open interest analysis, symmetry, rule of alternation, or whatever, then you can take the appropriate action and sell short the "b" wave top (or buy the "b" wave bottom) with the expectation of a move at least back to the start of the "b" wave.

20. The second wave often provides an excellent entry point at the 1 X 1 or the 1 X 2 Gann Angle lines drawn from the bottom of the 1st wave.

21. If you are unable to discern a probable pattern, do not force a pattern on the market. Let the market show you what the pattern is.

22. If intraperiod prices (those that have an open, high, low, and close) are inconclusive, connect the closing prices only. Sometimes, this procedure clarifies the wave count.

Elliott Wave Channeling Techniques

We cannot discover new oceans
unless we have
the courage
to lose sight of the shore.

The following discussion assumes that a bottom is in place and that an upward channel is in the process of forming. (Reverse the process, of course, for a market top.)

1. After the 2nd wave is completed, draw a line off the top of the 1st wave parallel to the line connecting the bottom of the 1st and 2nd waves.

2. Draw the 1 X 1 and 2 X 1 Gann Angle lines upward to the right from the top of the first wave.

3. Expect resistance at the end of the 3rd wave at one of these angle lines upon completion of five waves of the next lower degree.

4. Upon completion of wave 4, draw the steeper line from the bottom of wave 2 to the bottom of wave 4 or the bottom of wave 1 to the bottom of wave 4.

5. Draw two parallel lines (one off the top of wave 3 and one off the top of wave 1) parallel to the line you just drew in # 4 above.

6. Draw the 1 X 1 and 2 X 1 Gann Angle lines upward and to the right from the top of the 3rd wave.

7. Look for resistance after a five wave move around the nearest upper channel line that has been drawn as suggested in the guidelines above.

Gann Techniques

. . . when we have knowledge
of the Divine Law
of supply and demand
and know how to draw upon
the universal laws which supply
all our desires,
then we are free from fear and worry.
Therefore . . . seek the truth,
the Divine Law . . .
find it and be free.
- W. D. Gann

William D. Gann (1878-1955) was a legendary stock and commodities trader who developed a unique combination of precise
mathematical and geometric principles which he applied to his
trading.

He placed tremendous importance on historic highs and lows as
future resistance and support areas (thus the reason that you
will find historic high and low exchange prices in this publication). He stressed that a broken support level would become
resistance and that a broken resistance level would become
support, was a firm believer in the 50 percent retracement, and
felt that anniversary dates, especially one year forward of a
prominent top or bottom, were especially potent time targets
(thus the reason so many anniversary dates are listed throughout
the pages of "The Calendar Book").

The 360 degrees that make up a circle were equated to the days
of the year giving rise to the Gann Year which began on March
20th at 0 degrees next to the first day of spring. The circle was
divided into halves (180 degrees or 26 weeks), quarters (90
degrees or 13 weeks), sixths (60 degrees or 60 days), eighths (45
degrees or 45 days), 12ths (30 degrees or 30 days), and 16ths (22
1/2 degrees or 22 1/2 days). May 6th represented 45 degrees,
June 21st - 90 degrees, September 23rd - 180 degrees, December
21st - 270 degrees, and so on. (These dates are, of course, listed
in "The Calendar Book" as they occur). Since these dates were

natural harmonics of the 360 degree circle, they were thus said to represent especially important potential turning dates during the year.

They also reflect the important astronomical relationships of 30 degrees (semi-sextile), 60 degrees (sextile), 90 degrees (square), 120 degrees (trine), 180 degrees (opposition), 270 degrees (square), and 360 degrees (conjunction).

Combining time and price and the proportional relationships between the two was the basis for much of Gann's work. He projected tops and bottoms based on his method of squaring price and time and natural divisions thereof (i.e., when one unit of price equals one unit of time and its harmonic divisions). He would do this by taking a prominent high or low in a market, converting that figure into a calendar unit (days, weeks, months, or years), and projecting that time period forward.

For instance, if a record high had been established in a market at $ 100.00, Gann would count forward 100, 200, 300 and so on time periods to identify potential turning points. At these points, time and price were said to be squared.

Gann Numbers

*If you really do
put a small value upon yourself,
rest assured that the world
will not raise the price.*

Gann used several numbers in his work, but the number 7 and its multiples had special significance due to its repetitive use in the Bible. Hence, he would look for markets to make top or bottom on the 7th day, week, month, or year or on time periods ending with a 7 (the 17th, etc., time period).

The 49th time period was especially significant (square of 7) and was believed to be critical to trend continuation (the 49th day, week, month, year, etc.) as was the 77th ("The Calendar Book" thus lists the 49th and 77th week and month from significant market tops and bottoms on the right page of the calendar weeks in the "CIT Projections" section under "Gann").

Gann also looked for market turns on the important harmonics of the circle and would thus count forward from significant tops and bottoms by 30, 45, 60, 90, 120, 135, 150, 180, 210, 225, 240, 270, 300, 315, 330 and 360 days, weeks, months, or years and multiples of those numbers. ("The Calendar Book" of the Almanac thus lists these weekly and monthly turning point projections on the right page of the calendar weeks in the "CIT Projections" section under "Gann").

Twelve and its factors were also important numbers (12 houses in the Zodiac, 12 signs, 12 months in a year, 2 X 12 = 24 hours, 5 X 12 = 60 (sextile), 10 X 12 = 120 (trine), 12 X 12 = 144 (a Fibonacci number), 15 X 12 = 180 (opposition), 30 X 12 = 360 (conjunction), and so on.

As an example, examine the weekly chart of S & P 500 prices below. This chart was presented in The 1989 Almanac. The arrows mark projected Gann Cycle turning points obtained by counting forward from the August 25, 1987 high and the October 20, 1987 low. The down arrows on top above prices are associated with the August high while the up arrows on bottom below prices are associated with the October low.

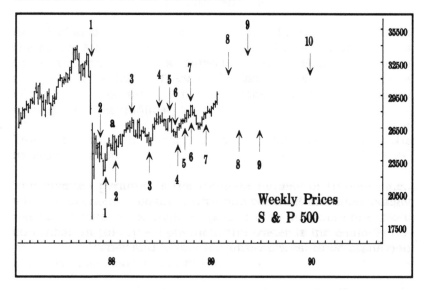

NOTE IN BOTH CASES THAT 6 OF THE 7 PROJECTED TURNING POINTS WERE EXACTLY ON OR WITHIN 1 PERIOD OF A PIVOT POINT!

Points 2, 3, 4, 5, and 6 on top marked major trend reversals that were definitely tradeable on an intermediate term basis.

Points 1, 2, 3, 4, and 6 (and, arguably, 7) on bottom marked major trend reversals that were definitely tradeable on an intermediate term basis.

The point market "a" in early 1988 was 180 weeks from the July 25, 1984 major stock market low and WAS marked as such on page 35 of The 1988 Almanac (just as other important Gann CIT cycle projections are listed on the right page of each year's "Calendar Book").

The numbers below correspond to those in the chart and represent the number of weeks from the 1987 pivot point;

Number	Weeks	Number	Weeks
1	7	6	52
2	12	7	60
3	30	8	77
4	45	9	90
5	49	10	120

The latter points in both groups projected turning points in 1989. Points 8, 9, and 10 on top projected turning points for the weeks ending 890217, 890519, & 891215. Points 9 and 10 on bottom projected turning points for the weeks ending 890414 & 890714.

Three of the five projected turning points occurred on or within one period of a significant high or low point!

It should be noted when doing this type analysis that the 90th period is especially significant as it is also quite close to the Fibonacci 89th period.

Also, the 144th period is the most powerful number of all being common to the Fibonacci Series, Gann, and the square of 12.

One could, of course, do the same type analysis from other major turning points in the stock market (for instance, the major 1984 low, the major 1982 low, the major 1974 low, and so on) in order to gain the benefit of Gann weekly Change-In-Trend (CIT) projections.

One could also, of course, do the same type analysis on other markets in order to gain the benefit of Gann weekly CIT projections.

And, when finished, one could then perform the same type analysis for all those markets and for all those major turning points on a MONTHLY basis in order to gain the benefit of MONTHLY Gann CIT projections.

But an easier way to obtain such information is to simply look in "The Calendar Book" of The Almanac where it is listed under "Gann" for each of the weeks and months of the year in the "Monthly Change-In-Trend Projections" and "Weekly Change-In-Trend Projections" sections.

A close examination of the weekly chart above and the indicated turning points should help explain why many traders find this information to be quite valuable!

Gann Lines

For forty years
I have studied and improved my methods.
I am still learning
and hope for greater discoveries
in the future.
- W D Gann

Gann would divide a market advance into 8ths and 3rds in order to estimate future support / resistance during market corrections / advances. He would then draw horizontal lines on his charts representing these retracement levels between the beginning of a market advance and the highest point the advance had achieved. The levels are noted below -

1/8	=	12.5 %
2/8	=	25.0 %
1/3	=	33.3 %
3/8	=	37.5 %
4/8	=	50.0 %
5/8	=	62.5 %
2/3	=	67.7 %
6/8	=	75.0 %
7/8	=	87.5 %
8/8	=	100.0 %

The 50 percent retracement was the most important with the next two in order of importance being the 37.5 % and the 62.5 % retracements. Each level was expected to provide support / resistance and, if broken, the next level of support / resistance would be the next line down (up).

The example below extends the analysis on the weekly S & P 500 Index.

This chart has been created by dividing the price drop from the August 25, 1987 high to the October 20, 1987 low into 1/8ths.

Note the support and resistance that the market experienced at the various levels as indicated by the numbers in the chart.

The 50 % retracement level is shown by line "A - A" in the chart.

Note how this retracement level stopped cold the initial upward thrust in late October, 1987 (point 1 in the chart).

Other important support / resistance levels are indicated by numbers 1 through 13 with 1, 2, 4, 5, 6, & 9 being virtual exact hits!

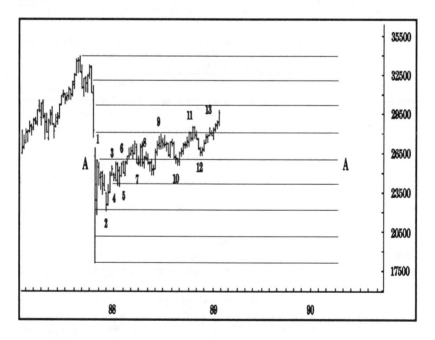

Gann Angles

The average man or woman nearly always
wants to buy low and sell high . . .
The farmer always wants to sell
what he produces at high prices and
wants to buy what he needs at low prices.
The laboring man wants high wages all the time and
low prices for what he buys to eat and wear.
This is a violation of a fundamental economic law
and it just will not work.
To make a success in speculation
you cannot expect to buy low and sell high.
You will make money when you do just the opposite
of what the average man or woman tries to do
and makes a failure and loses as a result
of what they are trying to do.
You will make profits when you learn
to buy high and sell low.
You must follow the trend in progress.
- W D Gann

Gann's geometric angles are trendlines drawn from prominent tops or bottoms at certain specific angles which represent the relationship between price and time.

One of Gann's most important theories was that, when price meets time, change is imminent. The angle line representing price and time in balance (and, hence, the most important angle line on a chart), is the 45 degree line.

In an uptrend, that line is drawn upward to the right from a market low. In a downtrend, it is drawn down to the right from a market high. On this line, one unit of price equals one unit of time. Price penetration of this line usually indicates a major trend reversal.

The next most important angle line is the 2 X 1 and the 1 X 2 followed by the 4 X 1 and the 1 X 4 and then the 8 X 1 and the 1 X 8.

The 3 X 1 and 1 X 3 were generally used on weekly and monthly charts.

The table below lists the various angle lines in descending order with their degree equivalents (read as time X price where 0 degrees = horizontal and 90 degrees = vertical).

1 X 8	=	82.50 degrees	a
1 X 4	=	75.00 degrees	b
1 X 3	=	71.25 degrees	
1 X 2	=	63.75 degrees	c
1 X 1	=	45.00 degrees	d
2 X 1	=	26.25 degrees	e
3 X 1	=	18.75 degrees	
4 X 1	=	15.00 degrees	f
8 X 1	=	7.50 degrees	g

The letters correspond with the Gann Angles drawn in the chart below which continues the weekly SP example.

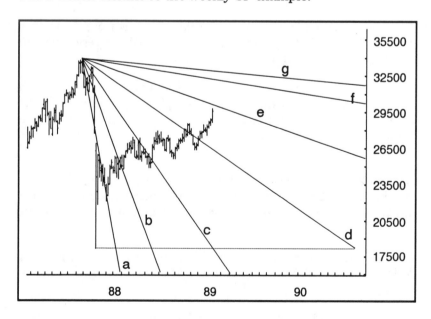

Note that a 1 X 8 or 82.50 degree line can be easily drawn on a chart by moving 1 unit of time to the right and 8 units up if the line is being drawn off a major low (move down, of course, if drawing from a major high). Other Gann Angles can then be drawn in similar manner.

Were these angles important to S & P 500 prices? A number of instances can be found to indicate that they certainly were!

For example, note how, after the initial bounce up to the 50 % retracement level, price then proceeded to follow line "a" (the 1 X 8) down into December.

Note how, when price finally broke the grip that line "a" had on the S & P 500 Index, that the rally carried EXACTLY to line "b" (see point 1 in the chart) from which a correction ensued.

Note, when price finally penetrated line "b" (the 1 X 4), how line "b" (which previously had provided resistance) SUPPORTED price (see point 2 in the chart).

Note that the ensuing rally carried EXACTLY to the next line, line "c" (the 1 X 2), from which a correction ensued (see point 3 in the chart).

Note, when price finally penetrated line "c" (see point 4 in the chart) how it moved up to the next resistance line which is "d" on the chart (the 1 X 1 or 45 degree).

Note how price initially resisted further rise EXACTLY at point 5 but that the resistance was only strong enough to last for 1 week.

After a brief correction, note how price accelerated upon penetration (see point 6 in the chart).

As you can probably gather from the above, when price penetrates one of these lines, it is said to be likely to continue its move to the next line of support / resistance.

When price is moving rapidly upwards (downwards), it has gotten ahead of time and an imbalance exists that will normally be corrected by price either dropping or time advancing (or both) until they again approach the 45 degree angle line.

Note that such is exactly what happened since the 1987 stock market decline! Price moved from the October, 1987 lows back to the 45 degree line from the top over the next 16 months.

Often several such Gann Fans are drawn off several major high / low points for analysis. In our weekly chart of the S & P 500, it would obviously make sense to draw such a fan in an upward direction off the low point on October 20, 1987.

When angle lines drawn off different points cross, the "cradle" that they create provides especially strong support or resistance.

Finally, the point at which the 1 X 1 meets with the horizontal drawn from the top or bottom of the move is said to provide an important turning date. In our chart above, this point would be where line "d" (the 1 X 1 or 45 degree) crosses the dotted horizontal line drawn off the October 20, 1987 low point @ 181.00.

Since the drop in the S & P 500 futures market covered 342.35 - 181.00 = 161.35 points, the point in the future where these two lines cross should be 161 weeks from the August 25, 1987 high (although some do plot this off the low price).

At this point, time and price are equal and are said to be "squared".

HOW TO USE - The above techniques are best applied when used in combination with each other. Once an important market move has occurred, the entire price range can be divided into eighths and the appropriate Gann lines drawn. The 2 X 1, 1 X 1, and 1 X 2 angle lines should then be drawn from significant tops and bottoms. The user then looks for coincidence or confirmation between the two methods when prices move to both a prominent angle line and a significant retracement line.

The examples that follow continue the S & P 500 example and show the squaring of price and time for S & P 500 weekly prices for the price decline from the August 25, 1987 high to the October 20, 1987 low.

The prices used for this example were both from the December, 1987 futures contract which was the nearest future at the time. The high price was 342.35 and the low price was 181.00 leaving a difference of 161.35 points.

As mentioned above, since this decline covered a little over 161 points, a properly drawn scale of 1 point = 1 week would result in price and time being squared 161 weeks later (specifically, during the week of 900928).

(Note that it is not possible on the quotation equipment being used in this example to draw such a line and that the scale being used is roughly 1.53 : 1).

Many practitioners draw a 45 degree angle to a chart on a "best fit" basis. In other words, if the service they are following is using a 1.53 : 1 scale in presenting weekly prices as in our example, they simply draw a 45 degree angle on the chart and naively call this line the point at which time and price are squared.

Such a 45 degree line drawn in such a manner is shown in the chart on the following page by the dotted line connecting the August 25, 1987 high and point "Z".

Note that, since this line intersects the horizontal line drawn off the October 20, 1987 market low at point "Z", it indicates that time and price have travelled equal amounts or are "squared" at this point. Such is obviously not the case, however, as the 161 point decline is not squared when equal to the 99 weeks (or so) traversed in time.

Nevertheless, I have spoken with many Gann practitioners who have used and continue to use Gann charts constructed on chart scales that are other than of a "purist" interpretation. These people apply their angles on a "best fit, eyeball" method and have apparently found the approach to be quite successful!

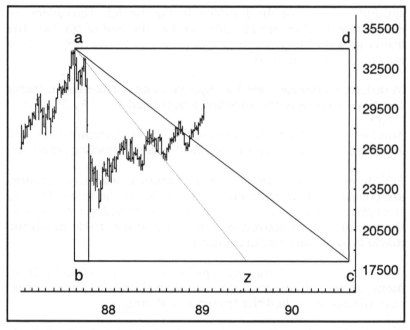

For the rest of our discussion, however, we shall use the "purist" approach (i.e., 1 unit of price = 1 unit of time).

Note in this chart that, since the high and the low are known, that the 2 horizontal lines ("a - d" and "b - c") can easily be drawn. Since the beginning of the move is also known, a vertical line ("a - b") can be drawn through this point. Finally, we can draw a 2nd vertical line ("d - c") through the September 28, 1990 weekly time point 161 weeks forward from the August 25, 1987 high.

NOTE THAT LINE "a - c" IS THE 45 DEGREE ANGLE LINE THAT DEFINES THE POINT WHERE PRICE IS EQUAL TO TIME FOR THIS MOVE!

Note that the 45 degree line bisects or splits the rectangle in the chart directly in half.

Note that dotted line "a - z" in the chart that is drawn at a 45 degree angle with a protractor does NOT square price and time.

Note that, since time and price are squared at point "c", and since time is equal to price at point "c", that line "a - b" therefore equals line "a - d" (though their lengths in the chart MAY be different, depending on the scale).

You are thus looking at a square in the above chart and NOT a rectangle IN TERMS OF PRICE AND TIME.

This should clarify the importance of proper chart scaling for you (and bring back fond memories of your lovable high school geometry teacher)!

In the next chart, we have turned vertically our horizontal Gann Lines discussed in the last section. We still divide the move into 1/8ths, it is just that we now divide the PROJECTED TIME required to square time with price into 1/8ths. This projected time in our weekly SP example is 161 weeks with the first line on the beginning of the move (August 25, 1987) and the last line on the end of the move (the week of September 28, 1990).

Note the 50 % COMPLETION level that occurs the week of 890317 which is similar to the 50 % RETRACEMENT level. Other percent-

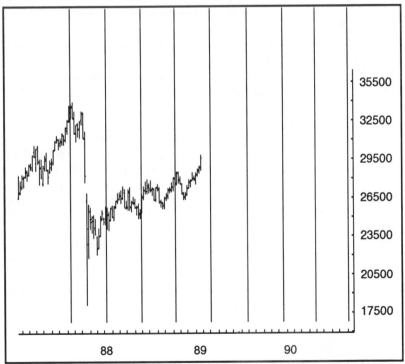

age completion levels can likewise be calculated (and are represented by the vertical lines).

Have these time periods been important to weekly S & P 500 prices? I think you can answer that question for yourself by inspecting the chart and the 1/8th time intervals!

The next step, as you may have already guessed, is to start combining some of the above Gann techniques.

For instance, in the chart below, the horizontal Gann lines for price have been combined with vertical Gann lines for time in order to arrive at both price support / resistance and time completion levels.

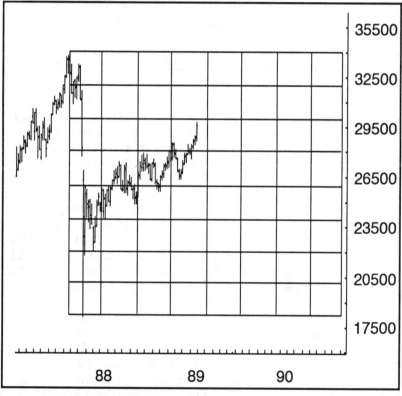

In the next chart, we have added Gann angles from the August 25, 1987 high to the Gann price and time lines.

You may want to inspect the interaction of these lines and angles yourself, but pay particular attention to point 1 (where the lines and angles both provided stiff resistance to further price progress), to point 2 (which marked rapid acceleration once both the lines AND the angles were broken and the key time interval had arrived), and point 3 (where both the lines and angles again combined to detour price right upon arrival of the next time interval).

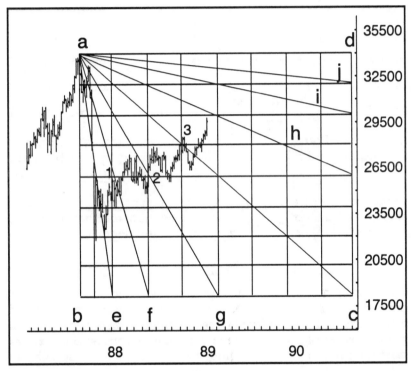

Note the symmetry of the angles and the lines. In other words, the second horizontal line from the top (line "j") intersects the week that time and price are squared (line "d - c") at the exact same place that line "a - j" (the 8 X 1) intersects the square of time and price (or line "d - c"). The same holds true, of course, for points e, f, g, c, h, and i in addition to j.

Now you should be able to see clearly what was meant by drawing an angle line by moving over 1 unit (or 1 box in this example) and then moving down 8 units (or 8 boxes). The same, of course, applies in different proportions to the other angles.

Finally, in the chart below, Gann Price and Time Lines have been combined with the Gann Fan drawn from the major August 25, 1987 high and a Gann Fan drawn from the major October 20, 1987 low.

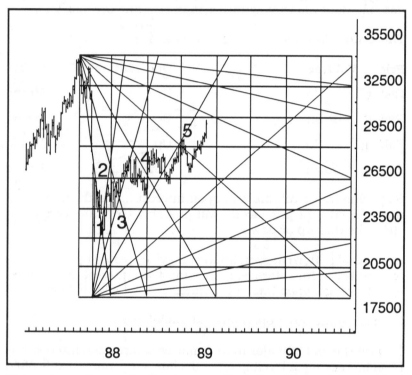

Note where the angle lines cross that they form the "cradles" mentioned earlier that provide especially strong support resistance to price.

Five such cradles are shown in the chart and are numbered 1 through 5.

This same type analysis can be applied to other weekly moves in the S & P 500. The move from August, 1984 to the August, 1987 high would be a good candidate as would the moves from the 1974 and 1982 lows to the 1987 high.

If one wished to completely analyze the stock market, similar analysis would be conducted on the Dow Jones Industrial, Transportation, and Utilities Averages, the New York Stock Exchange Index, the Value Line Index, and so on.

Additionally, the same type analysis can be conducted on S & P 500 monthly prices and S & P 500 yearly prices.

In the case of monthly prices, a 1-point-per-month scale would suggest over 13 years before price and time squared the move analyzed in our charts above (which just happens to be a nice Fibonacci number, doesn't it)?

The move could also be analyzed on a daily basis, too, but such is somewhat rare. Nevertheless, here are the dates on which prices will be squared (and multiples of those squares) based on the 161.35 point move discussed in the SP futures market. The dates are figured for both calendar and trading days.

Days	Calendar Days	Trading Days
161	880202	880414
162	880712	881201
161	881221	890725
161	890531	900312
162	891108	

Why were the price and time intervals discussed in this article divided into 8ths? Perhaps it was because of the natural division by two (i.e., 100 % / 2 = 50 %, 50 % / 2 = 25 %, 25 % / 2 = 12 1/2 % which is 1/8th).

More than likely, however, it is because of the fact that 360 degrees (the number of degrees in a full circle or 1 Gann year) divided by 45 degrees (the most important of the Gann angles) equals 8.

Should you use Gann's teachings to plan your trades? As always in this book, the answer is that only YOU can make that decision!

There are many traders who follow Gann and his works. He reportedly made $54 million or so trading markets during his career a long time before the Dow Jones Industrials ever thought about surpassing 1,000 and at a time when a 5 cent cigar lived up to its reputation.

Yet his estate was reportedly probated at only around $150,000 when he died in Florida. (Gann enthusiasts argue that such is what might be expected with proper estate planning). Also, an interview of Gann's son by Dr. Alexander Elder purportedly revealed that Gann made much of his funds by selling trading systems.

For those interested in further in depth Gann information, Robert Miner's home seminar course is very highly recommended. Many illustrations and examples are accompanied by audio tape and text which thoroughly explain concepts and application.

Mr. Miner additionally publishes "The Precious Metals Timing Report" which applies those concepts to current prices. Mention that you are an Almanac purchaser and free information and a sample copy will be sent. Contact Robert Miner, PO Box 35696A, Tucson, AZ 85740.

Combining Gann and Elliott

Nervous markets
usually don't go up.
- Alan Abelson

If Gann's method of analysis is strong enough to stand alone on its own merits . . .

If Elliott's method of analysis is strong enough to stand alone on its own merits . . .

Then shouldn't the combination of the two result in an even more powerful set of analytical tools?

The book, "Trading for Profit", explains the concepts and illustrates the use of the two techniques in combination. The author, Don Vodopich, also publishes a weekly newsletter, "Precision Timing". If you have interest in this area and would like a free sample copy of Mr. Vodopich's newsletter, mention The Almanac and contact

Precision Timing, Inc., PO Box 11722A, Atlanta, GA 30305 (404-231-3668).

Some Charts

If there's a way to do it better . . .
find it!
- Thomas A Edison

Look over the charts below.

If you're interested in finding out what generated the buy and sell signals, simply turn to the next section when done.

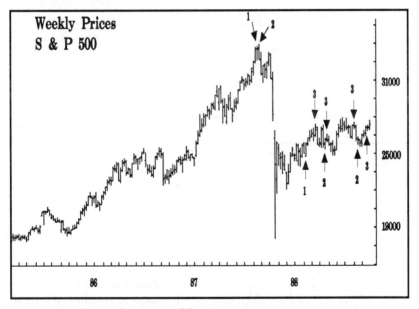

The chart above shows weekly SP prices.

The two strongest signals that were generated in 1987 are indicated by the down arrows in August, 1987, and are marked "1" and "2".

The strongest weekly signal in 1988 is noted by the up arrow as indicated by the "1" in the chart in February, 1988.

There were 2 signals of secondary strength as indicated by the 2 up arrows marked "2" in April and August, 1988.

There were 4 lesser signals as indicated by the arrows marked "3".

Note that 7 of the 9 signals either marked a key pivot point OR occurred during the period next to a key pivot point. One of those that "failed" (if you can actually call it a failure) is the August, 1988 "2". This signal obviously occurred quite near the market lows, however, from which stock prices recovered and rallied smartly for the next 2 months.

The signals noted in the following chart of daily cash S & P 500 closing prices were listed in The 1988 Almanac on page 254.

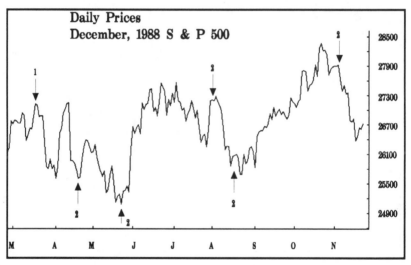

The "1" signal was for March 17, 1988, which marked the early spring closing high in this market.

This day (March 17, 1988 - the # 1 turning point day for the year) additionally MARKED THE HIGH IN THE ADVANCE / DECLINE LINE FOR THE ENTIRE YEAR !!!

I have NEVER, ANYWHERE seen ANY predictions given on ANY market 1 year in advance of their occurrence as was done in The 1988 Almanac that were as accurate as these turned out to be in 1988 !

And this impressive record continued!

For instance, during an interview with Bill Griffith on Financial News Network in early 1989, I reviewed the next two change-in-trend dates as projected by this trading technique.

The two dates are noted in the chart below by the arrows and were listed on page 326 of The 1989 Almanac.

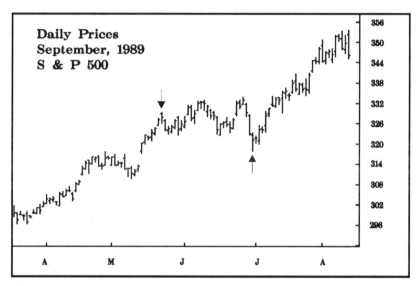

Can you spot the expanding triangle top and the subsequent selloff (It occurred from late May to late June)?

What would have provided an excellent exit signal after this selloff (See the basic chart section)?

Astronomical

Millionaires don't use astrology;
billionaires do.
- John Pierpont Morgan

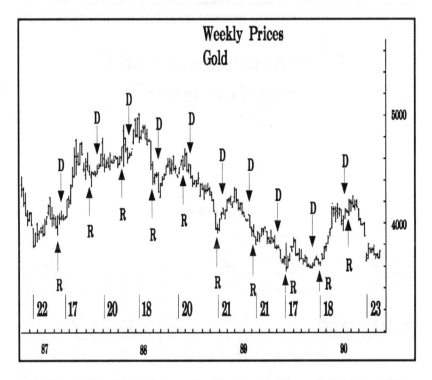

The above top chart shows the dominant 19 week linear cycle in the gold market at the bottom of the chart through early 1990.

The "up" arrows below weekly gold prices with the "R" note the weeks that Mercury went retrograde. Note how significant this event was to the gold market.

Note how this astronomical event parallels the 19 week gold cycle.

The "down" arrows above prices with the "D" note the weeks that Mercury went direct.

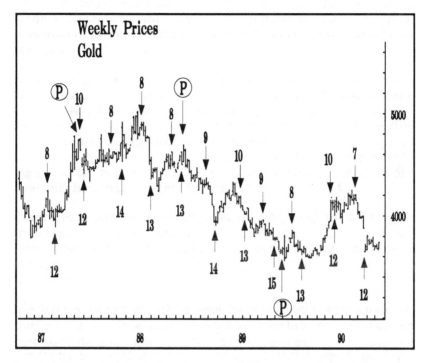

In the above chart, the "up" arrows below prices list the number of weeks that occurred after Mercury went direct. The 12 to 14 week period after this event has occurred has been quite important to this market. The 1987 through 1989 Almanacs listed this information and centered the projected turning points in the 13th week. The results in each of those years turned out to be quite significant in forcasting weekly ringed low points as can be seen in the chart. Note that all projected turns occurred within one week of a ringed low point.

The "down" arrows shown above prices in the above chart list the number of weeks that occurred after Mercury went direct last year. The 8 to 10 week period after this event has occurred has been quite important to this market. The 1987 through 1989 Almanacs listed this information and centered the projected turning points in the 9th week. The results in each of those years turned out to be quite significant in forcasting weekly ringed low points as can be seen in the chart. Note that all projected turns occurred within one week of a ringed low point.

As you can see, all of these projections were quite important to subsequent gold prices. In 10 of the 11 projections, upward movement in price was halted for the next month at the very least.

The "circled" arrows in the preceding chart with the "P" inside point to the 15th week after Pluto went retrograde over the past three years as projected in The 1987 through 1989 Almanacs.

As you can see, this information was quite timely indeed.

FROM THE PREVIOUS SECTION - The weekly S & P 500 signals were formed by simply adding together all the daily astronomical observations (aspects, retrogrades, directs, and new and full moons) for the week. The week with the most observations was rated 1, the week with the next most observations was rated 2, and so on. Note that the weeks with the stongest signals were the two weeks that were right at the very top of the stock market in 1987.

Additionally, the three highest days at the 1987 stock market top were also the days of very strong astronomical activity. Days that were included for signals were those that had at least two observations.

Such information is listed in "The Calendar Book" and can be found each year in the "Astronomical Points" section.

Arch Crawford of Crawford Perspectives was given quite a bit of publicity for the advice he gave his subscribers that they sell their stocks in late August, 1987 based on astrological signals. Mr. Crawford's advice demonstrates that some traders DO use such information to buy and sell securities. (This same information, it should be noted, was listed in The 1987 Almanac along with several other analytical techniques!)

I am perfectly convinced
that these decennial (economic) crises
depend upon meteorological variations
of like periods which again depend,
in all probability,
upon cosmical variations
of which we have evidence in the frequency
of sun-spots, amoras, and magnetic perturbations.
- William H. Jevons

(Mrs. Whelan, my high school English teacher, originally gave me the above as an example of a run-on sentence, but since it is pertinent to this section, it seemed an appropriate location in the Almanac to use it).

As difficult as it will be for many readers of this section to accept, many traders base their trading on the alignment of the sun and the planets.

Astronomical projections, such as the day of high tides, when planets will conjunct, eclipses, etc., are very precise and can be made years in advance. The science of astronomy should not be confused with such things as astrology (which studies peoples "signs", their horoscopes, etc.), cosmotology (which has nothing to do with Carl Sagan but instead involves something like hair-dressing), and so on.

The various relationships of the planets to each other as we view them in the sky are their "aspects". Change is anticipated when planets aspect. When they appear very close to each other in the sky, they are in conjunction. When they are vary far apart (i.e., one is rising in the east as the other sets in the west), they are in opposition.

The amount of the angle by which they are apart is measured in degrees. For instance, when they are in conjunction (close together), the angle separating the planets is 0 degrees. When they are in opposition (far apart), the angle between them is 180 degrees. Some of these aspects are said to be bullish, some bearish.

The major aspects are the conjunction (0 degrees and most bullish), sextile (60 degrees and bullish), square (90 degrees and bearish), trine (120 degrees and bullish), and opposition (180 degrees and very bearish).

Waxing aspects are those where the planets are moving away from each other towards opposition, while waning aspects move towards each other (towards conjunction).

Let's look at an example in the Gold market.

Gold tends to exhibit a fairly regular 19 week cycle across the lows. Over the three years ending in early 1990, this cycle had bottomed the week of 861121 (22 weeks after the last 19 week cycle low), 870320 (17 weeks), 870807 (20 weeks), 871218 (19 weeks), 880506 (20 weeks), 880930 (21 weeks), 890217 (20 weeks), 890609 (16 weeks), 891013 (18 weeks), 900216 (18 weeks) and 900615 (17 weeks). The average time period between cycle lows was 18.91 weeks with a range from 17 to 22 weeks. (Such a variation in range is very typical of linear time cycles and this cycle in particular).

These cycles were shown at the bottom of the first chart of weekly gold prices shown in this section.

Mercury is said to be one of the planets that "Rule" gold. Mercury goes retrograde (appears to be going "backwards" in the sky) every 19 weeks. This relationship has historically correlated very well with the gold market. Mercury's retrograde is shown in the first chart of weekly gold prices shown above by the "up" arrow below prices with the "R" below it.

Additionally, 8-10 weeks after Mercury goes direct (appears to be going "forwards" in the sky), gold has tended to crest. Mercury's direct is shown in the first chart of weekly gold prices above by the "down" arrow above prices with the "D" above it.

The 8-10 week periods are shown by the "down" arrow above prices in the second chart above of weekly gold prices as they were projected in The 1987, 1988, and 1989 Almanacs and as they occurred through early 1990.

Also, 12-14 weeks after Mercury goes Direct, gold has tended to bottom. These relationships are displayed in the second chart shown above of weekly gold prices as they were projected by The

1987, 1988, and 1989 Almanacs and as they occurred through early 1990.

This information was not listed in The 1990 Almanac but was reintroduced in The 1991 Calendar Book due to subscriber requests. When using these listings, one should note that the projections are made by week number so that one can easily turn to the appropriate week of the year to correlate the expected change-in-trend listed in "The Calendar Book" in the "Astro Points" section.

One should expect the change-in-trend to occur the week before, the week of, or the week following the projected change when using this information.

Additionally, 13-15 weeks after Pluto goes retrograde, gold has a tendency to make a major change in trend. This information is also listed in "The Calendar Book" in the "Astro Points" section.

Were one to truly historically correlate aspects with major market turning points, it would be necessary to use an Ephemeris (which lists major aspects and other heavenly information) and to study when the various aspects of the different planets had occurred versus the ensuing price action in a manner similar to what has been done above.

RULERS OF COMMODITIES

COMMODITY	RULER
Cattle	Mars, Saturn, Taurus
Cocoa	Pluto
Coffee	Neptune, Mars, Pluto
Copper	Venus, Taurus, Libra
Corn	Sun, Mercury, Uranus, Taurus
Cotton	Neptune
Financials	Jupiter, Saturn, Venus, Taurus
Gold	Moon, Sun, Leo
Heating Oil	Mars, Sun, Neptune, Aries, Leo

Live Hogs	Saturn, Uranus, Taurus
Lumber	Saturn, Capricorn
Oats	Mercury, Virgo
Oil	Neptune, Pisces
Orange Juice	Sun, Leo
Platinum	Neptune, Uranus
Pork Bellies	Saturn, Neptune, Taurus
Silver	Moon, Cancer
Soybeans	Venus, Taurus
Soybean Oil	Venus, Neptune, Taurus
Soybean Meal	Moon
Sugar	Venus, Jupiter
Wheat	Venus, Jupiter, Mercury, Virgo

Saturn squared with Neptune means high interest rates.

Jupiter in conjunction with Neptune is bearish for the financial world.

Mars squared with the Sun means higher metals prices.

Planetary movements involving the following planets are perceived as being -

BULLISH - Jupiter (most bullish), Venus, and the Sun

BEARISH - Saturn (most bearish), Mars, Neptune

NEUTRAL - Mercury, Uranus, and the Moon

As stated earlier, each year's "Calendar Book" lists the strongest astronomical signals of the year. The reader should note, however, that these listings are based on aspect frequency only (i.e., the number of events occurring on a particular day or during a particular week) and do not include such interpretation as whether a particular aspect is likely to be bullish or bearish for a particular market.

True planetary observers or financial astrologers, of course, are not only going to observe the NUMBER of aspects in a given period, but are also going to concentrate on WHICH PLANETS are forming WHAT TYPE of an angular relationship. From this information, they not only ascertain which markets should be involved and the time of the expected turning point, but also the direction of the expected move.

The 1990 Calendar Book began to list not only "true" aspectivity data, but also that which included such additional information such as eclipses or planets traversing their zodiac signs and the like.

Additionally, particulary important dates for both the "true" and "other" listings were verbally summarized during each weekly section beginning with The 1990 Calendar Book.

An example of how these turning points were used by the author in a real time example comes from "The Almanac Reports" and involves the August 2nd and August 18th, 1988 astro turning points.

In the July 28, 1988 issue of "The Almanac Reports," we wrote "This coming Tuesday, August 2, is a key turning point date of secondary significance" and thus prepared for a potential upcoming change-in-trend.

In the August 2nd issue of "The Almanac Reports," we were short one September, 1988 S & P 500 futures contract @ 27390 and suggested adding additional short contracts in the September S&P 500, the September Value Line, and the September NYSE Index contracts " . . . on the first day that the Basic Charting Technique is completed with stops above the high of the move."

This technique entered short positions on August 3rd @ 27405 in the S & P 500, @ 24870 in the September Value Line, and @15495 in the September NYSE.

In the August 17th issue of "The Almanac Reports" we wrote "In light of the importance to markets of past (astro) turning point dates, one should be particularly sensitive to market reversals."

Stops were lowered in the August 17th issue which allowed us to write in the August 19th issue that we had been stopped out of positions in the September Value Line and September NYSE on August 18th and in the September S & P 500 on August 22nd.

Per contract profits from these transactions were $ 5,275.00 in the Value Line, $ 3,025.00 in the NYSE, and $ 13,825.00 in the S & P 500 for a total of $ 22,175.00.

The August 22nd issue of "The Almanac Reports" then included the following chart of 15 minute prices in the September S & P 500 with the suggestion that long positions be entered on a break of the downtrend line shown in the chart and the high of the previous 15 minute period. Note that the Elliott Wave was used to provide additional supportive information indicating that a corrective wave was about to end.

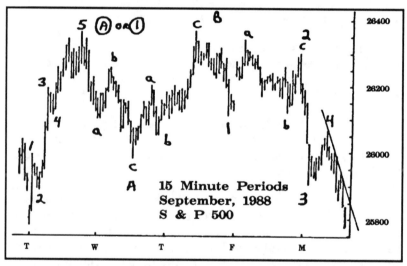

A second contract was added in the August 25th issue as were long positions in the September NYSE and Value Line indexes. Stops were raised in the September 12th issue of "The Almanac Reports" and were elected (unfortunately) the next day for a profit of $ 1,000.00 in the NYSE, $ 1,450.00 in the Value Line, and $2,075.00 in the S & P 500 indexes. The final stop on the September S & P 500 contract was elected September 15th for a $ 2,900.00 profit.

Thus, the total profit from this astro turning point trade was $7,425.00 (gross) and the total for the two astro turning point dates of August 2nd and August 18th was $ 29,600.00.

The next example of how these turning point dates were used to anticipate market change comes from the November 2nd issue of "The Almanac Reports" that discussed the upcoming November 4th turning point date by stating that "We are close to the November 4th (Saturday) turning point date. I feel at this time that this turning point date will be of greater significance to the BD (US Treasury Bond market) than the stocks."

The following five minute bar chart on December, 1988 US Treasury Bond prices was issued with the suggestion to enter short positions @ 9106 with a 9206 stop.

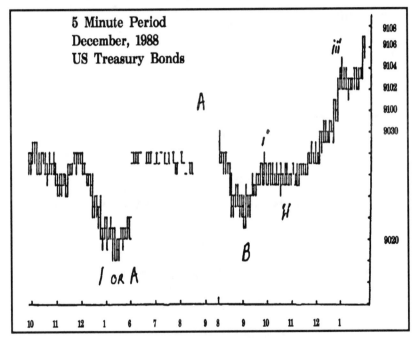

Prices would peak on Friday, November 4th, 1988 at 9114 and would drop sharply over four points through the rest of the month.

Our trade would be stopped out on November 11th for a $2,312.50 gross profit.

A daily chart of December, 1988 US Treasury Bonds follows. The down arrow shows the November 4th turning point date discussed above and demonstrates its importance to this market.

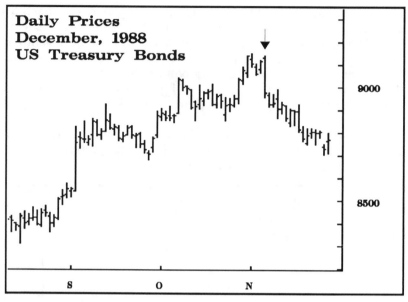

Can you spot the FND Slammer in this market?

Linear Time Cycles

*It is much more dignified
to say we're moving in cycles
rather than running around in circles
even though it comes out
to about the same thing.*

In 1875, an Ohio farmer by the name of Samuel Benner wrote a slim book called "Benner's Prophecies of Future Ups and Downs in Prices". The essence of his book was contained in his assertion that various commodity prices such as corn, hogs, and pig iron fluctuated in relatively consistent and repetitive patterns and that, as a result of these patterns, economists and producers could predict optimum periods for production, purchases, sales and investments. Benner's statements were among the first that identified definite cycle lengths for agricultural prices.

The theory of cyclical analysis is that events will occur within a cycle to move prices in the direction of the cycle. The basic drawback of fundamental analysis is that the events causing changes in supply and demand are not known until after the fact and, consequently, after tops and bottoms have occurred. Cycles help traders pick the direction of price moves before the news comes out. Instead of asking WHICH WAY or HOW FAR a market will go, cycles ask WHEN it will arrive or WHEN the move will begin. Time cycle analysts thus contend that TIME is the dominant determining factor in market analysis.

At the very least, other technical tools can be improved by incorporating cycle analysis. Cycle analysis can (and should) be used on a "tops down" approach. For instance, the multi-year cycles listed in the Calendar Book can be used for major trend orientation. Weekly price data can then be used to identify intermediate cycles of the 20 week to 75 week range or so and can be used for intermediate trend orientation. Weekly data of the 5 to 20 week range can then identify shorter term intermediate cycles. Finally, daily price data can be used for short term trend direction by using the basic trading cycles of the 20 to 40 day variety. (The author has even traded a five hour cycle in the S & P 500 futures contract).

Since the trend of each cycle is determined by the direction of its next longer cycle, the idea is to use the shorter cycle to time market entry only when the direction of all the cycles line up. In other words, when the long and intermediate term cyclical trends are up and the short term daily cycle is due to bottom and turn up, the trader would want to enter long positions on the break of a trendline or chart pattern, trading system buy signal, moving average upturn, penetration of a recent significant high point, an on balance volume or relative strength index price/line divergence (or any of several other oscillators), and so on.

Most markets have at least five DOMINANT cycles. The Almanac summarizes and lists those dominant cycles in the "Summary of Cycles" section of "The Calendar Book." In Almanacs prior to 1990, the cycles were graphically projected into the upcoming year through the use of time bands drawn in advance of actual price movement. By the time the 1990 Calendar Book was written, so many linear time cycles were being listed in the "Summary of Cycles" section that it was felt that the reader might be discouraged due to too much information. Therefore, the Cycle Indexes were introduced to help readers more easily filter the overall effect of the many various cycles listed in the Almanac.

The Cycle Indexes attempt to present the overall effect or summary of all upward and downward tugs and pulls of all the weekly and monthly cycles followed by The Almanac. The reader should pay particular attention to the major peaks and troughs projected by these indexes in attempting to discern major changes in trend that are likely to occur over the forthcoming period of time.

An important note on cycles is that the entire time band of a cycle can "shift" forwards or backwards in time to compensate for previous cycles that are either longer or shorter than normal duration. (On occasion, they will even seem to disappear). It is a common feature of cycles to correct themselves as time passes, however. Hence, a cycle that runs short one period might then make an adjustment by "shifting" and running longer on its next repetition.

Edward R. Dewey, considered the father of cyclical analysis, made two major observations regarding cycles. First was that many seemingly unrelated phenomena shared the same cycle length, some of the most common being 5.91 years, 8 years, 9.2 years, 9.6 years, and 18.2 years. For instance, the 5.91 year cycle is evident in business failures, cotton prices, grouse abundance, pig iron prices, and sunspots, among others.

Second was that these seemingly unrelated events not only shared the same cycle length, but that the cycles almost invariably turn at the same time as other cycles of the same length (some reaching lows while others reach highs).

Dewey's conclusion was that there seemed to be a pulse to the universe that caused these cycles and accounted for their pervasive presence throughout so many areas of human activity.

Some of the principles of cycles are stated in the principles of summation, harmonicity, synchronicity, proportionality, variation, and nominality. These may not be available at your local shopping mart but can probably be found with a little effort in any city library. The one worth discussing here is the nominal cycle model which generally summarizes a set of harmonically related cycle lengths that affects markets.

YEARS	MONTHS	WEEKS	DAYS
18			
9			
	54		
	18	78	
	9	39	
		19.5	
		10	70
		5	35
			17

(Remember to clarify between calendar and trading days with the above being calendar days.)

Since cycles are usually measured across the lows, most variations in cycles occur at the peaks and not at the troughs. It is these variations that can provide clues as to the trend of the next larger cycle. If the cycle crest occurs at the midpoint, there is no overriding trend influence present and the bullish and bearish forces are said to be in balance. If the crest is to the left of the cycle midpoint, left translation has occurred, a bearish trend is present (prices have spent more time going down than up), and the cycle is more apt to extend by a small amount. The opposite applies to bull markets which tend to experience shorter cycles (hence, as we wrote in The 1988 Almanac, cycle dominance in the stock market was in the process of shifting from the 46 month to the 40 month cycle as the dominant cycle).

HOW TO USE - If you think you are in a major bull market, right translation should occur. Hence, the number of days correcting the advance should not exceed the number spent in the advance (generally speaking). If it does, left translation has occurred and the entire advance should be reevaluated. The same also applies to analysis of successive cycle lows. For example, a long term cycle should experience a series of smaller cycles that have higher ending low points than the beginning low points if in a bull move.

One might also note that cycle analysis generally seems to work best in bull markets.

USEFUL HINT ON THE USE OF CYCLES - One of the problems in using cycles is being able to assess where you are in relation to the underlying cycles. I personally find that wall charts are quite helpful in solving this problem and use a series of large charts that cover the last 10 years for about 25 different markets. Time windows can be plotted and change-in-trend reversal time bands projected.

A special cycle often used by traders because of its repeated mention in the Bible is a PROJECTION cycle and is the cycle of seven. These traders expect prices to reverse on the seventh hour, day, week, month, etc.

Cycles and Drought

When the well's dry,
we will know the worth of water.

It has long been observed and is supported by tree ring data from the Western United States that widespread drought strikes the Great Plains and prairies about every twenty years. Evidence suggests that this phenomenon is affected by a modulation of atmospheric precipitation that occurs in phase with a lunar tide of 18.6 years. This lunar cycle occurred this century in 1917.5, 1936.1, 1954.7, and 1973.3. It next is scheduled in 1991.9 and is caused by cyclic behavior between the moon and the sun.

The 11 year cycle related to sunspot activity and its correlation with drought is discussed in the section on sunspots.

When these two waves are closely aligned, yield shortfalls of crops are particularly acute. Close alignment occurred in 1936 and was followed shortly thereafter by the Midwestern dust bowl days. In 1954, the two cycles were closely aligned and again we experienced a period of severe dryness.

The cycles both will be in close alignment in the early 1990s. Will this period again be one of severe drought? There are too many variables in climatology to say for sure. Some important ones are reviewed in this book.

In the absence of further volcanic activity, the effects of the El Chicon volcanic eruption in Mexico will surely continue to lessen over the next few years. Will this lessening of ash combine with the greenhouse effect to increase temperatures at the same time that sunspot activity is increasing and the lunar cycle occurs? There are certainly several different indicators pointing in that very direction.

Prior to the 1988 drought experience, the last major drought in the United States began in 1970 in northern Mexico and southwest Texas, advanced northward with growing severity, and abruptly ended in 1977 shortly after the Governors of Western states met in an emergency drought-inspired session.

These droughts usually experience not only decreased yields, but also acreage abandonment and have a significant effect on the American economy. The 1988 drought, for instance, is estimated to have decreased GNP for that year by 1.1 %.

What is especially interesting about these cycles is that they tend to parallel general real estate activity. Indeed, United States real estate activity cycles have averaged 18.9 years in length.

Even more remarkable is the fact that the years in which building activity reaches a minimum or trough are approximately coincident with the years in which tides are at maximum levels and are thus roughly coincidental with a decrease in agricultural output.

Cycles and Politics

Politicians are the same all over.
The promise to build a bridge
even when there is no river.
- Nikita Krushchev

Henry Adams first postulated a 12 year political cycle in the United States upon examining the first 36 years of the republic's existence in the 1800s. Arthur M. Schlesinger Jr. in "The Cycles of American History" found that this cycle faded in the late 1800s but that a cycle of roughly 30 years reflects changes in the national mood and commitment as opinion alternates between public purpose and private interest. Indeed, he used the cycle to predict the beginning of a new conservative epoch beginning in 1978. He goes on to further argue that the rhythmic "bursts of innovation and reform" that characterized the administrations of Presidents Theodore Roosevelt, Franklin Roosevelt, and John F. Kennedy will reappear at the end of this current phase.

According to this theory, this period should occur shortly before or after 1990 and should be accompanied by a sharp change in the national mood, commitment, and direction.

The existence of this 30 year cycle is said to be explained by the span of a generation. Since political ideals are formed during roughly the 17th to 25th year, when one's generation comes to power roughly 30 years later, it carries forth the ideals of younger years. The generation that inherits power in the 1990s will thus be the one whose opinions were formed during the leadership of John Kennedy. President Reagan's generation will have their time in about 2010.

Supporters of this theory point to the 1986 mid-term election and the unexpected Democratic gains in the Senate as the first sign of the emergence of the next phase of the cycle and further support its existence recently with the Iran/Contra scandals, the 1987 Wall Street crash, the exposure of the televangelists, the revolt against deregulation on the stock exchanges, in the banking and savings and loan industries, in the airline industry, and in the telephone industry, the revulsion against greed as the basis of American ethics, the defeat of Supreme Court nominee Robert Bork, the Republican intra-party quibbling over the INF treaty, repudiation of the Yuppie movement, the abandonment of the Reagan agenda by President Reagan himself, the reelection of a liberal Senate and House in the 1988 elections, and so on.

At the time of this writing, the end of the current phase appears to have occurred in July, 1990, with President Bush's popularity at an approval rating of over 70%.

It should be noted that for several years, Almanacs have stated: "The cycle is not expected to come full flood until the early 1990s and should, over the next few years, mark a retreat from what survived of the Reagan agenda."

If the cycle continues, we will have a Democratic President in 1992 (1996 at the latest).

The Kondratieff Wave

He who knows nothing
is confident
of everything.

The Kondratieff Wave is a roughly 52-55 year cycle of economic activity in which economic expansion rises to a peak that then gives way to a roughly 10 year period of gradually declining activity. This plateau period is culminated by a severe deflationary depression.

The peak in expansion is normally accompanied by high inflation and commodity prices. Adherents point to the Bible and the Jubilee in which all debts were forgiven every 50 years and to the burning of Mayan cities as supportive evidence of the long term existence of the cycle throughout the world.

In the United States, the Wave reached peaks in 1814, 1864, and 1920 with an idealized peak of the next cycle in the mid-1970s. Many argue that this peak occurred prior to the 1973-74 slowdown while others point to the ensuing inflation of the late 1970s and argue that the peak occurred in roughly 1981. Still others believe that the trough of this cycle has already passed with the end of the early 1980's deflation in 1985-1986. Although such would be the preferred experience, the extreme level and continued buildup of worldwide debt argues against such an easy resolution to the problem. Instead, according to the Wave, regardless of when the actual peak occurred, we should now (in the late 1980s) be near the end of the plateau period.

Many compare this period to those past and note such similarities as the following;

In all prior periods, as in this one, debt has continued to grow as inflation lessened. Deflation became more dominant. The 10 year period following the peak has sociologically been a false "period of good feelings" (witness the Era of Good Feelings, Reconstruction, the Roaring 20s) and has created a false sense of security.

Tax reduction has historically occurred during this period along with a buildup of foreign debt, violent currency fluctuations, a farming depression, a southern land boom and bust (Florida then, the Southwest now), a booming stock market, high personal and corporate debt (add junk bonds, government, and third world debt this time), the rise of trade protectionism (Smoot-Hawley in the 1920s, the 1988 Trade Protection Bill now), the "Cult of the Rich" has captivated the public (Great Gatsby then and Dallas, Dynasty, Life Styles of the Rich and Famous, etc., now), there is a fascination with crime (Al Capone, John Dillinger then and The Godfather, Miami Vice, etc., now), a movement to the right occurs politically (Fascism then, Jerry Falwell, the Moral Majority, etc., now), there is a creationist/evolutionary swing (the Scopes "Monkey Trials" then, Right to Life now), and so on.

In the 1870s, debt was built around the railroads. In the 1920s, it was built around Latin American and German debt. Now the biggest debtor is the United States Government.

In the 1930s, gold and Homestake Mining were superior investments despite the crash.

In the 1987 Almanac we wrote, "If the Kondratieff Wave depression is to be, what would signal its onset? How about when stocks peak and gold bottoms? When?

How about 13 years off the 1974 stock market lows, 55 years off the 1932 stock market lows, and 7 years off the 1980 gold market highs - - - in short, 1987 ! ! !"

Perhaps the Elliott Wave interpretations of the next 2 charts of the monthly cash CRB Index tell the present situation best.

Are we at the end of a major corrective process that favors a severe deflationary move down to the roughly 160 area in the CRB Index (as suggested by the first chart) . . .

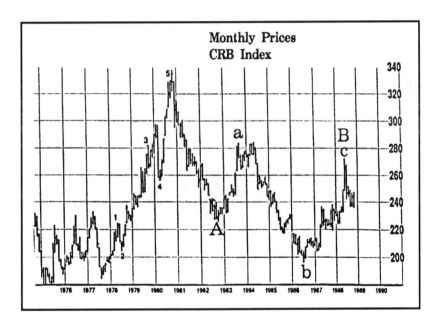

Or have we just begun a move upwards that will carry DRAMAT-ICALLY HIGHER over the next several years (as suggested by the second chart) . . . ?

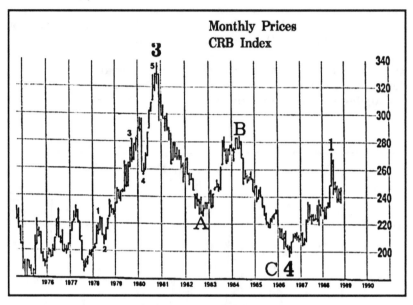

Monthly Prices
CRB Index

The Lunar Cycle

The effect of the moon
is on men,
not on wheat itself
nor upon any of the manipulations
that occur in the transportation
or handling of the grain.
We find it affecting wheat
more intensely
than any other commodity . . .
- Buron H. Pugh

Perhaps Burton H. Pugh discovered something in his early 1900 studies on wheat and lunar phases. In order, there appears to be some statistical correlation in the grains, meats, and metals to this phenomena.

The individual commodities that seem to be most sensitive to this strategy appear to be Wheat, Corn, Soybeans, Soybean Oil, and Silver. The basic strategy calls for buying the full moon, selling the new moon.

For Sugar, sell when the moon is at its greatest declination north. The time period for the declination is thirteen days.

Cocoa tends to rally about 75% of the time at the start of a new moon.

The phases of the moon are listed on the left-hand page of "The Calendar Book" and are listed at Central Standard Time (unadjusted for Daylight Savings Time).

The following text and chart below is from The 1988 Almanac;

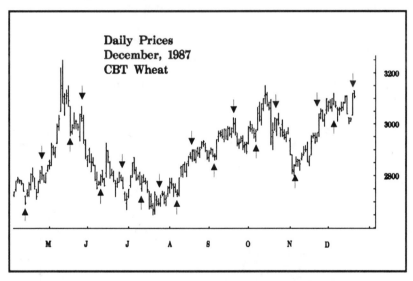

Daily Prices
December, 1987
CBT Wheat

If Mr. Pugh's quote above is true, then it should hold for December, 1987 Wheat just as Mr. Pugh wrote about December, 1897 Wheat. With that in mind, the exact date of the full and new moon phases are marked on the chart below. I think one would have to admit that some of these trades are pretty darn good.

"Simply using the closing prices at the end of the day produced a gain of $ 1,262.50 before commissions and slippage for seventeen trades. If $ 50.00 is assumed for commissions and slippage, the net profit was $ 412.50. If $ 100.00 is assumed for commissions and slippage, the net profit is $ -437.50.

"If the execution price is on the opening price of the phase change day, the profit was $ 2,250.00 ($ 1,400 after commissions of $50.00 per trade and $ 550.00 after commissions of $ 100.00). Note that no stops or timing systems were used in this example.

"For instance, using a 15 cent price objective and a 10 cent stop would improve results by $ 875 on the approach that uses closes and by $ 2,087.50 on the approach that uses opening prices only. Hence, under the simple approach listed, the results, had one used either of these two methods over this 8 month period, would have ranged between $ 437.50 and $ 3,487.50, depending upon slippage, versus a margin requirement of $ 500.00.

"Perhaps you can come up with a better entry / exit method!"

What if you had read the above in The 1988 Almanac and had traded Wheat prices based on the Lunar Cycle in 1988?

The chart below shows hypothetical exit and entry days for December, 1988 Wheat.

Using the closing prices only, 18 trades were generated, 15 of which were profitable ($ 12,175), three of which were losses ($-1,962.50), for a total gross profit of over $ 10,000!

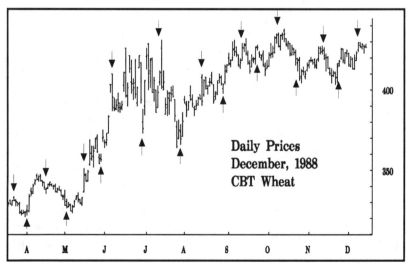

Daily Prices
December, 1988
CBT Wheat

Summary of Cycles

Trust to time:
it is the wisest
of all counselors.
- Plutarch : Lives, c. 100

Let's look at an example of how one might use the cyclical information in "The Calendar Book" to make timely decisions in the stock market. The example that follows shows weekly prices for the Dow Jones Industrial Averages through year end, 1989. The example we will use analyzes the weekly cyclical stock market information as it was presented for the first half of 1990 in "The 1990 Calendar Book."

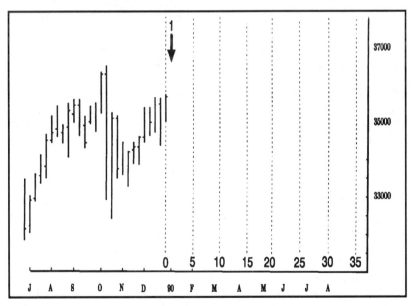

The vertical lines drawn in the chart above correspond with the week of the year as listed in "The Calendar Book" (i.e., the vertical line labeled with a "5" corresponds with the 5th week of the year. "Week 5" in "The Calendar Book" contains information that pertains specifically to that week).

The chart shows prices as 1989 ended with the extreme volatility and downward thrust of October, 1989 the dominant feature in the chart. Many analysts were quite bullish at that time, the normal new year optimism prevailed, and so on.

The following information was listed on page 323 of the "Cycle Index" section of The 1990 Almanac (Calendar Book).

SP   20 WK HI   Weeks 1, 21, & 41

This information told readers that, in the S & P 500 index, the 20 week linear time cycle was expected to peak or make a high during the year on or around the 1st week of the year, the 21st week of the year, and the 41st week of the year.

(We knew this was so by looking at the symbols listed during each week of the year in The Calendar Book and deciphering that "SP" represents the S & P 500 stock market index, that "20 WK" tells us that we are analyzing a 20 week cycle, that "HI" tells us that this cycle is consistent across the highs or peaks of the stock market, and that "Weeks 1, 21, & 41" tell us which weeks of the year the 20 week cycle in the stock market is expected to peak).

Of course, we could also turn to Week # 1 on page 49 in The 1990 Calendar Book and see the same information presented in a slightly different manner. Here in the "Weekly Linear Cycles" section we can find the listing

*SP HI 20 - 3 / 5.

This information tells us much about the various cycles for each market listed in the "Cycles Index" section of The Almanac and makes it possible for one to keep current regarding The Almanac's cyclical information by simply turning the pages in "The Calendar Book" to the current week of the year. (Then, if one desires a listing of all the different cycles projected in the book for a specific market, one can turn to the "Cycles Index" section at the back and obtain that listing).

The "SP HI 20" portion of the information tells us the obvious - that the S & P 500 stock market index is expected to be near a high or peak in prices during this weekly time period (we know that it is weekly because it is listed under the "Weekly Linear Cycles" section). The "20" tells us that this peak occurs roughly every 20 weeks and tells us by being listed during the current week that the 20 week cycle should peak during this time period or week. (If the "HI" were not present in the above listing, we would know that the cycle was automatically projecting a LOW).

In the preceding chart, we have drawn a downward arrow during this period (the first week of 1990) which, of course, occurs the first week after the vertical dotted line labeled with the "0". (This "0" line marked the end of the previous year. The chart thus shows prices updated through the end of the year as they appeared to the trader at that time). The rest of the "*SP HI 20 - 3 / 5" information pertains to the cycle's "time band".

A time band is formed by simply taking a percentage of the length of the cycle with the most common time band being the 10 percent time band. In our example, 10 percent of a 20 week cycle is 2 weeks. The 10 percent time band thus states that price for this 20 week high cycle is most likely to peak during the period encompassing the 2 weeks prior to and the 2 weeks following the week of the expected high. Hence, the two weeks before, the week of, and the two weeks after total five weeks within which the 20 week cycle is expected to peak.

In "The Calendar Book," we represent the first week when the cycle first enters the 10 percent time band as "1 / 5". The second week is represented as "2 / 5" with the last week being represented as "5 / 5" (thus indicating that the following week would be outside the time band since it would be represented as "6 / 5". Since such is the case, the "6 / 5" and those weeks beyond are obviously not listed). The center week of this particular time band is thus the third of five weeks which is represented in our example as "3/5".

Hence, one can turn to any week of the year in "The Calendar Book" and quickly ascertain which cycles are projected to be within a 5 or 10 percent time band that particular week AND how far into that time band price has progressed.

THE CENTER WEEK OF THE TIME BAND IS THE WEEK THAT THE CYCLE WILL IDEALLY PEAK (OR BOTTOM)!

Centered weeks are ALWAYS represented with odd numbers (i.e., in our example, 3 is the center week of a 5 week cycle time band for a 20 week cycle). A 30 week cycle would thus have a 7 week

10 percent time band with the centered week being the week marked "4 / 7". A 40 week cycle would have a 9 week 10 percent time band with the centered week being the week marked "5 / 9" and so on.

The Almanac also defines a 5 percent time band with an asterisk. Such may be found in our example where the asterisk preceding the "SP" defines this week as being both within the 10 percent AND 5 percent time bands. Whereas the 10 percent time band for a 20 week cycle will cover 5 weeks, the 5 percent time band will cover only 3 weeks.

The centered week will, of course, always be within both the 5 AND 10 percent time bands and will thus be marked with an asterisk. Note, however, that an asterisked week is NOT NECESSARILY the centered week.

In our chart below, we have replaced the "down" arrow from our previous chart with a vertical mark representing the centered week for our 20 week projected stock market cycle high. We have also drawn a horizontal line encompassing the two weeks preceding and the two weeks following this centered week. The drawing that results thus represents the 10 percent time band for the 20 week cycle centered on the 1st week of 1990 as projected in "The 1990 Calendar Book."

Note that the time band is drawn above year end prices since the expectation is that an intermediate to major HIGH is being projected.

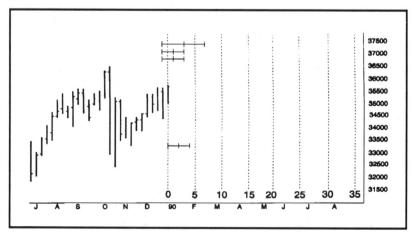

If we were to look further at the cycles listed during the first week in "The 1990 Calendar Book," however, we would note that the 20 week high cycle was not the only listing.

In fact, we would see THREE cycles projecting immediate highs - the 18 week, the 20 week, and the 32 week cycles.

10 percent time bands representing these three projected cycle highs have also been drawn in the chart above prices. Note that the time bands for the two shorter cycles project the same period for the high therein strengthening the expectation that the high is likely to be significant. Note, too, that these two cycles overlap the longer 32 week cycle which is drawn on top and together suggest that the 32 week cycle is likely to peak early in its time band rather than late OR that a "double top" will quickly be experienced in the early weeks of the year.

(One might notice, too, that the smaller cycles projecting peaks have been drawn below the longer cycles. The opposite is the case with cycles projecting lows. Although all cycles projecting lows are, of course, drawn BELOW price, here the longer cycles are drawn on the bottom with the shorter cycles directly on top. Hence, as one proceeds vertically away from price, one encounters longer and longer time band projections).

We also note that "The 1990 Calendar Book" is projecting a low to quickly follow the centered peaks in the first week of the year as the 24 week cycle bottoms. This low is centered in the second week of the year and the information allows us to draw the projected 10 percent time band below prices. This has been done in the chart that follows.

Two weeks go by placing us in the third week of the year. We note that the 18 and 20 week cycles have made their expected highs as projected by The Almanac. We can now, therefore, mark the cyclical highs for those cycles with vertical marks above prices as noted in our chart following.

The 32 week cycle high is still unresolved, however. All we can say at this point is that it is LIKELY to have occurred coincident with the 18 and 20 week cycle highs. Since the time band has not concluded, however, and CLEARLY resolved the cycle high, we will leave the time band as drawn in the chart for now.

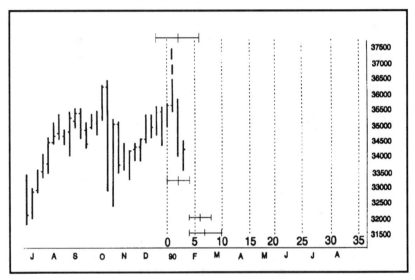

(By the way, if you purchased "The 1990 Calendar Book," you DID sell your portfolio of stocks into these highs, didn't you???)

Additionally, it appears from price action that the 24 week cycle low projected for the 2nd week of the year in "The 1990 Calendar Book" MAY have already occurred given the price action this week and the close well off the lows of the week.

In looking ahead, we notice that the 16 and 33 week cycles are soon expected to make intermediate to major cyclical lows and that the 10 percent time bands for these two cycle lows both begin next week, the 4th week of the year.

We thus draw the time bands below prices for these two cycle lows as shown in the chart below with the 16 week cycle on top, the 24 week in the middle, and the 33 week on the bottom. Note that these time bands suggest that further lows are yet to come. A rational conclusion is that it is thus likely to expect AT LEAST a retest of this week's lows prior to a potential market reversal.

In fact, we turn now to the "Cycles Index" section at the back of the book and notice that there are several cyclical highs projected in Spring, 1990, suggesting that these cycle lows should be followed by rising prices until spring when the 18 and 21 week cycle highs are again projected to peak.

Is it possible that this market will bottom in early February and then rally in the face of such poor price action, with most advisers bearish, with the savings and loan crisis deepening, with interest rates rising, the dollar falling, and so on?

Let's see what happened and how our cyclical projections turned out! The chart below shows prices through week 7, 1990. We are now able to definitely mark the 32 week cycle high at the beginning of the year as has been done with the third mark above prices. It also appears that the 24 week cycle low appeared during the 3rd week of the year as suspected during the discussion accompanying the previous chart.

We can also conclude that the 16 week cycle has bottomed 1 week early during the 5th week of the year as marked by the vertical dash.

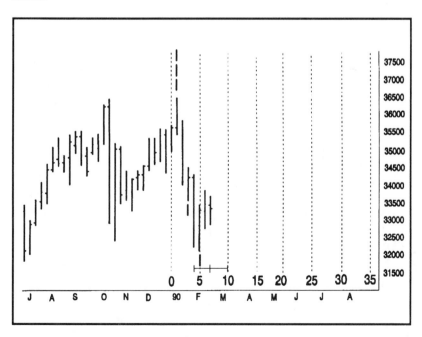

It is still a little premature to conclude that the 33 week cycle has also bottomed, however, since there are still 3 weeks left in the 10 percent time band.

We thus leave the 10 percent time band drawn in the chart as is shown.

Since the 24 and 16 week cycles have both bottomed one week prior to the centered week, we must conclude that a rally may be in order since bull markets will usually bottom early in their time bands.

The ideal situation would involve a successful retest of the early February lows thereby forming a double bottom.

In the chart below, it is now the 10th week.

Note that our successful retest has occurred and that prices have since rallied. Since we are at the end of the 10 percent time band, we can conclude that the retest marked the low of the 33 week cycle and that it appeared 1 week after the ideal center of the cycle.

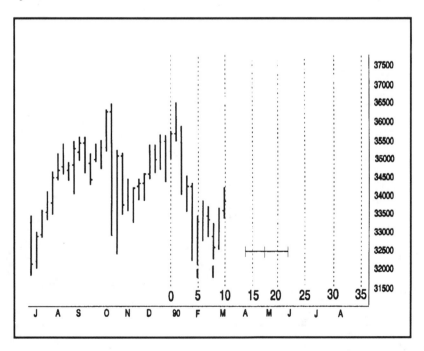

Although price has since rallied, we note that our next cyclical projection in "The 1990 Calendar Book" is for an intermediate to major cycle low in early May as the 44 week cycle bottoms.

We thus draw this 10 percent cycle time band below prices and center the time band on the 18th week of the year as listed in "The Calendar Book."

In the chart below, it is now the 17th week of the year.

Price is breaking hard into our projected 44 week cycle low due next week and we need to be looking forward and plotting our next strategy should this projected cycle low occur on time as expected.

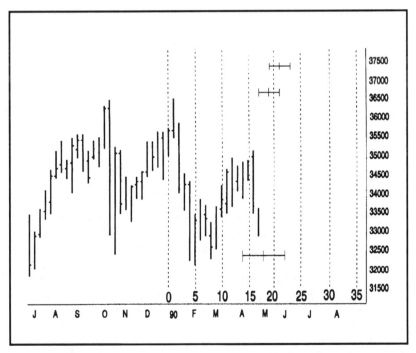

We note that the next projected cycles are the 18 and 20 week cycles which are centered in and project peaks during weeks 19 and 21. 10 percent time bands for these cycles are shown above prices in the chart and suggest a bottom shortly followed by a move up into the cyclical peaks.

In the chart below, we are in the 19th week of the year.

The Calendar Book has the 18 week cycle high projected for this week, but price is exceptionally strong and the 20 week cycle high is not projected to be made for another two weeks.

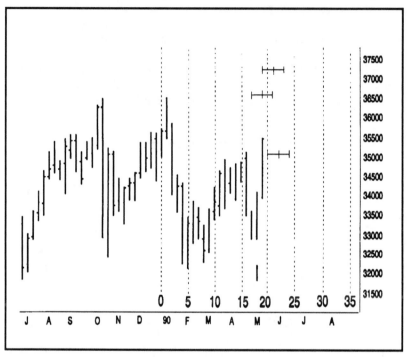

We do note that the 16 week cycle is then expected to bottom very shortly thereafter suggesting a period of volatility.

Also, the 44 week projected low in "The 1990 Calendar Book" appears to have occurred on the centered 18th week of the year and can now be marked as such. This marking is also shown in the chart above.

We have moved ahead to the 24th week of the year in the following chart.

The period has been quite volatile over the past month as suggested by the previously discussed cycle analysis.

We can label the peaks of the 18 and 20 week cycle highs and for the 16 week cycle lows but neither the peaks nor the troughs are well defined on a weekly chart and are subject to interpretation.

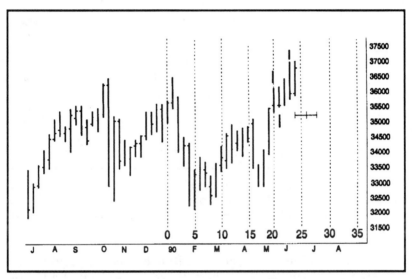

The cycles do suggest an intermediate term low just immediately ahead, however, as listed during this current 24th week of the year for the 24 week cycle. This cycle is centered during the 26th week of the year and we have just entered this week the 10 percent time band. The time band is drawn below prices in the chart above .

In the next chart, we are in the 28th week of the year. Given the strong upward movement this week, it is quite clear that the 24 week cycle has occurred on the centered week as projected by "The 1990 Calendar Book." This week is marked as such in the chart by the vertical dash.

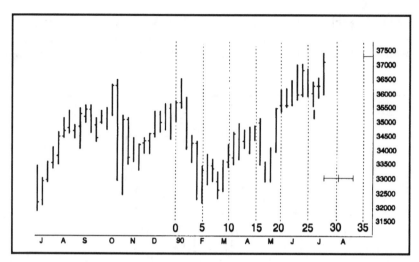

The next major low is also projected by the 10 percent time band drawn below prices. This time band centers the 38 week cycle during the 31st week of the year which is the first week in August, 1990.

Note that two additional cycle high time bands are projected for late August by "The 1990 Calendar Book" for peaks in the 18 and 32 week cycles shortly thereafter. These peaks are centered on the 37th and 35th weeks of the year, respectively.

IMPLICATIONS - There are several implications suggested by the use of the cyclical projections in "The Calendar Book" of "The $upertrader's Almanac."

1. The long term stock market INVESTOR should attempt to time PURCHASES during those periods of projected cyclical lows. The greater the number of cycles projecting the low (as at the February lows in our example above) the greater the probability that the anticipated low is likely to be one of major importance.

2. The intermediate term stock market INVESTOR should attempt to time PURCHASES during those periods of projected intermediate term cyclical lows and should raise cash by EXIT-ING the market or REDUCING COMMITMENTS during those periods of intermediate anticipated cyclical highs.

3. The stock market TRADER should attempt to margin his account to the maximum extent acceptable given the individual's

risk tolerance by making PURCHASES at major cyclical lows with margin used to a lesser extent at less important intermediate term and short term cyclical lows. Positions should at least be EXITED at major cyclical highs and margin commitments due to long positions at least reduced to zero. At intermediate and short term market highs, margin positions should at least be reduced to no more than 25 percent. Many stock market traders will, of course, wish to at least exit all positions and will even reverse positions by selling short at cyclical highs.

4. The INSTITUTIONAL TRADER will want to enter short hedges with options, futures contracts, and so on at intermediate and major cyclical projected highs. Cash should be raised and later reemployed at intermediate and major cyclical lows.

REFINING TIMING OF ENTRY AND EXIT POINTS - Entering and exiting positions should be done on a "tops down" basis by lining up daily cycles with monthly and weekly cycles in order to determine the most opportune entry and exit time periods.

Additional confirming evidence (such as chart patterns, trendlines, Elliott Wave analysis, divergence, and the like) should then be used to provide actual entry points once the opportune TIME has been defined.

5. Similar analysis should be performed on other markets with purchases and long hedges made at cyclical lows while short hedges and outright short sales should be initiated at cyclical highs.

Market Profile

Don't fall in love with your positions.
They can break your heart.

The Market Profile and the Liquidity Data Bank are reports disseminated by the Chicago Board of Trade. They purport to contain market information that formerly was available only to the trader standing in the pit. Some active traders consider the two reports to be a major breakthrough in market understanding and claim that they offer a logical and organized set of price and volume data from which traders can base trading decisions.

The CBOT Market Profile is an information service composed of two parts;

1.) a graphic, or profile, of current market activity organized in terms of price and time, and

2.) the Liquidity Data Bank which is a summary of the volume traded at each price.

The volume information in the LDB details which prices were accepted or rejected by the market.

The profile graphic organizes the market in half-hour time periods and uses letters of the alphabet to plot price activity occurring in a given half-hour period. The first half-hour period is given the letter "A", the second the letter "B", and so on. An example follows.

Price	8:30	9:00	9:30	10:00	10:30	11:00	11:30
100:02	– –	– –	– –	– –	– –	– –	– –
100:01	– –	– –	– –	– –	– –	– –	G-Above
100:00	– –	– –	– –	– –	– –	– –	G-Value
99:31	– –	– –	– –	– –	– –	– –	G
99:30	– –	– –	– –	– –	– –	– –	G
99:29	– –	– –	– –	– –	– –	– –	G
99:28	A	AB	AB	AB	AB	AB	ABG
99:27	A	AB	ABC	ABC	ABCE	ABCE	ABCEG
99:26	A	AB	ABC	ABCD	ABCDE	ABCDEF	ABCDEFG
99:25	A	AB	ABC	ABCD	ABCDE	ABCDEF	ABCDEFG
99:24	A	AB	ABC	ABCD	ABCDE	ABCDEF	ABCDEF
99:23	A	AB	ABC	ABCD	ABCDE	ABCDEF	ABCDEF
99:22	A	AB	ABC	ABCD	ABCD	ABCDF	ABCDF
99:21	A	A	AC	ACD	ACD	ACDF	ACDF
99:20	A	A	AC	AC	AC	AC	AC
99:19	– –	– –	C	C	C	C	C-Below
99:18	– –	– –	– –	– –	– –	– –	Value
99:17	– –	– –	– –	– –	– –	– –	– –

Time

Example 1. The construction of a treasury bond profile.

If the market trades only briefly in a given price range, it denotes rejection by the market of that price. On the other hand, if the market trades in a range for an extended time, it denotes market acceptance of that price. This acceptance of price by the market forms what is called the value area. This area is said to contain 70% of the day's trading activity.

When price and value diverge, as it did in the above example by trading above 100 late in the day, a trading opportunity arises. Price must either return to the value area or must lead value to a new value area. Once the day's value area is formed, the following day's price action can be compared to the first day's value area.

Trading FND Slammers

I do not think much
of a man
who is not wiser today
than he was yesterday.
- Abraham Lincoln

This section has the ability to pay for The Almanac many, many, many times over by itself (but, of course, so do many of the other sections in the book).

The following technique does not require a fancy computer in order to experience success. You do not need to spend a lot of time studying reports, reading "tout" sheets", becoming an expert, etc. All you need do is identify and pay attention to two things;

A. upcoming first notice days (FND - or, if FND follows the last trading day (LTD), the upcoming LTD) and

B. a bear market.

Here is what to do -

1.) Locate a bear market (i.e., one that is making new lows) - a bull or neutral market will not do.

2.) Identify the upcoming FND (or LTD) for the next expiring contract.

3.) Sell short on trading system short sale signals, on breaks to new lows, on the thrust technique (see index), on intraday chart breaks, on chart formation breaks, etc.

4.) Enter the trading system stop or other appropriate stop point.

5.) Pyramid the position on successive short sale signals or breaks to new lows.

6.) Close the position the day before FND (or LTD).

If you will use this technique only this year, you should be able to build at least five major positions per half annum and more in deflationary periods.

A follow-up method also exists, and that is to trade the long side just after the long liquidation into FND occurs (see the lumber example below although ANY of the following trades could have been used to show a post-FND bounce). Note that the FND bounce is best played in the next contract out and not the contract that has just experienced the liquidation pressure (which makes sense as the liquidating trade would be subject to delivery if entered on the long side).

Why does this phenomenon exist?

Simply because long positions are subject to a delivery notice on FND whereas short positions are not (delivery is initiated at the option of the short).

Usually, a large number of traders believe that the market is oversold and HAS to go up (and in most instances, they are 100% correct - their timing is just a little bit off, they are holding the wrong contract and are running out of time). As FND approaches, these weak players must exit or have 10,000 Live Hogs (or whatever) running around in the middle of their living room.

So guess what happens? Everyone KNOWS that the market HAS to go UP, so they hold onto their contracts, FND approaches, and they are forced to liquidate all at the same approximate time.

Do the shorts care? Sure they do! They care about how low the price will go and how much money they might make and often even join in the selling to help things out a little bit.

Now on which side do you want to be?

You might doubt the importance of the FND liquidation discussion above and feel that it is being overblown - in other words, that the liquidation must be due to new fundamental information that has just entered the market, good crops, bad crops, the latest guru's buy or sell signal, and so on.

But look at the sugar example below. Prices dropped from about 9.00 cents to about 7.75 cents IN 4 DAYS. This was a whopping

14 % of the TOTAL VALUE of the market and over 150 % of the margin.

Why did this happen?

If we look back to this period of time, traders were VERY bullish Sugar. Hence, going into contract expiration and FND, most traders were long (commercial interests, on the other hand, were VERY short).

Commercials (dealers) are the STRONG hands in a market, the public constitutes the WEAK hands. The result?

A classic FND Slammer!!!

What happened directly afterwards? Prices bottomed THE NEXT DAY and within 2 months rose to new six year highs as they traded at over 15 cents in July, 1988.

Traders who predicted a rise in sugar in 1988 called the market correctly, but if they were caught in the May FND Slammer liquidation, they chose the wrong contract and were forced to reenter the market in either July or one of the more deferred months at a steep premium in order to continue to participate.

Did the above have anything to do with hurricanes, Cuban sugar, import quotas, force majure on shipping cargoes, increased demand, etc.?

NOT HARDLY!

Although the examples that follow are all from late 1988, many such examples can be found in ANY six month period. Note how representative these examples are of several different industry groups.

Since FND in sugar follows LTD, the arrow in this FND Slammer of May, 1988 sugar actually points to LTD.

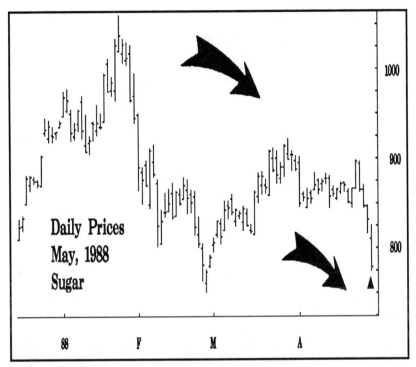

Daily Prices
May, 1988
Sugar

Sometimes experienced traders will take delivery of a commodity and store it when it gets slammed. Sugar is not a good candidate for this approach, however, as it can be delivered at any port in the world.

The FND slammer in December, 1988 Oats shown on the next page occurred the day prior to FND (which is the day depicted by the up arrow in the chart below).

This is the typical experience as most brokerage firms are calling their clients and pressuring them to liquidate by the close of business of the day preceding FND. One of the ways this pressure evinces itself is through DRAMATICALLY increased margins by the brokerage firm.

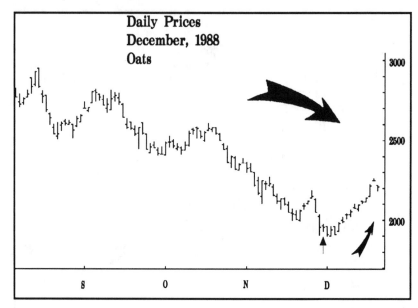

Note the post FND bounce.

This example from the Soybean Complex in December, 1988 Soybean Oil is similar to the December Oats example above.

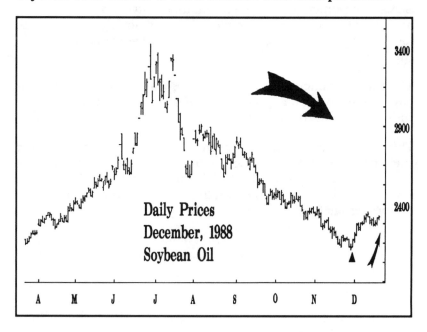

Although pork bellies and live hogs have no FND, FDD serves the same purpose since longs are still subject to delivery after FDD.

The arrow in the December, 1988 Live Hog chart below points to FDD.

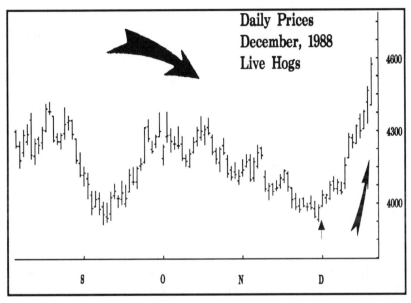

Note the bounce that occurred immediately afterwards. This rally accounted for about 16.5 % of the live hog price. Do you really suppose that 16.5 % of the Live Hog supply in the United States all of a sudden became quarantined, diseased, or otherwise vanished in the but fourteen days after FDD?

Or was this simply another example of an FND Slammer?

Do you think that Slammers only occur in the meats, grains, and soft commodities?

Then look at the next chart of June, 1988 US Treasury Bond prices and note the liquidation that took place right into FND day (marked by the up arrow). This phenomena has happened many times in the BD market over the past 10 years (although it does not occur in the Currencies or Stock Indexes).

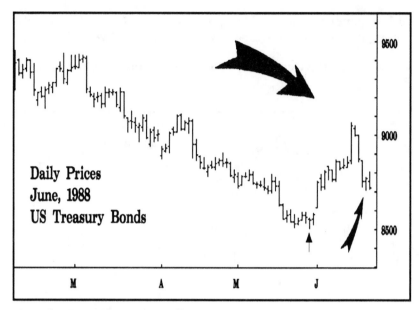

Daily Prices
June, 1988
US Treasury Bonds

Note the Post Slammer Rally!

How about the metals?

Note the lows in October, 1988 gold that occurred in the fall right on FND!

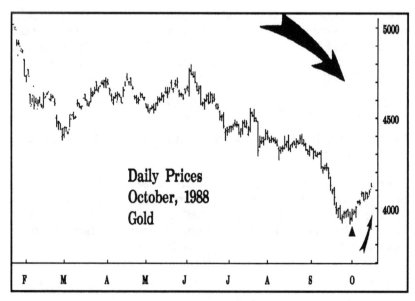

Daily Prices
October, 1988
Gold

In both the US Treasury Bond and gold examples, the contract getting slammed made new lows on FND day while the back (deferred) contracts did not, setting up a classical divergence pattern. This divergence, especially when it occurs on or within one day of FND, is a VERY STRONG sign that the Post Slammer Rally is preparing to occur in the deferred contract.

Note the bounce in both these contracts after the Slammer!

Need I tell you where the long term downtrend in the August, 1988 pork belly chart shown below ended?

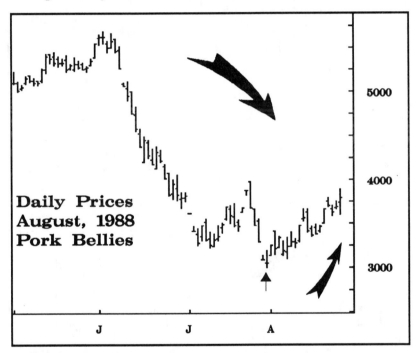

**Daily Prices
August, 1988
Pork Bellies**

In the lumber market, FND occurs the day after LTD and LTD occurs on the first business day prior to the 16th of the month.

Hence, the slam in our next example of November, 1988 lumber occurred into LTD on November 15th, 1988 as shown in the chart that follows.

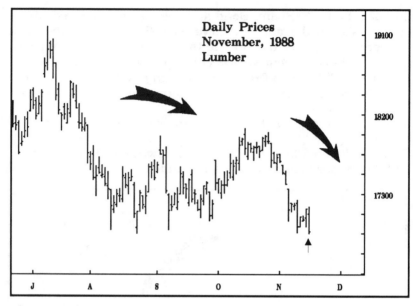

Daily Prices
November, 1988
Lumber

The next chart shows January, 1989 lumber, the next available lumber contract after the November, 1988 lumber contract expired. The same LTD for the November, 1988 lumber contract is marked by the up arrow.

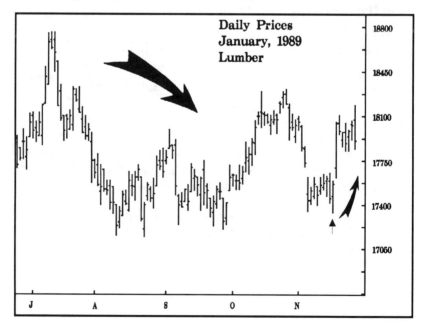

Daily Prices
January, 1989
Lumber

Note the low made the day after the arrow (i.e., on FND).

Note the Post Slammer Rally that occurred in the LBF contract after the LBX liquidation had been completed.

A FND Seasonal Slammer is formed when a market downtrend into a FND aligns with a down seasonal.

A FND Cyclical Slammer is formed when a market downtrend into a FND aligns with the time band of an expected cycle low.

Where can one obtain timing information pertaining to first notice days, last trading days, first delivery days, last delivery days, and so on?

Glad you asked!

"The Calendar Book" of "The $upertrader's Almanac" lists such information in the weekly sections of the book on the exact dates that such events occur!

Hence, one need only turn the pages of "The Calendar Book" to locate such events in markets experiencing bearish trends.

"The Calendar Book" additionally identifies specific potential FND Slammers that the trader should monitor throughout the year in the weekly section of the book.

Priority is placed upon those Slammers that have a chance of aligning with seasonals and cycles listed in the book and therein have the possibility of developing into FND Seasonal Slammers and FND Cyclical Slammers.

An example of both a FND Seasonal Slammer and a FND Cyclical Slammer comes from "The 1990 Calendar Book" where, on page 55 (Week 2), it was stated that "One should monitor trades # 26 and # 29 for the possibility that they will develop into FND Slammers".

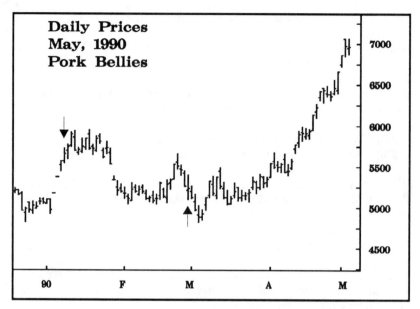

Daily Prices
May, 1990
Pork Bellies

Trade # 29 listed the down seasonal in May Pork Bellies that suggested weak prices from January 7th to February 28th. These dates are indicated by the down and up arrows in the chart.

First Notice Day in March Pork Bellies also occurred on February 28th as listed on page 84 of "The 1990 Calendar Book."

The March 5, 1988 low at 4837 in this chart occurred within the five percent time band of the 22 week cycle projected low and within the ten percent time band of the 29 week cycle projected low.

These projected cycle lows were listed on page 91 (and on other weekly pages in the book) under the "Weekly Linear Cycles" section.

"The 1990 Calendar Book" had thus listed information that projected a down seasonal into late February and major intermediate term cycle lows projected in late February or early March.

With such a confluence of important events occurring around FND, is it any wonder that liquidation occurred but three days from FND?

Note the rally that occurred in the next contract out as shown in the chart. Once the two overlapping cycles had bottomed, the weak seasonal had run its course, and the FND Slammer had washed out the final weak long positions, the market absolutely exploded.

The post FND Slammer rally that occurred moved prices up over $ 8,000 per contract versus a margin of but $ 1,000 in the next two months.

If you purchased "The 1990 $upertrader's Almanac," were you able to profit from the above information?

Cause and Effect

CAUSE :	**SUPPLY INCREASES**
EFFECT :	Price should decline
REASON :	More product is available for the same amount of demand
EXCEPTION :	Demand increases faster than supply

CAUSE :	**SUPPLY DECREASES**
EFFECT :	Price should increase
REASON :	Less product is available for the same amount of demand
EXCEPTION :	Demand decreases faster than supply

CAUSE :	**DEMAND INCREASES**
EFFECT :	Price should increase
REASON :	More demand exists for the same amount of product
EXCEPTION :	Supply increases faster than demand

CAUSE :	**DEMAND DECREASES**
EFFECT :	Price should decline
REASON :	Less demand exists for the same amount of product
EXCEPTION :	Supply decreases faster than demand

CAUSE :	**INTEREST RATES INCREASE**
EFFECT :	Financial instruments (BD, MB, & TN) should decline in price
REASON :	Long term financial instruments maintain an inverse relationship of price to yield
EXCEPTION :	A rate increase in the short end can be perceived as being anti-inflationary which drives long term yields down

CAUSE :	**INTEREST RATES INCREASE**
EFFECT :	Financial instruments (CD, ED, & TB) should decline in price
REASON :	Short term financial instruments maintain an inverse relationship of price to yield
EXCEPTION :	If the increase causes a panic, prices of short term instruments will rise from a flight-to-quality

CAUSE :	**INTEREST RATES INCREASE**
EFFECT :	Economic growth should slow
REASON :	The cost of doing business has increased causing cancellation of marginally profitable projects
EXCEPTION :	The increases are not sufficient to slow growth or the rate of inflation is above the level of interest rates

CAUSE :   **INTEREST RATES INCREASE**

EFFECT :   Inflationary expectations should decrease

REASON :   Implies less demand for goods and services

EXCEPTION :   Increases are not perceived as sufficiently strong to arrest the inflationary spiral

CAUSE :   **INTEREST RATES INCREASE**

EFFECT :   Commodity prices should decline

REASON :   Implies less demand for goods and services

EXCEPTION :   Product shortages still exist or tangible assets are perceived as being more valuable to hold in a high inflation / severe dollar depreciation environment

CAUSE :   **INTEREST RATES INCREASE**

EFFECT :   CRB Index should decline

REASON :   The CRB Index directly reflects commodity price movements

EXCEPTION :   The increases are not perceived as being sufficient to slow down business expansion, inflation, or both

CAUSE :   **INTEREST RATES INCREASE**

EFFECT :   Stock prices should decline

REASON :   The increased cost of doing business implies less economic growth and, therefore, less corporate profitability

EXCEPTION :   The increase is perceived as being the last in this round of increases or is perceived as creating a better long-term business environment

CAUSE :	**INTEREST RATES INCREASE**
EFFECT :	Currency prices should decline
REASON :	More foreign investment is attracted to higher US interest rates
EXCEPTION :	Dollar-denominated assets are not perceived as having sufficient value to induce the investment

CAUSE :	**INTEREST RATES INCREASE**
EFFECT :	Metals prices should decline
REASON :	The increased cost of doing business implies less economic growth and, therefore, less demand for metal
EXCEPTION :	The precious metals sector will rise in tandem with interest rates in an inflationary environment as interest rates rise when it is perceived as a store of value or a hedge against inflation

CAUSE :	**INFLATION INCREASES**
EFFECT :	Prices of goods and services in general should increase
REASON :	Higher prices are required to offset the higher costs of production including, but not limited to, wages, raw materials, and the cost of money (interest)
EXCEPTION :	The producer holds prices in order to maintain or enlarge market share or prevent a loss to foreign competitors

CAUSE :	**INFLATION INCREASES**
EFFECT :	Commodity prices should increase
REASON :	Commodity prices are one of the main ingredients of inflation
EXCEPTION :	The inflation is caused by other factors, such a rapid wage increases, a depreciating currency, raw material shortages, government policies, excess monetary stimulus, excess fiscal stimulus, and so on

CAUSE :	**INFLATION INCREASES**
EFFECT :	Financial instruments (BD, CD, ED, MB, TB, & TN) should decline in price
REASON :	A higher return is required to offset the increased erosion of the financial instrument's income stream
EXCEPTION :	The increases cause panic in the financial markets and trigger a flight-to-quality into short term financial instruments (TB)

CAUSE :	**INFLATION INCREASES**
EFFECT :	Real (inflation-adjusted) economic growth should slow
REASON :	Higher inflation implies higher interest rates and reduced growth
EXCEPTION :	The relationship is not highly correlated

CAUSE :   **INFLATION INCREASES**

EFFECT :   Stock prices should decline

REASON :   Higher inflation implies higher interest rates
                     and reduced growth as the quality of earn-
                     ings deteriorates

EXCEPTION :   The relationship is not highly correlated

CAUSE :   **INFLATION INCREASES**

EFFECT :   Currency prices should rise

REASON :   Higher prices imply that each dollar will
                     purchase a lesser amount of goods and
                     services therefore requiring a lower dollar
                     to compensate for the higher prices

EXCEPTION :   The increase in inflation is perceived as
                     being at or near the end of the inflationary
                     cycle or political, economic, or military events
                     in other nations are not perceived as being
                     secure leading to a flight-to-quality (Dollars)

CAUSE :   **INFLATION INCREASES**

EFFECT :   Metals prices, especially precious metals,
                     should rise

REASON :   The precious metals sector is perceived as a
                     store of value which protects against declines
                     in the value of paper money

EXCEPTION :   It sometimes occurs that the precious metals
                     sector is NOT perceived as a store of value
                     which protects against declines in the value
                     of paper money

CAUSE :   **DOLLAR DECREASES**

EFFECT :   Foreign currencies should increase

REASON :   Currencies maintain an inverse relationship to the Dollar

EXCEPTION :   Not all currencies increase.

CAUSE :   **DOLLAR DECREASES**

EFFECT :   US Dollar Index should decrease

REASON :   This increase should occur by definition

EXCEPTION :

CAUSE :   **DOLLAR DECREASES**

EFFECT :   Economic growth should increase

REASON :   The price of US goods becomes more competitive to foreigners as the Dollar declines leading to increased exports

EXCEPTION :   A time lag is required to effect the relationship, it can be offset by a perception of inferior quality, foreign trade barriers may prevent increased exports, or the domestic economy may slow faster than the increased export demand

CAUSE :   **DOLLAR DECREASES**

EFFECT :   Inflationary expectations should increase

REASON :   The price of foreign goods becomes more expensive to Americans as price increases are required to offset the lower value of the Dollar

EXCEPTION :   The foreign producer holds prices in order to maintain or enlarge market share or offsets the currency fluctuation with increased efficiencies of production

CAUSE :   **DOLLAR DECREASES**

EFFECT :   Commodity prices should increase

REASON :   Increased inflationary stimulus is implied as
                  foreign demand for the same amount of
                  goods increases

EXCEPTION :   Increased foreign demand may not be
                  sufficient to overcome increased supply

CAUSE :   **DOLLAR DECREASES**

EFFECT :   CRB Index should increase

REASON :   The CRB Index directly reflects commodity
                  price movements

EXCEPTION :   Increased foreign demand may not be
                  sufficient to overcome increased supply

CAUSE :   **DOLLAR DECREASES**

EFFECT :   Financial instrument prices should decline

REASON :   Greater inflationary and higher growth
                  pressures are implied making less valuable
                  the fixed income stream from an income
                  producing asset

EXCEPTION :   A severe unchecked drop may cause a
                  flight-to-quality in Treasuries

CAUSE :   **DOLLAR DECREASES**

EFFECT :   Metals prices, especially precious metals, should rise

REASON :   The precious metals sector is perceived as a store of value which protects against declines in the value of paper money

EXCEPTION :   It sometimes occurs that the precious metals sector is NOT perceived as a store of value which protects against declines in the value of paper money or a foreign nation may need to sell precious metals reserves to raise cash

CAUSE :   **DOLLAR DECREASES**

EFFECT :   Grain and Bean prices should increase

REASON :   Greater export demand is implied by the cheaper Dollar

EXCEPTION :   Sufficient supply exists in the hands of foreigners to offset the implied demand increase

CAUSE :   **DOLLAR DECREASES**

EFFECT :   Stock prices should increase

REASON :   The decrease implies greater foreign demand for US goods and, therefore, greater corporate profitability along with more attractive prices for assets to foreign acquires

EXCEPTION :   A time lag is required to effect the relation-ship, it can be offset by a perception of in-ferior quality, foreign trade barriers may pre-vent increased exports, or the domestic economy may slow faster than the increased export demand

CAUSE :   **DOLLAR DECREASES**

EFFECT :   Trade deficit should narrow

REASON :   Lower prices for US goods to foreigners increases foreign demand and, therefore, exports

EXCEPTION : Foreign productivity increases, technological advances, or protected markets may prevent the narrowing from occurring

CAUSE :   **ECONOMIC GROWTH INCREASES**

EFFECT :   Financial instruments should decline

REASON :   Implies greater demand for money to finance the expansion and, thus higher interest rates to allocate available investable funds

EXCEPTION : Capacity utilization is particularly low, productivity increases are particularly high, the national savings rate is sufficiently high to supply the funds needed for investment, or foreign investment supplies needed capital

CAUSE :   **ECONOMIC GROWTH INCREASES**

EFFECT :   Commodity prices should increase

REASON :   Greater demand is implied for goods, services, labor, and raw materials

EXCEPTION : Can be offset with increasing supply availability due to opening of new mines, increases in agricultural acreage, technological advances, productivity advances, and government programs that increase supply

CAUSE :   **ECONOMIC GROWTH INCREASES**

EFFECT :   Inflationary expectations should increase

REASON :   Greater demand is implied for goods, services, labor, and raw materials

EXCEPTION :   Can be offset with investment that results in increases productive capacity

CAUSE :   **ECONOMIC GROWTH INCREASES**

EFFECT :   Metals prices, especially industrial metals, should increase

REASON :   Greater demand is implied for available production

EXCEPTION :   Can be offset with production increases or foreign supply

CAUSE :   **ECONOMIC GROWTH INCREASES**

EFFECT :   Dollar should increase in price

REASON :   Foreign investment is attracted to expanding economies

EXCEPTION :   Offset if the growth increases inflationary expectations

CAUSE :   **ECONOMIC GROWTH INCREASES**

EFFECT :   Stock prices should increase

REASON :   Implies increased profitability for US firms

EXCEPTION :   Profitability can be offset by more rapidly increasing costs in an inflationary and highly competitive environment

Record Prices

Our senses can grasp nothing that is extreme;
...too much truth stuns us.-
Blaise Pascal, Pensees, I, 1670

The following are the highest prices at which the following markets have traded in the left columns, with lowest prices in the right columns. (Please note that the contract that recorded the record high price was not always the spot contract, especially in carrying charge markets.) Those dates beginning with a "9" indicated a price in the 1890's.

BDM	860415	105.15	**BDZ**	810928	55.05
BOV	741001	51.00	**BOV**	681011	6.91
BPN	720517	2.6130	**BPZ**	850226	1.0185
CN	801128	419 .250	**CU**	960908	19. 500
			CAI	860224	.6759
CCN	770718	5379.22 (-244.00)			
CFU	770414	340.17			
CLX	901010	41.15	**CLK**	860401	9.75
CPZ	881208	164.75			
CTV	730924	99.00			
DMZ	880104	.6610	**DMH**	850226	.2881
EDU	860902	94.36	**EDH**	820216	82.84
FCJ	790418	95.15			
GMZ	860417	102.03			
GOC	800121	1026.40	**GOV**	760825	99.70
GOY	800121	1031.90			
HOU	791203	115.00	**HOQ**	860714	29.95
JYZ	881202	.008650			
LBU	790824	287.30			
LCJ	900416	80.55			
LHQ	820820	68.00			
MBM	860401	103.17	**MBM**	871019	70.03
NYU	891009	209.20	**NYU**	820806	55.85
OU	880628	394	**OZ**	321203	13 .875
OJX	771116	220.00			
			PAZ	691206	31.65
PBQ	750814	105.10			

PLL	800305	1189.50	**PL**	590110	50.50
SN	730605	1290	**SX**	390815	65.75
SFZ	871231	.8210			
SMN	730605	413.50	**SMV**	580127	41.70
SUH	741121	66.00			
SPU	900605	374.90	**SPU**	820809	101.15
SVL	800117	5240.00			
TBZ	761220	95.81	**TBZ**	801211	82.90
TNU	860829	105.13	**TNZ**	820623	68.00
ULU	900823	111.00	**ULV**	860728	30.00
VLM	891009	319.90	**VLH**	820809	110.50
WH	740226	645	**WZ**	321125	41

The following listing shows record high and low prices and the date on which they occurred. The record high price is listed in the "HIGH" column and the record low price in the "LOW" column. The date on which the record price occurred is listed just to the left of the price column.

The contracts analyzed in this study are listed in the "BEGIN" and "END" columns. For instance, the first contract "BDH" (March US Treasury Bonds) analyzes all March contracts beginning with the March, 1978 contract ("7803" in the "BEGIN" column) and ends with the March, 1989 contract ("8903" in the "END" column). The study thus includes twelve years of March US Treasury Bond prices which is from the first day of trading of the contract at the Chicago Board of Trade.

Many traders use this information to define major long term support and resistance levels, begin major Fibonacci, Gann, or other counts, begin cycle studies, and so on.

Many thus also find it quite important to know that, although the all-time high for the March bond contract was attained on April 17, 1986 at 102.29, the March, 1978 bond contract also peaked at 102.28 on September 19, 1977.

If you would like to have such detailed information, The Almanac makes its historical computer printout sheets which individually analyze in detail all the years in the "Record Prices" study shown below. This study consists of over 200 pages of such information and is complete through the end of the most recent calendar year.

The cost of these computer printouts is $ 75.00. They may be ordered at the back of the book in the "Additional Products" section should you have interest.

FINANCIALS - BD, ED, MB, TB, TN

CONTRACT	BEGIN	END	DATE	HIGH	DATE	LOW
BDH	7803	9003	860417	102.29	810928	55.20
BDM	7806	9006	860417	105.15	810928	56.08
BDU	7809	9009	860417	104.20	810909	56.12
BDZ	7712	8912	860417	103.25	810928	55.05
EDH	8203	9003	860902	94.32	820216	82.84
EDM	8306	9006	861205	94.15	820625	83.97
EDU	8309	9009	860902	94.36	840530	84.55
EDZ	8312	8912	860902	94.41	840629	84.84
MBH	8603	9003	870305	101.05	850924	80.04
MBM	8606	9006	860401	103.17	871019	70.03
MBU	8509	9009	860401	103.01	880111	81.01
MBZ	8512	8912	861204	101.18	871019	73.00
TBH	7703	9003	761203	95.13	800317	83.95
TBM	7606	9006	761203	95.40	810514	83.35
TBU	7609	9009	761203	95.15	810825	84.30
TBZ	7612	8912	761220	95.81	801211	82.90
TNH	8303	9003	870305	105.06	820623	68.03
TNM	8206	9006	860416	105.08	820625	68.13
TNU	8209	9009	860829	105.13	820623	68.01
TNZ	8212	8912	861204	105.13	820623	68.00

METALS - CP, GO, PA, PL, SV

CONTRACT	BEGIN	END	DATE	HIGH	DATE	LOW
CPF	7301	9001	890124	160.00	721110	46.10
CPH	7303	9003	890303	155.00	721117	47.10
CPK	7305	9005	800212	153.00	721109	47.80
CPN	7307	9007	800213	153.00	721117	48.35
CPU	7309	9009	800212	153.00	821109	49.05
CPZ	7212	8912	881208	164.75	721117	46.05
GOG	7502	9002	800121	973.20	760825	100.50
GOJ	7504	9004	800121	986.50	760825	101.50
GOM	7506	9006	800121	999.80	760825	102.10
GOQ	7508	9008	800121	1013.10	760825	101.00
GOV	7510	9010	800121	1026.40	760825	99.70
GOZ	7512	8912	800211	981.00	760825	100.00
PAH	8303	9003	831220	174.00	821101	64.50
PAM	8306	9006	831220	173.75	821103	65.45
PAU	8309	9009	890414	180.00	821104	66.00
PAZ	8212	8912	831220	178.00	821101	63.50
PLF	7301	9001	800305	1148.50	721030	126.00
PLJ	7304	9004	800305	1189.50	721030	127.90
PLN	7307	9007	800305	1071.50	721102	133.20
PLV	7310	9010	800305	1113.50	721102	135.50
SVF	7301	9001	800118	5036.0	720531	157.6
SVH	7303	9003	800122	4493.5	711101	140.9
SVK	7305	9005	800122	4530.5	711229	149.4
SVN	7307	9007	800121	4467.5	720228	158.2
SVU	7309	9009	800122	2500.0	720918	174.0
SVZ	7212	8912	800122	2405.0	711103	137.5

CURRENCIES - BP, CA, DM, SF, JY

CONTRACT	BEGIN	END	DATE	HIGH	DATE	LOW
BPH	7603	9003	810121	2.4475	850226	1.0345
BPM	7606	9006	810120	2.4660	850226	1.0235
BPU	7509	9009	810120	2.4715	850226	1.0190
BPZ	7512	8912	801103	2.4485	850226	1.0185
CAH	7803	9003	770526	.0946	860204	.6759
CAM	7806	9006	770922	.9316	860204	.6845
CAU	7809	9009	771220	.9165	860204	.6809
CAZ	7812	8912	770929	.9307	860204	.6785
DMH	7603	9003	871231	.6426	850226	.2881
DMM	7606	9006	871231	.6494	850226	.2905
DMU	7509	9009	871231	.6555	850226	.2925
DMZ	7512	8912	880104	.6610	850226	.2971
JYH	7803	9003	871231	.008590	821104	.003620
JYM	7806	9006	881125	.008485	770610	.003650
JYU	7809	9009	881125	.008580	820813	.003760
JYZ	7712	8912	881202	.008650	821104	.003600
SFH	7603	9003	871231	.7955	850226	.3408
SFM	7606	9006	871231	.8040	850226	.3439
SFU	7509	9009	871231	.8120	850226	.3480
SFZ	7512	8912	871231	.8210	850226	.3525

STOCKS - NY, SP, VL

CONTRACT	BEGIN	END	DATE	HIGH	DATE	LOW
NYH	8303	9003	891009	204.20	820809	58.45
NYM	8206	9006	891009	206.70	820809	59.25
NYU	8209	9009	891009	209.20	820806	55.85
NYZ	8212	8912	891009	201.95	820809	58.10
SPH	8303	9003	891010	369.05	820809	101.85

SPM	8206	9006	891010	373.20	820810	103.20
SPU	8209	9009	900605	374.90	820809	101.15
SPZ	8212	8912	891010	364.50	820809	101.40
VLH	8203	9003	891010	311.50	820809	110.50
VLM	8206	9006	891009	319.90	871023	111.00
VLU	8209	9009	900103	309.05	820809	110.60
VLZ	8212	8912	891010	311.50	820809	109.90

OIL - CL, HO, UL

CONTRACT	BEGIN	END	DATE	HIGH	DATE	LOW
CLF	8401	9001	830802	32.15	860714	10.45
CLG	8402	9002	830804	32.00	860714	10.50
CLH	8403	9003	840516	31.30	860714	10.55
CLJ	8404	9004	840516	31.45	860305	11.49
CLK	8405	9005	840328	31.10	860401	9.75
CLM	8306	9006	840516	31.50	860401	9.95
CLN	8307	9007	840516	31.70	860401	10.15
CLQ	8308	9008	830713	31.92	860401	10.30
CLU	8309	9009	830802	32.35	860714	10.10
CLV	8310	9010	900920	35.00	860714	10.10
CLX	8311	9011	901010	41.15	860714	10.25
CLZ	8312	8912	830802	32.21	860714	10.40
HOF	8101	9001	810227	112.00	860714	33.85
HOG	8102	9002	810304	113.00	860714	34.50
HOH	8103	9003	810406	114.70	860714	32.25
HOJ	8104	9004	810410	112.76	861029	38.80
HOK	8105	9005	810410	113.00	860714	30.90
HOM	8106	9006	810107	109.20	860401	31.33
HON	8107	9007	810107	109.80	860401	31.40
HOQ	8108	9008	810128	110.00	860714	29.95
HOU	8109	9009	810817	110.25	860714	30.55
HOV	8110	9010	810817	111.25	860714	31.50

HOX	8111	9011	810225	108.50	860714	32.40
HOZ	8012	8912	810225	110.25	860714	33.30
ULF	8601	9001	851121	80.00	860728	30.75
ULG	8502	9002	851125	79.10	860725	31.50
ULH	8503	9003	850221	79.50	860725	31.90
ULJ	8504	9004	850327	83.99	860725	32.30
ULK	8505	9005	850424	86.50	860723	32.70
ULM	8506	9006	850523	83.80	860401	34.10
ULN	8507	9007	850620	85.90	860401	33.75
ULQ	8508	9008	850712	85.15	860731	30.25
ULU	8509	9009	900823	111.00	860728	30.75
ULV	8510	9010	900924	106.30	860728	30.00
ULX	8511	9011	900928	101.70	860728	30.00
ULZ	8512	8912	851111	81.00	860728	30.20

FIBER - CT, LB

CONTRACT	BEGIN	END	DATE	HIGH	DATE	LOW
CTH	7303	9003	800915	97.00	720822	27.05
CTK	7305	9005	801229	97.67	720908	27.59
CTN	7307	9007	801229	97.05	720822	27.85
CTV	7310	9010	730924	99.00	720822	27.70
CTZ	7212	8912	800912	96.96	720908	26.59
LBF	7401	9001	790911	251.00	741003	98.50
LBH	7403	9003	790221	248.70	741003	101.70
LBK	7405	9005	790515	246.00	741003	106.50
LBN	7407	9007	830506	252.50	741003	111.00
LBU	7309	9009	790824	287.30	790913	111.00
LBX	7311	8911	791002	265.00	741003	94.60

MEAT - FC, LC, LH, PB

CONTRACT	BEGIN	END	DATE	HIGH	DATE	LOW
FCF	7901	9001	790418	91.350	780123	46.250
FCH	7803	9003	790320	93.850	770817	40.900
FCJ	7804	9004	790418	95.150	770817	41.025
FCK	7805	9005	790418	94.000	770817	41.200
FCQ	7808	9008	790418	92.850	770822	41.900
FCU	7809	9009	790418	92.200	771103	41.900
FCV	7810	9010	790418	90.000	771021	42.000
FCX	7811	8911	790416	90.300	771122	44.100
LCG	7102	9002	890208	75.850	701209	27.100
LCJ	7104	9004	900416	80.550	701209	27.825
LCM	7006	9006	790427	79.750	690725	26.650
LCQ	7008	9008	900813	79.425	690910	27.150
LCV	7010	9010	901001	80.450	701209	27.900
LCZ	7012	8912	891220	79.150	701209	26.600
LHG	7002	9002	801202	62.700	710111	15.800
LHJ	7004	9004	801223	61.500	710111	15.750
LHM	7006	9006	900529	67.450	710111	17.450
LHN	7007	9007	900521	65.325	710111	18.250
LHQ	7008	9008	820820	68.000	710111	18.625
LHV	7010	9010	820908	64.875	710831	17.925
LHZ	7012	8912	751002	65.600	701029	15.900
PBG	7002	9002	751003	104.100	710111	22.575
PBH	7003	9003	751003	100.150	710111	22.600
PBK	7005	9005	750922	96.500	710111	23.250
PBN	7007	9007	750915	94.950	710723	20.700
PBQ	7008	9008	750814	105.100	710729	19.750

FOOD - CC, CF, OJ, SU

CONTRACT	BEGIN	END	DATE	HIGH	DATE	LOW
CCH	7303	9003	770307	4499.37	720822	668.21
CCK	7305	9005	770318	4442.27	730122	668.43
CCN	7307	9007	770718	5379.22	730122	666.67
CCU	7309	9009	770718	5009.95	730122	672.84
CCZ	7212	8912	770718	4541.48	720822	660.50
CFH	7403	9003	770414	329.05	750303	49.00
CFK	7405	9005	770414	337.50	750411	45.25
CFN	7407	9007	770414	339.88	750411	47.00
CFU	7409	9009	770414	340.17	750411	48.30
CFZ	7312	8912	770413	334.00	750411	49.50
OJF	7301	9001	900115	201.00	770111	37.40
OJH	7303	9003	900122	206.50	770111	37.50
OJK	7305	9005	900123	205.85	770111	38.50
OJN	7307	9007	900123	205.40	770111	39.70
OJU	7309	9009	880812	203.50	770111	41.00
OJX	7311	8911	771116	220.00	721018	41.40
SUF	7401	9001	741120	65.00	841231	2.87
SUH	7303	9003	741121	66.00	850620	3.34
SUK	7305	9005	741120	63.44	850430	3.05
SUN	7307	9007	741120	60.05	850628	2.30
SUV	7310	9010	741120	53.55	850620	2.74

GRAINS - C, O, W, WK, WM

CONTRACT	BEGIN	END	DATE	HIGH	DATE	LOW
CH	6903	9003	801128	410 1/4	680930	106
CK	6905	9005	801128	418	680930	109 1/2
CN	6907	9007	801128	419 1/4	680909	104 3/8
CU	6909	9009	801128	407	710921	109 1/2

CZ	6912	8912	741004	400	710921	112 3/8
OH	7503	9003	880628	367 3/4	860710	108
OK	7505	9005	880628	340	860417	94 1/4
ON	7507	9007	880628	393	860722	95
OU	7509	9009	880628	394	770816	98 1/2
OZ	7412	8912	880628	389 1/4	860710	105 1/2
WH	6903	9003	740226	645	680930	123 3/4
WK	6905	9005	740226	636	690328	125 1/8
WN	6907	9007	740226	585	690630	124 1/2
WU	6909	9009	740226	582	690728	119 1/2
WZ	6912	8912	740226	582	690728	125 1/4
WKH	7703	9003	801022	540	770822	236
WKK	7705	9005	801022	548 1/2	860710	233
WKN	7607	9007	801022	544	770613	227
WKU	7609	9009	801022	550	770815	225
WKZ	7612	8912	801022	515 1/2	770823	231
WMH	8103	9003	801120	519 1/2	861219	259 1/2
WMK	8105	9005	801120	537	870105	255 1/2
WMN	8107	9007	801120	538	870807	275 1/2
WMU	8109	9009	801120	545	871103	285 1/2
WMZ	8012	8912	810220	500	860917	254

SOYBEAN COMPLEX - BO, S, SM

CONTRACT	BEGIN	END	DATE	HIGH	DATE	LOW
BOF	6901	9001	741004	47.87	680930	7.00
BOH	6903	9003	741004	46.76	681009	7.07
BOK	6905	9005	741004	45.88	681009	7.15
BON	6907	9007	741004	45.12	681009	7.22
BOQ	6908	9008	740731	47.40	681009	7.17
BOU	6909	9009	740730	44.90	681008	7.05
BOV	6910	9010	741001	51.00	690611	6.98

BOZ	6912	8912	741004	48.85	690611	6.97
SF	6901	9001	880623	1034	690318	236 7/8
SH	6903	9003	880623	1023	690502	240 5/8
SK	6905	9005	770422	1076.50	690605	244 3/8
SN	6907	9007	730605	1290	690729	247 3/4
SQ	6908	9008	730726	1175	690903	245 5/8
SU	6909	9009	880623	1070	681004	240 1/2
SX	6911	8911	880623	1046	690729	233 1/2
SMF	6901	9001	880623	313.00	691112	66.30
SMH	6903	9003	880623	308.00	691112	67.35
SMK	6905	9005	730510	321.50	691112	68.60
SMN	6907	9007	730605	451.00	691112	69.70
SMQ	6908	9008	730605	413.50	691112	70.40
SMU	6909	9009	710712	365.00	690911	69.10
SMV	6910	9010	880623	322.00	690307	66.75
SMZ	6912	8912	880623	318.00	690819	66.50

Chapter 5

Spreads

Carrying Charges

*The long leg of a bull spread must be
in the spot month if the spread
is to profit from price increases caused
by fear of tight supplies.*

Carrying charges represent the costs of storing the physical commodity, the cost of insurance, and the interest cost (prime + 1%) over the period stored. Not all commodities have carrying charges (for example, the perishables [LC, FC, LH, and potatoes] do not).

Carrying charge information is vital to a spread trader because if one were to enter into a spread of buying the lower nearby and selling the deferred, one would want to know the maximum risk (namely full carrying charges). If buying the deferred and selling the near, carrying charges will allow profit objectives to be established were the spread to widen in your favor.

(In reality, storable commodity spreads historically only rarely have approached full carrying charges and are normally contained by about 70 percent of full carry (record-high interest rates have allowed more frequent occurrence of full carry in the early 1980's, however, as product owners have been more reluctant to hold inventory at costly levels).

Since prices fluctuate rapidly and interest rates change, the carrying charges are going to change also. Hence rather than list the carrying charges, here is the formula plus the storage cost for a few commodities:

*Carrying Charge = (Spot Price x Interest Cost / 12 +
Storage + Insurance) x # of Months*

When divided by the number of months involved, the resulting figure is the Cost of Carry and is the theoretical monthly decline in the value of deferred contracts from full Carrying Charge value if cash prices remain stable.

Interest rate future spreads (Bonds and Notes) are based on the current yield of the underlying cash instrument and the expected repurchase rate in the future month. Currency spreads are based on the interest rate differential between US rates and rates of the country in question. Stock spreads are based on such factors as dividend yields, T-bill rates, holding period, etc. The perishable commodities mentioned above have no limit as to the discount a nearer month can go to a deferred one. TBs, CDs, and EDs have no carrying charges but instead trade off market expectations of future interest rates.

Here are some recent storage and insurance costs:

Soybeans and all grains	-	4.92 cents	/bushel	/month
SM	-	$210	/contract	/month
CP	-	$ 75	/contract	/month
OJ	-	$34.50	/contract	/month
CL	-	$150	/contract	/month
CF	-	$86	/contract	/month
SV	-	$7.50	/contract	/month
BO	-	$54	/contract	/month
CT	-	$125	/contract	/month
PB	-	$190	/contract	/month
HO	-	$336	/contract	/month
CC	-	$25	/contract	/month
GO	-	$2	/contract	/month

There are additional one-time handling charges as follows:

CP - $50   OJ - $40.50   CF - $168.75   CC - $100

HOW TO TRADE CARRYING CHARGES - The two variables in the carrying charge formula are interest rates and prices. Hence, IF ALL OTHER THINGS ARE EQUAL, when prices or interest rates are increasing, expect the spreads to widen (buy the deferred and sell the near).

Source/Product Spreads

People seldom improve when they have
no other model but themselves to copy after.
- Goldsmith

The most popular of the source/product spreads is the Soybean Crush. The Soybean Crush is the process which converts 1 bushel of Soybeans into 11 pounds of Soybean Oil, 48 pounds of Soybean Meal, and 1 pound of waste. The value of the products in cents per bushel minus the price of one bushel of Soybeans is normally the way the spread is plotted. The correct way to establish a Soybean Crush spread is long 12 SM, long 9 BO, and short 10 S contracts (the "Big Crush"). The "Little Crush" is formed by buying 1 SM, 1 BO, and selling 1 S. The best time of the year to enter into the Soybean Crush spread is in June by trading next year's March or May products versus same month Beans. For processing to be profitable, the combined prices of SM and BO must exceed the cost of the S by about 15 cents per bushel at a minimum. Hence, a general rule of thumb is that one would want to reverse the Soybean Crush spread and buy products, sell Soybeans (the "Reverse Crush") if the spread approached the above price level.

A second popular source/product spread is the Cattle Crush. This spread is normally computed by subtracting the combined dollar value of 1 FC and 1 C from the dollar value of 2 LC contracts. The spread is formed by buying the FC and C and selling the LC.

A third source/product spread is the Crack spread, obtained from "cracking" one barrel of oil in the refinery process. A typical barrel of CL will produce about 18.9 gallons of Gasoline (45% of the total yield) and 7.1 gallons of Heating Oil (17% of the total yield) for a total of 62% of each barrel. The crack spread is normally formed by selling 3 contracts of CL versus buying 1 contract of HO and 2 contracts of UL although there are other variations.

Chapter 6

Mother Nature and The Markets

The Greenhouse Effect

Almighty and merciful Father,
we pray Thee send to us
such seasonable weather
that the earth may,
in due time,
yield her increase
for our use and benefit.
- The Book of Common Prayer, 1662

(The following article is from The 1987 & 1988 Almanacs BE-FORE it became fashionable to be concerned about the effects of Global Climate Change).

Much attention has been given the last few years to what Swedish Nobel laureate Svante Arrhenius in 1896 termed the "greenhouse effect". The term refers to sunlight that passes through the atmosphere, reaches and warms the surface of the Earth, is radiated back into the atmosphere as infrared radiation (heat), and is trapped in the atmosphere by ever-increasing amounts of carbon dioxide and certain other gases instead of being released into space. The trapping of this heat is similar to the way a blanket traps heat and gradually increases worldwide temperature.

The process is basically beneficial as the air traps enough heat to keep the earth's surface about 54 F degrees warmer on average than it would be without an atmosphere. Mars, for instance, with a thin atmosphere deficient in carbon dioxide (CO_2), shivers at about -60 F degrees while Venus, which lies beneath a thick blanket of the gas, is searingly hot at 900 F.

Concern on Earth arises that CO_2 concentrations will increase to levels that will produce a general warming or "greenhouse effect". Indeed, many news stories have painted a bleak picture of cities like Charleston, South Carolina, submerged, of the nation's breadbasket transformed into a desert, of New York City enjoying the same average temperature that Daytona Beach, Florida, now experiences, and of congressmen arriving by boat at Capitol Hill as polar ice caps melt and raise sea levels.

The Carbon Dioxide Buildup

The carbon dioxide buildup is caused by

1.) the burning of fossil fuels (US utilities, for instance, produce approximately 8 % of worldwide emissions while the US in total produces about 25 % of total worldwide emissions),

2.) the leveling of tropical forests (currently at a rate of 3,000 acres per hour), and

3.) other activities.

Deforestation and especially the leveling of tropical forests is particularly important because trees and vegetation are normally natural "sinks" for carbon dioxide (i.e., they have historically REMOVED carbon dioxide from the atmosphere through the process of photosynthesization). In recent years, however, they have actually become net PRODUCERS of CO_2 as forests are burned and decompose and, in the process, produce more atmospheric CO_2 than they consume.

Historical Research

Since 1851, researchers at East Anglia have demonstrated that the earth's average temperature has risen by approximately 1 F degree as CO_2 concentrations rose 10 percent from 1850 to 1940 (with a cooling period of about .36 F degree then following that lasted from 1940 to 1965). During this same period, sea levels rose by about 1 foot.

By studying such things as gas bubbles trapped in glacial ice, scientists have estimated that CO_2 made up 250 - 290 parts per million (ppm) of the atmosphere in the less industrialized world that existed before 1850 and around 200 ppm during the Ice Ages. These concentrations compare to 315 ppm in 1958 when Charles David Keeling began a monitoring program atop the Mauna Loa volcano in Hawaii and about 340 ppm currently (around an 8 % rise in the last 30 years alone).

Waiting for the "Signal"

Some thus now feel that the trend is in the process of accelerating rapidly and point to such evidence as the melting of two-thirds of the Athabasca Glacier in the Canadian Rockies since 1870 or the approximately 100 X 20 mile ice berg that split from Antarctica in late 1987 as evidence of the existence of the greenhouse effect.

Others, however, are not convinced and are expecting a carbon dioxide "SIGNAL" to rise above background random noise in the 1990s to truly confirm the theory. The event these observers are awaiting is a rise in the average global temperature that can be pinned unequivocally to man's activities.

Should the concentration pass 400 ppm (expected in the next 50 years), the atmosphere will have returned to a state it has not seen for well over 1 million years. But it could go even higher. In 1983, the National Academy of Sciences projected that the CO_2 level will rise to 600 ppm within the next 50 to 100 years.

Such a concentration would require two events to occur;

1. First, sufficient fossil fuel will have to be burned and,

2. Second, the CO_2 will have to stay in the air (which about 58% of the CO_2 produced by burning has done since precision monitoring began in 1958).

Natural Removal of CO_2

The CO_2 that does not remain in the air is removed through such natural processes as photosynthesis, absorption by limestone formations, and through the oceans. Since deforestation has caused terrestrial ecosystems to be a net source of CO_2 in recent years, the oceans are assumed to be swallowing more CO_2 than normal estimates would assume. (The oceans contain 55 times as much carbon as does the atmosphere and 20 times as much as do land plants). Small changes in the oceans' capacity to store carbon can thus dramatically alter the rate of growth of the greenhouse effect. Although the oceans theoretically can dissolve 2,250 times as much CO_2 as there is in the atmosphere today, in reality this cannot happen because the top surface layer of the ocean, in contact with the air, would become saturated and prevent additional gas from being dissolved. Also, since oceanographers and chemists cannot explain how the seas manage to absorb as much CO_2 as they do, they can only assume that present absorption rates will continue.

A lesser absorption rate will, of course, result in more CO_2 in the atmosphere and accelerate the warming process. Much of the CO_2 absorption rate will thus depend upon the natural ability of the oceans to recycle water through their currents and deposit carbon to lower levels.

The oceans have a warm underwater current that flows to the poles about 300 feet below the surface. Upon reaching the poles, the water is cooled, sinks, and then returns back to tropical climes. It is during the sinking period that CO_2 is carried out of the atmosphere and deposited in sediments on the sea floor. The entire cycle, traced by tracking carbon 14 and tritium as a result of Pacific Ocean nuclear tests, is estimated at about 500 years. This long circulation time and imprecise knowledge of how the warm surface water interacts with cold water from the depths make it very difficult to determine how much CO_2 and heat the oceans can take up, let alone how the ocean's circulation is affected.

Warmer oceans would result in greater volumes of sea water evaporating. Since water vapor is an even more efficient absorber of infrared energy (heat) than CO_2, it, too, could exacerbate the warming by increasing the humidity. Additionally, when the Earth warms up, the high latitudes warm up much more than the low latitudes. A faster rise in temperature in the higher latitudes will reduce the temperature differential between the equator and the poles which will tend to stall ocean and wind currents and hasten the warmup.

Thus, as oceans warm, their capacity to hold CO_2 diminishes, effectively "snowballing" the greenhouse effect.

Effects of Other Gases

Although most attention has been given to the effect of CO_2 on the atmosphere, other gases also contribute to the greenhouse effect. In fact, these gases are accumulating more rapidly than CO2. Methane, for instance, has been rising at 1 % per year for each of the last 3 decades. These gases are potentially more dangerous than CO2 because they remain in the atmosphere for many years and are potent absorbers of heat. As a group, they are already 60 % as influential as CO2 on Earth's atmosphere and within 50 years will, at current rates, equal or exceed CO2's influence.

The effect of these gases has the potential of increasing temperatures faster than most models now predict. The main culprits are methane, ozone, nitrous oxide, and several chlorofluorocarbons (Freons).

Offsetting Factors

The main offsetting factor to the greenhouse effect is simply that plants generally grow better in climates with higher CO2 concentrations. When the concentration of CO2 is below 280 ppm, CO2 is probably the main limiting factor to plant growth. For every 10 ppm above 280, however, growth is generally stimulated between 0.5 % and 2.0 %. Also, when more carbon dioxide is available, plants use water more efficiently. Some thus hope that an atmosphere richer in CO2 could lead to higher food yields in the future and that enhanced plant growth could slow the rise in CO2 and global temperatures. In some varieties, however (soybeans, for example), the growth would produce more carbon compounds and relatively fewer compounds high in nitrogen.

A second offsetting factor is the cloud cover. An increase in cloud cover would be expected to provide a shading (or cooling) effect. With a warmer environment, more water will evaporate into the air, changing the area, height, water content, and reflectivity of clouds. More precipitation (7-11 % above present levels is expected) would thus likely occur worldwide.

Cloud cover is thus one of the largest swing factors in the entire equation describing future effects of the Greenhouse effect on earth. But scientists are not sure what types of clouds might form and it DOES make a difference. The reason is that high altitude or cirrus clouds (those that look like fine strands of cotton fiber) absorb infrared energy and thereby contribute to the warming effect while cumulus clouds, or those soft, white, billowy cotton puffs of the mid-altitudes, allow infrared energy to pass through.

A third offsetting factor (which acts like cloud cover) are aerosols and dust thrown up by volcanic activity. Since 1958, for instance, there have been two unusually large volcanic eruptions (Mount Agung in 1963 and El Chichon in 1982). These two eruptions cooled the planet although the effect does tend to be a temporary one.

One model that accounts for these eruptions has temperatures rising after 1985 by 1 F degree by the early 1990s and almost 2 F degrees by 2000. If correct, the Earth will be warmer than it has been for thousands of years by the end of the century. In fact, some point to the recent African and Southeastern United States droughts (1986) as being typical of what to expect in the post-El Chichon, CO_2-driven warming period.

Implications

So what are the implications of all this information? Projections call for temperature increases of about 3 to 8 degrees within 50 - 100 years, NOT CONSIDERING THE OTHER GREENHOUSE GASES. This increase may not sound like much, but consider the following;

In the Corn Belt, an increase of only 3 F degrees would TRIPLE the frequency of periods of 5 days or more exceeding 95 F degrees. Such conditions at critical stages in the growing season are known to harm corn and lead to reduced yields. Omaha, Nebraska, which currently averages three days per year of greater than 100 F degrees, would be expected to average twenty per year by 2030. Washington, DC, would go from one to twelve days per year.

Changes in the timing and amount of precipitation will almost certainly occur if the climate warms, affecting agriculture and hydroelectric resources. Soil moisture, which is critical during early planting and growth periods, will change. In fact, temperature and soil moisture maps at Princeton University of a world with double the present concentration of CO_2 are similar to those of the United States dust bowl days of the 1930s. This loss of water in the US would likely be worsened by a northward shift of the rain belts.

As an example of how little a change is needed to effect change, it is estimated that a 3 1/2 F rise in temperature and a 10 % decrease in precipitation could cut the flow of the Colorado River by 40 % and leave most of the Western states without enough water. The Rio Grande basin would be the hardest hit with a fall of 75 %. Additionally, a small change in the mean temperature would likely generate a large change in the frequency of such extreme events as droughts, freezes, floods, and hurricanes.

Sea levels would likely rise by about 3 feet by the year 2030. Most of these increased water levels would arise from the Antarctic and Greenland ice sheets and glaciers. (Were the North Pole to melt entirely it would have no influence on water levels since ice displaces just about its own volume of water when floating). These changes in water levels will be nowhere near as rapid as the possible changes in temperature over the next century, however, since ice has a high level of thermal inertia and melts very slowly.

The most dramatic scenario is that the West Antarctic ice sheet could slide into the sea if the buttress of floating ice separating it from the ocean were to melt, raising the average sea level 16-19 feet. A 12 foot rise would inundate vast tracts of farmland in the Netherlands, Bangladesh, Thailand, Kampuchea, Vietnam, and China. Half of Florida and Louisiana would be covered by the ocean (but don't go long Orange Juice futures yet).

Naturally occurring climate swings have brought down societies in the past (the Anasazi Indians of the American Southwest, for example, from decreased rainfall). 13 million Bangladeshis live on ground that is less than 10 feet above sea level. Do you suppose they would be politely allowed to file into India and Burma if the flooding starts?

Of course, some areas of the world will benefit from the greenhouse effect while others will not. Great Britain, for example, which derives its temperate climate from the Gulf Stream, might experience a climate change to one similar to other places of the same latitude (like the Aleutian Islands) were the stream to slow because of more equal temperatures at the poles and the equator. The northernmost reaches of the Earth's land masses would likely benefit from the warming (Canada, Alaska, Iceland, Scandinavia, the Soviet Union, and Japan). Iceland could conceivably double its sheep production as a result of increased grazing land. The North American grain belt would shift northward into Canada as the warming produced drier, hotter conditions in the American Midwest. Forests would advance almost to the northernmost points of the lands encircling the pole. Thus, the regions that would suffer the most would tend to be the developed countries of the richer northern hemisphere (the grain-growing region of the United States, most of Europe, and the most fertile regions of the Soviet Union).

Summary

So why have such a long-term discussion in such a short-term oriented profession as trading? The answer is simple - the greater understanding we have of the world we live in, the greater we should collectively be able to plan for and adjust to future changes that occur (not withstanding being able to appreciate the reasons for a warming trend over the next several years, should it occur).

Additionally, should events unfold the way they appear to have the greatest chance of occurring, one will not be surprised by a warmer tendency. Such preparation should allow the farmer to be more willing to plant earlier, if need be, and the trader to be more willing to justify long positions during key growing periods.

Of course, you may think that the above is just some grandiose theory that does not apply to your farm, your city, or your state, and that it will "go away" IF it ever arrives.

And perhaps you're correct! But consider this;

Five of the warmest years ever recorded since records have been kept have occurred since 1978 !!!

1980, 1981, and 1983 stand out as the three warmest years EVER recorded !!!

Perhaps now a rereading of the Almanac's previously published "Outlook" sections is in order and will have more meaning.

If that outlook is correct, then we should expect periods of dryness to be magnified over the next several years as the general trend now appears to be towards a warmer climate.

Or to quote this same section in The 1987 Commodity Trader's Almanac, "Beans in the teens? They're coming !"

1988 Update

The Greenhouse Effect was NOT, by itself, responsible for the 1988 warming and drought! It simply does not have the ability to cause such a dramatic change in temperatures as that which occurred in 1988. The 1988 dry spell was due more to the changing jet stream caused by the 1986-87 El Nino.

The Greenhouse effect DOES appear to be with us, however, and should accentuate the warmer temperatures expected into the early 1990s.

One additional problem is that even if the industrialized world freezed CO_2 emissions tomorrow, the growing industrialization of third world countries would soon overtake the lessened emissions of the industrial countries.

Volcanic Activity and the Climate

*Everybody talks about the weather
but nobody does anything about it.
- commonly ascribed to Mark Twain
(Samuel L. Clemens) but not found
in his published works*

Of a much shorter orientation is the level of volcanic activity. When volcanoes erupt, they shoot both visible ash and invisible sulfur dioxide into the air. Under the right conditions, the sulfur dioxide gas can react with water vapor in the upper air in the presence of sunlight to form a haze of tiny sulfuric acid droplets. This process allows a volcanic cloud to renew itself and, sometimes, even grow as it circles the earth. The cloud that is created by the eruption blocks out sunlight and has a cooling effect on the earth.

One of the first to recognize the effect of volcanic eruptions on climate was Founding Father Benjamin Franklin who observed and documented the effects of the 1783 eruption of Laki in Iceland while serving as ambassador to France. A blue haze that drifted across Europe and into parts of Asia followed this eruption. The winter of 1783-84 was unusually severe and Franklin proposed in a paper read before the Literary and Philosophical Society of Manchester that a connection existed between the haze, the cold winter, and the volcanic eruption in Iceland the previous year.

Some of the more powerful volcanic eruptions have been Tambora (Indonesia, 1815), Krakatoa (Indonesia, 1883), Santa Maria (Guatemala, 1902), Katmai (Alaska, 1912), Gunung Agung (Bali, 1963), and El Chichon (Chiapas, Mexico, March 28, 1982).

The Tambora eruption caused the famous "Year Without a Summer" when snow and freezes ruined crops in New England in June and August. The Krakatoa explosion spread dust into the stratosphere that cooled the earth for several years. The El Chichon eruption created one of the largest aerosols ever recorded. Followers of the aerosol theory point to the severe El Nino that followed soon afterwards and the devastating drought in Asia, Africa, and Australia as evidence of the power that volcanic eruptions can exert on world weather patterns and offer the Mount St. Helens eruption as the cause of the 1980 US drought.

Other recent eruptions have been the Columbian volcano on November 13, 1985 (which, by this theory, triggered the February, 1986 El Nino alert by the National Weather Service), the Augustine volcano in Alaska on March 27, and the eruptions in Hawaii in late 1986. Most recent were the Redoubt eruptions in Alaska.

Of particular importance in analyzing volcanic activity is the latitude of the volcanic eruption. Low-latitude volcanoes shade the equator, decreasing the temperature in what is usually the hottest zone. High-latitude volcanoes, on the other hand, make the nearest pole even colder and increase the temperature differential between the pole and the equator. It is this difference in temperatures in these two parts of the world that influences weather patterns with the patterns becoming more violent the greater the difference.

Because of the effect that increased temperature differentials between the polar regions and the equator can have on worldwide climate (causing stronger tradewinds and more severe weather patterns), the serious student will monitor volcanic activity to anticipate change in normal climatic patterns.

Volcanic activity has experienced a dramatic increase over the last decade. The aerosols produced by this activity were augmented in recent years by the dust and ash produced by the Northwestern United States forest fires during the dry period of 1987-88. This greater amount of particulate matter is still exerting a minor cooling effect upon the environment. This effect has resulted in a cooler climate than would have otherwise been experienced.

Sunspots

A sunset
is a sunrise
on the other side of the world.

In 1925, G. E. Hale and Seth Nicholson observed that Northern and Southern hemisphere sunspots are of opposite magnetic polarity. Nicholson further added in 1937 that the polarity reverses every 11 years giving rise to a complete cycle every 22 years. The cycle has varied from 20.8 to 27 years in length since 1755 and last peaked in 1980 (sunspot cycle number 21).

The 11 year sunspot cycle was due to bottom in 1986 in a major Minimum and bottomed on schedule. As the 11-year sunspot cycle tends to alternate peaks and, since cycles 19 and 21 were very high (around 170 mean sunspots), the next peak, due in 1991, would normally be expected to be lower than the previous one.

The sun was extremely inactive in the mid-1980s. The period is similar to the mid 1960's when ideal weather conditions occurred most of the time in the corn / soybean belt. Winters were quite harsh, especially in the eastern United States where snowfall was quite a bit above normal. Since 1986, however, the increase in sunspots has been particularly rapid and has coincided with much warmer weather.

History is replete with sunspot minima correlating with cooling climate. In the so-called "Little Ice Age", for instance, which chilled the earth from 1400 to 1850, the coldest of those years coincided with a period of minimum sunspot activity called the Maunder minimum.

A 90-100 year sunspot cycle also exists that reached maximum values around 1750, 1860, 1950, and is next anticipated around 2032 when Saturn and Uranus again synod behind the sun. Activity reaches minimum values (1670, 1800, 1900) when Saturn and Uranus synod in front of the sun, an event last due in 1988.

Drought has often followed two years after the sunspot minima.

Perhaps especially ominous is the fact that the Sun's critical mass will be off center from the solar system's barycenter (center of mass) in 1992 and that this event has corresponded historically with some very dry periods!

Finally, Ned Dewey published that earthquakes increase around the peak of a solar sunspot cycle.

El Nino Weather Patterns

In fair weather
prepare for foul.
- Thomas Fuller

The term "El Nino" originally was given by 19th-century Peruvian fishermen to a warm coastal current which runs southward along the coast of Ecuador around the Christmas season. In the last 30 years, El Ninos have occurred in 1957, 1963, 1965, 1969, 1972-73, 1975, 1976, 1982-83, and in 1986-87. The 82-83 El Nino has been described by scientists as being a once-in-a century event.

The 1986 El Nino actually began around October, 1986, although there were some early signs of it beginning in early 1986. In fact, in February, 1986, the National Weather Service issued an El Nino alert and Columbia University's Center for Climatic Research, developers of the first-ever forecasting model for El Ninos, predicted that the El Nino would peak in October / November and disappear by early 1987. By summer, 1986, however, it appeared to have aborted. The real episode then began late in the year with the effect finally easing by year end, 1987.

El Nino conditions frequently lead to weather and crop related havoc, especially during the second year of such conditions. The two areas and crops most affected by El Ninos are Wheat in Australia (which tends to receive below-average rainfall during an El Nino) and Corn in Argentina (which tends to receive above-average rainfall). The timing of the rainfall with respect to the stage of crop development determines the effect on crop yields. South Africa and Australia suffered from the worst drought since the 1972 El Nino during the 1982 El Nino.

The most severe effects of the 1986-87 El Nino have included drought in India and the Pacific Northwest. The Indian drought was caused by the weakening of the Indian Monsoon, a normal El Nino occurance. Reductions in rainfall also occurred in such areas as Indonesia, the Philippines, and several Pacific Islands. The high pressure El Nino system pushed the normal movement of storms in the northern Pacific Ocean northward into Alaska and northern British Columbia, by-passing the Northwestern US and leading to severe dryness.

If this effect continues into the late winter, it causes the jetstream to bring cold air from Canada into the US, resulting in a colder winter. If it continues into spring, it causes a wetter planting season.

One of the major causes of El Ninos is rising ocean temperatures. The warm water proceeds to warm the air above, causing it to rise and increase circulation. The changes in large-scale atmospheric pressure patterns affect the "southern oscillation".

Westerly winds then push the warmed waters east from the Indian and tropical Pacific Oceans to the coast of South America.

The warm water promotes the growth of plankton which smothers fish by depriving them of oxygen. Anchovies have been especially sensitive during past El Ninos and have experienced large population reductions. As other fish feed on the anchovies, an El Nino effects the entire food chain.

The arrival of the El Nino is marked with by a drop in fish catches along the coast of Peru and Ecuador and by heavy winter and spring rains at Guayaquil, Ecuador. The process normally lasts about 18 months and occurs every 2 to 7 years.

HOW TO TRADE - Since Peruvian anchovies are a source of protein, soybeans have been the market most affected during an El Nino event. The lack of Monsoon rains can additionally affect the sugar crop of India and, especially, the Phillipines.

Since the next El Nino is likely to occur in 1991-92 or so, if our outlook for some other weather-related events holds true (i.e., the sunspot cycle, the drought cycle, and the greenhouse effect) then it is possible that an early 1990s El Nino could occur at exactly the wrong time (is there ever a right one?) and could have the effect of magnifying the effects of the other events.

Chapter 7

Computer Applications

Computerized Approaches

In evaluating trading systems,
even a broken clock is right
twice a day.
- Edward Dobson

With their ability to crunch data, computers can be of enormous benefit in analyzing markets TO THOSE WHO KNOW HOW TO USE THEM PROPERLY.

Computers are basically used for three purposes;

1.) to test methods historically to see how a given trading technique "would have done" and to include modifications that can perhaps improve the method,

2.) to update and analyze markets daily, and

3.) to update and analyze markets in a "live environment".

In testing methods historically, one must begin first with some data to analyze. Although many feel that only the last six month's data is sufficient to study, we feel that those results that have withstood the vagaries of at least two long term cycles (each of 3 to 6 years or so, depending on the market) are more likely to provide the user with long term success. This requirement would mean that one would need prices back into the late 1970s at a minimum. It should also be noted that many major price movements began in the early 1970s when the Russians began their grain buying binge, gold was demonetized, the Vietnam War was fought, and so on. Hence, if one uses prices from about 1970 forward in one's data base, 85% of everything that is likely to happen in most market environments is likely to be contained in those prices.

Once a basic trading approach is expressed mathematically as a formula, the method is optimized by running several different parameters to find the "best fit(s)" for a particular market. The process usually begins with large increments in the parameters.

After a profit "cluster" area is located, the parameters are then broken down to smaller amounts around the "clustered" area.

For instance, if one were optimizing a dual moving average trading system, the initial matrix might appear as in the chart to the right.

15	2	-1	-4
10	5	1	-2
5	2	0	-1
	20	30	40

Once the most profitable area had been located (at 10 and 20 in our example), the matrix would then be magnified to include smaller parameters, as in the following chart (with a final optimized profit given by parameters 9 and 21).

12	2	3	2	2	3
11	3	5	4	4	5
10	3	4	5	6	6
9	2	5	6	8	7
8	3	5	6	7	6
	18	19	20	21	21

(The number of days in the matrix for the short term moving average are given by the left column while the bottom row gives the number of days for the long term moving average. The cell contains the profit in thousands of dollars for each appropriate moving average.)

If only one parameter were being optimized, the profit would be plotted in a line against the corresponding parameter value. If three were being used, a three-dimensional matrix would be used. Beyond three dimensions, the matrix must be described mathematically.

One variation of the above would place in each cell the profit less the worst drawdown achieved during the time period analyzed. Another variation would divide the profit by the worst drawdown and would then compare the resulting rates of return.

Once the optimization study is completed, the routine can be run over the period being analyzed by using the optimized parameters. Exact prices for entry and exit can be recorded and tabulated chronologically. This type of a computer run is termed a simulation of actual trading results and typically includes such useful information as total profit, worst drawdown, wins, losses, average win, average loss, and so on.

Once one has settled on a routine or system (be it by the process of optimization or not), the need to collect and update the data necessary to generate entry and exit signals arises. This updating process can be done by hand simply by obtaining the needed prices from your broker at the end of the day or from the newspaper the next morning. Many traders use a data service, however, that supplies prices either over the phone lines via a modem or satellite dish.

Once the prices have been updated, the system can analyze the data and supply the appropriate orders for the following day. Some of these routines are quite simple, some are exceedingly complex. In either case, once the method of following price has been determined, one can automate the approach to where everything from the data load to a complete set of printed reports is done automatically every trading day. Some will use a spreadsheet for these functions, but most prefer a dedicated computerized system.

Computrac is perhaps the granddaddy of computer systems for traders. In addition, they have a strong and active users group that supports and annually updates their service. Once a year, the members gather and share ideas, trading techniques, and so on. If you cannot attend their annual meetings (which are open to members and non-members alike), cassette tapes can be purchased of the presentations and discussions. If you will

mention that you are an Almanac purchaser, a free demonstra-
tion diskette, information regarding this year's seminar, and
information on last year's tapes will be forwarded. Contact Mr.
Timothy Slater, Computrac, PO Box 15951, New Orleans, LA
70175-5951 (800-535-7990)

The Technician/Meta Stock is a newer arrival but also supplies
a high-quality product. Both of these systems can fulfill the
requirement of daily analysis (besides performing many other
functions) and are recommended for those traders interested in
computerized commodity trading. A new product released this
past year is "The DownLoader-Lotus Signal". Their book on
market indicators, "The Market Indicator Interpretation Guide",
explains technical indicators and how they are used. A demon-
stration diskette and 30 page manual can be obtained for $ 5.00.
If you will mention that you are an Almanac purchaser, a 10
percent discount on all purchased products will apply. Contact
Ms. Christine L Thompson, Equis International, PO Box 26743,
Salt Lake City, UT 84126 (800-882-3040).

What if you don't want to go through the process of obtaining a
data base and doing computer runs for the next umteenth days?
Then perhaps you will want to use someone else's routine and
program it so that it can be run each day on a computer (for
instance, you may wish to use some of the ideas in this book). If
you do, however, you are proceeding on the blind-faith assumption that the routine will work. Hence, even in this instance, it is
still better to run the past simulation study to verify purported
results.

A second choice is to purchase a dedicated computer trading
system. These types of systems have routines in them and,
usually, some historical data that can be run to verify past
results. Some of these programs are in the "toolbox" or "black
box" category.

Finally, you may wish to have a "live environment" system if you
have the time to trade during the day. Such a system will provide
you with tick-by-tick data and enable one to graph and analyze
charts with different types of dedicated studies at varying levels
depending on the system. More than one trader has told me that
the addition of such software has helped their entry/exit execution considerably.

Chained Contracts

The difference between
a successful person and others
is not a lack of strength,
not a lack of knowledge,
but rather a lack of will.
- Vince Lombardi

When doing optimization and simulation studies on historical futures data, one runs into the problem of discontinuity of data. To best explain the problem, simply think of the price of your favorite stock over this past year. Note how continuous the data is from one day to the next. In futures, the continuity of data is broken with the expiration of each contract.

Thus, when doing historical analysis, one must allow for these breaks which occur anywhere from four times per year in the financials and currencies to twelve times per year in the energy complex.

In order to adjust for these breaks in data, the concept of a continuous daily data stream was born. The most popular approach continuously takes an average of two forward contracts in order to produce a "chained" series of data over a long period of time. Since one does not trade an average of forward contracts, however, we prefer to use a different chaining technique that uses actual spot contract price relationships during the period that the contract is the spot contract.

When this approach is used, an adjustment is made each time the current spot contract is "rolled forward" to the next contract. The adjustment is equal to the difference between the closing prices of the old spot and new spot contracts on the day of change. All past historical data is adjusted by this differential. The effect is to create a long chain of spot contract prices.

When building these contracts, I like to include, in addition to the chained prices, the actual spot futures prices along with the contract volume and open interest and total market volume and open interest. Additionally, I find it helpful if the cash price is also stored along with the spread price between the spot and a deferred contract.

The key to constructing these contracts is to perform an analysis of when liquidity moves from the old spot to the new spot contract. This analysis can be done by comparing volume and open interest data between the two contracts and then determining the best time to roll the contract forward. The change is rounded off to the nearest Friday.

Continuity of data is not the only problem that exists when analyzing data. Another problem exists in the TYPE of data that is stored. Different data types can cause compatibility problems. For instance, if you have a program that requires Computrac data and another that requires CSI data, you potentially have a problem running one (or both) of the programs if your data is not compatible with the system's format.

Additionally, when performing any type of analysis, don't forget to include a "slippage" assumption on a per-trade basis. Slippage is a somewhat relative term, for some brokers fill orders better than do others. Also, since slippage includes commissions, and since commissions vary, slippage will differ from one trader to another.

On average, a $ 50.00 slippage assumption is reasonable for most realizing, of course, that if a trader is paying an average of $ 75.00 commission per trade, he has already dictated a higher slippage assumption as defined by this higher commission alone (and that does not include the "skid" or bad fills on trades, either)!

Chapter 8

Additional Products

Additional Products

*Every job
is a self-portrait
of the person
who did it.
Autograph your work
with excellence.*

We have several products available that are designed to assist the varied interests of traders from the research-oriented to the day trader!

Here is a brief description of our other products;

1. All spread and seasonal trades in The Almanac originated from our "Quarter Month Spread Analysis" or "Quarter Month Seasonal Analysis" sheets which are unique in the industry. Over 3,000 spreads and seasonals in over 1,000,000 possible combinations are analyzed in compiling the seasonal information presented in this book. If you would like to see how these studies originate and possibly purchase some of these sheets (they are available by group - i.e., meats, grains, etc.), then request either The Spread Packet or The Seasonal Packet. Both are free to Almanac purchasers.

2. Other products originate from these studies. The first is "The Spread Investment Letter" which each month presents an especially attractive spread and also lists 75-150 updated spread seasonals. The seasonal spreads are broken down into one of three portfolio groupings and ranked in order of their past historical profitability on an annualized expected rate-of-return basis. We believe that "The Spread Investment Letter" established a record for newsletter profitability on a one-contract-per-recommendation basis in July, 1988 when the one month profit topped $ 150,000. A one month trial can be ordered from The Spread Packet (see # 1 above) which is free to Almanac purchasers.

3. The "Seasonal Trade Portfolios" present a series of seasonal trades designed for (approximately) a $ 15,000 portfolio and updated quarterly. The portfolios are paid on a percentage-of-

profits basis after an initial deposit. These portfolios contain the author's best seasonal work. If you are interested in further information, ask for "The Seasonal Portfolio" letter which is free to Almanac purchasers.

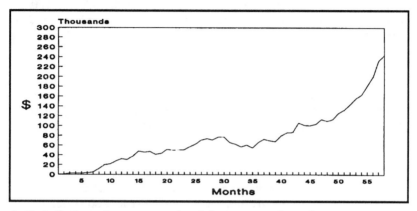

4. Detailed analysis on each of the seasonal trades presented in The Almanac is available from our "Spread History Printout" and "Seasonal Trade Printout" sheets which are explained and for which examples are presented at the front of "The Calendar Book" at the end of the "How to Use the Seasonals" section. An order form is available at that location that pertains to that year's seasonal trades.

5. The 10-IN-1 S & P 500 Day Trading System was originally briefly offered in 1987 and has not been actively advertised since. The system is a pattern recognition approach. If you would like further information, request the 10-IN-1 S & P 500 Day Trading System brochure which is free to Almanac purchasers (when available).

6. Historical contract price information can be ordered which lists individual contract historical high and low prices for forty or so markets. This information will be of value to the research-oriented or Gann-oriented trader and costs $ 75.00 (over 200 pages). Additional information can be found in the section on "Record Prices".

7. The MOB Control is a special report that discusses the intricacies of The 1988 Almanac's Trade of the Year, the Municipal Bond / US Treasury Bond spread (the MOB spread). This report

costs $ 25.00 for Almanac purchasers. The value of the report is that it is timeless in nature and not just applicable to 1988.

8. The Little Colonel is a special report that discusses the intricacies of The 1989 Almanac's Trade of the Year, the Corn / Wheat spread. This report costs $ 25.00 for Almanac purchasers. The value of the report is that it is timeless in nature and not just applicable to 1989.

9. The Bean Spread is a special report that discusses the intricacies of The 1990 Almanac's Trade of the Year, the Soybean / Wheat spread. This report costs $ 25.00 for Almanac purchasers. The value of the report is that it is timeless in nature and not just applicable to 1990.

10. The TED Spread is a special report that discusses the Almanac's Trade of the Second Half of the Year for 1990 and costs $ 25.00 for Almanac purchasers. This report is also timeless.

11. I have received several inquiries regarding doing a seminar over the past few years and am honored to think that anyone would feel that I would have anything to teach them in the few hours we could spend together. I originally planned on doing some seminars in 1989 but was constrained by time and my ongoing legal battles with the National Futures Association and whether or not I have the right to publish this book in America. If time allows and a seminar schedule is released, you will be contacted so long as you are on our mailing list.

12. Are you experiencing difficulty with your trading? Through 1988, I did some private consulting in Tulsa on weekends that were private but fairly expensive. I canceled all such appointments in 1989 and have not since resumed this service. If you are having difficulty, however, or need to upgrade your trading approach or improve your trading methods or habits, I am available on a limited number of Saturdays throughout the year in your hometown for private consultation. This service is quite expensive, but if you are interested, request the letter for private consultation.

13. As you may have noticed throughout The Almanac, in 1988 and 1989, I additionally provided a followup service to assist traders in applying the wealth of information that The Almanac

offers to real time situations. This service is called "The Almanac Reports" and is not produced on any set schedule, but is sent as market conditions dictate. The service is most effective if received over facsimile transmission and does NOT (usually) include analysis of specific seasonal trades in the book since that information would be redundant.

"The Almanac Reports" is geared towards education and enabling you to fully "stand on your feet" and use the information in The Almanac on your own by the time you finish the study period. Back issues of "The Almanac Reports" are suggested, especially "The 1988 Almanac Reports." The cost is $ 75.00 for each year, either 1988 or 1989.

Future Almanac Reports are expected to last one month of each year with two objectives in mind; first, to provide Almanac purchasers with current examples of how to apply the information in the book to real time situations and, second, to provide examples for the next Almanac. It is expected that these Reports will be available in either July, August, or September of each year. Time did not allow the Reports to be issued in 1990.

14. Many have written over the past few years asking if I personally would manage their account. I am not presently managing public accounts in the United States and trade only for our family accounts. It is possible, however, that I may sponsor a fund that would be managed by others. If you have interest in this area, indicate such interest below and sales brochures will be sent should the situation arise. (Remember, however, that the actual offering will only be made by prospectus).

15. I plan to write a few reports that periodically, on an unscheduled basis, identify important market junctures that provide trading opportunities on a short, intermediate, and long term basis. The cost of these reports is $ 25.00 each. There is no subscription fee. The program is quite simple. We send you the report. So long as you pay for the last report, you will be sent the next report. All subscribers begin with report # 1 (even though this report is now outdated). If you like what you see, then AFTER you have received the first report, send in your $ 25.00 and the next CURRENT report will be sent. To activate this program, simply request Report # 1, The Sugar Report, on the following page.

16. If you do not have a current copy of The $upertrader's Almanac (Calendar Book), it may be ordered below. This is the book that contains the timing information (seasonals, cycles, and so on) that pertain to the current year.

17. Finally, hopefully you won't mind sometime during the year sending in the questionnaire on the following page.

If you have obtained our book from a friend and would like to be on our mailing list, simply fill out the following questionnaire. We generally send four quarterly updates per year at no charge to Almanac purchasers with timely and important information included.

We supply a complete set of books each year to the three people who provide the most helpful suggestions or criticisms about our books. These testimonials may include true stories of how The Almanac has helped one's trading or any other matter relating to the books.

TO REALLY IMPROVE YOUR ALMANAC, YOU SHOULD

_____

_____

_____

_____

THE MOST HELPFUL ITEM HAS BEEN

_____

_____

_____

_____

THE LEAST HELPFUL ITEM (I can't believe you included it in your book) HAS BEEN

_____

_____

_____

_____

NAME _____

ADDRESS _____

CITY STATE ZIP_____

Please forward the following;   Cost

(Circle the # of appropriate item)

1.	Seasonal Spread Packet	(Free)
2.	Seasonal Trade Packet	(Free)
3.	The Seasonal Portfolio Letter	(Free)
4.	10-IN-1 S & P 500 Day Trading System Brochure	(Free)
5.	Historical Contract Price Information	@ $ 75.00
6.	The MOB Control Report	@ $ 25.00
7.	The Little Colonel Report	@ $ 25.00
8.	The Bean Spread	@ $ 25.00
9.	The TED Spread	@ $ 25.00
9.	Seminar Brochure when available	(Free)
10.	Private Counselling Letter	(Free)
11.	The 1988 Almanac Reports	@ $ 75.00
12.	The 1989 Almanac Reports	@ $ 75.00
13.	This year's Almanac Report brochure (1 month only) when available	(Free)
14.	Report # 1, The Sugar Report	(Free)
15.	The $upertrader's Almanac (Calendar Book)	@ $ 99.00
16.	Managed Fund Information when available	(Free)

Total Cost Enclosed_____

To whom should we send information on the next Almanac?

1. Name _____

Address _____

City State Zip _____

2. Name _____

Address _____

City State Zip _____

3. Name _____

Address _____

City State Zip _____

4. Name _____

Address_____

City State Zip _____

(Thank you for your support of our product!)

Market Movements, Inc.
5212 E. 69th Place
Tulsa, OK 74136
(918) 493-2897

Acceleration
The rate of change in speed of thrust or velocity (usually the second derivative of speed in the calculus).

Accommodation Trading
Wash trading entered into by a trader, usually to assist another with illegal trades.

Account Sale
A statement sent by a broker to a customer when a transaction is closed out.

Accrued Interest
The unpaid interest that has accumulated since the most recent coupon payment which the buyer owes the seller.

Accumulation
Acquisition under the cover of small trades by smart money as prices fall. Accumulation helps to signal that a bottom has been reached or is near and that an upside breakout is imminent.

Acid Test
A method which tests the fineness of gold by subjecting it to various acids.

Acreage Allotment
Limitations on the planted acreage of some basic crops.

Active
A market characterized by heavy trading volume.

Actuals
The physical, or cash, market; the physical goods underlying a paper contract.

Afloat
Actuals on board ship enroute to their destination.

Agencies
Securities issued by an agency of the federal government (e.g., FNMA, GNMA, etc.).

Agent
A firm or individual acting on behalf of another (the principal) who is subject to the principal's control and authority. The agent usually receives a

fee or commission and usually does not act as a principal in the transaction (i.e., may not profit from a mark-up).

Aggregation

The policy under which all positions owned or controlled by one trader or group of traders are combined to determine reporting status and speculative limit compliance.

All or Any Part

A provision that the total amount of a given order, or any lesser amount, may be executed at the specified price.

All or None (AON)

An order which is to be executed only if all of it can be executed at one specific price (as opposed to a fill-or-kill order).

Allowances

The discounts allowed for grades or locations or a commodity that are lower or higher than the par or a basis-grade or location specified in the futures contract.

Alloys of Gold

Mixtures of gold with metals such as copper, silver, zinc, etc.

Altered Coin

A coin which has been altered in any way other than normal wear after being struck at the mint.

AMEX

American Stock Exchange.

Amortization

The process of fully paying off indebtedness by installments of principal and earned interest over a definite time.

Amplitude

Amount of vertical rise or fall in price over a specified period of time.

Angle

A measure in degrees from the horizontal on a price chart of various key angles (such as 45 degrees) which Gann Theory considered to be support/resistance levels for a price trend. When an angle line is broken upside by the trend, the next significant angle line becomes the new resistance level and the line just broken becomes the new support level.

Animal/By-Product Spread The value difference between a live animal contract and one of its slaughter by-products (i.e., Live Hogs/Pork Belly).

Anniversary Dates Significant market dates occurring one year, or multiples of one year, following a major high or low in the market. Followers of W. D. Gann place special emphasis on these dates and look for new highs or lows to occur on them.

Anticipatory Hedge A long anticipatory hedge is initiated by buying futures contracts to protect against a rise in the price of an asset to be purchased at a later date. A short anticipatory hedge is initiated by selling futures contracts to protect against the decline in the price of an asset to be sold at a future date. Also can be used to protect against a rise in interest rates of an anticipated fixed-rate liability or a future repricing on a variable-rate liability.

Anticipatory Indicator A trading technique which predicts market events in advance.

Aphelion The point in its orbit when a planet is furthest from the sun.

API American Petroleum Institute

API Gravity Gravity (weight per unit volume) of oils as measured by the API scale.

Apogee The point in its orbit when the moon is furthest from the earth.

Appreciation	The increase in value of an asset.
Approved Delivery Facility	Any bank, stockyard, mill, store, warehouse, plant, elevator or other depository that is authorized by an exchange for the delivery of commodities tendered on futures contracts.
Arbitrage	Simultaneous purchase of cash or futures in one market against the sale of cash or futures in the same or a different market to profit from a difference in prices.
Arbitrage (cash market)	In the financial markets, can refer to buying one security and selling another security with similar maturity and coupon in an attempt to profit from price distortions.
Arbitrage (futures market)	The simultaneous purchase of one commodity against the sale of another or against a cash instrument in order to profit from distortions from usual price relationships. Variations include the simultaneous purchase and sale of different delivery months of the same commodity, of the same commodity and delivery month on two different exchanges, and the purchase of one commodity against the sale of another commodity.
Arbitration	A forum for the fair and impartial settlement of disputes that the parties involved are unable to resolve between themselves.
Ascending Node	The point of a planet's orbit at which it crosses the plane of the earth's orbit extended to meet the celestial body from south to north.
Asked	The offering price at which a seller will sell.
Aspect	The angular relationship between the

Right Ascensions of any two planetary bodies as seen from the Earth
(The Moon and the Sun are considered planetary bodies for this purpose). These angles have special
names, the most important being
conjunction, opposition, sextile,
square and trine.

Assay

To analyze an ore to determine its
nature and purity.

Asset

On a balance sheet, that which is
owned or receivable.

Associated Person

An individual who solicits orders,
customers, or customer funds on behalf of a Futures Commission Merchant, an Introducing Broker, a
Commodity Trading Adviser or a
Commodity Pool Operator and who
is registered with the Commodity Futures Trading Commission.

At The Market

An order to buy or sell at the next
available price.

Auction Line

In the Market Profile, a vertical line
on the left-hand side of a daily chart.
The first half-hour's and subsequent
periods' price-trading ranges of high
to low prices are entered here. Also,
dealings on a securities exchange
where a two-way auction is
continuously in effect.

Averaging Down

A practice whereby traders add to
their positions as the market moves
down against them.

Averaging Period

The period over which data is averaged
for determining the trend of a market indicator.

Away

A trade that is done through another
firm away from the first firm.

B/D

Barrels per Day - usually used in

	connection with a refiner's production capacity or an oilfield's rate of flow.
Back Spread	Buy the back month, sell the near month.
Backwardation	A futures market condition in which the nearby months are premium to the distant months.
Balance of Payments	A record in balance sheet form showing the value of all the economic transactions between residents, business firms, governments, and any other institutions in a country and the rest of the world.
Balance of Trade	The difference between the total value of exports and imports which creates a trade deficit when imports exceed exports.
Balance Point	A pivotal price of the market.
Balance Point Line	A line drawn through the halfway point of two or more swings.
Balance Sheet	A condensed financial statement showing the nature and amount of a company's assets, liabilities, and capital on a given date. The balance sheet shows in dollar amounts what the company owns, what it owes, and its stockholders' ownership in the company.
Bankers' Acceptance (BA)	A debt instrument, payment on which is guaranteed by a bank through "acceptance."
Bar, Bar Chart	A bar chart shows the development of price over time in a market. Each vertical bar represents a single trading period and it extends from the lowest to the highest priced trade during that period. A small tick to the left shows the price of the first

trade and a tick to the right shows the price of the last trade made during that period.

Barrel

A volumetric unit of measure for crude oil and petroleum products equivalent to 42 U.S. gallons.

Barron's Confidence Index

An index designed to identify investors' confidence in the level and direction of security prices.

Basis

The difference between a cash price of a commodity and the futures price at a specific time and place.

Basis Grade

The grade of a commodity used as the standard of the contract.

Basis Point

Expression of yield, where each basis point equals 1/100 of a percentage point.

Basis Risk

The risk resulting from a change in basis while one is hedged in the futures market while holding inventory. This risk cannot be hedged against.

Bastard Hedge

Using a substitute for what should be a regular hedge.

Batch

A measured amount of oil or refined product in a pipeline.

Batching Sequence

The order in which product shipments are sent through a pipeline.

Bear

One who believes that prices will decline.

Bear Market

A market in which prices are declining.

A news item is considered bearish if it is expected to produce lower prices.

Bear Spread

A spread that consists of a short position in the nearby contract and a long position in the distant contract.

Bear Trap

A market phenomenon in which the market appears to be declining, prompting sellers to sell, only to rally, trapping the unwary sellers.

Bearer Bond

A bond that does not have the owner's name registered on the books of the issuing company and that is payable to the holder. Coupons are attached and ownership is evidenced by possession.

Bid

An offer to buy a specific quantity at a stated price - opposite of the offer.

Bid and Ask

The prices at which a market may be bought or sold at a given moment on the exchange floor. One can sell at the bid and buy at the ask.

Bid and Asked

The bid price is the highest price anyone has declared that he wants to pay at a given time - the asked price is the lowest price anyone will take at the same time. The price difference between the bid and asked price is called the spread.

Big Board

A popular term for the New York Stock Exchange, Inc.

Billon

An inferior silver alloy containing less than 50% of pure silver.

Birth Chart

A "snapshot" of the planetary positions taken when a person is born or when a trade, corporation, or market is initiated.

Blems

Large mounds of raised metal on a counterfeit coin.

Blue Chip

A company known nationally for the quality and wide acceptance of its products or services and for its ability to make money and pay dividends.

Blue Sky Laws

A popular name for laws enacted by various states to protect the public against securities frauds. The term is believed to have originated when a judge ruled that a particular stock had about the same value as a patch of blue sky.

Board of Trade

Generically describes an exchange or association of persons who are engaged in the business of buying and selling any commodity or receiving the same for sale on consignment. Also, specifically refers to the Chicago Board of Trade.

Bona Fide Hedger

A classification or definition which may be established by the Commodity Futures Trading Commission for regulation purposes. The definition typically includes the industries which are viewed as having a bona fide hedging potential in their use of futures contracts.

Bond

An IOU or certificate representing debt issued by a corporation, municipality, state, or the federal government. The issuer promises to pay back investors (lenders) the full loan amount (known as the face value) at a stated time (called the maturity date). In addition, the issuer pays lenders a fixed annual interest rate (known as the coupon rate) at regular intervals, usually every six months.

Bond Indenture

A legal statement enumerating duties of the issuer and rights of the holder.

Book Transfer

Transfer of title from the seller to the buyer without the physical movement of product.

Book-Entry Securities

Computerized records at the Fed

consisting of the names of member banks, the securities they own, and the securities they are holding.

Booking the Basis

A forward pricing sales arrangement in which the cash price is determined either by the buyer or the seller within a specified time. At that time, the previously agreed basis is applied to the then-current futures quotation.

Boom Market

A market in which buying demand greatly exceeds selling pressure.

Bottom

A point in time when price is lower than prices either before or after that time.

Bottom Out

The point in time at which a bear market reaches its lowest price, or market bottom, and a reversal of the general market trend can be expected.

Bought the Spread

Paid money out to buy a spread.

Box

The area of a point-and-figure chart into which the technician places one X or O representing a given amount of price increase or decrease.

Box Size

The amount of price increase or decrease represented by a box on a point-and-figure chart.

Breadth Indicator

A measure of the proportion of stocks rising in an upward market or falling in a declining market.

Break

A rapid and sharp decline in prices.

Break Down

When price breaks out in a downward direction.

Breakout

Overcoming resistance, especially from a congestion area. It is the point at which prices penetrate a previous high, low, or some other support/resistance point on an intra-day or inter-day basis. Occasionally the penetration creating the breakout is only temporary, in which case it is known as a "false breakout."

Broad Tape

A term commonly applied to news-wires carrying price and background information on securities and commodities markets, in contrast to the exchange's own price transmission wires, which use a narrow "ticker tape."

Broker

An agent or one who buys and sells futures contracts for the account of others and is paid a fee or commission. The term may refer to (1) a Floor Broker - a person who actually executes orders on the trading floor of an exchange, or (2) an Account Executive, Associated Person, Registered Representative or Customer's Person - the person who deals with customers in the offices of a Futures Commission Merchant, Introducing Broker, or Securities Broker, or (3) a Futures Commission Merchant, Introducing Broker, or Securities Broker.

Brokerage

A fee charged by a broker for execution of a transaction, usually on an amount-per-transaction or a percentage-of-the-total-value-of-the-transaction basis.

BS & W

Bottom sediment and water, often found in crude oil and residual fuel.

Bubble

A flat or inclusion within a diamond.

Bucketing

The illegal practice of accepting orders to buy or sell without executing such orders or the illegal use of the customer's principal without disclosing the fact of such use.

Bulge	A rapid advance in prices.
Bull	One who believes that prices will rise.
Bull Market	A market in which prices are rising. A news item is considered bullish if it is expected to bring higher prices.
Bull Spread	A spread that consists of a long position in the nearby contract and a short position in the distant contract. However, in precious metals, if a trader anticipates a significant rise in prices, he will sell the nearbys and buy the deferred contracts.
Bull Trap	A market phenomenon in which the market appears to be rising, prompting buyers to purchase contracts, only to decline, trapping the unwary buyers.
Bullion	Gold which is at least .995 fine available in the form of ingots, bars or wafers.
Bullion Coins	Contemporary gold coins minted continuously in large numbers and having a low premium over bullion.
Buoyant	A market in which prices have a tendency to rise easily with a considerable show of strength.
Buy In	A purchase to cover a previous sale; also called short covering.
Buy on Close	To buy at the end of the trading session within the closing price range.
Buy on Opening	To buy at the beginning of a trading session within the opening price range.
Buy Order	An order placed with a broker to purchase at the market (that is, at the best price available) or at an-

other specified price.

Buy Order Limit A price level which a trader determines. If price passes that level, the trader automatically buys into the market. A trader may leave a standing order with a broker regarding buy levels referred to as an open order or Good-'til-Cancelled (GTC) order.

Buy-Back A repurchase agreement (RP or repo).

Buying Hedge Buying futures contracts to protect against a possible increase in the price of commodities that will be needed in the future.

Buying the Spread Usually means establishing a "bull spread" or going long the front contract month and selling the deferred contract month in anticipation of rising prices. This definition is backwards for the precious metals where the front months usually rise slower than the deferred contracts when prices are rising.

C & F Cost & freight paid to port of destination.

C.E.A. Commodity Exchange Act which has been replaced by the Commodity Futures Trading Commission (CFTC), the regulatory agency which oversees commodity exchanges and all regulated futures contracts.

C.I.F. Cost, insurance, and freight paid at the point of destination, included in the price quoted.

Call The period in which the price for each futures contract is established. For example, an opening call.

Call Rule An exchange regulation under which an official bid price for a cash commodity is competitively established at the close of each day's trading.

Callable

A bond or preferred stock issue, all or part of which may be redeemed by the issuing authority under definite conditions before maturity.

Callable Bond

A bond that is redeemable by the issuer prior to maturity - for example, most Treasury bonds are callable five years before maturity at a specific price.

Carat

A unit of measurement in which precious stones and pearls are weighed.

Cardinal Square

A square composed of numbers spiraling outward, starting with the lowest all-time price (or the start of prices can be used) and increasing by some fixed increment. Significant angles drawn from the center of this square (at, for example, 90 and 45 degrees) are supposed to point out significant support and resistance levels.

Cargo

In sugar, usually 10,000 tons.

Carry (cost of carry)

The financing of a commodity or cash security until it is sold or delivered which can include storage, insurance, and assay expenses or financing costs in repos, bank loans, or dealer loans.

Carry (Negative)

The condition in which the cost of financing is more than the return on the instrument.

Carry (Positive)

The condition in which the cost of financing is less than the return on the instrument.

Carry Order

An order that simultaneously liquidates an existing position and initiates a new position in the same direction in a later contract month. This is used to roll over or switch a position that has matured into a new distant position.

Carry-Over
That part of current supplies of a commodity comprised of stocks from previous production/marketing seasons, and current production less current consumption.

Carrying Broker
A member of a commodity exchange, usually a clearinghouse member, through whom another broker or customer clears all or some trades.

Carrying Charge Spread
The most basic spread structure, spot cash price plus increased monthly prices which include interest, insurance, storage, and handling. Applies only to storable commodities.

Carrying Charges
The cost of storing a physical commodity over a period of time including insurance, storage, and interest on invested funds as well as other incidental costs. A carrying charge market exists when there are higher futures prices for each successive contract maturity. If the carrying charge is adequate to reimburse the owner of the physical commodity, it is called a full carrying charge.

Carryover
Part of the current crop production that will be carried to the next crop year, or that part of current supplies of a commodity comprised of stocks from the previous crop year's production.

Cash
The price of a physical commodity.

Cash Commodity
The physical or actual commodity as distinguished from the futures contract that is based on the physical

commodity.

Cash Forward Contract

The purchase or sale of a commodity in the cash market for delivery at a later date.

Cash Instrument

Refers to the underlying security for which futures are traded.

Cash Market

A market in which transactions for purchase and sale of the physical commodity or financial instrument are made under whatever terms are agreeable to the buyer and seller and are legal under law and the rules of the market organization, if such exists. "Cash market" can refer to an organized, self-regulated central market, an over-the-counter type of market, (in which buyers, sellers, and/or dealers compete in decentralized locations), or to such other methods of purchasing and selling the physical commodity as are prevalent in the industries using that commodity.

Cash Price

The price in the marketplace for actual cash or spot commodities to be delivered via customary market channels.

Cash Settlement

A transaction for immediate payment, usually the same day by wire transfer.

Cat Cracker

A large refinery vessel for processing reduced crudes or other feed-stocks in the presence of a catalyst, as opposed to the older method of thermal cracking.

Catalyst

A substance which promotes a chemical reaction, but does not itself enter into the reaction.

Catapult

A pattern found on a point-and-figure chart when a string of X's or O's breaks far above or below the previous price range.

CBOT   Chicago Board of Trade.

Certificate of Deposit (CD)   A time deposit usually with a bank or savings institution having a specific maturity which is evidenced by a certificate.

Certificated Stock   Stocks of a commodity that have been inspected and found to be of a quality deliverable against futures contracts. They are stored at the delivery points designated as regular or acceptable for delivery by the commodity exchange.

CFO   Cancel Former Order.

CFTC   The 1974-established federal regulatory agency that administers the Commodity Exchange Act. The CFTC is the federal oversight agency which monitors the futures and commodity options markets to detect and prevent commodity price distortion and market manipulation and to protect the rights of customers who use the markets for either commercial or investment purposes.

Channels   Two parallel lines which contain price movements on a bar chart. These parallel lines can be straight or curved but they represent support and resistance lines extended into the future.

Chart Trading   Using graphs and charts to analyze market behavior and forecast price movements. Technical traders are often chart traders or chartists.

Charting   The use of graphs and charts in the technical analysis of futures markets to plot price movements, volume, open interest or other statistical indicators of price movement in the hope that such graphs and charts will help one anticipate and profit from price trends. Contrasted with fundamental analysis.

Cheap

Colloquialism implying that a market is underpriced.

Cheap Spread

Small traders trying a low margin or cheaper method to trade a high margin requirement market.

Churning

Excessive trading that results in the broker deriving a profit from commissions while disregarding the best interests of the customer.

Clean Cargo

Refined products - all refined products except bunker fuels and residuals.

Clear

In futures the clearing member of an exchange "clears" trades for its customers when it maintains records of all trades and settles margin flow on a daily "mark to market" basis. It is the clearing member firm that deals directly with the clearinghouse.

Clearances

Refers to the quantity of a commodity which has moved out of a particular port or ports on a specified date or to trades cleared by commodity clearinghouses.

Clearing

The procedure through which trades are checked for accuracy after which the clearinghouse or association becomes the buyer to each seller of a futures contract, and the seller to each buyer.

Clearing Member

A member of the clearinghouse or association. All trades of a non-clearing member must be registered and eventually settled through a clearing member.

Clearinghouse

The part of all futures exchanges

through which all futures trades
made during the day are reconciled,
settled, guaranteed, and later either
offset or fulfilled through delivery of
the commodity. It may be a fully
chartered separate corporation
rather than a division of the exchange itself.

Climax Day   A daily reversal pattern having a long
thrust and closing near the high if
up (or low) for the day.

Close   The end of the trading session. On
some exchanges, the close lasts for
several minutes to accommodate
customers who have entered buy or
sell orders to be consummated "on
the close."

Close Only   A day order to be executed at the
market on the close.

Close Out   The liquidation of a market position.

Closing Price   The price last quoted on a trading day.

Closing Range   A high and low range of prices at
which futures transactions occurred
during the close of the market. Buy
and sell orders at the close can thus
have been filled at any point within
such a range.

CME   Chicago Mercantile Exchange.

Coin Gold   Gold that is used in coins generally
alloyed with small amounts of other
metals.

Collateral   Securities or other property pledged
by a borrower to secure repayment
of a loan.

Collectibles   Tangible goods often purchased as
investments, including coins,
stamps, books, antiques, etc.

Commercial   A company that merchandises or

processes cash grain and other commodities.

Commercial Grain Stocks   Domestic grain in store in public and private elevators at important markets including grain afloat in vessels or barges in harbors of lake and seaboard ports.

Commercial Paper   An unsecured debt instrument issued by a corporation with a fixed maturity, typically for a short-term period (30,45,60,or 90 days). It is priced at a discount from par and is redeemable at par on the maturity date.

Commission   The fee charged by a broker for making a trade on behalf of customers. Also sometimes used to refer to the Commodity Futures Trading Commission.

Commission House   A company that buys and sells for the accounts of customers.

Commission Merchant   One who makes a trade for either another member of the exchange or for a nonmember client. The trade is made in the commission merchant's own name making him liable as principal to the other.

Commitment or Open Interest   The number of contracts in existence at any period of time which have not as yet been satisfied by an offsetting sale or purchase or by actual contract delivery.

Commodity Credit Corporation   A government-owned corporation established in 1933 to assist American agriculture. Major operations include price support programs, supply control and foreign sales programs for agricultural commodities.

Commodity Exchange Act   The federal act that provides for federal regulation of futures trading.

Commodity Pool	An enterprise in which funds contributed by a number of persons are combined for the purpose of trading futures contracts or commodity options.
Commodity Pool Operator (CPO)	An individual or firm who accepts funds, securities, or property for trading commodity futures contracts and combines the customer funds into pools. CPOs must register with the CFTC, and are closely regulated.
Commodity Trading Adviser	Commodity Trading Advisers are required to be registered with the CFTC and to belong to the NFA. A CTA, for compensation or profit, directly or indirectly advises others as to the value of or the advisability of buying or selling futures contracts or commodity options. The CTA may issue analysis or reports concerning commodities and/or may place trades for other people's accounts.
Competitive Bid	A bid tendered in a Treasury or municipal auction by an investor for a specific amount of securities at a specific yield or price. Noncompetitive bidders usually pay the average of all bid prices.
Compound Interest	Interest earned on the principal and on interest already earned.
Confirmation	A notice a clearing firm sends to its customers daily to confirm each transaction reflecting any trades occurring on the previous day.
Confirmation Statement	A statement sent by a commission house to a customer when a futures position has been initiated. The statement shows the number of contracts bought or sold and the prices at which the contracts were traded. Sometimes combined with a Purchase and Sale statement.

Confirming Indicator

An indicator belonging to a minor or ancillary price prediction technique which serves to confirm signals already given by other techniques.

Congestion

In technical analysis, an extended area of limited price fluctuations within a narrow range.

Conjunction

An aspect of two heavenly bodies occurring when there is 0 degrees between their respective Right Ascensions.

Consumer Price Index

A measure of the average level of prices in a fixed market basket of goods and services bought by urban wage earners and clerical workers and by all urban consumers compared to the average level in a base period.

Contango

A carrying charge market or a market that closely reflects full carry.

Contract

In the case of futures, an agreement between two parties to make and, in turn, accept delivery of a specified quantity and quality of a commodity at a certain place by a specified time.

Contract Grades

Commodities meeting standardized specifications listed in exchange rules - those that can be used to deliver against a futures contract.

Contract Market

A board of trade designated by the Commodity Futures Trading Commission to trade futures on a particular commodity. It is commonly used to mean any exchange on which futures are traded.

Contract Month

The month in which a futures contract may be fulfilled by making or taking delivery.

Contract Specifications

The quality specifications set forth in

or Grade	the rules of an exchange that must be met when delivering the physical product against the futures contract.
Contract Trading Volume	The total number of contracts traded in a commodity or commodity delivery month during a specified period of time.
Contract Unit/Lot	The actual amount of a commodity designated in a given futures contract.
Contrary Opinion	A market theory based on the notion of doing the opposite of what the majority of the participants in the market are doing. Contrary opinion is particularly useful in pinpointing market reversals when prices become oversold and overbought as measured by taking a consensus of traders.
Controlled Account	Any account for which trading is directed by someone other than the owner.
Conversion	The sale of a cash position and investment of part of the proceeds in the margin for a long futures position. The remaining money is placed in an interest-bearing instrument. This practice allows the investor/dealer to receive high rates of interest and take delivery of the commodity if needed.
Conversion Contract	A contract for the purchase or sale of a commodity at a price to be based on a designated futures but with the basis still not fixed. Fixation will occur within a specified time at the then prevailing commercial basis (in relation to the future on which the conversion contract is based) for the quality of the commodity at the time and place of delivery stipulated.

Conversion Factor

A figure published by the CBOT used to adjust a T-Bond hedge for the difference in maturity between the T-Bond contract specifications and the T-Bonds being hedged.

Corner

An occurrence of the past whereby one or more individuals bought up the available supply of a commodity future and/or the physical and could then set the price at which those who had previously sold short must cover their contracts. The strategy is now illegal on all exchanges. It also means to secure such relative control of a commodity or security that its price can be manipulated or, in the extreme, obtaining contracts requiring delivery of more commodities or securities than are available for delivery.

Corporate Taxable Equivalent

The amount of yield necessary on a par bond to produce an identical after-tax yield to maturity as that offered by the premium or discount bond with which it is being compared.

Correction

A situation in which the market moves against the prevailing trend before trend reassertion without disturbing the long-term trend.

Cost of Production Spread

Essentially used by commercial hedgers to hedge their cost of feed and sale of animals to insure costs and solidify gross sales revenue (i.e., Corn/Cattle or Corn/Hogs).

Counterfeit Coin

Coins or blanks produced by casting or other methods outside of the mint.

Country

Refers to a place relatively close to a farmer where he can sell or delivery his crop or animals.

Coupon

A percentage of a bond's face value

which is the annual rate of return
the bondholder will receive from the
issuer. Also, a sticker attached to a
bearer bond which can be torn off
and presented for payment.

Coupon Bond

A bond with interest coupons
attached. The coupons are clipped
as they come due and are presented
by the holder for payment of interest.

Coupon Rate

The rate of interest stated on a bond
to be paid to the purchaser by the issuer of the bond.

Cover

A purchase to offset a previous
transaction with an opposite transaction of equal size.

Covered Interest Arbitrage

Purchasing an instrument denominated in a foreign currency and hedging
the resulting foreign exchange risk
by selling the proceeds of the investment forward for dollars in the interbank market or going short that
currency in the futures market.

Covering

The buying of securities or commodities to close a short position.

Crack Spread

A type of commodity/product spread
involving the purchase of crude oil
futures and the sale of gasoline and
heating oil futures.

Cracking Spread

When refiners refine crude oil into its
major by-products, heating oil and
gasoline, they are "cracking" the
crude oil. The profit margin difference is the processing margin and
can be traded either way. A trader
puts on a crack spread when he anticipates the processing margin narrowing and puts on a reverse crack
when he anticipates the margin
widening.

Credit Risk

The risk that an issuer of debt securities or a borrower may default on his obligations.

Creditor

A person or firm that extends credit by loaning money, by selling property on credit, by selling goods on credit, by furnishing credit cards, and so on.

Creditworthiness

A creditor's measure of a consumer's past and future ability and willingness to repay debts.

Crescendo Effect

Momentary buying or selling resulting from a triggering of stops, often just after the open. This phenomenon usually occurs just prior to a trend reversal.

Crop Report

Periodic reports issued by the Department of Agriculture estimating the size and condition of major U.S. crops.

Crop Year

The year based on the period from one harvest to the next harvest. The crop year is standardized for each commodity although harvest may overlap several months between different regions where the crop is grown.

Cross Hedge

Hedging a cash market risk in one commodity or financial instrument by initiating a position in a futures contract for a different but related commodity or instrument. A cross hedge is based on the premise that although the two commodities or instruments are not the same, their price movements correlate.

Cross Trading

Offsetting or noncompetitive matching of the buying order of one customer against the selling order of another. This practice is permissible only when executed as required by the CEA, CFTC, and rules of the contract market.

Cross-Rate

In foreign exchange, the price of one currency in terms of another currency in the market of a third country.

Crossover

When the faster of the two indicators which are plotted together overtakes the slower. Crossovers usually give potential buy-sell signals.

Crude Oil

A mixture of hydrocarbons that exists in liquid phase in underground reservoirs and remains liquid at atmospheric pressure after passing through surface separating facilities.

Crude Oil Stocks

Stocks of crude oil and lease condensate held at refineries, in pipelines, at pipeline terminals, and on leases.

Crush

In soybeans, crush is the process by which soybeans are converted to soybean oil and soybean meal. A 60-pound bushel of soybeans yields 48 pounds of soybean meal and 11 pounds of soybean oil with 1 pound of waste. Also refers to a spread that consists of long soybeans, short soybean meal, and short soybean oil. An exact (big) crush is 10 soybean contracts versus 12 meal and 9 oil contracts. The little crush involves 1 contract of each. In cattle, the crush is a spread that consists of long feeder cattle, long corn, and short live cattle. An exact cattle crush is three feeder cattle contracts and two corn contracts versus five live cattle contracts.

Crusher

One who extracts oil from oilseeds like soybeans or sunflowers or a spread broker who specializes in oilseeds and their products.

Currency Futures

Instruments to manage the risk or exposure involved in foreign trade.

Currency Spread

Buying a commodity in a weak monetary country and selling a commodity in a strong monetary country (ie., Buy London Copper/Sell New York Copper; D-Mark/Japanese Yen; British Pound/Canadian Dollar; U.S. Dollar Index/Swiss Franc; ECU/U.S. Dollar Index). These spreads are very difficult for American traders unless they are well versed in both currency histories and commodities.

Current Account Balance

The difference between the nation's total exports of goods, services, and transfers and its total imports of the same items.

Current Coins

Gold coins which were legal tender in the period of circulating gold currency.

Current Coupon

A bond with a recently issued coupon or a coupon close to the yields currently offered on new debt instruments of similar maturity and credit risk.

Current Delivery

The futures contract which matures and becomes deliverable during the present month.

Current Issue

The most recently auctioned and usually most actively traded short-term debt instrument.

Current Yield

The return on an asset calculated by dividing the annual coupon payments by the actual purchase price of the asset. Accrued interest is typically omitted in the calculation.

Cushion Bond

A callable high-coupon bond that sells at a slight premium. Its above average yield protects or cushions it

	against a decline in price and rising interest rates.
Customer's Man	An employee of a commission house who solicits or accepts and handles orders for purchase or sale.
Cycle Size	The number of lines in a cardinal square less one, representing twice the number of "coils" in the spiral.
Cycles	Recurring price changes of equal time spans.
Cyclical Industry	An industry whose sales and profits are sensitive to changes in the level of economic activity.
Daily Price Limit	The maximum advance or decline from the previous day's settlement permitted for a contract in one trading session. This limit is set by the exchange upon which the instrument is being traded.
Daily Range	The maximum daily range permitted in a market's price.
Day Order	A buy or sell order which is automatically canceled if it is not filled during the day it is entered.
Day Trader	A trader who will normally initiate and offset a position within a single daily trading session.
Deadweight Tons	Total carrying capacity of a ship in tons when loaded to the appropriate freeboard during the summer season.
Dealer	A principal in all transactions, buying and selling for his own account. Also an individual or firm in cash market who acts as principal in transactions.
Debenture	A debt instrument which is secured only by the general credit of the issuer.

Debt Securities

Loans, evidenced by an agreement to pay back the principal plus interest at a specified time.

Deck

All of the unexecuted orders in a floor broker's possession.

Declination

The celestial latitude, or degrees north or south of the equator, of a heavenly body's position. North declination is positive and south declination is negative.

Declination Factor

The sum of the declinations of Venus and Mars.

Deep Discount Bond

A bond that sells well below face value because of its low coupon rate or low credit rating. The low rate also makes it less likely to be called than bonds paying higher rates.

Default

The failure to perform on a futures contract as required by exchange rules, such as a failure to meet a margin call or to make or take delivery. Also refers to failure to make timely payment of interest or principal on a debt instrument.

Deferred Contracts

Those futures contract which call for delivery in the most distant months instead of nearby months.

Deferred Delivery Contract

An agreement between a buyer and seller of the physical commodity to transfer possession and title to the product at some future date. Contracts for deferred delivery are distinguishable from futures contracts.

Deflation

A decline in the general price level.

Deliverable Grade

A commodity or financial instrument that meets standard specifications required by the exchange as acceptable for delivery against a futures contract.

Deliverable Stocks
Stocks that are in storage and certified as deliverable against a short futures position.

Delivery
The process and time at which funds and the physical commodity change hands upon expiration of a futures contract. The possibility that delivery can occur causes cash and futures prices to converge. As the time for delivery approaches, the price difference between cash and futures narrows until finally, in the delivery month, prices in both markets are about the same.

Delivery Area
The points specified in an exchange's rules as to where delivery of the physical commodity can be made.

Delivery Instrument
A document used to effect delivery on a futures contract, such as a warehouse receipt or shipping certificate.

Delivery Month
The month in which settlement is to be made in accordance with a futures contract.

Delivery Notice
The written notice given by the seller of intention to make delivery against a short futures position on a particular day.

Delivery Point
The place(s) at which the cash commodity may be delivered to fulfill an expiring futures contract.

Delivery Price
The price fixed by the clearing house at which deliveries on futures are invoiced. Also, the price at which a futures contract is settled at the time of delivery.

Demurrage
Compensation paid for detention of a ship during loading or unloading beyond the scheduled time of departure.

Depositary

A subsidiary of the Chicago Board of Trade Clearinghouse which supervises the issuance of Depositary Receipts and Demand Certificates. The Depositary collects Demand Certificates and holds them as bailee until they are exchanged for Depositary Receipts. The Depositary also collects storage funds from holders of outstanding DRs and remits storage payments to issuers of outstanding DRs.

Depositary Receipt

A document guaranteeing the existence of a given quantity and quality of commodity in storage. In certain futures contracts, warehouse receipts rather than wet barrels are delivered against a futures contract.

Depreciation

A fall in the value of a monetary unit in terms of purchasing power.

Depression

A period of greatly reduced business activity characterized by widespread unemployment and low production.

Descending Node

The point of a planet's orbit at which it crosses the plane of the earth's orbit extended to meet the celestial body from north to south.

Designators

Up or Down notations written beside a day's OBV when that figure tops a previous high or goes below a previous low.

Devaluation

A formal "official" decrease in the exchange rate by a country.

Diamond

A chart pattern which usually occurs at major tops. Prices trade in a range which widens out and then narrows into a diamond shape which can either signal a reversal or a consolidation.

Diesel Fuel

Distillate fuel oil used in compression-ignition engines.

Differential Activity Volume(DAV)
A daily indicator used with tic volume which is derived from the difference between the number of upticks and the number of downticks.

Differentials
Price differences between classes, grades, and locations of different stocks of the same commodity.

Discount
Can refer to the amount a price would be reduced to purchase a commodity of lesser grade, the price differences between futures of different delivery months, or cash grain prices that are below futures.

Discount Bond
A bond selling below par.

Discount Broker
A broker who charges lower commissions on transactions.

Discount Rate
The add-on rate of interest charged to Fed member banks for borrowing at the discount window.

Discount Securities
Non-coupon-bearing debt instruments issued at a price below par and redeemed at maturity for full face value.

Discount Window
A "window" available to Fed members that allows them to borrow against collateral. Use of this facility is often discouraged by the Fed, sometimes by charging a surcharge.

Discounting
The process of determining present value.

Discretionary Account
An arrangement by which the owner of the account gives written power of attorney to someone else, usually a broker or Commodity Trading Adviser, to buy and sell without prior approval of the account owner. Often referred to as a managed account or

controlled account.

Disintermediation

A dislocation of investment funds from one vehicle to another. For example, with the advent of money market funds, banks and savings and loans suffered disintermediation when savings were withdrawn to invest in the money market funds.

Dispersion

Deviation from the average.

Disposable Personal Income

Personal income less personal tax and nontax payments to government.

Distant

The contract of a spread that is the furthest in the future.

Distillate

Liquid hydrocarbons usually water-white or pale-straw in color and of high API gravity recovered from wet gas by a separator that condenses the liquid out of the gas stream.

Distillate Fuel Oil

A general classification for one of the petroleum fractions produced in conventional distillation operations. It is used primarily for space heating, on-and-off highway diesel engine fuel, and electric power generation.

Distribution

A condition occurring in rising markets when smart money begins dumping stock in order to take profits and which signals that a top has been reached and a breakdown is imminent.

Diversification

Trading a number of different positions and/or markets for the purpose of spreading and reducing risk.

Doctor Test

A qualitative method of testing light fuel oils for the presence of sulfur compounds and mercaptans.

Dollar Bonds

A type of municipal revenue bond whose price quotes are given in dollars instead of a yield basis.

Dollar Cost Averaging
A policy of buying investment instruments at regular intervals with a fixed dollar amount.

Dollar Price
Percentage of face value at which a debt instrument is quoted.

Domestic Crude Oil
Crude oil produced in the United States or from its outer continental shelf.

Dominant Future
The future having the largest number of open contracts.

Don't Know
An expression used to denote that a party "does not know" or recognize a particular transaction.

Double Bottom/Top
Two extended lows/highs of equal strength signalling the reversal of a bull/bear market.

Double Eagle
A former US $20 gold coin from the USA bearing an eagle on the reverse side.

Double-Up
When traders close out a position and immediately initiate an opposite position.

Down
The amount by which one time period's price closes below the previous period's price.

Downstream
An industry term referring to commercial petroleum operations beyond the crude production phase.

Downtick
A trade which takes place at a lower price than the immediately preceding transaction.

Ductility
The property of a metal that allows it to be drawn or stretched into thin wire.

Dumping
Selling goods in a foreign country

cheaper than they are sold at home.

Eagle
A former US $10 coin bearing an eagle on the reverse side.

Ease Off
A minor and/or slow decline in the prices of a market.

Eclipse, Annular
An eclipse in which sunlight shows around the moon.

Eclipse, Lunar
Opposition of sun and moon with the moon at or near node.

Eclipse, Solar
Conjunction of sun and moon with the moon at or near node.

Econometrics
The application of statistical and mathematical methods in the field of economics in testing and quantifying economic theories and the solution of economic problems.

Efficient Market Hypothesis
Presumes that all information and news relevant to a market is already accounted for in its price or, conversely, that the market price already reflects everything known in the marketplace.

Elasticity
A characteristic of markets which describes the interaction of supply, demand, and price. A market is said to be elastic in demand when a price change creates an increase or decrease in consumption and elastic in supply when a change in price creates change in the production or supply.

Electrum
A natural light-yellow alloy of gold and silver.

Elliott Wave Principle
A system for interpreting and forecasting price movement based on the concept of five waves in the direction of the main trend followed by three corrective waves against the

trend.

Elongation Apparent angular distance of a member of the solar system from the sun as seen from the earth.

End-User The ultimate consumer of products.

Entry Signal A signal given by a trading technique showing at what price or when a trader should initiate a position.

Ephemeris An almanac of planetary, lunar, and solar positions.

Equilibrium Price A price that equates supply and demand.

Equinox, Fall Sun passes from northern to southern hemisphere.

Equinox, Spring Sun passes from southern to northern hemisphere.

Equity The dollar value of a trading account if all open positions were offset at the going market price.

Equivalent Bond Yield The annualized yield on a short-term, discount instrument adjusted so as to be comparable to the annualized yields on coupon-bearing securities.

Equivalent Taxable Yield The yield required on a taxable security to provide the investor with the same after-tax return as he would receive by owning a tax-exempt security.

Erratic A market that moves rapidly, changes direction quickly, and is irregular in its action.

Euro Lines Credit lines granted by foreign banks or offshore branches of U.S. banks for Eurocurrencies.

Eurobonds Bonds, not necessarily denominated in the currency of the issuer, that are issued outside the United States, usually in Europe. Also, bonds issued in Europe by a foreign institution but outside the boundaries of the capital market of its own country.

Eurodeposits

Certificates of deposit issued by a U.S. bank branch or foreign bank located outside the United States.

Eurodollar Time Deposits

U.S. dollars on deposit outside the U.S., either with a foreign bank or a subsidiary of a U.S. bank. The interest paid for these dollar deposits generally is higher than that for funds deposited in U.S. banks because the foreign banks are not backed by the U.S. government.

Eurodollars

Deposits denominated in U.S. dollars at banks and other financial institutions outside the United States. Although this name originated because of the large amounts of such deposits held at banks in Western Europe, similar deposits in other parts of the world are also called Eurodollars.

Even Lot

A unit of trading in a market established by an exchange to which official price quotations apply.

Even Money Spread

Buying and selling two positions at the same time.

Even Up

To close out, liquidate, or cover an open position.

Ex-Pit Transaction

Trades executed, for certain technical purposes, in a location other than the regular exchange trading pit or ring.

Ex-Store

Selling term for commodities in a warehouse.

Excess

The amount by which the equity in a

margin account exceeds the margin requirement. This excess can be withdrawn at any time and/or be invested in the security of the customer's choice.

Exchange
An association of persons engaged in the business of buying and selling.

Exchange Certified Stocks
Stocks of commodities held in depositories or warehouses certified by an Exchange approved inspection authority as constituting good delivery against a futures contract position.

Exchange Control
Governmental restrictions on transactions in foreign exchange.

Exchange for Physicals
Where the holder of a long futures position and the holder of a short futures position agree to the delivery of product in a manner that varies from an exchange's specifications.

Exchange Rate
The price of one currency stated in terms of another currency.

Exchange Rate Futures
Futures contracts for currencies.

Execution
Occurs when a customer's order has been either partially or completely filled.

Execution by Outcry
The practice on many exchanges of executing orders verbally and publicly.

Execution Indicator
A market technique which generates signals telling the trader either when or at what price level to buy, sell, or close out positions.

Exotic Spreads
Buying and selling two different commodities that are quasi-related but are not given spread margin considerations by the exchanges (i.e., New York Gold/Treasury Bonds).

Expiration Date

The last day that an option may be exercised.

Exposure

The amount a trader would stand to lose on a position if that position were closed out at that moment.

Exponentially Smoothed Moving Average

A moving average which gives diminishing weight to days further and further into the past. The weighting factor is an exponentially decreasing fraction.

F.O.B.

Free on Board - the transportation cost to the point of destination is not included in the quoted price of the product.

Face Value

The value of a bond that appears on the face of the bond unless the value is otherwise specified by the issuer. Face value is ordinarily the amount the issuer promises to pay at maturity. Face value is not an indication of market value but is sometimes referred to as par value.

Factor Slippage

Refers to the phenomenon that a hedge or arbitrage ratio can be slightly distorted due to the fact that there can be a change in the cheapest deliverable instrument. This change will cause the market to begin tracking another instrument with a different delivery factor from the one originally used to calculate a hedge or arbitrage ratio.

Fade

A trader "fades" an indicator by doing the opposite of what a normal interpretation of its signals would dictate. This is not the same as ignoring the indicator because the trader actually takes action based on the indicator.

Fail

The situation wherein one side of a trade does not live up to the contractual obligations of the trade.

Familiar Spreads
Another name for common or well publicized spreads. Also, spreads used extensively by system books (ie, Wheat/Corn; Gold/Silver; T-Bill/Eurodollar; London Silver/2 New York Silver).

Fan
A series of three lines connecting a single high (in falling price action) or low (in rising price action) with three consecutively lower highs or higher lows. When price breaks the third fan-line contrary to the major trend, a reversal breakout is signaled.

Fast Market
Transactions in the pit or ring that take place in such volume and with such rapidity that price reports and price quotations fall behind.

Federal Budget Receipts
In the unified budget concept, covers receipts, net of refunds, of all Federal agencies and trust funds.

Federal Debt Limit
A limit imposed by law on the aggregate face amount of outstanding obligations issued, or guaranteed as to principal and interest, by the United States except such guaranteed obligations as may be held by the Secretary of the Treasury.

Federal Deposit Insurance Corp.
An agency of the federal government that insures accounts at most commercial banks and mutual savings banks.

Federal Expenditures
Federal purchases of goods and services, transfer payments, grants-in-aid to state and local governments, net interest paid and subsidies less current surplus of government enterprises.

Federal Funds
Reserve balances that depository institutions lend each other, usually on an overnight basis. Also, member banks' deposits held by the Federal

Reserve.

Federal Funds Rate

The rate of interest charged for the use of federal funds.

Federal Reserve Bank

An agency of the U.S. government established to implement monetary policy as set forth by its seven governors. The policies are administered through its twelve regional banks. Typical operations consist of buying and selling securities on the open market, where it conducts transactions not only for its own account, but also for foreign central banks. Repos and/or the purchase of securities are used to add reserves to the banking system, while reverse repos and/or selling securities are used to drain reserves.

Federal Tax Receipts

Differ from tax receipts chiefly in that business taxes are included on an accrual basis.

Fedwire

The Federal Reserve funds transfer system. Fedwire is used for transferring reserve account balances of depository institutions and government securities.

Feed Ratio

The relationship of the cost of feed expressed as a ratio to the sale of animals, such as the corn/hog ratio. These serve as indicators of the profit return or lack of it in feeding animals to market weight.

Feedstock

The supply of crude oil, natural gas liquids, or natural gas to a refinery or petrochemical plant or the supply of some refined fraction of intermediate petrochemical to some other process.

Fibonacci

Italian mathematician who formulated a series of numbers based on adding the previous two numbers, starting with one. Market days, based on taking the market count from previous highs and lows, are widely followed by technical analysts.

Fibonacci Ratio

Any ratio between two successive numbers in the series 1,1,2,3,5,8...which approaches .618 or 1.618. This ratio is sometimes useful for determining the length of successive waves.

Fictitious Trading

Wash trading, bucketing, cross trading, or other schemes to give the appearance of trading.

Fiduciary

One who acts for another in financial matters.

Field Trend

Rising, Falling, or Doubtful notations written when cluster-patterns of Up and Down designators have been zig-zagging downward, upward, or in neither direction, respectively. If cluster patterns are zig-zagging downwards, the Field Trend is falling. If the patterns are zig-zagging upwards, the Field Trend is rising. If the Up-Down designations are not in gear with each other, then the Field Trend is doubtful.

FIFO

First-in-first-out; an inventory accounting method.

Fill

Refers, as a noun, to the execution of an order (e.g., "The trader received his fill") and, as a verb, to the process of executing an order (e.g., "The order was filled immediately.").

Fill or Kill

An order to be immediately executed or canceled (FOK).

Finance Charge

The total dollar amount paid to get credit.

Financial Futures

Contracts calling for future delivery of currencies or interest rate instruments.

Financial Leverage

The use of borrowed funds to acquire an asset.

Financing Cash Position

Short-term borrowing, usually through repos, by which dealers or traders obtain the capital to support inventory.

Fine Gold Content

The weight of pure gold in a coin as calculated by multiplying the coin's gross weight by its fineness.

Fineness

Proportion of pure gold or silver in an alloy expressed in parts-per-thousand by weight.

Fingerprints

Blems, clashes, marks, chips, pits, scratches or other defects on a die which repeatedly reproduce themselves on coins struck by that particular die.

Finished Leaded Gasoline

Contains more than 0.05 gram of lead per gallon or more than 0.005 gram of phosphorus per gallon.

Finished Unleaded Gasoline

Contains not more than 0.05 gram of lead per gallon and not more than 0.005 gram of phosphorus per gallon.

First Hands

Refers to the original owner of a product or commodity.

First Notice Day

The first day on which notices of intent to deliver a commodity in fulfillment of an expiring futures contract can be given to the clearinghouse by a seller and assigned by the clearinghouse to a buyer. First Notice Day varies from contract to contract.

Fiscal Policy

The setting of taxes, government spending, and public borrowing to influence economic activity.

Fiscal Year	An accounting year for a business or government that does not necessarily begin in January.
Fixed Rate	A traditional approach to determining the finance charge payable on an extension of credit. A predetermined and certain rate of interest applied to the principal.
Fixing the Price	In an "on call" transaction, the determination of the exact price at which a physical product will be involved.
Flag	Two parallel lines of highs and lows drawn at angles to the current trend. Indicates consolidation and further work prior to resumption of the current trend.
Flash Point	The lowest temperature at which a liquid will generate sufficient vapor to produce a flash when exposed to a source of ignition.
Flat	Trading without accrued interest.
Flat Book	A policy whereby commercial firms are almost always fulled hedged, i.e., their positions in the futures market reflect their commitments in the cash market.
Flat Market	Exists when all the delivery months of a particular market are at or about the same price.
Flight Capital	A movement of funds legally or illegally from one country to another caused by fear of inflation, confiscation, or exchange controls.
Flip	When a trader closes out a position and simultaneously opens the opposite position.
Floating Inventory	Products that have been purchased by a dealer that are on board a

vessel in transit. If the dealer succeeds in finding a buyer for the shipment before it arrives, the need for him to pay to store is eliminated.

Floor Broker

A member who is paid a fee for executing trades for clearing members or their customers. He must be licensed by the CFTC and the exchange upon which he trades and is permitted to trade for his own personal account.

Floor Trader

Members of an exchange on the trading floors that trade for themselves; sometimes called scalpers or locals.

Flop Over

A new parallel with the same width as previous channel.

Fool's Gold

Popular name for iron pyrite.

Force Majeure

A standard clause which indemnifies either or both parties to a transaction whenever events reasonably beyond the control of either or both parties occur to prevent fulfillment of the terms of the contract.

Forecasting

The processes of predicting the future.

Foreign Crude Oil

Crude oil produced outside the United States.

Foreign Currency

The standard unit of the official medium of exchange of a sovereign government other than the United States Government.

Foreign Currency Futures Contract

A foreign exchange contract that is standardized with respect to size and settlement date and is traded on a commodity exchange.

Foreign Exchange Rate

The price of one currency denominated in another currency.

Foreign Exchange Risk

The risk associated with holding a long position in a currency (perhaps a receivable) or a short position in a currency (perhaps a payable).The risk is that exchange rates can change adversely, thereby causing a net loss even though the commercial transaction giving rise to the risk makes economic sense.

Forward

In the future.

Forward Contract

A cash market transaction in which two parties agree to the purchase and sale of a market at some future time under such conditions as the two agree. Those who use forward contracts expect to make or take physical delivery of the merchandise or financial instrument. Each contract is tailored specifically to the needs of buyer and seller. Trading is generally done by phone in a decentralized marketplace. In contrast to futures contracts, the terms of forward contracts are not standardized, the contract is not transferable, and it can usually be canceled only with the consent of the other party.

Forward Fed Funds

Fed funds traded for deferred delivery. This is a cash forward transaction, not a futures contract.

Forward Forward Contract

An agreement under which a deposit with a fixed maturity is agreed upon at a fixed price for deferred delivery.

Forward Market

Refers to informal (non-exchange) trading of products to be delivered at a future date.

Forward Months

Futures contracts, of those currently traded, calling for later or distant delivery.

Forward Purchase or Sale

A purchase or sale of an actual product for deferred delivery.

Forward Rate

The rate associated with the purchase

or sale of a currency for a specific deferred delivery date.

Forward Shipment A contract covering cash products to be shipped at some future specified date.

Fossil Energy Energy derived from crude oil, natural gas, and coal.

Fraction A separate, identifiable part of crude oil; the product of a refining or distillation process.

Free Supply The part of supply that is available to the market and not under the shelter of government programs. Producers are eligible to receive loans for their grain at specified loan levels.If the market price falls below the loan rate, producers are induced to turn their grain over to the government, reducing free supply.

Freight Rate The charge for transporting goods.

Fuel Oil The heavy distillates from the oil refining process.

Full Faith and Credit Debt State and local debt for which the credit of the government, implying the power of taxation, is unconditionally pledged.

Full Moon When the Moon is opposite the Sun in the sky and is fully luminated.

Full-Coupon Bond A bond priced at or close to par because its coupon is as high as recently issued coupons or prevailing market rates for similar maturities.

Fully Disclosed An account carried by the Futures Commission Merchant in the name of the individual customer; opposite of an omnibus account.

Fundamental Analysis Analysis based on the economic

factors affecting supply and demand and their influence on market prices.

Fungibility

The characteristic of total inter-changeability.

Fungible

Interchangeable. Products which can be commingled for purposes of pipe-line shipment.

Futures

Contracts calling for a cash commodity to be delivered and received at a specified future time, at a specified place, and at a specified price.

Futures Commission Merchant (FCM)

An individual or organization which solicits or accepts orders to buy or sell futures contracts and accepts money or other assets from custom-ers in connection with such orders. Must be registered with the Com-modity Futures Trading Commission.

Futures Contract

An agreement to make or take delivery of a standardized amount of a com-modity during a specific month at a price established by open auction in a trading pit under terms and condi-tions set by a federally designated contract market where the trading is conducted.

Futures Industry Association (FIA)

The national trade association for the futures industry.

Futures Market

A market in which contracts for the future delivery of commodities or fi-nancial instruments are traded. Can refer to a specific exchange or the market in general.

Futures Price

The price of a particular futures con-tract is determined by open competi-tion between buyers and sellers on the trading floor of a commodity ex-change.

G.T.C. Order

Good Till Canceled - A customer's order to his broker to buy or sell at a specified price, the order to remain in effect until it is either executed or canceled.

Gann

An early 20th-century theoretician and analyst who formulated market rules based on laws of the universe.

Gaps

Gaps are areas on the bar chart where no trades are made. There are four types of gaps and each have significance: breakaway, common, exhaustion, and runaway (measuring) gaps.

Gasohol

A blend of finished motor gasoline and alcohol in which 10 percent or more of the product is alcohol.

Gasoil

European designation for No. 2 heating oils and diesel fuels.

Gasoline, raw

The untreated gasoline-cut from the distillation of crude oil.

Gasoline, straight-run

The gasoline-range fraction distilled from crude oil.

General Obligation Bonds

Municipal bonds secured by the issuer's pledge of its full faith, credit, and taxing power, as opposed to revenue bonds, which only pledge the income from a certain project to pay interest and principal.

Gilt-Edged

High-grade bonds issued by a company that has demonstrated its ability to earn a comfortable profit over a period of years and pay its bondholders interest and principal without interruption.

Give Up

At the request of the customer, a brokerage house which has not performed the service is credited with the execution of an order. Also, in the trading pit, a broker "gives up"

the name of the firm for which he
was acting to another member with
whom a transaction has just been
completed.

GNMA

Mortgage-backed securities for which
the Government National Mortgage
Association (GNMA) has guaranteed
the timely payment of principal and
interest. GNMAs are issued with a
life of 30 years, but because the underlying mortgages can be paid
down ahead of schedule, the average
life of GNMAs is approximately 12
years.

Gold Backing

Backing of a nation's circulating
currency by official gold reserves.

Gold Standard

A system under which a country backs
its paper currency by law with a
stated quantity of gold.

Golden Number

Denoting the year in the 19-year cycle
of the moon. The moon phases occur
on the same dates every nineteen
years.

Good Delivery

Delivery in which all contract specifications have been met (i.e., proper
documentation, signatures, timely
delivery at the proper place, etc.).

Governments

U.S. Treasury securities.

Grades

Various qualities of a product.

Grading Certificates

A formal paper setting forth the
quality of a product as determined
by authorized inspectors or graders.

Grain (PM)

The earliest unit of weight, originally
a grain of wheat, barley, or corn.

Grain Futures Act

The federal statute which regulated
trading in grain futures effective
June 22, 1923.

Greenwich Time	The mean solar time of the meridian of the city of Greenwich, England, used as the prime basis of standard time throughout the world.
Gross Debt (BC)	All long-term credit obligations incurred and outstanding whether backed by a government's full faith and credit or nonguaranteed, and all interest-bearing short-term credit obligations.
Gross National Product	The market value of a nation's total output of goods and services.
Gross Processing Margin	For soybeans, refers to the difference between the cost of soybeans and the combined sales income of the soybean oil and meal which results from processing soybeans.
Gross Weight	Total weight of a coin or bar.
Guided Account	An account that is part of a program directed by a Commodity Trading Adviser (CTA) or Futures Commission Merchant (FCM). The CTA or FCM plans the trading strategies but the customer is advised to enter and/or liquidate specific trading positions. Approval to enter the order must be given by the customer.
Haircut	Refers to special margin rates for floor traders or to the spread in a repo transaction. Also refers to a term signifying that only a portion of the full value of an asset can be used to meet a specific requirement.
Hallmark	A mark or set of marks used in England since about 1300 to indicate the fineness and the maker of gold and silver articles.

Handle	The portion of a price quote that is assumed to be understood by all active traders. For instance, in a 91.14-91.16 bid/ask bond market, the quote might be "bid 4, ask 6". The handle would be 91.1.
Hardening	Describes a price which is gradually stabilizing or indicates a slowly advancing market.
Head and Shoulders	A chart price pattern associated with trend reversals. In a bull market, the pattern is characterized by a left congestion area followed by a charge to new highs and then a second congestion area around the same price level as the first, but below the price high of the peak.
Heating Oil	Synonymous to No. 2 Fuel Oil, a distillate fuel oil for domestic heating or used in moderate capacity, commercial-industrial burners.
Heavy	A market in which prices are demonstrating either an inability to advance or a slight tendency to decline.
Heavy Crude	Crude oil with a high specific gravity and a low API gravity due to the presence of a high proportion of heavy hydrocarbon fractions.
Hedge	Using the futures market to reduce the price risks inherent in buying and selling cash products.
Hedging	The sale of futures against the physical product as protection against a price decline or the purchase of futures against forward sales as protection against a price advance. Hedging is often used to offset the risks associated with the fluctuating value of inventory.
Hidden Spread	When one has numerous outright positions, liquidating some of them

may result in two outright positions falling into a preferential spread margin situation. Usually this occurs by chance. Computers compute the lowest rate of margin requirements allowed by exchange clearing house rules to gain customer favor.

High

Highest price at which an instrument sold during the trading period.

High-Balling

Bidding up the price of a market in an attempt to generate buy stop orders.

Historical Spread

A spread put on to establish a trading objective from historical research and relationships (i.e., Gold/Silver Ratio; Long Term Municipal Bond Index/T-Bond).

Historical Volatility

The range of price fluctuation over a sample period of time used as a measuring guide.

Hit

A trader who agrees to sell at the bid price quoted by another trader is said to have "hit the bid", whereas one who has lost is said to have "taken a hit."

Ignition Point

Temperature to which a substance can be heated before it will burn.

Import/Export Spread

Buying and selling the same commodity in two different countries to profit from differences due to tariffs, import quotas, or levies (i.e., World Sugar #11/Domestic Sugar #12).

Impulse Wave

A wave or cycle of waves which carries the current trend further in the same direction.

In Sight

The amount of a particular commodity that arrives at terminal or central locations in or near producing areas.

Incentive Payment Plan Usually describes the cash subsidy paid to agricultural producers by the U.S. government.

Indenture A written agreement under which bonds and debentures are issued setting forth the maturity date, interest rate, and other terms.

Industrial Metal Spread Spreads designed to play the difference between industrial metals as opposed to precious metals (i.e., Copper/Aluminum; London Copper/New York Copper; L.M.E. Lead/L.M.E. Zinc/L.M.E. Nickel).

Inelasticity A characteristic that describes the interdependence of the supply, demand, and price. A market is inelastic when a price change does not create an increase or decrease in consumption; supply and demand are relatively unresponsive to changes in price.

Inferior A conjunction in which the planet is between the sun and the earth.

Inflation A rise in the general price level.

Inflation/Precious Metals Spread Spreading the consumer price index to a precious metal for long term trend patterns (i.e., Consumer Price Index/COMEX Gold; Consumer Price Index/C.R.B. Futures Price Index - 27 commodities).

Initial Margin Customers' funds required at the time a future position is established to assure performance of the customers' obligations. Margin in commodities is not a down payment as it is in securities.

Inside Day A day with both the high and the low between the previous day's high and low.

Institution

An organization holding substantial investable assets, often for others.

Institutional Customer

In the financial instruments market, roughly analogous to the commercial customer in the grain trade.

Integration

A term which describes the degree in which one given company participates in all phases of the industry.

Inter-Crop Spread

In the same commodity, buying and selling two different crop months (i.e., July Corn/December Corn).

Inter-Delivery Spread

Buying and selling two different months of the same commodity. This is the most widely known spread (i.e., July Corn/September Corn).

Inter-Grain Spread

Buying and selling equal quantities of any two grain contracts (i.e., Corn/Oats).

Intercommodity Spread

A spread that consists of a long position in one commodity and a short position in another commodity.

Interest

Payments made by a borrower to a lender for the use of his money.

Interest Rate Parity

Traditional theory of foreign exchange which states that the forward premium or discount on one currency relative to another is directly related to the interest rate differential between the two countries.

Interest Rate Spread

Buying and selling any two interest rate contracts to benefit from their yield and time structures (i.e., GNMA/T-Bond; T-Bill/T-Bond; T-Bill/Eurodollar; C.D./T-Bill).

Intermarket Spread

A spread that consists of a position in one market and an opposite position for the same commodity in a different market (i.e., Kansas City Board of Trade wheat/Chicago

Board of Trade wheat).

Intermediate Cycle/Action Movements lasting several weeks or months and which make up major cycles.

Intramarket Spread A spread that consists of opposite positions in different contract months of the same commodity. An intramarket spread can involve contracts of the same crop year or contracts of different crop years (i.e., July Cotton/December Cotton is an old crop/new crop intramarket spread).

Introducing Broker (IB) A firm or individual that solicits and accepts commodity futures orders from customers but does not accept money, securities, or property from the customer. An IB must be registered with the Commodity Futures Trading Commission and must carry all of its accounts through an FCM on a fully disclosed basis.

Inverted Market A market in which futures prices for nearby delivery months of a commodity are selling at a premium in comparison to the most distant months. This definition would not necessarily hold true for financial instrument futures which are priced as a function of the cash yield curve.

Inverted Market Spread Front months are at a premium to the deferred months.

Investment The use of money for the purpose of making more money - to gain income or increase capital or both.

Investor An individual whose principal concerns in the purchase of a security are regular dividend income, safety of the original investment, and capital appreciation.

Invisible Supply

Uncounted stocks of a product in the hands of wholesalers, manufacturers, and producers which cannot be identified accurately - stocks outside commercial channels but theoretically available to the market.

IOM

Index and Option Market.The Chicago Mercantile Exchange's division set up to trade stock index futures and options.

Island Formation

A bar chart pattern that is formed at the extremes of a market move when the price gaps in the direction of the trend and stays there for one or more days. The momentum of the trend having been exhausted then results in the price gapping back the other way against the trend. Thus, at its extreme the price is isolated on both sides like an island.

Jet Fuel

Kerosene-type; quality kerosene product used primarily as fuel for commercial turbojet and turboprop aircraft engines.

Job Lot

A trading unit which is smaller than a full-contract unit.

Jobber

A trader on an exchange floor who attempts to scalp a profit from small price fluctuations.

Junk Bond

A high-risk, high-yield corporate or municipal bond that is rated BB or lower by Standard & Poor's or Ba or lower by Moody's. Issued by companies with questionable financial strength, with short track records, or as a means of financing a corporate takeover.

Kansas City Board of Trade

First futures exchange to offer stock index futures. Home of the Value Line Index futures contract which commenced trading in February,

	1982. Prior to that time, it was known primarily as a grain exchange.
KCBT	Kansas City Board of Trade.
Kerb	Pertaining to London sugar trading. Also refers to telephone or any other dealings outside the ring that are beyond the regular trading sessions.
Key Reversals	One day action in which the market opens violently in the direction of the major trend, moves to new price levels not reached previously, and then reverses direction and closes in the opposite direction. High volume is a signature of this formation.
Krugerrand	A gold coin consisting of one ounce of gold issued by the Union of South Africa.
L	The fourth category in the Federal Reserve's method of reporting money supply.
Labor Force (BLS)	All persons 16 years of age or over who are employed or unemployed according to established criteria.
Labored Move	Price pattern confined to a slanting narrow channel.
Lagged Moving Average	A moving average which is recorded on the price chart under the price several days ago. This is thought to compensate somewhat for the fact that the moving average is an indicator of past activity.
Landed Mill	A term of sale meaning delivered at the mill with all charges paid.
Landed Price	The actual cost of oil to a refiner, taking into account all costs from the place of production or purchase to the refinery.
Large Traders	A large trader is one who holds or

controls a position in any market equaling or exceeding the reporting level.

Last Trading Day

The last day for trading or offsetting a position which can be different than regular trading hours. Traders must either liquidate their positions or actually make or accept delivery as trading ceases for the current delivery month.

Law of Demand

Exhibits a direct relationship to price. If all other factors remain constant, an increase in demand leads to an increased price while a decrease in demand leads to a decreased price.

Law of Supply

Exhibits an inverse relationship to price. If all other factors hold constant, an increase in supply causes a decreased price while a decrease in supply causes an increased price.

Leading Indicator

A signal given by a major market analysis technique which forecasts future price movements or market action.

Leg

One side or position of a spread.

Lender of Last Resort

As the nation's central bank, the Federal Reserve has the authority and financial resources to act as "lender of last resort" by extending credit to depository institutions or to other entities in unusual circumstances involving a national or regional emergency where failure to obtain credit would have severe adverse impact on the economy.

Leverage

The ability to control a large dollar amount of a product or cash instrument with an investment of a comparatively small amount of capital (margin). In the futures market the margin is merely a good faith performance bond while in the cash or securities markets, the margin is an actual down payment on equity.

Leverage Contract

A standardized agreement calling for the delivery of a product with payments against the total cost spread out over a period of time. Principal characteristics include: Standard units and quality of a product and of terms and conditions of the contract; payment and maintenance of margin; close out by offset or delivery (after payment in full); and no right to or interest in a specific lot of the product. Leverage contracts are not traded on exchanges.

Leverage Dealer

The principal to every leverage transaction who may function as a market maker.

Leverage Transaction Merchant

The firm or individual through whom leverage contracts are entered. LTM's must be registered with the Commodity Futures Trading Commission.

Libor

The London Interbank Offered Rate. Usually, European banks offer a "scale" of different rates for Eurodollar deposits which differ for various maturities. As with the prime rate in the United States, the LIBOR may vary from institution to institution.

Licensed Warehouse

A warehouse approved by an exchange from which a commodity may be delivered on a futures contract.

Life of Contract

The period during which trading can take place between the start of trading in a particular contract and the last trading day.

Life of Delivery

The period between the first and last trades in any futures contract.

LIFO

Last-in-first-out; an inventory accounting method.

Lifting

Refers to tankers and barges taking on cargoes of oil or refined product at a terminal or transshipment point.

Lifting a Leg

The act of closing out one leg of a spread leaving an outright position open. Liquidating one side of a long-short spread or arbitrage prior to closing the other side. Also called "legging out."

Light Crude

Crude oil with a low specific gravity and high API gravity due to the presence of a high proportion of light hydrocarbon fractions.

Light Ends

The more volatile products of petroleum refining.

Limit Move

The maximum that a futures price can rise or fall from the previous session's closing price according to rules set by each exchange.

Limit Only

The definite price stated by a customer to a broker restricting the execution of an order to buy for not more than or to sell for not less than the stated price.

Limit Order

An order in which a specific price is set. A purchase order will not be executed above this price and a sell order will not be executed below it. A limit order can also be set to specify time constraints as to the time of execution.

Limited Partnership

A partnership composed of one or more general partners with professional expertise willing to assume unlimited liability and several or a large number of limited partners, usually without expertise, with investable funds but unwilling to as-

	sume liability beyond the extent of their investment. There are registered limited partnerships, registered with the SEC, and private placement limited partnerships that are exempt from registration. For tax purposes and cash distributions the limited partners are treated as individuals with all the benefits flowing directly through to them as certain IRS criteria are met.
Limited Risk Spread	A bull spread that is limited in its potential adverse movement against the trader by full carry. This possibility only occurs for storable commodities.
Liquid Market	A market which involves a large number of buyers and sellers able to trade substantial quantities at small price differences. In a liquid market, buying and selling can be accomplished quickly and easily.
Liquidate	To exit a long position or bull spread.
Liquidating Market	A market characterized by longs selling their positions.
Liquidating Only	Exchanges have the right to disallow any new positions and require that any trading that is done be only for liquidation purposes. When this occurs, the market is said to trade for "liquidation only."
Liquidity	Refers to a market which allows quick and efficient entry or exit at a price close to the last traded price. This ability to liquidate or establish a position quickly is due to a large number of traders willing to buy and sell. The market is said to flow like liquid, or have liquidity.
Liquidity Data Bank	A Market Profile distribution with further details on volume traded at

each price level. Volume is further broken down into local trader volume and hedger volume.

Liquidity Risk

The risk a financial institution faces when it has an imbalance in its asset-liability maturity structure - usually a factor when assets are longer in maturity than liabilities, exposing the institution to the risk that funds may not be available in the future in sufficient quantity to finance assets.

Loan Prices

The price at which producers may obtain government loans for their crops.

Loan Program

Primary means of government agricultural price support operations in which the government lends money to farmers at preannounced rates with the farmers' crops used as collateral.

Local

Term used to denote a 'jobber' in the US markets.

Local Bottom

A bottom that is not necessarily of major significance, formed when one period's price level is below the preceding and succeeding periods.

Local Top

A top that is not necessarily of major significance, formed when one period's price level is above the preceding and succeeding periods.

Locals

Floor traders who trade for their own accounts.

Lock Limit

A situation that occurs when demand to buy or sell is so great that it is impossible to find someone to take the opposite position. This happens when the market has moved the daily trading limit and can go no further until the following trading day.

Lock-Limit Day	A session in which the market opens up or down the limit and stays there all day with very little business transacted. This situation follows surprise changes in crop forecasts or unforeseen climate developments such as a freeze.
Locked Market	A market is "locked" when the bid price equals the offered price. To be distinguished from lock limit.
Locked-in Profits	A strategy for protecting profits in a cash, futures, or options position in the futures market by purchasing an offsetting position.
Long	As a noun, a trader who has pur chased futures contracts or the cash commodity or financial instrument (depending upon the market under discussion) and has not yet offset that position. As a verb (going long), the action of taking a position in which the trader has bought without taking the offsetting action.
Long Bonds	Bonds with a long current maturity, usually 15 years or more.
Long Hedge	The purchase of futures contracts as a protection against a rise in the price of a commodity.
Long Position	A position in which the trader has bought an instrument that does not offset a previously established short position.
Long The Basis	A trader who has purchased cash or spot goods and hedged them with sales of futures - owning the actual commodity and short futures.
Long Ton	A avoirdupois weight measure equalling 2,240 pounds.
Lot	In futures trading, refers to the unit

of trading.

Low

Lowest price at which an instrument sold during the period.

M1

Money supply as measured by the sum of currency in circulation plus demand deposits in commercial banks, traveler's checks, and other checkable deposits (including the net of demand deposits due to foreign commercial banks and official institutions).

M2

M1 plus overnight repurchase agreements and Eurodollars, MMMF balances (general purpose and broker/dealer), MMDA's, and savings and small time deposits.

M3

M2 plus large time deposits, term repurchase agreements, and institution - only MMMF balances.

Maintenance Margin

The minimum level at which the equity in a futures account must be maintained. If the equity in an account falls below this level a margin call will be issued and funds must be added to bring the account back to the initial margin level. The maintenance margin level generally is 75% of the initial margin.

Major Cycle

A bull-bear swing of important dimension spread out over several years.

Major Market Index

Traded on the Amex, an index that measures stock market performance through changes in the share prices of 20 leading "blue chip" corporations.

Make A Market

An individual or firm "makes a market" when he (it) is willing to buy and sell for his (its) own account.

Malleability

The property of some metals of being

extended in all directions by ham-
mering without cracking or breaking.

Manifest

A document issued by a shipper
covering oil or products to be trans-
ported by truck.

Manipulation

Illegally buying or selling a security
for the purpose of creating the false
or misleading appearance of active
trading or for the purpose of raising
or depressing the price to induce
purchase or sale by others.

Margin

The collateral that must be deposited
by the trader with a brokerage firm
to protect the firm from a loss on the
position. These funds are deposited
by both the buyer and the seller of
the futures contract. In the cash
market, the term may refer to the
profit spread a dealer makes on a
transaction.

Margin Call

A call from a clearinghouse to a
clearing member or from a broker or
firm to a customer to bring margin
deposits up to a required minimum
level.

Margin Call Spread

Maintenance margin calls can be met
by traders spreading against a losing
position to reduce the margin requirement and not be forced out of a
position that they believe in.

Mark To Market

The revaluing of a security, commodity,
or futures contract reflecting the
most current actual market value.
All futures accounts are marked to
market daily after the close of the
market.

Market Bottom

A bottom of major significance that
only happens once in many years. At
a market bottom, the price reaches
levels which it rarely, if ever, has
reached before and, after the bot-

tom, it rises without returning to the bottom. A market bottom signals the end of a bear market.

Market If Touched (MIT)

An order to buy or sell "at the market" (price) if a specified price is touched. An MIT order can be used to take profits or to establish a new position.

Market on Close (MOC)

An order to buy or sell at the end of the trading session at a price within the closing range of price.

Market on Opening

An order to buy or sell at the beginning of the trading session at a price within the opening range of prices.

Market Order

An order to buy or sell as soon as possible at the best price available when the order hits the trading floor.

Market Price

Market price is the last reported price at which an instrument traded.

Market Profile

A statistical distribution of price activity over discrete time intervals which form bell-shaped profiles. The implication is that certain statistical distributions occur with greater frequency than do others.

Market Top

A top of major significance that only happens once in many years. At a market top, the price reaches levels which it rarely, if ever, has reached before, and after the top, it falls without returning to the top. A market top signals the end of a bull market.

Market Value

The price at which a commodity or security can presumably be purchased or sold.

Matched Sale-Purchase Agreements

When the Federal Reserve makes a matched sale-purchase agreement, it sells a security outright for immediate delivery to a dealer or foreign cen-

	tral bank, with an agreement to buy the security back on a specified date at the same price.
Maturity	The point in time when a futures contract can be settled by delivery of the actual commodity.
Maximum Price Fluctuation	The maximum amount futures contract prices can move up or down during a specific trading session.
Member Bank	A depository institution that is a member of the Federal Reserve.
Member Firm	A securities brokerage firm organized as a partnership or corporation and owning at least one seat on the exchange.
Member's Rate	Commission charged for the execution of an order for a person who is a member of the exchange.
Mercaptans	Sulphur compounds often present in refined products which impart an undesirable odor.
Meridian	A great circle of the celestial sphere passing through its poles and the zenith of a given place.
Metal Account	Instead of taking delivery of metal bars or coins, a customer can have his claim to a particular quantity of precious metal credited to a metal account.
Metal Merchant	In the metal trade, a firm which serves metal producers and consumers as buyer, seller, agent, or banker, or a combination of any or all of these roles.
Metric Ton	A weight measure equal to 1,000 kilograms, 2,204.62 lbs, and 0.9842 long tons.

MGE   Minneapolis Grain Exchange.

Mid-Line   The horizontal line on an oscillator
                                 chart which marks the division be-
                                 tween negative and positive momen-
                                 tum.

Middle Distillate   Term applied to hydrocarbons in the
                                 so-called "middle range" of refinery
                                 distillation. Examples are heating
                                 oil, diesel fuels, and kerosene.

Minimum Price Fluctuation   Also referred to as a point or "tick."
                                 It is the smallest allowable incre-
                                 ment of price movement in a given
                                 market.

Minor Action   A market movement lasting one or
                                 several days, occasionally useful in
                                 analyzing intermediate trends.

Mint   Place where coins are struck by
                                 authority of the government.

Mint Mark   A small mark inscribed on a coin to
                                 identify the mint.

Mogas   Industry abbreviation for motor gasoline.

Momentum   A technical indicator that measures
                                 the rate of change of prices or trad-
                                 ing volume.

Momentum Index   A running chart of daily momentum
                                 fluctuations on a given momentum
                                 period. The values of the chart are
                                 normalized so that they range be-
                                 tween -1 and 1.

Momentum Period   A set period over which the techni-
                                 cian figures each day's momentum.

Monetary Policy   Management of the money supply by
                                 the Feds to keep the amount of avail-
                                 able credit in line with the needs of
                                 the economy in order to influence in-
                                 terest rate levels and the economy's
                                 course.

Money
Anything which serves as a medium of exchange, a measure of value, and a store of value which is commonly acceptable.

Money Market
The market in which short-term debt instruments are traded.

Money Spread
Spreading two related products, not necessarily equal in size or price (i.e., Soybean Oil/Soybean Meal; T-Bills/T-Bonds; Heating Oil/Crude Oil).

Moon's Age
The number of days since the previous new moon.

Mortgage Bond
A bond secured by a mortgage on a property. The value of the property may or may not equal the value of the mortgage bonds issued against it.

Motor Gasoline
A complex mixture of relatively volatile hydrocarbons, with or without small quantities of additives, that have been blended to form a fuel suitable for use in spark-ignition engines.

Motor Oil
Refined lubricating oil, usually containing additives, used as a lubricant in internal combustion engines.

Moving Average
A method of filtering or smoothing price action. An indicator which the technician usually plots on the same chart as price and which is the daily average of prices (systematically: highs, lows, close or combinations of all three) over a fixed period.

Multiplier
The number by which an index contract quoted value must be multiplied by in order to establish its total value. For instance, the multiplier for the S & P 500 is $ 500.00.

Municipal (Muni) Notes
Short-term notes issued by municipalities (e.g., tax anticipation notes

(TANs), bond anticipation notes (BANs), or revenue anticipation notes (RANs)).

Municipal Bond

A bond issued by a state or a political subdivision, such as a county, city, town, or village. The term also designates bonds issued by state agencies and authorities. In general, interest paid on municipal bonds is exempt from federal income taxes and from state and local income taxes within the state of issue.

N.F.A.

National Futures Association.

NAFTA

National Association of Futures Trading Advisers - The national trade association of Commodity Pool Operators, Commodity Trading Advisers, and related industry participants.

Naptha

A volatile, colorless product of petroleum distillation used primarily as paint solvent, cleaning fluid, and blendstock in gasoline production to produce motor gasoline by blending with straight-run gasoline.

Naphthenes

One of three basic hydrocarbon classifications found naturally in crude oil used in petrochemical feedstock (e.g., cyclopentrate, methy-, ethyl-, and propylcyclopentane).

Narrowing

Gaines in a nearby contract relative to the distant contract in a normal market. Thus, the difference between the two contract prices becomes smaller.

National Futures Association (NFA)

Authorized by the Congress in 1974 and designated by the CFTC in 1982 as a "registered futures association", the NFA is the industry-wide self-regulatory organization of the futures industry.

Native Gold	Refers to the natural and rate occurence of gold in a pure state in nature.
Nearby	The contract (or leg) of a spread that is closest to expiration.
Nearby Delivery Month	The futures contract closest to maturity.
Nearbys	The nearest delivery months of a futures market.
Neckline	In a bull market the line connecting the local lows just before and after a head formation. When it is broken to the downside after the right shoulder has formed it confirms the reversal. The opposite is true in head and shoulders bottoms.
Negative Carry	The net cost incurred when the cost of finance is greater than the return on the asset being carried.
Negotiable	Readily transferable title of a security.
Net Asset Value	The value of each unit of participation in a commodity pool which is basically assets minus liabilities plus or minus the value of open positions when marked to the market divided by the number of units.
Net Change	The change in the closing price from one trading period to the appropriate price the next trading period.
Net National Product	The market value of the net output of goods and services produced by the nation's economy.
Net performance	A change in net asset value exclusive of additions, withdrawals and redemptions.
Net Position	The net total number of instruments either bought or sold which have not been offset by opposite trades.

Netback

Net FOB cost of product offered on a delivered or CIF basis. It is arrived at by subtracting from the landed price all costs of shipment from the port or origin.

Neutral Approach

The strategy an investor employs when it is thought that the price trend is sideways.

New Crop

The supply of a commodity that will be available after harvest.

New Money

In a Treasury refunding, the amount by which the sum of money being raised is greater than the par value of the securities maturing.

New York Futures Exchange

The NYFE (pronounced "knife") which is a subsidiary of the New York Stock Exchange and the first exchange to trade index options and index futures side-by-side.

No. 1 Fuel Oil

A light distillate fuel oil intended for use in vaporizing pot-type burners.

No. 2 Fuel Oil

A distillate fuel oil for use in atomizing-type burners for domestic heating or for moderate-capacity, commercial-industrial burner units.

No. 4 Fuel Oil

A fuel oil for commercial burner installations not equipped with pre-heating facilities. It is used extensively in industrial plants.

Node

Either of the two points where the moon's orbit intersects the ecliptic.

Nominal Price Quotations

Computed price quotation for a period in which no actual trading took place which is usually an average of bid and asked prices.

Non-Member Trades

Speculators and hedgers who trade on an exchange through a member but do not hold exchange memberships.

Non-Trend Day	A Market Profile day in which no clear distribution pattern emerges and whose profile resembles a large clump.
Nonfinancial Domestic Credit	Credit market funds raised by non-financial sectors including funds raised by Federal, state, and local governments, corporate bonds, mortgages, consumer credit, and open market paper.
Normal Day	A Market Profile day in which the dis tribution pattern resembles a pot belly. During the opening periods, the range varies widely and retraces later settling down and trending toward a closing objective at around the midpoint of the day's range.
Normal Market	A market that reflects carrying charges where the nearby contracts are discounted in relation to the distant contracts.
Not Held Basis Order	An order whereby the price may trade through or better than the trader's desired level but the broker is not held responsible if the order is not filled.
Note	In a Treasury issue, a note is a debt instrument with a maturity between 1 year and 10 years. In municipals, maturities range between a month and a year and pay no interest until maturity.
Notice Day	Any day on which notices of intent to deliver on futures contracts may be issued.
Notice of Delivery	A notice given through the clearinghouse expressing an intention to deliver the commodity.
NYCE	New York Cotton Exchange.

NYSE	The New York Stock Exchange, the largest securities exchange in the United States.
NYSE Composite Index	A market-weighted average of the value of all the stocks traded on the New York Stock Exchange.
Occultations	Eclipses of stars by the moon.
Octane Number	A measure of the resistance of a fuel to pre-ignition when burned in an internal combustion engine.
Odds	Percent of expected change of the market price.
Offer	An indication of willingness to sell at a given price - opposite of bid.
Offset	Closing out or covering an open futures position by making an equal but opposite futures transaction - the liquidation of a long or short position.
Oil	Crude petroleum and other hydrocarbons produced at the wellhead in liquid form.
Old Crop	Supply from previous harvests.
Old Crop/New Crop Spread	A spread that consists of a position in the new crop year and an opposite position in the old crop year (a type of intramarket spread).
Omnibus Account	An account carried by one Futures Commission Merchant (FCM) with another FCM in which the transactions of two or more persons are combined and carried in the name of the originating FCM rather than of the individual customers.
On Track	A type of deferred delivery in which the price is set f.o.b. seller's location and the buyer agrees to pay freight

	costs to the destination. Also sometimes refers to products that are loaded in railroad cars "on track."
On-Call Transaction	Sale of physicals at a price based on a specific number of points "on or of" a specified futures month.
On-Stream	Term used for a processing plant, refinery, or pumping station that is operating.
One-sided (one-way) Market	A market in which only the bid or the offer is firm.
OPEC	The Organization of Petroleum Exporting Countries, oil-producing and exporting countries that have organized for the purpose of negotiating with oil companies on matters of oil production, price and future concession rights. Current members are: Algeria, Ecuador, Gabon, Indonesia, Iran, Iraq, Kuwait, Libya, Nigeria, Qatar, Saudi Arabia, United Arab Emirates, and Venezuela.
Open	The period at the beginning of the trading session officially designated by the exchange during which all transactions are considered made "at the opening."
Open Contracts or Positions	Contracts which have been initiated but that have not yet been liquidated by subsequent sale or purchase or by going through the delivery process. Also called open interest.
Open Interest	Futures contracts that haven't been liquidated by purchase or sale of offsetting contracts or by delivery or acceptance of the physical commodity. Open Interest is equal to the total number of long positions in the market or the total number of shorts but not a combination of the two.

Open Order

An order that stays open to be filled until the specified price is reached or the order is canceled - also called "good (un)till canceled (GTC)."

Open Outcry

The auction system used in the trading pits on the floor of the exchange. All bids and offers are made openly and loudly by public, competitive outcry and hand signals in such manner as to be available to all members in the trading pit at the same time.

Open Trade Equity

The unrealized gain or loss on open positions.

Opening Range

The range of prices at which transactions took place at the opening of the market. Buy and sell orders at the open will have been filled at any point within such a range.

Operable Distillation Capacity

The maximum amount of input that can be processed by a crude oil distillation unit in a 24-hour period which includes any shutdown capacity that could be placed in operation within 90 days.

Opportunity Cost

The foregone return a trader "could have earned" had he not selected another alternative.

Opposition

An aspect which occurs when two heavenly bodies are on opposite sides of the sky (180 degrees apart).

Original Margin

Term applied to the initial deposit of margin money required of clearing member firms by clearinghouse rules or to the initial margin deposit required of customers by exchange regulations.

Origins

Refers to countries where the softs are grown.

Oscillator A momentum index which is used to predict overbought/oversold conditions in the market.

Outright A net long or short position in a market.

Outside Day A day with both high and low beyond the previous day's high and low.

Overbought A conclusion reached by technical traders when it appears from chart patterns that prices have increased too far, too fast. If a market is overbought, technical traders would forecast a price decline to be imminent.

Overnight Delivery Risk In the cash markets, a risk that payment or delivery on one side of a transaction may be made without knowing until the next day whether funds have been received in an account on the other side.

Oversold A technical opinion that the market price has declined too steeply and too fast in relation to underlying fundamental factors. The market is said to be oversold when speculative long interest has been greatly reduced and the speculative short interest increases.

P & S A purchase and sales statement sent by a broker to his client showing both the purchase and sale of a position that has been closed out.

PAD Districts Petroleum Administration for Defense Districts - a regional grouping of the 50 states and the District of Columbia into 5 districts for the purpose of petroleum administration.

Paper Profit An unrealized profit on a position still held which becomes a realized profit or loss only when the position is closed out.

Par	100 percent of face value.
Pass-Through	A security on which the payments of interest and principal are passed through by an agent to the holder of the security (e.g., GNMA mortgage-backed pass-through certificates).
Pattern	Based on yearly patterns, not necessarily seasonal, but designed to take advantage of usage and supply variations.
Pattern Recognition	A technical method of forecasting future prices by superimposing similar price patterns from the past onto future price action.
Paydown	When the amount of money received in a Treasury refunding exceeds the par value of the maturing securities.
Pennant	A flag whose sides converge to the right - usually a consolidation pattern.
Percentage Range	A market analysis technique which compares a given day's closing price with the range of closing prices over a given period. Proximity to the top or bottom of this range expressed as a percentage provides buy or sell signals.
Perigee	Moon reaches point in its orbit closest to the earth.
Perihelion	Planet reaches point in its orbit closest to the sun.
Period	A fixed amount of time over which the price range is figured.
Petrochemical	An intermediate chemical derived from petroleum, hydrocarbon, liquids or natural gas (e.g., ethylene, propylene, benzene, toluene, and xylene).

Petroleum	A generic name for hydrocarbons including crude oil, natural gas liquids, natural gas and their products.
Physical Commodity	The actual physical product as opposed to futures.
Pipeline	A pipe through which oil, its products, or gas is pumped between two points, either offshore or onshore.
Pit	A specially constructed arena on the trading floor of some exchanges where trading in a futures contract is conducted by open outcry. On other exchanges, the term "ring" designates the trading area for futures contracts.
Pivot	Reversing or changing direction - same as turning point.
Point	Can mean 1% (100 basis points), 32/32nds in the bond market, or the minimum fluctuation in a futures contract. (It is inappropriate to use the term point to refer to 1/32nd of a point in bonds).
Point and Figure Charts	Charts especially used by short term traders that show with Xs and Os price changes of a minimum amount regardless of time period involved.
Point Balance	A statement prepared by Futures Commission Merchants to show profit or loss on all open contracts by computing them to an official closing or settlement price.
Point-and-Figure	A charting method, using Xs and Os, that also generates "buy" and "sell" signals.
Polarization	Measures the degree of purity as the state of refined sugar is approached - above 99 degrees is considered refined or white sugar.

Pork Bellies

One of the major cuts of the hog carcass that, when cured, becomes bacon.

Position

A commitment to go long (buy) or short (sell) in a market. Also the amount of instruments owned (long position) or owed (short position).

Position Limit

The maximum position, either net long or net short, in one commodity future or in all futures of one commodity combined which may be held or controlled by one person as prescribed by an exchange or by the Commodity Futures Trading Commission.

Position Month

The month preceding delivery month.

Position Trader

A trader who either buys or sells instruments and holds them for an extended period of time as distinguished from a shorter term trader or even a day trader.

Position Trading

An approach to trading in which the trader either buys or sells contracts or securities and holds them for an extended period of time.

Positive Carry

The net gain earned over time when the cost of financing is less than the return on the asset being financed.

Positive Leverage

The total yield from the investment is greater than the cost of the debt financing.

Posted Price

The price an oil purchaser will pay for crude of a certain API gravity from a particular field or area.

Prearranged Trading

Trading between brokers in accordance with an expressed or implied agreement or understanding.

Precious Metal Spread

Any combination of four precious metals contracts - platinum, gold, palladium, and silver. Silver has changed to an industrial metal, having been phased out as a circulating coin metal years ago (i.e., Gold/Platinum; Platinum/Palladium; Gold/Silver/Platinum; Gold/Silver).

Premium

The amount by which an index futures contract exceeds the price of the actual index, the amount by which the market value of a debt security exceeds its par value, or the yield differential which one issuer must pay over and above competitive issues in order to attract investors.

Premium Spread

Nearby month reflects tightness of supply whenever it goes to a premium to the deferred month.

Premium Bond

A bond selling above its par.

Prepayment

A payment made before its scheduled payment date.

Price Action

Price movement, on graphs, for a day or some other time period.

Price Limit

The maximum price advance or decline from the previous day's settlement price permitted in one trading session.

Price Manipulation

Any planned operation, transaction, or practice calculated to cause or maintain an artificial price.

Price Weighted Index

A stock index weighted by adding the price of one share of each stock included in the index and dividing this sum by a constant divisor. The divisor is changed when a stock split or stock dividend occurs because these affect the stock prices.

Price-Fixing Spread

Buying and selling two different but related commodities on the basis of normal or historic relationships or

ratios. Actually a form of dollar averaging two commodities by historical
price/quantity switch methods.

Primary Dealer   A firm which makes a market in government debt securities acting as a prin-
cipal in the trades. The Fed
conducts its open market operations
only through primary dealers.

Primary Markets   The principal market for the purchase
and sale of a cash product.

Primary Movement   Receipts and shipments of grain at
primary markets, the first major col-
lecting point in commercial channels.

Primary Stocks   Stocks of crude oil or petroleum
products held in storage at (or in)
leases, refineries, natural gas processing plants, pipelines, tankfarms,
and bulk terminals that can store at
least 50,000 barrels of petroleum
products or that can receive petroleum products by tanker, barge, or
pipeline. "Primary Stocks" excludes
stocks of foreign origin that are held
in bonded warehouse storage.

Prime Rate   The interest rate charged by major
banks to their most credit-worthy
customers.

Principal   The corpus of the amount borrowed
or the face amount of par value of a
debt instrument. Also an individual
or firm which buys and sells for his
or its own account.

Private Wires   Wires leased by various firms and
news agencies for the transmission
of information to branch offices and
subscriber clients.

Productivity   The amount of physical output for
each unit of productive output.

Profile   The visual shape of a daily chart.

Profit Taking	Often used to explain a downturn in the market following a period of rising prices.
Progressed Chart	An astrological chart showing the relations among the entity's birth chart with a chart of planets adjusted by a time progression factor imposed on it.
Prompt Barrel	Product which will move within three to four days.
Prompt Month	Month in which contractual obligations must be fulfilled.
Prompt Shipment	To be shipped within four to six weeks.
Provisional Price	The tentative price at which call cotton is invoiced prior to determination of the final price.
Public	Non-professional speculators as distinguished from hedgers and professional speculators or traders.
Public Elevators	Grain elevators in which bulk storage of grain is provided for the public for a fee.
Purchase and Sale Statement	A statement sent by a commission house to a customer when a futures or options position has been liquidated or offset. The statement shows the number of contracts bought or sold, the prices at which the contracts were bought or sold, the gross profit or loss, the commission charges, and the net profit or loss on the transaction. Sometimes combined with a confirmation statement.
Purchase Price	The total actual cost paid by a person for entering into a transaction including price, commission, and/or any other direct or indirect charges.
Pyramiding	The use of unrealized profits on existing futures positions as margin to in-

crease the size of the position, normally in successively smaller increments.

Quotation The actual price or the bid or ask price at a particular time. Often called a quote.

Rally An upward movement of prices.

Range The difference between the high and low price of an instrument during a specific period, usually a single trading session.

Ratio Spread A spread that consists of the price of one instrument divided by the price of a different instrument (e.g., Gold/Silver Ratio).

Raw Material/by-Product Spread Buying and selling the base material and its resultant by-product(s) (i.e. Soybeans/Oil and Meal or Crude Oil/Heating Oil and Gasoline).

Raw Material/One Product Spread Offsetting one side of the raw material with only one by-product (i.e., Crude Oil/Gasoline).

Reaction A price movement counter to the ongoing trend.

Realizing Accepting a profit either by a liquidating sale or covering a short sale.

Recession An economic downturn with two or more quarters of reduced gross national product after adjustment for inflation.

Recovery An increase in prices following a substantial decline.

Rectangle Either a reversal or continuation pattern which is bounded by parallel horizontal lines.

Red Gold An alloy of 1/4 copper and 3/4 gold.

Reduced Crude Oil Crude oil that has undergone at least one distillation process to separate some of the lighter hydrocarbons. Reducing crude lowers its API gravity.

Refiner Acquisition Cost The cost to the refiner, including transportation and fees, of crude oil.

Refiner-Marketer A marketer of gasoline and/or heating oil who operates his own refinery.

Refinery A plant used to separate the various components present in crude oil and convert them into usable products or feedstock for other processes.

Reforming Process The use of heat and catalysts to effect the rearrangement of certain of the hydrocarbon molecules without altering their composition appreciably.

Refunding The act of issuing new debt and using the proceeds to retire existing debt.

Refunding Periods The period when U.S. government securities reach maturity and must be refinanced.

Registered Bond A bond that is registered on the books of the issuing company in the name of the owner. It can be transferred only when endorsed by the registered owner.

Registered Commodities Rep (RCR) An individual who is authorized to solicit and handle customer business for his or her firm. The individual must be registered with the CFTC and is often referred to as a commodity broker or account executive.

Registered Security A security which will pay the owner whose name appears on the face of the certificate.

Regressive Tax A tax whose rate declines as the tax base increases.

Regular Issuer

A refiner or marketer with storage facilities in the delivery area that satisfies an exchange's requirements in terms of financial capability, capacity, and location, authorized to issue Depositary Receipts for delivery on the exchange, and required to provide wet barrels when presented with a Demand Certificate.

Regularity

Term used to describe a processing plant, warehouse, mill, vault, or bank that satisfies exchange requirements in terms of financing, facilities, capacity, and location and has been approved as acceptable for delivery of commodities against futures contracts.

Regulated Commodities

Those commodities over which the Commodity Future Trading Commission has regulatory supervision for the purpose of seeing that commodity trading is conducted in the public's interest.

Regulation T

The federal regulation governing the amount of credit that may be advanced by brokers and dealers to customers for the purchase of securities.

Regulation U

The federal regulation governing the amount of credit that may be advanced by a bank to its customers for the purchase of listed stocks.

Regulations (CFTC)

The regulations adopted and enforced by the federal overseer of futures markets, the Commodity Futures Trading Commission, in order to administer the Commodity Exchange Act.

Reinvestment Rate

The rate at which funds from the maturity of an asset or the sale of an asset can be reinvested. Also refers to the rate that can be obtained on an investment of coupon payments until an instrument matures.

Relative Strength Index (RSI) An arithmetic measure of the degree to which a market is overbought or oversold.

Reparations Compensation payable to a wronged party in a futures or options transaction. The term is used in conjunction with the Commodity Futures Trading Commission's customer claims procedure to recover civil damages.

Reportable Positions The number of open contracts specified by the Commodity Futures Trading Commission at which one must begin reporting total positions by delivery month to the authorized exchange and/or the CFTC.

Reporting Limit The number of futures contracts above which a trader must report daily to the exchange and the Commodity Futures Trading Commission. The report must include position by commodity, by delivery month, and purpose of the trading.

Repurchase Agreement (repo) An agreement under which one party agrees to "sell" a security today and also commits to buy it back on an agreed-upon date and at an agreed-upon price. The difference in the original sales price and the subsequent repurchase is in effect interest for a loan. Repos are a very popular means by which dealers finance inventory.

Reserve Requirements The percentages of deposits that member banks are required to maintain with the Fed.

Residual Fuel Oil Very heavy fuel oils produced from the residue from the fractional distillation process rather than from the distilled fractions.

Residuals

A term used to describe oils that are "leftovers" in various refining processes.

Residue

The non-volatile components of crude oil which flow out of the bottom of a fractionating column during fractional distillation.

Residue Gas

Gas that remains after processing in a separator or a plant to remove liquids contained in the gas when produced.

Resistance Level

A price level where sellers are expected to enter the market to slow or stop advances.

Resting Order

An order away from the market, waiting to be executed.

Retail

End buyers, such as individuals or institutions, who intend to resell inventory.

Retender

The right of holders of futures contracts who have been tendered a delivery notice through the clearinghouse to offer the notice for sale on the open market, thereby liquidating their obligation to take delivery under the contract.

Retrograde

The movement of a celestial body seen as backward to that of the general motion of similar bodies.

Revaluation

A formal "official" increase in the exchange rate or price of currency.

Revenue Bond

A municipal bond which is secured by the income it is expected to receive from a certain project as opposed to a general obligation bond which pledges its full taxing power as security.

Reversal

The point at which trend changes direction.

Reversal Chart

A "point and figure" chart which plots changes in market direction only if a reversal exceeds a certain magnitude.

Reverse Crush

A spread opposite to a Soybean or Cattle crush spread.

Reverse Repurchase Agreement

The purchase of securities with the understanding that these securities will be resold to the original seller in the future.

Rich

Slang for a security that is relatively overpriced.

Right Ascension

Celestial longitude, or east-west position in the sky, of a heavenly body that is measured in hours, minutes and seconds.

Ring

A circular area on the trading floor of an exchange where traders and brokers stand while executing futures trades. Some exchanges use pits rather than rings.

Risk

Degree of uncertainty of return due to possible adverse price or interest rate fluctuations.

Risk Capital

Capital in excess of basic living expenses and savings.

Risk/Reward Ratio

The potential loss compared to potential gain in a strategy expressed as a ratio.

Roll

A switch that simultaneously liquidates an existing position and initiates a new position in a different contract month.

Roll Back

A roll from a distant contract into a nearer contract.

Roll Forward

A roll from a nearer contract into a more distant contract.

Round Turn

The process of offsetting a long or short position by liquidation or delivery. Most futures commission houses only charge commissions on the round turn.

Rounded Bottom/Top

A long, curving pattern which signals the end of a bull/bear market more common in bottoming markets than topping markets which is typified by very low volume except on upside breakouts from the pattern.

Rule of 72

A handy formula for figuring the number of years it takes to double principal using compound interest by dividing the interest rate into the number 72.

Rule Of Three

A general rule that places the breakout point prior to the resumption of a trend at the third attempt to penetrate support or resistance.

Rules(NFA)

The standards and requirements to which participants who are required to be Members of the National Futures Association must subscribe and conform.

Runaway Market

A fast move of the price in one direction.

Running Bales

A term used in the cotton trade to designate the number of bales of cotton as they come from the gin in varying weights.

Running Market

A market where price is generally going either up or down, as opposed to a trading market.

Sample Grade

In commodities, usually the lowest quality of a commodity too low to be acceptable for delivery in satisfaction of futures contracts.

Scale Down (or Up)

To purchase or sell on scale down means to buy or sell at regular price intervals in a declining market. To buy (sell) on scale up means to buy (sell) at regular price intervals as the market advances (declines).

Scalper A speculator on the floor of an exchange who buys and sells contracts for his own account usually basing his decisions on very small price fluctuations. The scalper is usually willing to buy at the bid price and sell at the offer price with equanimity thus providing liquidity.

Season or Lifetime High-Low The highest and lowest prices recorded for each contract maturity from the first day it was traded to the present.

Seasonal Effect The regular tendency for commodity prices and open interest to increase or decrease at certain times of the year.

Seasonal Spread Designed to benefit from seasonal trends from growing, harvesting, and climatic influences.

Seasonality Price patterns that occur at approximately the same time each year.

Seat A traditional figure of speech for a membership on an exchange.

SEC Securities & Exchange Commission, which regulates the securities industry.

Secondary Market The market in which previously issued financial instruments continue to be sold and resold.

Segregated Account A special account used to hold and separate customers' assets from those of the broker or firm.

Sell Order Limit A price level order which a trader determines. If price passes that level, the trader automatically sells the

market. A trader may leave a standing order with a broker regarding
sell limit orders.

Seller's Option The right of a seller to select, within
the limits prescribed by a contract,
the quality of the commodity delivered and the time and place of delivery.

Selling Pressure A situation where there appears to
be more contracts offered for sale
than there are purchase orders to
buy them.

Semilogarithmic Paper Graph paper on which one axis is
expressed in logarithms.

Settle The market is said to "settle" after
the "settlement price" for a particular trading session is established.
This price is derived by the exchange
by using a weighted average of trade
prices that took place during the
"close" (closing range). Settlement
prices are usually available for quot-
ing purposes 15 to 30 minutes after
the close. The term also describes
the process of "evening up" after the
market has closed.

Settlement Refers to the official final closing price
of the day and also to how a futures
contract is delivered with all index
futures having a cash settlement provision.

Settlement Price The single closing price determined
by each exchange's price committee
of directors used primarily by the exchange clearinghouse to determine
the need for margin capital. Determines both margin calls and invoice
prices for deliveries. "Settlement
price" is also often used as an approximate equivalent to the term
"closing price." The close in futures

trading refers to a very brief period of time at the end of the trading day during which transactions frequently take place quickly and at a range of prices immediately before the bell. Therefore there frequently is no one closing price but a range of closing prices. The settlement price is the closing price if there is only one closing price but when there is a closing range, it is as near to the midpoint of the closing range as possible consistent with the contract's price increments.

Sextile

An aspect which occurs when two heavenly bodies are one-sixth of a full circle apart in the sky (60 degrees apart).

Shake-out

Stops being run, but with no continuation - a false break-out.

Short

A trader who has sold, speculating that prices will decline. He is "short" until he liquidates by buying or accepts delivery. The short seller sells the security first and then buys it back later, hopefully at a lower price.

Short Hedge

Selling futures to protect against possible decreased prices of commodities.

Short Position

A position in which the trader has sold that does not offset a previously established long position.

Short Sale

A sale of an instrument not owned by the seller in the expectation of declining prices.

Short Squeeze

A situation in which "short" traders are unable to buy the cash product to deliver against their positions and so are forced to buy offsetting futures at prices much higher than they would ordinarily be willing to pay.

Short the Basis

A trader who has sold cash or spot goods and hedged them by purchasing futures - being short the cash market and long futures.

Short Ton

A measure of weight equal to 2,000 pounds.

Size

The magnitude or dollar volume of a trade. A trader who is making a large bid or offer is said to be "doing size."

Small Traders

Traders who are not required to file reports of their transactions or positions.

Soft

A description of a price which is gradually weakening.

Solar Cycle

A period of 28 years at the end of which the days of the month return to the same days of the week.

Sold-Out Market

When liquidation of a weakly-held position has been completed and offerings become scarce the market is said to be sold out.

Solstice, Summer

Point at which the sun is farthest north of the celestial equator and enters Cancer.

Solstice, Winter

Point at which the sun is farthest south of the celestial equator and enters Capricorn.

Sour/Sweet Crude

Industry terms which denote the relative degree of a given crude's sulfur content.

Source/Product Spread

A spread between a commodity and one or more of its products.

Sovereign

A British 1 pound gold coin with a fine gold content of 7.32 grams.

Special Accounts

When a market position becomes reportable it is sometimes referred to as a "special account."

Speculation

Buying or selling in hopes of making a profit. Like gambling, it carries a connotation of a high degree of risk but unlike gambling, it is made with an "educated guess."

Speculator

A person who trades in commodity futures for a purpose other than hedging. Involves the sale and purchase or purchase and sale of commodity futures contracts or of the physical commodity. The futures speculator (unlike the commercial hedger) seldom has a position in the cash market. The speculator absorbs the risk inherent in price fluctuations in return for a profit opportunity and thereby adds liquidity to the marketplace.

Spike Reversal

Similar to a reversal day except that the price 'spikes' well above or below previous highs or lows before moving sharply in the opposite direction.

Spot

An outgrowth of the phrase "on the spot," it usually refers to a cash market price for stocks of the physical commodity that are available for immediate delivery. Spot is also sometimes used in reference to the futures contract of the current month in which case trading is still "futures" trading but delivery is possible at any time.

Spot Commodity

The physical commodity as distinguished from the futures contract.

Spot Market

Market being traded for immediate delivery.

Spot Price

The price at which the cash product is selling. For grains, the term is cash price.

Spread

The difference between bid and offer prices, the difference between yields or prices of two cash instruments, the price differential between two futures contracts, or, finally, the profit margin a dealer works for in a transaction.

Spread Order

An order to buy one instrument and sell another at a specified price difference or premium (e.g., "buy a March Bond, sell a June Bond with the June 20/32nds premium to the March").

Spreading

Generally the purchase of one instrument against the sale of another in the expectation that the price relationships between the two will change so that a subsequent offsetting sale and purchase will yield a net profit.

Spreadsheet

Software that presents financial statements, investment reports, or other information laid out across many rows and columns. A change in any number automatically updates related data on the spreadsheet.

Square

An aspect which occurs when two heavenly bodies are one quarter of a full circle apart in the sky (90 degrees apart).

Squeeze

Situation in which those who are short cannot repurchase their positions except at a price substantially higher than the value of these positions in relation to the rest of the market.

Standard & Poor's 500 Stock Index

A market value weighted stock index first introduced in 1957 and traded as a futures contract on the Chicago Mercantile Exchange since April, 1982.

Stationary

Halt in the apparent movement of a planet against the background of the

	stars just before the planet comes to opposition.
Stock Index Future	A futures contract pegged to a stock market average.
Stock Market Spread	Any combination of different stock indexes (i.e., Standard and Poor Stock Index/Value Line Stock Index; TSE 300 Index/ NYSE Index; London F.T. Stock Exchange 100 Index/ S & P Index).
Stop Limit Order	A type of stop order in which a price limit is placed above or below the market and may or may not be filled. For instance, a buy stop limit order must be executed at or below the specified price, when that price is triggered.
Stop Order	An order that becomes a market order when a particular price level is reached. Sometimes referred to as a stop loss order, a buy stop order is placed above the market.
Stop-Buy Point	A price entry point placed above the current market price which becomes a market order to buy if touched.
Stop-Loss Order	An open order given to a brokerage firm to liquidate a position when the market reaches a certain price so as to prevent losses from mounting.
Stop-Sell Point	A price entry point placed below the current market price which becomes a market order to sell if touched.
Straddle	A straddle is often a spread initiated between two different markets. It is also an old cotton market term for spread.
Straddle-Up Spread	Legging into a spread one position at a time which is usually done by traders to lock in a loss.

Straight-Run

Refers to a petroleum product produced by the primary distillation of crude oil.

Street Book

A daily record kept by futures commission merchants and clearing members showing details of each futures transaction including date, price, quantity, market, commodity, and the person for whom the trade was made.

Strong Hands

When used in connection with delivery for commodities on futures contracts, the term usually means that the party receiving the delivery notice probably will take delivery and retain ownership of the commodity.

Suitability Rule

The rule of fair practice that requires a member to have reasonable grounds for believing that a recommendation to a customer is suitable on the basis of his financial objectives and abilities.

Sulfur

An element that is present in some crude oil and natural gas as an impurity in the form of its various compounds.

Superior

Indicates that the sun is between the planet and the earth.

Support Area

Same as resistance area, except they each are at opposite sides of buying or selling pressure. A price range where an increase in the demand for an instrument is expected - a barrier to price decline.

Support Level

A price level where buyers are expected to enter the market to slow or stop declines.

Surplus

The excess of a product on hand over actual or prospective requirements.

Swap	In foreign exchange, buying a currency in the spot market and simultaneously selling it forward.
Swing	Distance between two pivots points.
Swing Chart	The swing chart operates with a trend line swinging between the bottoms and tops of daily prices and with stop-sell and buy-order points.
Switch	A roll from one month to another which can be done at the market or at a specified difference. When used by hedgers, this tactic is referred to as "rolling forward the hedge."
Synodic Month	The time required of the moon to pass through its lunar phases and return to the start, averaging 29 days, 12 hours, 44 minutes and 2.8 seconds.
Syzygy	The nearly straight-line configuration of three celestial bodies.
Tails	The two extreme ends of a normal day Market Profile chart.
Taking A View	Having an opinion as to where a market is likely to move and then acting on the conviction.
Tariff	A schedule of rates or charges permitted a common carrier or utility.
Tax Straddle	A spread put on expressly for shifting tax exposure from one year to the next. Still allowed, but with many qualifications.
Technical Analysis	Analysis based on market action through chart study, moving averages, volume, open interest, oscillators, formations, and other technical indicators which concerns factors within the market.

Technical Condition of a Market	Supply and demand factors that have important short-term influence on the market but that should have no major trend-setting significance.
Technical or Rally Decline	A price movement resulting from conditions developing within a market itself such as changes in open interest, volume, extent of recent price movement and approach of the first notice day. In a technical rally or decline, market participants are usually reacting to signals generated from technical analysis rather than the supply and demand conditions in the physical market.
Technical Position	Term used to indicate internal market conditions. When the market is sold out or is over-sold, its technical position is said to be strong.
Telephone Man	Man assigned to a telephone post on the floor of the exchange by a member firm to receive and transmit orders to the firm's floor broker.
Tender	When a seller gives notice to a clearinghouse (through his broker) that he intends to fulfill his futures contract by delivering the physical commodity.
Tender Price	A term used to designate the spot cash price when delivering.
Term Repo	A repurchase agreement for a specified period of time. Most repos are done for a very short time period (usually overnight) but term repos are entered into for longer periods (e.g., 3 days, 1 week, 30 days, 60 days, etc).
Terminal Elevator	An elevator located at a point of greatest accumulation in the movement of agricultural products which stores the commodity or moves it to the processors.

Terminal Market   Term synonymous with futures
                                   market in the United Kingdom.

The Desk   The trading desk at the New York
                                   Federal Reserve Bank through which
                                   open market purchases and sales of
                                   government and federal agency secu-
                                   rities are made. The desk maintains
                                   direct telephone communication
                                   with major government securities
                                   dealers.

Thin Market   A market with a low trading volume
                                   and poor liquidity.

Three and Four   Name given to using spread
Dimension Analysis   differences to catch reversals in the
                                   market through monthly price
                                   spread divergences.

Thrift Institution   A general term often used for mutual
                                   savings banks, savings and loan as-
                                   sociations, and credit unions.

Throughput   A term used to describe the total
                                   amount of raw materials that are
                                   processed by a plant such as an oil
                                   refinery in a given period.

Tick   The smallest possible change in price,
                                   either up or down.

Ticker Tape   A continuous paper tape transmis-
                                   sion of price, volume, and other trad-
                                   ing and market information which
                                   operates on private wires leased by
                                   the exchanges.

Tide   The alternate rising (or high) and
                                   falling (or low) of the seas and
                                   oceans that occurs twice a day and
                                   is caused by the gravitational attrac-
                                   tion of the sun and the moon occur-
                                   ring unequally on different parts of
                                   the earth.

Tight Market   A tight market, as opposed to a thin
                                   market, is one in which volume is

heavy, trading is active and highly competitive, and spreads between bid and ask prices are narrow.

Time of Day Order

This is an order which is to be executed at a given minute in the session.

Time-Price-Opportunity Count

A counting of frequency of distributions of price occurrences as defined by letters above and below a center line. Evaluation of the balance allows for further evaluation of the Market Profile directional implications.

To-Arrive Contract

A type of deferred shipment in which the price is based on delivery at the destination point and the seller pays the freight in shipping it to that point.

Token Coin

A piece of stamped metal with an intrinsic value lower than its face value.

Tola

A traditional unit of weight for gold in the Middle East and India.

Tonne

Refers to a metric tonne, which is 2,204.6 pounds.

Top

A point in time or price when price is higher than prices either before or after that time.

Top-Out

The point in time or price at which a bull market reaches its highest price, or market top, and a reversal of the general market trend can be expected.

Total Return

The return on an investment that includes price appreciation, dividends, interest, and any tax benefits.

Trade Balance

The net amount of goods exported or imported.

```
              MARKET-MOVEMENTS
              5212-E.-69-PLACE
              TULSA-OKLA.-74136
                918-493-2897


DATE 12/30/91            TIME 07:02 PM


 ITEM: 025   SALE     $139.00
ACCT: 5415305033303166  0392
RESP:  AUTH/TKT 075086



 I AGREE TO PAY ABOVE TOTAL AMOUNT
 ACCORDING TO CARD ISSUER AGREEMENT


X_____

 SIGNATURE


  RETAIN THIS COPY FOR YOUR RECORDS
```

Trade Date	The date on which a transaction takes place.
Trade Deficit	Refers to the amount by which merchandise imports exceed merchandise exports.
Trade House	A firm that buys and sells for the accounts of customers as well as for its own account.
Traders	Generally refers to either people who trade for their own account or to employees of dealers or institutions who trade for their employer's account.
Trading Range	A narrow band within which prices trade characterized by resistance at the top of the range and support at the bottom of the range. Prices usually make substantial moves once they break out of a trading range.
Trading Hours	The different exchanges' determined hours trading which varies from one exchange to another.
Trading Limit	The maximum price change permitted in one session. Beyond this limit trading may not take place but may still continue at the limit or within the range of the limit. Can also mean position limit.
Trading Market	A market situation that happens when price moves equally up and down for a period without showing a strong tendency to move in one direction or another.
Trailing Stop	Raising a sell stop or lowering a buy stop to protect profits as a market moves in one's favor which may be arrived at by using chart points, a moving average, on a percentage move basis, or by some other method.

Transaction Account

A checking account or similar account from which transfers can be made to third parties.

Transaction Costs

Consists primarily of commission costs but may include margin and interest costs under certain conditions.

Transfer Payments

Payments to individuals by government and business for which no goods or services are currently rendered.

Transfer Trades

Entries made upon the books of futures commission merchants for the purpose of (1) transferring existing trades from one account to another within the same office where no change in ownership is involved, (2) transferring existing trades from the books of one commission merchant to the books of another commission merchant where no change in ownership is involved, (3) exchanging futures for cash commodities, or (4) exchanging futures positions, one of which was taken to fix the price of a commodity involved in a call sale.

Transferable Notice

A term used on some contract markets to describe a notice of delivery.

Transit

The passing across a meridian on a celestial body by another celestial sphere.

Transit Chart

An astrological chart composed of an entity's birth chart with a chart of current planetary positions imposed on it.

Treasury Bills

Short-term U.S. government debt instruments with maturities of one year or less which are sold at auction by the Fed with 3-, 6-, or 12-month maturities. Bills are sold at a discount from par with the interest earned being the difference between

	the face value received at maturity and the price paid.
Treasury Bonds	Treasury bonds are coupon-bearing debt instruments issued and guaranteed by the U.S. government with maturities beyond 10 years. Interest is paid semiannually.
Treasury Issues	Bonds, notes, and bills issued by the U.S. government and backed by its full faith and credit. They are considered the safest and highest quality investments available.
Treasury Notes	Treasury notes are coupon-bearing debt instruments issued by the Treasury with maturities of not less than 1 year and not more than 10 years. The semiannual payment of interest and principal on notes is fully guaranteed by the government.
Trend	The tendency of prices to move in one direction more rapidly than another - the general direction a market is moving.
Trend Day	A Market Profile day in which the profile resembles a bow shape due to two (and rarely three) distinct distribution patterns. Price moves slowly but steadily in one direction.
Trend Line	A line on a swing chart which follows the bottoms or tops of daily price bars switching between the tops and bottoms at reversal points.
Trending Market	A market where price is either going up or down as opposed to a trading market.
Trine	An aspect which occurs when two heavenly bodies are one-third of a full circle apart in the sky (120 degrees apart) generally considered to be a favorable event.

Troy Ounce

A unit in the Troy system of weights used for precious metals based on a pound of 12 ounces and an ounce of 20 pennyweights or 480 grains.

Ullage

Expressed either in absolute volumetric terms or as an overall percentage of capacity, ullage refers to the amount of available space in a given storage container.

Underlying Futures Contract

The futures contract which may be purchased or sold upon the exercise of an option.

Unwinding

Liquidating a position or spread.

Uptick

A trade which takes place at a higher price than the immediately preceeding transaction.

Value Area

In Market Profile, a clustering of trade activity around a range of prices. The narrower the range and/or the greater the clustering of trades the greater the significance of that price level.

Value Line Stock Index Futures

The first stock index futures introduced. Traded at the Kansas City Board of Trade, the Value Line Index futures, based on the Value Line Index, is comprised of both second-tier and blue-chip stocks. The Value Line contract enjoys the reputation as the most volatile of the three major stock index futures.

Variable Limit

An expanded allowable price range set by the exchange when market volatility causes prices to reach and settle at the normal daily trading limit for (usually three) successive trading days. In such situations the trading range is typically expanded by 50 percent. Once the market fails to close at the expanded limit, the normal limit is automatically reinstated.

Variation Margin

A call for additional margin deposits made by a clearinghouse to a clearing member while trading is in progress and current price trends have substantially reduced the margin deposits.

Variation Margin Call

A demand for money issued by a commission house to bring the equity in an account back up to the initial margin level.

Velocity

The amount by which price changes over time or the rate at which money balances turn over in a period for expenditures on goods and services.

Vendor

A seller of commodity-industry related products.

Vertical Integration

Refers to a condition in which a company produces raw material, transports it, refines or processes it, and markets the product, all as one integrated operation.

Viscosity

A method of measuring a given liquid's resistance to flow, usually decreasing with increasing temperatures.

Visible Supply

The amount of a commodity that can be accounted for and computed accurately usually because it is being kept in major known storage places.

Volatility

A measure of the market instability usually by price measurement. Markets which are subject to frequent large price changes are said to be highly volatile.

Volume

The total number of instruments traded in a given period.

Waning Moon

From Full Moon to New Moon including the 3rd and 4th quarters.

Wash Sales

An illegal process in which simultaneous purchases and sales are made in the same market, on the same exchange, and in the same month. No actual position is taken, although it appears that trades have been made.

Wash Trading

Entering into, or purporting to enter into, transactions to give the appearance that purchases and sales are being or have been made but usually not resulting in a change in the trader's market position.

Wasting Asset

A financial instrument whose time value runs out as it reaches its maturity or settlement date.

Waxing Moon

From New Moon to First Quarter to Full Moon including the 1st and 2nd quarters.

Weak Hands

When used in connection with delivery of commodities on futures contracts, the term usually means that the party probably does not intend to retain ownership of the commodity.

Weathered Crude

Crude oil which has lost an appreciable quantity of its volatile components owing to natural causes during storage and handling.

Wedge

A narrowing triangle within which price stays as it moves up and down. A rising wedge usually signals a reversal in a previous bull or bear market.

Weighting

A method of evaluating the price performance of individual stocks compared with the movement of the total stock market. This method involves either assigning equal weights to equal price changes or determining the relative importance of each stock in accordance with market value.

Wet Barrel

An actual barrel of product already physically in storage at the time of a given transaction as opposed to a "paper barrel" which appears only as a credit in an accountant's ledger.

Wet Barrel Delivery

A futures market delivery mechanism involving the transfer of the physical commodity during the delivery month. Contrasted with a warehouse receipt delivery mechanism.

Whipsaw

A trader is said to be "whipsawed" when he takes a position and immediately the market moves against the position enough to trigger a liquidation at a predetermined loss, only to have the market then turn around and move in the direction that would have allowed the trader to profit in the first place. This usually occurs because the trader is setting stop loss orders too close to the market.

White Gold

An alloy of 75% gold and either 15% nickel and 10% copper or 25% palladium.

Winter Wheat

Wheat that is planted in the fall, lies dormant during the winter, and is harvested beginning about May of the next year.

Wire House

A commission house with branch offices connected by telephone, teletype, telegraph or cable.

Without

The term "without" indicates a market in which there is either a bid without an offer or vice versa (e.g., in a bear market the quote might be "150 offered without").

WOW

Waiting on Weather.

Yellow Gold

An alloy of 1/5 copper, 1/5 silver, and 3/5 gold.

Yield

The production of a piece of land (e.g., his land yielded 100 bushels per acre) or the return provided by an investment.

Yield (Current)

Interest earned divided by the price of a security.

Yield Curve

A chart in which yield levels are plotted on the vertical axis and the term to maturity of debt instruments of similar credit worthiness (usually governments) is plotted on the horizontal axis.

Yield to Maturity

The rate of return earned by a debt instrument held to maturity. In this calculation it is assumed that interest payments can be reinvested at the coupon rate, which obviously may not be accurate. Capital gains or losses are also considered.

Zero-Coupon Bond

A bond that pays no annual interest, is sold for less than face value, and is redeemed at full value upon maturity.

Zodiac

An imaginary belt in the heavens usually 18 degrees wide that includes the paths of all the planets except Pluto and is divided into 12 constellations (configurations of stars) called signs each claiming 30 degrees of longitude. Used for astrological purposes only.

Index